East German intelligence and Ireland, 1949–90

D1425479

Manchester University Press

East German intelligence and Ireland, 1949–90

Espionage, terrorism and diplomacy

Jérôme aan de Wiel

Manchester University Press

Copyright © Jérôme aan de Wiel 2014

The right of Jérôme aan de Wiel to be identified as the author of this work has been asserted by him in accordance with the Copyright, Designs and Patents Act 1988.

Published by Manchester University Press
Altrincham Street, Manchester M1 7JA, UK
www.manchesteruniversitypress.co.uk

British Library Cataloguing-in-Publication Data is available

Library of Congress Cataloging-in-Publication Data is available

ISBN 978 1 5261 0741 1 paperback

First published by Manchester University Press in hardback 2014

This edition first published 2017

The publisher has no responsibility for the persistence or accuracy of URLs for any external or third-party internet websites referred to in this book, and does not guarantee that any content on such websites is, or will remain, accurate or appropriate.

Printed by CPI Group (UK) Ltd, Croydon CR0 4YY

To Klaus Brinkmann (1943–2009, †Berlin)

There are many secrets; don't try to resolve them all.

(Dejan Stojanović, Serbian poet)

Contents

Figures

All photographs are contained in Stasi file MfS-HA IX, no. 2451. The author wishes to acknowledge the BStU's permission to publish. Figures captions are translations of the original Stasi captions.

Tables

Acknowledgements

Several people made very precious contributions to this book.

The very first person I would like to thank is Christian Schwack from the Bundesbeauftragte für die Unterlagen des Staatssicherheitsdienstes der ehemaligen Deutschen Demokratischen Republik (BStU, the Federal Commissioner for the Records of the State Security Service of the Former German Democratic Republic) in Berlin. Quite simply without his help this book would never have seen the light. Herr Schwack undertook the research in the labyrinthine archives of the former Stasi and over a period of about three years he managed to unearth over 6,000 photocopies of original documents. His commitment to and interest in this project is everything a researcher can hope for. I also benefited from his very valuable insights into the Stasi. A great source of help was also the remarkable website of the BStU which assisted me in my analysis of Stasi documents. Edgar Uher, a former diplomat of the East German Ministry of External Affairs and also an officer of the Hauptverwaltung Aufklärung (HVA, main directorate of foreign intelligence in the Stasi) kindly agreed to help me. In his capacity as diplomat and agent, Herr Uher specialised in Irish affairs and thus gave me most valuable explanations regarding East Germany's interest in Ireland and Northern Ireland and also regarding the inner workings of the HVA and the Ministry for External Affairs. His unpublished memoirs provided me with original information.

Reiner Oschmann, the former correspondent of *Neues Deutschland* in London, shared with me his experiences as a journalist in Ireland and explained to me the finer details of the East German press. Wolfgang Döhnert of the Allgemeiner Deutscher Nachrichtendienst (ADN, general German news agency from the GDR) also related his experiences in Ireland and Northern Ireland, and his meetings with Irish and Northern Irish personalities. Both journalists have the most pleasant recollections of the island. So does Dr Joachim Mitdank, the last East German Ambassador to Ireland (based in London). Dr Mitdank detailed the intricacies of East German foreign policy for me and gave me his impressions on Ireland and different personalities he met there.

I also would like to take this opportunity to thank all the archivists in the Bundesarchiv-Militärarchiv (military archive) in Freiburg am Breisgau, the Deutsches Rundfunkarchiv (the archive of German broadcasting) in Potsdam-Babelsberg, the Auswärtiges Amt (the archive of the Foreign Office) in Berlin and the Stiftung Archiv der Parteien und Massenorganisationen der DDR im Bundesarchiv (SAPMO-BA, the Foundation Archives of Parties and Mass Organisations of the GDR in the Federal Archive) in Berlin. It is a pleasure to do archival research in Germany. In my now long experience of working in European archives, it is not often that twenty-five boxes of documents are ready for consultation on arrival.

Professor Keith Jeffery of Queen's University, Belfast, the author of a seminal study of MI6, read the manuscript and gave me very valuable advice and insights. Professor (emeritus) Dermot Keogh, a specialist in the history of Irish foreign policy, and Professor Geoffrey Roberts of the School of History in University College, Cork, a specialist in Soviet history, were most encouraging in this project. I greatly benefited from their advice. The Research committee of the School helped me financially. It was much appreciated. As usual, I could rely on the expertise and knowledge of the archivists in the National Archives of Ireland in Dublin. I am most grateful to the archivists in the North Atlantic Treaty Organization (NATO) in Brussels who repeatedly managed to unearth relevant documents. I also would like to thank the two anonymous peer reviewers of Manchester University Press who made most useful and pertinent comments. I was fortunate to work with Tony Mason, Lianne Slavin, Dee Devine and Paul Clarke of Manchester University Press who were encouraging and supportive in this project. I greatly appreciated their guidance. Martin Barr was a copy-editor every author can only wish for, paying attention to every detail.

My wife, Sabine Egger, was always patient when I asked her to translate some difficult passages in 'Stasi-German' despite her own very busy academic timetable. She was a source of strength for me. The Senate of the National University of Ireland helped the publication of this project by providing generous financial assistance. Many thanks to them. Finally, I should like to mention my friend the late Klaus Brinkmann. Berlin – East or West – had but few secrets for Klaus. He passed away before the completion of this book. I always enjoyed his hospitality and his rather off-the-beaten-track history walking tours. This book is dedicated to his memory.

Abbreviations

The following is a list of the most frequently used abbreviations.

AD	Action directe (France)
ADN	East German news agency
AfNS	Amt für Nationale Sicherheit (Office of National Security)
BAOR	British Army of the Rhine
BfV	Federal Office for the Protection of the Constitution (West Germany)
BKA	Federal Criminal Office (West Germany)
BND	Federal Intelligence Agency for threats from abroad (West Germany)
BStU	archive of the former Stasi in Berlin
CIA	Central Intelligence Agency (USA)
CPI	Communist Party of Ireland
CSCE	Conference on Security and Cooperation in Europe
DEA	Department of External Affairs (Ireland, until 1971)
DFA	Department of Foreign Affairs (Ireland, since 1971)
FBI	Federal Bureau of Investigation (USA)
GRU	Foreign Military Intelligence of the Soviet Army General Staff (USSR)
G2	Irish military intelligence
HA-III	department in charge of telecommunication and radio intelligence (Stasi)
HA-VI	department in charge of border controls and tourism (Stasi)
HA-XXII	department in charge of terrorism (Stasi)
HVA	Main Directorate of Foreign Intelligence (Stasi)
INLA	Irish National Liberation Army
KGB	Committee for State Security (USSR)
LKA	State Criminal Office (West Germany)
MfAA	East German Ministry of External Affairs

MfS	Ministerium für Staatssicherheit (Ministry of State Security, known as Stasi)
MI5	Security Service (UK)
MI6	Secret Intelligence Service (UK)
NATO	North Atlantic Treaty Organization
NVA	National People's Army (East Germany)
OIRA	Official Irish Republican Army
PIRA	Provisional Irish Republican Army
PLO	Palestine Liberation Organization
RAF	Red Army Faction (West Germany)
SED	East German Communist party
SF/WP	Sinn Féin/the Workers' Party
Stasi	*see* MfS
WISK	West German Ireland Solidarity Committee
WP	Workers' Party (Ireland)
ZAIG	Central Evaluation and Information Group (Stasi)

Introduction

In July 1967, Erich Mielke was handed a report on Frank Ryan. As a former veteran of the Spanish Civil War, the head of the Stasi was immediately interested by the case of this IRA man who had volunteered to serve in the International Brigades in Spain to fight against the fascist Franco. It might have reminded him of his good self. The report was all about repatriating Ryan's remains, buried in a cemetery in Dresden, to Ireland. At first sight, there was nothing wrong with handing over the body of a former comrade to his family. But there was a problem: why had Ryan been buried in *Nazi* Germany in 1944? And so began the extraordinary story of the process of establishing diplomatic relations between the German Democratic Republic (GDR), or East Germany, and Ireland, which must be unique in the annals of the history of diplomacy. In the East German Ministry of External Affairs, it became known as 'corpse diplomacy'. Ryan could never have imagined that one day he would be at the centre of Irish–East German relations, nor that he would also become the main source of inspiration for a well-written East German political thriller in which the Stasi agents were the heroes.

The same year, 'Bettina' joined the Stasi. The person would remain known under this cover name as the 39 million index cards in the archive of the former Stasi in Berlin do not reveal the person's identity, just a registration number: XV/92/67. 'Bettina' was active in the Bonn area, the former capital of the former West Germany. What is known is that 'Bettina' was a member of a Stasi unit that targeted ministries including the department of telecommunications of the West German army, the Bundeswehr. This provides a vital clue and explains where 'Bettina' in all likelihood obtained a plan for the extension of the Irish telephone network in 1983. 'Bettina' might also know what this plan was doing in West Germany. 'Fichte' was another agent whose name could not be established, except for the registration number, XV/1762/71. This is a pity because if 'Fichte' is still alive, he or she might have accepted to say how the pump and turbine plans of Poolbeg Generating Station, also known as Pigeon House, near Dublin were obtained in 1969. There was as well this mole in the Belgian Foreign Ministry in Brussels, 'Angestellter'. This civil servant transmitted to East Berlin Belgian documents on Ireland and Northern Ireland. According to former East German spies, 'Angestellter' was particularly active and good.

In the 1980s, the Provisional Irish Republican Army (PIRA) began a bombing campaign against the British Army of the Rhine (BAOR). A handful of Irish migrants living in West Germany appeared to support the PIRA and also the Irish National Liberation Army (INLA). There was an association called Westdeutsches Irlandsolidaritätskomitee, the West German Ireland Solidarity Committee (WISK), based not far way from Frankfurt am Main. What were its activities? Soon the Stasi found out pretty much everything there was to know. In 1986, HA-XXII, the Stasi department in charge of terrorism, found out that the PIRA was about to buy arms in the town of Ferlach in Austria. A major source of information for the Stasi on PIRA activities in West Germany were the different police institutions in West Germany which it had seriously infiltrated. So it was that it got wind of an anti-PIRA operation led by the West German federal police code-named 'Operation HARP' in 1989.

Due to legal considerations and the protection of third persons, the archive of the former Stasi in Berlin often blacks out names in documents that are given to researchers. There was no exception for this book, but the archive did send the author one document without blacked-out passages containing the name of an Irish individual who, according to information collected by the Stasi, was meant to initiate contacts between the PIRA and the Venezuelan terrorist Carlos 'the Jackal' who was then a regular visitor to East Berlin and other Eastern European capitals. The Romanian intelligence services too had contacts with Carlos and at least on one occasion set up an arms deal between the Carlos group and the PIRA somewhere in the suburbs of Bucharest.

The above stories are snippets of information contained in the 6,000 photocopies that the Bundesbeauftragte für die Unterlagen des Staatssicherheitsdienstes der ehemaligen Deutschen Demokratischen Republik (BStU, the Federal Commissioner for the Records of the State Security Service of the Former German Democratic Republic, Stasi) in Berlin sent to me. Research for this book was not hampered by the thirty-year restriction rule on archives which does not apply as far as Stasi material is concerned. This is most definitely a very rare commodity in the field of history, let alone in the field of intelligence studies. Indeed, if there is one aspect for which the Cold War is famously known it is espionage. When I was contemplating a research project on the relations between Ireland and the GDR, I considered possible sources and contacted the BStU to ask if there was any relevant material concerning Ireland and Northern Ireland. Once my identity was established and when I was vetted, as it were, the BStU was willing to undertake the research for me in the gigantic and labyrinthine archive left by the Stasi. My approach was straightforward: I asked the BStU to send me photocopies of all original documents containing the words Ireland, Northern Ireland, Irish, Ulster, Dublin, Belfast, Irish Republican Army, Irish National Liberation Army and so on, and also the names of several individuals. The research took over three years in total and yielded over 6,000 photocopies. The Stasi material was in turn complemented by documents, notably from the Soviet military intelligence, found in the Bundesarchiv-Militärarchiv (the German military archive) in Freiburg am Breisgau where the papers of the former East German military intelligence are located.

The idea to do research on Ireland during the Cold War, a rather under-researched area, began in 2006 when I became the main researcher for a project entitled 'Ireland and European Integration in a Comparative International Context, 1945–1973', financed by the IRCHSS (Irish Research Council for the Humanities and Social Sciences) and under the supervision of Professor (emeritus) Dermot Keogh of the School of History in University College, Cork (UCC). The aim of this project was to analyse Ireland's relations with the founding member states of the European Communities (EC) at political, economic and cultural levels. While in Germany, I began to toy with the idea of also researching a project on Ireland's relations with a country behind the Iron Curtain, the former GDR. I envisaged studying Ireland's relations with East Germany on the same lines as the IRCHSS project, namely focusing on political, economic and cultural levels.

Why the GDR in particular? Relations between Ireland and Germany throughout the twentieth century have been the object of several studies. For example, in 2008 I published a book called *The Irish Factor, 1899–1919: Ireland's Strategic and Diplomatic Importance for Foreign Powers*, in which I developed the relations between Imperial Germany and Ireland.[1] The inter-war period was analysed by Mervyn O'Driscoll in *Ireland, Germany and the Nazis: Politics and Diplomacy, 1919–1939*.[2] Germany's relations and attempts to influence the Irish republican movement against Britain during the Second World War was first studied by Enno Stephan in 1965 in his book *Spies in Ireland*,[3] and then by Mark M. Hull in 2003 in *Irish Secrets: German Espionage in Wartime Ireland 1939–1945*.[4] Post-war relations between the Federal Republic of Germany (FRG), or West Germany, and Ireland have been analysed by O'Driscoll in *Ireland through European Eyes: Western Europe, the EEC and Ireland, 1945–1973*,[5] O'Driscoll being a member of the said IRCHSS project team. The very active Centre for Irish–German Studies in the University of Limerick has done much work on cultural and literary contacts between the two countries like for example Joachim Fischer's *Das Deutschlandbild der Iren 1890–1939* (the image the Irish had of Germany, 1890–1939).[6] So, this left the GDR to complete Ireland's relations with the Germanys during the twentieth century.

Books and articles on Ireland's involvement in the Cold War are not that many. Dermot Keogh's 'Ireland, the Vatican and the Cold War: The Case of Italy, 1948'[7] gives an in-depth insight on how the Irish Catholic Church and government made their contribution in helping the Christian Democrats to defeat the Communists during the Italian general election. Bernadette Whelan's authoritative study *Ireland and the Marshall Plan, 1947–57* relates how Ireland benefited from and responded to Washington's plan to assist Western Europe in its economic recovery and avoid the spreading of Communism.[8] In *A Diplomatic History of Ireland 1948–49: The Republic, the Commonwealth and NATO*,[9] Ian McCabe meticulously analyses Ireland's decision not to become a member of the North Atlantic Treaty Organization (NATO). Till Geiger's 'Trading with the Enemy: Ireland, the Cold War and East–West Trade, 1945–1955'[10] is a ground-breaking study of Ireland's trade relations with countries behind the Iron Curtain during the early years of the Cold War. Eilís Ward examines the arrival of Hungarian refugees in Ireland after the failed uprising in Budapest in '"A Big Show-off to What We Could Do": Ireland and the Hungarian Refugee Crisis of 1956'.[11] It proved difficult for the Irish authorities to organise the stay of the refugees.

Paula L. Wylie's *Ireland and the Cold War: Diplomacy and Recognition 1949–63* is a ground-breaking study of successive Irish governments' recognition policy towards certain countries, notably the GDR.[12] Ireland's independent stance which sometimes upset the United States and gained the admiration of the non-aligned bloc is related in detail by Joseph Morrison Skelly in *Irish Diplomacy at the United Nations, 1945–1965*.[13] Catherine Manathunga has paid attention to Ireland's nuclear disarmament initiatives in the United Nations in 'The Evolution of Irish Disarmament Initiatives at the United Nations, 1957–1961'.[14] So has Evgeny M. Chossudovsky in 'The Origins of the Treaty on the Non-Proliferation of Nuclear Weapons: Ireland's initiative in the United Nations'.[15] This arguably was Minister for External Affairs

Frank Aiken's finest hour as he was largely at the origin of this treaty, signed in Moscow in July 1968. The Soviets had much respect for him.

For the later period of the Cold War, Robert McNamara has studied the Irish government's attitude towards the conflict in Vietnam in 'Irish Perspectives on the Vietnam War'.[16] He concludes that the Irish had become far less idealistic as they used to be and that they largely adopted a pro-American stance, more reflective of NATO member states than of a neutral country. It certainly was a reflection of Ireland's tough anti-Communist stance. The country might well have been neutral but was definitely pro-NATO as Taoiseach Seán Lemass had made clear in the 1960s when his government made the decision to apply for membership of the European Economic Community (EEC). Despite Lemass and his successors' pro-West declarations, Trevor Salmon takes a critical look at the country's defence relationship with Britain and NATO in 'The Changing Nature of Irish Defence Policy'.[17] He essentially argues that Ireland had to become more realistic about existing and emerging threats, and jettison some of its stubborn neutrality. In a very valuable chapter entitled 'Northern Ireland, NATO and the Cold War',[18] Geoffrey R. Sloan assesses the strategic value of the island. He stresses the vital role of Northern Ireland for NATO and also that some British strategists believed that Ireland was defenceless and thus constituted a gap in NATO's defence. Opinions on Northern Ireland's strategic value fluctuated during the Cold War but in 1972 the British government was adamant that the 'Troubles' should not pose a security threat to Britain and present an opportunity for a foreign power to destabilise the United Kingdom. As this book shows, that was precisely what the Soviets wanted to do in 1972 during the KGB's 'Operation SPLASH'. Patrick Keatinge has made regular contributions on Ireland's foreign relations in *Irish Studies in International Affairs* which provide valuable insights.[19]

Regarding bilateral relations between Ireland and Eastern European countries, Stephen White in 'Ireland, Russia, Communism, Post-Communism'[20] details the beginning of the relations between Ireland, the Irish Free State as it was known back then, and the Soviet Union. He writes that over the decades the Soviet Union was more or less interested in Ireland, but that under Leonid Brezhnev's leadership (1964–82) interest in the country was definitely being revived owing to the 'Troubles' in Northern Ireland. The Soviets were of the opinion that the origins of the conflict were purely economic and that it was a colonial war. The PIRA was not liked in Moscow as it was deemed to be inspired by 'religious fanaticism and anti-communism'. According to the Soviets, only the Communist Party of Ireland (CPI) had the answer to the problem, but Soviet patience and support for the CPI eventually petered out. In 'The Soviet Union in Irish Foreign Policy',[21] Michael Ó Corcora and Ronald J. Hill explore the establishing of diplomatic relations between the Soviet Union and Ireland, and also issues of Irish public opinion towards Moscow. The Irish people were rather apathetic or suspicious and the Irish Church was vehemently anti-Communist. By and large, the Irish trade union movement was not supportive of the Soviet Union, but economic lobbies, like the farmers, eventually pressured the government into opening trade links with the Soviets. Generally, Ireland did not particularly like the Soviet Union as it considered this country to be a colonial power with a hold over Eastern Europe. Eventually, the decision to open diplomatic relations was taken in 1973.

Gabriel Doherty has written a detailed study of Ireland's food aid programme to an economically stricken Poland in the early 1980s at a time when that country was rocked by political events that were the creation of the independent trade union Solidarność (Solidarity) in which Lech Wałęsa played a key role and the subsequent *coup d'état* led by General Wojciech Jaruzelski. Doherty describes Ireland's efforts with the European Community as being motivated by humanitarian, development and security concerns. Included is an analysis of Irish policy towards Poland between 1921 and 1980.[22]

The opening of diplomatic relations between Ireland and the GDR occurred in 1980 at a time when East–West tensions increased seriously. Damian Mac Con Uladh has written two pioneering studies. In 'The Poor Relations: The GDR and Ireland', he pertinently argues that to get a good understanding of Irish–East German relations it is necessary to go further than just focusing on diplomacy and foreign policy. Relations between the Socialist Unity Party (SED), or the East German Communist party, and the CPI played a central role, as did exchanges between so-called Friendship societies in the two countries and also trade.[23] In a chapter entitled 'The GDR and Northern Ireland',[24] Mac Con Uladh explains that the GDR considered the Northern Irish conflict to be a colonial struggle. The PIRA's strategy and outlook was strongly condemned by the East German media although it did support Bobby Sands and the hunger strikes of 1980–81 as the CPI had decided to support them. The Protestant/unionist community was systematically described as being reactionary and right-wing.

As previously mentioned I decided to take the same approach as in the IRCHSS project and analyse East-German–(Northern) Irish relations at political, economic and cultural levels, initially believing that the amount of available primary sources would be rather limited.

I considered my sources and found more material than anticipated in the National Archives of Ireland, Dublin, the Irish military archive in Cathal Brugha Barracks, Dublin, the archives of the Communist Party of Ireland in the Gilbert Library, Dublin, the Dublin Diocesan Archive, the Stiftung Archiv der Parteien und Massenorganisationen der DDR im Bundesarchiv (Foundation Archives of Parties and Mass Organisations of the GDR in the Federal Archive), Berlin, the Auswärtiges Amt-Politisches Archiv (archive of the German Foreign Office), Berlin, the Deutsches Rundfunkarchiv (archive of German broadcasting), Potsdam-Babelsberg, the Evangelisches Zentralarchiv (archive of the Evangelical Church in the former GDR), Berlin, the Konrad-Adenauer-Stiftung (archive of the German Christian-Democratic Party), Sankt Augustin, the Regionalarchiv Ordinarien Ost (archive of the Catholic Church in the former GDR), Erfurt, and the online newspaper archive of the Staatsbibliothek zu Berlin, Preußischer Kulturbesitz Zeitungsinformationssystem. Also, there was relevant material in the archive of NATO in Brussels, which has been declassified, and in the online archive of the American Central Intelligence Agency (CIA), to my mind a model for other intelligence agencies to adopt if ever they decide to make their files available to research, which is not a foregone conclusion.

As is well known, for a very long time Ireland was considered to be a springboard for an attack on Britain by foreign continental powers, that is to say Spain, France and Germany. In the *Irish Factor, 1899–1919*, I portrayed some of the intelligence activities of the Germans and the French.[25] Reinhard R. Doerries wrote about Imperial Germany's support for the Irish republicans during the First World War, especially about the relations between the Germans and Roger Casement.[26] As shown above, Enno Stephan and Mark M. Hull concentrated on German intelligence activities during the Second World War. Eunan O'Halpin, a leading expert in intelligence and security issues in Ireland, wrote extensively on intelligence issues within an Anglo-Irish-American context.[27] By contrast, spying activities involving (non-English speaking) foreign powers regarding Ireland and Northern Ireland during the Cold War have remained largely unexplored. In that sense, this book offers a totally new insight.

From a German point of view, this study is rather original. As Wolfgang Krieger points out, there has been but little interest shown in the history of German intelligence. In fact, he speaks of 'neglect' and attributes this to several reasons. Unlike the American CIA, the security and intelligences services of Germany, or the former West Germany, have not declassified material. Also, there is the particular 'psychological atmosphere' in Germany. After the Second World War, military and security studies were neglected and frowned upon by some political quarters. Moreover, Krieger writes that 'it is understandable that the Germans associated war so extensively with death, destruction and humiliation' unlike the Anglo-Saxons, which explains why in the United States and the United Kingdom war and intelligence studies are much more popular. But Krieger stresses that there is one exception: studies on the Stasi. Excellent books have been produced since the fall of the Berlin Wall. However, he explains that most studies are confined to the Stasi's activities within East Germany.[28] Yet, the Stasi most definitely ventured abroad. As Jens Gieseke, an expert on the history of the Stasi, writes, its main target abroad was first and foremost West Germany.[29]

Owing to the important mass of primary sources I decided to focus especially on East German intelligence activities, hence the title of this book. The following structure was adopted. Part I is entitled 'Relations between Ireland and East Germany'. It is an analysis of the political, economic and cultural links between the two countries, and also perceptions and portrayals by the media. For example, how did the *Irish Times*, the *Irish Independent* and the *Irish Farmers Journal* describe life behind the Berlin Wall? Was it all negative? In turn, what did *Neues Deutschland*, *Neue Zeit*, *Berliner Zeitung* and the *Weltbühne* think of Irish culture and what attitude did they adopt towards Bloody Sunday in (London)Derry in 1972 and the hunger strikes in Northern Ireland in the early 1980s? The East German television sent journalists to report not only on the conflict in Northern Ireland but also on the socio-economic conditions in Ireland. Was it all propaganda? A handful of Irish idealists settled in the GDR and attention is paid to their activities. The activities of the Ireland–GDR Friendship Society are also examined.

A large section is devoted to the long and extraordinary process of establishing diplomatic relations between Ireland and the GDR. It had become a point of honour, if not an obsession for the East German leader, Erich Honecker. The unpublished manuscript of Edgar Uher, a former East German diplomat and HVA (the Stasi's foreign intelligence department) officer gives a unique insight into what happened behind the scenes. The eventual opening of official diplomatic relations in 1980 did not bring about a much needed change in the balance of trade between the two countries as Dublin had hoped. For decades, Ireland's balance of trade with Eastern Europe and the Soviet Union was negative. The reasons why are explored. Another interesting issue is the uneasy *ménage à trois* that developed between Honecker's SED, the CPI and Sinn Féin/the Workers' Party (SF/WP). The Soviets had told the East Germans to drop the CPI and focus on SF/WP as this party looked more promising from an electoral point of view. How did East Berlin handle this delicate situation as it was on very good terms with the CPI leader, Michael O'Riordan?

Although the book is divided into two parts, the parts are connected as the Stasi was omnipresent, be it in assessing PIRA activities and getting confidential documents on the one hand, or reviewing a book based on Frank Ryan's life, analysing media duels between East and West Germany concerning Northern Ireland and reporting words of Irish businessmen visiting the Leipzig Fair on the other hand.

In Part II, attention is focused solely on intelligence activities: reading and listening about Ireland and Northern Ireland; spying on Ireland; recording information on Northern Ireland in the central databank for persons; and watching the PIRA, the INLA and BAOR. Thus, documents and findings are presented in a rather thematic way, except the history of Irish terrorist activities in West Germany. This approach has the advantage of showing how an intelligence service actually operates. The book will no doubt shatter some stereotype notions and clichés. Those who believe that intelligence services are only interested in secret documents, secret invasion plans, secret alliances and so on might be in for a rude awakening. Of course the Stasi was looking for classified and highly sensitive material but not only as the hundreds of press cuttings, the photocopies of books, the transcripts or radio and television broadcasts and so on do testify. There was also industrial espionage like acquiring telephone extension plans and turbine and pump plans, and also assessments of the Irish steel market. It has been possible to identify some of the sources and agents that provided information on Ireland and Northern Ireland, though not all.

In an nutshell, Part II explores the following issues: what kind of information on Ireland and Northern Ireland was obtained; where this information was obtained; who were the people behind the code names and registration numbers of agents and sources; how the obtained information was assessed in East Berlin; how the Stasi watched the activities of Irish terrorists in West Germany and their attacks on BAOR and what were HA-XXII's assessments of the evolving situation; what were the relations between the PIRA, the INLA, the Red Army Faction (RAF), the Revolutionary Cells, Carlos the Jackal and groups that supported Irish republicans in West Germany like the WISK. Certain Irish and British authors assert that the Stasi might have provided support to the PIRA or the Official IRA (OIRA).[30] These assertions have been investigated and answers are given. The Stasi material sheds light on this rather forgotten aspect of the Troubles, namely the PIRA's campaign against BAOR.

The SIRA documents show that there was interaction between the KGB (Committee for State Security, that is to say Soviet intelligence) and the Stasi. SIRA is the acronym for System der Informationsrecherche der Aufklärung (Information Research System of the HVA). The HVA (Hauptverwaltung Aufklärung) was the foreign intelligence department of the Stasi led by the legendary Markus Wolf, known for years in the West as 'man without a face', arguably the greatest spymaster ever. Information on Ireland and Northern Ireland was exchanged. But the KGB was not alone in its interest in Irish and Northern Irish affairs in the Soviet Union. There was the GRU also. The latter was the Foreign Military Intelligence of the Soviet Army General Staff. It took a very serious interest in the development of the conflict in Northern Ireland in 1972. The German military archives in Freiburg am Breisgau reveal that the GRU notified East German military intelligence that the conflict was weakening BAOR's strength. This in all likelihood prompted Yuri Andropov, the then head of the KGB, to agree to send arms to the OIRA as Michael O'Riordan, the very republican leader of the CPI, had been asking for since 1969 according to revelations in Boris Yeltsin's book, *The View from the Kremlin*. It would seem that the arms were delivered during 'Operation SPLASH' at a time when détente was a fashionable word. The archives of the former KGB are out of bounds. However, information on Ireland and Northern Ireland written by defectors or former agents exists. But evidently a clearer picture can only emerge if access to KGB material ever becomes open to research. Emerging also is a rather unexpected Romanian link involving arms deals between the Carlos group and the PIRA. It remains unclear whether it was the Securitate which was behind it or the Departamentul de Informatii Externe (DIE, Department of External Information, or Romanian foreign intelligence).

It is hoped that the reader will be persuaded that Ireland, the island on the fringe of Western Europe, was not without interest for the Stasi.

Notes

1 J. aan de Wiel, *The Irish Factor, 1899–1919: Ireland's Strategic and Diplomatic Importance for Foreign Powers* (Dublin: Irish Academic Press, 2008).

2 M. O'Driscoll, *Ireland, Germany and the Nazis: Politics and Diplomacy, 1919–1939* (Dublin: Four Courts Press, 2004).

3 E. Stephan, *Spies in Ireland* (Harrisburg, PA: Stackpole, 1965).

4 M. M. Hull, *Irish Secrets: German Espionage in Wartime Ireland 1939–1945* (Dublin: Irish Academic Press, 2003).
5 M. O'Driscoll, 'West Germany', in M. O'Driscoll, D. Keogh & J. aan de Wiel (eds.), *Ireland through European Eyes: Western Europe, the EEC and Ireland, 1945–1973* (Cork: Cork University Press, 2013), pp. 9–74.
6 J. Fischer, *Das Deutschlandbild der Iren 1890–1939* (Heidelberg: Winter, 2000).
7 D. Keogh, 'Ireland, the Vatican and the Cold War: The Case of Italy, 1948', *Irish Studies in International Affairs*, vol. 3, no. 3 (1991), pp. 67–114.
8 B. Whelan, *Ireland and the Marshall Plan, 1947–57* (Dublin: Four Courts Press, 2000).
9 I. McCabe, *A Diplomatic History of Ireland 1948–49: The Republic, the Commonwealth and NATO* (Blackrock: Irish Academic Press, 1991).
10 T. Geiger, 'Trading with the Enemy: Ireland, the Cold War and East-West trade, 1945–55', *Irish Studies in International Affairs*, vol. 19 (2008), pp. 119–42.
11 E. Ward, '"A Big Show-off to Show What We Could Do": Ireland and the Hungarian Refugee Crisis of 1956', *Irish Studies in International Affairs*, vol. 7 (1996), pp. 131–41.
12 P. L. Wylie, *Ireland and the Cold War: Diplomacy and Recognition 1949–63* (Dublin: Irish Academic Press, 2006).
13 J. M. Skelly, *Irish Diplomacy at the United Nations, 1945–1965* (Dublin: Irish Academic Press, 1997).
14 C. Manathunga, 'The Evolution of Irish Disarmament Initiatives at the United Nations, 1957–1961', *Irish Studies in International Affairs*, vol. 7 (1996), pp. 97–113.
15 E. M. Chossudovsky, 'The Origins of the Treaty on the Non-Proliferation of Nuclear Weapons: Ireland's Initiative in the United Nations', *Irish Studies in International Affairs*, vol. 3, no. 2 (1990), pp. 111–35.
16 R. McNamara, 'Irish Perspectives on the Vietnam War', *Irish Studies in International Affairs*, vol. 14 (2003), pp. 75–94.
17 T. Salmon, 'The Changing Nature of Irish Defence Policy', *The World Today*, vol. 35, no. 11 (Nov. 1979), pp. 462–70. See also: T. Salmon, *Unneutral Ireland: An Ambivalent and Unique Security Policy* (Oxford: Clarendon Press, 1989).
18 G. R. Sloan, *The Geopolitics of Anglo-Irish Relations in the 20the Century* (London and New York: Continuum, 1997), pp. 239–75.
19 See for example: P. Keatinge, 'Ireland's Foreign Relations in 1989', *Irish Studies in International Affairs*, vol. 3, no. 2 (1990), pp. 137–65.
20 S. White, 'Ireland, Russia, Communism, Post-Communism', *Irish Studies in International Affairs*, vol. 6 (1997), pp. 155–61.
21 M. Ó Corcora & R. J. Hill, 'The Soviet Union in Irish Foreign Policy', *International Affairs*, vol. 58, no. 2 (spring, 1982), pp. 254–70.
22 G. Doherty, 'Ireland, Europe and the Provision of Food Aid to Poland 1980–81', *Irish Studies in International Affairs*, vol. 24 (2013), pp. 1–19.

23 D. Mac Con Uladh, 'The Poor Relations: The GDR and Ireland', in J. Fischer, P. Ó Dochartaigh & H. Kelly-Holmes (eds.), *Irish–German Studies* (yearbook of the Centre for Irish–German Studies), 1. 2001/2002 (Trier: Wissenschaftlicher Verlag), pp. 73–87.

24 D. Mac Con Uladh, 'The GDR and Northern Ireland', in S. Berger & N. LaPorte (eds.), *The Other Germany: Perceptions and Influences in British–East German Relations, 1945–1990* (Augsburg: Wißner-Verlag, 2005), pp. 91–105.

25 See also J. aan de Wiel, 'French Military Intelligence and Ireland, 1900–1923', *Intelligence and National Security*, vol. 26, no. 1 (February 2011), pp. 46–71; J. aan de Wiel, 'Austria-Hungary, France, Germany and the Irish Crisis from 1899 to the Outbreak of the First World War', *Intelligence and National Security*, vol. 21, no. 2 (April 2006), pp. 237–57.

26 R. R. Doerries (ed.), *Prelude to the Easter Rising* (London: Frank Cass, 2000).

27 See for example E. O'Halpin, *Defending Ireland: The Irish State and Its Enemies since 1922* (Oxford: Oxford University Press, 1999); E. O'Halpin, 'Intelligence and Anglo-Irish relations, 1922–73', in E. O'Halpin, R. Armstrong & J. Ohlmeyer (eds.), *Intelligence, Statecraft and International Power* (Dublin: Irish Academic Press, 2006), pp. 132–50.

28 W. Krieger, 'German Intelligence History: A Field in Search of Scholars', *Intelligence and National Security*, vol. 19, no. 2 (summer 2004), pp. 185–98.

29 J. Gieseke, 'East German Espionage in the Era of Détente', *Journal of Strategic Studies*, vol. 31, no. 3 (June 2008), pp. 395–424, 406.

30 A. Glees, *The Stasi Files: East Germany's Secret Operations Against Britain* (London: Free Press, 2004), pp. 126–7, 216; E. Moloney, *A Secret History of the IRA* (London: Penguin, 2007), p. 137; B. Hanley & S. Millar, *The Lost Revolution: The Story of the Official IRA and the Workers' Party* (London: Penguin, 2010), p. 404.

Part I

Relations between Ireland and East Germany

1

History of the relations between Ireland/ Northern Ireland and the GDR

Ireland adopts the Hallstein doctrine

Before embarking upon this journey in the archives of the Stasi, it is necessary to give a picture on the relations between Ireland and the former German Democratic Republic (GDR, or East Germany) to set the scene. After the defeat of Nazi Germany in May 1945, the Soviet Union occupied the eastern area of the country. Serious disagreements between the Western Allies and the Soviets led to the division of Germany which would last until 1990: in May 1949, the Federal Republic of Germany (FRG, or West Germany) saw the light, followed in October by the GDR. The FRG became part of NATO (North Atlantic Treaty Organization) in May 1955. A few days later, the GDR was among the founding member states of the opposing military alliance, the Warsaw Pact although the country still had to establish a formal army. That was done the following year in 1956 when the Nationale Volksarmee (NVA, national people's army) saw the light and after Moscow denounced 'the remilitarisation of the Federal Republic'.[1]

Ireland had remained neutral during the Second World War although the large extent of its secret cooperation with the Western Allies led some to question if the country could really be described as having been neutral and redefined its wartime attitude as rather having been non-belligerent.[2] In the immediate post-war years, Ireland became officially a republic in 1949 and left the British Commonwealth. It also refused to join NATO as the then government deemed that joining the Atlantic Alliance would imply the recognition of Northern Ireland and the acceptance of partition.[3] However, despite Ireland remaining officially neutral during the emerging Cold War, it was firmly anchored in the West. It did not take long for the Irish to cross swords with the Soviets as Moscow refused Irish membership of the United Nations (UN) in 1946. Andrei Gromyko, the Soviet Permanent Representative to the United Nations, was not impressed by the war record of certain countries against Nazi Germany, Ireland among them.[4] He was clearly not aware of Ireland's secret cooperation but in fairness to him he could not have known. It would appear that in fact the Soviets were thinking of the balance of power in the United Nations and therefore blocked the admission of certain countries. Ireland eventually joined in 1955.[5]

Once Ireland was in the United Nations, the attitude of the Irish delegation varied according to who was in power in Dublin although the country did not waver in its support for the West. When John A. Costello was Taoiseach (Prime Minister) between 1954 and 1957, the objective was to help the West to win the Cold War. Ireland was staunchly behind the United States. When Éamon de Valera took over from 1957 until 1959, the Irish delegation in the United Nations sought to lessen East–West tensions, adopted an independent role and supported African and Asian countries that struggled for independence. Yet, it was never neutralist. During the area of Seán Lemass, the Irish delegation tried to promote a stable international situation that would be in the country's economic interests. Lemass himself was an Atlanticist who stood squarely behind President John F. Kennedy during the Cuban missile crisis in 1962. During an official visit to Bonn, he explained that although Ireland was not a member of NATO, it was firmly on the West's side. During de Valera and Lemass's terms in office, Frank Aiken was Minister for External Affairs. Aiken's main aim was the reduction of tensions between the superpowers in which the United Nations should play a key role. He advocated a troop withdrawal scheme from Central Europe which was unsuccessful. Yet he was successful in his initiatives in nuclear non-proliferation. The Non-Proliferation Treaty was eventually signed in Moscow in 1968 and was his finest hour.[6]

Besides the mainstream politicians, the Catholic Church was the spearhead of the anti-Communist struggle in the country and Irish Communists were kept under surveillance. John Charles McQuaid, the Archbishop of Dublin, was pro-NATO and was kept regularly informed about Communist activities within his archdiocese while the Catholic Information Bureau, headed by two bishops, kept and upgraded lists of known Communists.[7] The West German embassy in Dublin had noticed McQuaid's very strong denunciations of 'Godless Communism' and his threats of excommunication against those Catholics who joined Communist organisations or who published and distributed Communist books, newspapers and pamphlets.[8] On occasion, the police cooperated with the church. On 14 November 1967, the Special Detective Unit of the Garda Siochána (Irish police) wrote a report on Michael O'Riordan, the Irish Communist leader, who had participated in the 50th anniversary of the October Revolution of 1917 in Moscow. The detectives managed to get a copy of O'Riordan's speech. Their subsequent report was then forwarded to McQuaid.[9] There was clearly collusion between some in the Garda Siochána and the ecclesiastical authorities.[10] Irish democracy took no chances with what it considered to be potential enemies of the far left.

The participation of Irish citizens in activities behind the Iron Curtain was taken extremely seriously. In October 1951, when it became known that a handful of young Irish people might have participated in the World Festival of Youth in East Berlin, some deputies asked Aiken in the Dáil (Lower House in the Irish Parliament) 'if he is aware that citizens of the Republic of Ireland of immature age attended the youth rally in Berlin held in August of this year and fraternised with the avowed enemies of Christianity'. Aiken replied that 'no passports were granted for the express purpose of attending the youth rally in Berlin last August but, as far as I am aware, 18 holders of Irish passports issued over the past four years attended the Berlin rally'.[11] Clearly, the Department of External Affairs (DEA) kept a record on the movements of Irish citizens. Perhaps the Irish authorities were right to be concerned. This World Festival of Youth had been carefully rehearsed and mass parades on the very large-scale took place in various places in East Berlin. According to Anne Applebaum, the event marked 'the zenith of High Stalinism ... and put East Germany on display on an international stage for the first time'. Also massively present was the Stasi, eager to collect as much information as possible and scouting for possible new sources and agents, notably among the West German participants.[12]

Those who received East German literature were monitored by the Department of Defence. In March 1957, the Department informed the DEA that a bookshop called New Books Ltd located at 16a Pearse Street in Dublin and also members of the Irish Workers' League (IWL, Communists) and the Irish–Soviet Friendship Society were in possession of the following 'propaganda material': *Democratic German Report* (Berlin), *Democratic German Republic Magazine* (Leipzig), *German Democratic Republic* (Dresden) and *Women of the Whole World* (Berlin).[13] The same month, the Department of Justice replied to a query of the DEA that 'we have no evidence that propaganda material is being sent to this country by the Government of the Soviet Zone of Germany but we are aware that certain individuals are in receipt of propaganda material from East German trade union sources and from various cultural groups in East Germany'.[14] The Department of Justice took its mission to root out Communism most seriously as back in January 1953 the DEA had notified its relevant consulates that 'in no circumstances ... is a visa to be granted to an Eastern European without reference to the Department of Justice'.[15]

The West German government advocated non-recognition of the GDR and claimed to be the only valid and true representative of the whole of Germany. This became known as the so-called Hallstein doctrine and non-recognition became the norm in the West. Frank Aiken was strongly in favour of German reunification and the Irish government adopted Bonn's doctrine. This was appreciated by the West Germans,[16] although they criticised Ireland's insular tendencies and neutrality as they believed Western Europe should be strongly united to face the Soviet Union.[17] Consequently, Dublin kept relations with the GDR at a strict minimum and took great care not to stand in Bonn's way in intra-German relations. The Irish government rejected the GDR's application for membership of various international organisations which was a way for the East Germans to obtain some sort of recognition. In 1954, for instance, it objected to East Germany's membership of the World Meteorological Organization (WMO).[18]

East Berlin made strenuous efforts to obtain *de facto* and *de jure* recognition in the West, including Ireland. One approach consisted in sending official letters, hoping to get an acknowledgement in return and then try to build relations. Generally, the East German authorities took the occasion of the anniversary of some historic event or a current political development to make an approach. On 31 May 1965, the East German Ministry of External Affairs sent the DEA a 'Manifesto on the occasion of the 20th anniversary of the Liberation'; in other words, the end of the Second World War and the defeat of Nazism. In it, the Western powers were accused of having imperialist aims in Germany and of having partitioned the country and that 'we in the German Democratic Republic, we in the East of Germany, have consistently walked the path of peace. We have done everything necessary for peace.' By contrast, the FRG was 'the continuation of the Hitler state' and 'the spirit of militarist servitude and imperial conquest is increasingly permeating all pores of West German life and threatens to re-contaminate broad masses with chauvinism'.[19] The Irish government's standard reply to letters from East Berlin was to give no reply.

In November 1956, Minister for External Affairs Liam Cosgrave directed the department to send a new circular entitled 'Recognition of States' to the Irish missions abroad. Regarding China, it was explained that Ireland only recognised the nationalist government based in Formosa and not Mao Zedong's government, while it recognised *de jure* the Soviet Union without, however, recognising the incorporation of Estonia, Latvia and Lithuania. Regarding Poland, it was reiterated in the circular that only its pre-war government, now in exile, was recognised. As far as Albania, Bulgaria, Czechoslovakia, Hungary, Romania and Yugoslavia were concerned, '*de jure* recognition is accorded to the Governments of all these States'. As regards Germany, the situation was very clear: 'The Government of the Federal Republic of Germany is recognised as the only Government in Germany. Missions should be particularly careful to avoid any contact with representatives of the so-called "German Democratic Republic".'[20]

The Irish government eagerly endorsed NATO's decision not to accept as valid passports issued by the East German authorities. Only so-called Temporary Travel Documents (TTD) issued by the Western Allies in West Berlin could be accepted. These were not granted to East German officials. So it was that in 1953, the poet and playwright Berthold Brecht, who was a delegate of the East German section of the PEN Club, an association that promoted intellectual exchanges between writers worldwide, was not allowed to go to Dublin to attend a PEN congress.[21] In September 1965, the East German football club ASK Vorwärts was due to play a match against Drumcondra FC in Dublin. On this occasion, the Irish refused the display of East German insignia and the playing of the GDR anthem.[22] The handful of Irish Communists north and south of the border campaigned for the recognition of the GDR. In 1955, they claimed to have collected 10,000 signatures in a pro-recognition petition organised in Northern Ireland.[23] Their efforts were in vain.

The Irish government was kept well informed of the developing situation in the two Germanys by its diplomats. In September 1954, Conor Cruise O'Brien, then a young diplomat before he became the well-known intellectual and journalist, was in Berlin where he witnessed a demonstration against fascism in which East German Prime Minister Otto Grotewohl and Soviet General Alexander Gundorov participated. According to him:

> throughout these prolonged proceedings the mass of the demonstrators, or such sections of them as I could see, looked very bored indeed. Some of them yawned openly, very few did more than raise a most perfunctory clap when the speaker paused for a reaction from his audience. References to Russia and the remarks of the Russian General himself were received with even less enthusiasm than tributes e.g. to President [Wilhelm] Pieck [of the GDR].[24]

Coming so soon after the uprising of 17 June 1953 when Soviet tanks had put a violent end to the revolts of the East German working class, those people whose interests they were precisely meant to defend, Cruise O'Brien's remark was not surprising.

Other Irish reports dealt with the political difficulties experienced by Christians in East Berlin,[25] the West German government's attitude towards the East German regime,[26] and general impressions of the Soviet sector of Berlin.[27] In July 1955, T. J. Kiernan, the Irish Minister Plenipotentiary in Bonn, was invited to visit a so-called 'reception camp' in West Berlin as thousands of East Germans, especially young people, were leaving the GDR. He witnessed the screening of these refugees by the Western Allies as they had to be sure that no spies were among them. Kiernan observed that the refugees were becoming 'a major problem in West Berlin' as they had to be given employment. [28]

While an Iron Curtain isolated East Germany from West Germany, people were still able to move freely in Berlin as there were no strict border controls between the western and eastern sectors owing to agreements between the Soviets, Americans, British and French. This meant that tens of thousands of dissatisfied East Germans could reach the West by simply travelling to East Berlin and then cross into the western sector. Although this posed serious logistical problems for the West German authorities, these refugees constituted an important source of cheap labour as the FRG was experiencing its *Wirtschaftswunder* (economic miracle) in the 1950s. By contrast, East Germany was being bled dry of its population at an alarmingly rapid rate. By 1961, 3,500,000 had gone to the West while only 500,000 had gone to the East. Most of these East Germans were skilled workers and intellectuals.[29] Irish newspapers were well aware of the unfolding humanitarian crisis.[30]

If this exodus was set to continue, Walter Ulbricht would become the head of an empty country. Eventually, the leader of the GDR found a solution: the building of a wall around West Berlin. In the early hours of 13 August 1961, East Berliners woke up to find themselves cut off by barbed wire from the Western sector while at the same time bricklayers were erecting a wall under the watchful eyes of the Volkspolizei.[31] Over the years the Berlin Wall would become the world's most sophisticated and lethal border. East–West tensions increased, Western leaders denouncing the latest Communist atrocity and standing on the high moral ground. In reality, the building of the Wall stabilised the international situation as the focus of the Cold War shifted away from Berlin. For the GDR, it led to an improvement in its domestic situation.[32]

The Irish government was alive to the deteriorating situation in East Germany. Shortly before the building of the Wall, it was explained in a report that the policy of collectivisation was leading to food shortages. There was resistance to collectivisation and also some industrial unrest. Now, the East German authorities were trying to stem the flow of people leaving the country. The report's conclusion read: 'None of these harsh measures has availed, however, to dry up the refugee stream. Since the East German puppet State was created in October 1949, no fewer than 2,634,699 East Germans have, by fleeing the East Zone, "voted with their feet" against the Communist tyranny'.[33] Then Ulbricht came up with his solution. On 19 August 1961, six days after the beginning of the building of the Wall, Brian Ó Ceallaigh, the Irish chargé d'affaires in Bonn, reassuringly wrote that 'there is little or no war psychosis here'. Nevertheless, not everybody was reassured. Ó Ceallaigh added: 'There are, of course, some pessimists. We have felt an increase over the past weeks in the number of enquiries received from individuals and firms who want to settle in Ireland.'[34] Ireland was being perceived by some as a zone that would be spared by a possible East–West conflict. It is to be noticed that this perception would last until the final phase of the Cold War in the 1980s. Some officers in the Bundeswehr (West German army) had thought about evacuation plans and bought houses in Ireland.[35]

In December 1960, the West German Ambassador in Dublin reported to the Foreign Office in Bonn that 'Ireland was ideologically-speaking clearly on the West's side'.[36] It was therefore to be expected that sometimes the West German government asked the Irish government for support. On one particular occasion, the West German embassy asked the DEA to look after East German refugees that might reach Ireland by jumping ship. It explained that there was a 'continued suppression of German nationals in the Soviet-occupied Zone of Germany and especially [an] increased oppression of Christian faith'.[37] The Irish authorities were only too happy to help.

From time to time, the Irish authorities were also approached by West German anti-Communist groups. For example, in October 1958, the Irish embassy in Bonn received a letter from the Volksbund für Frieden und Freiheit (people's league for peace and freedom). The Volksbund warned that Dennoch-Verlag, a publishing company based in the FRG that reproduced pictures made by handicapped artists, was in fact 'an enterprise set up by a Communist to serve Communist purposes'. The company had a network with representatives abroad and the Volksbund gave the name and address of a man living in Cork cautioning that any 'assistance extended to this firm would be tantamount to support given to the Communist Party'.[38]

However, it should be stressed here that the West German Foreign Office discouraged and dismissed all kinds of comparisons between Northern Ireland and the Soviet-occupied Zone of Germany lest the British should be offended.[39] The West German position towards Irish partition was also shared by the East Germans. Despite the fact that East German newspapers condemned it, the issue played no practical part in the formulation of East German policy towards German partition. Dr Joachim Mitdank, the last East German Ambassador to Ireland (based in London) remarked that it was not relevant.[40] As will be seen shortly, the GDR intended to remain a separate state and Stasi documents confirm this. In the meantime, some trade relations had developed between Ireland and the East bloc.

Minimal trade relations

Ireland's trade policy with the East bloc reflected its foreign policy approach. In the immediate post-war years, Ireland's trade with Eastern Europe was simply insignificant. Imports from the East represented 1.5 per cent of the country's total imports and exports to the East represented 0.5 per cent. In 1949, Ireland imported East German goods for a total value of £13,946; in 1950, £12,001; in 1951, £96,723 and in 1952, £127,952. Under these circumstances, the US Congress, which had imposed severe trade restrictions and sanctions on trade with the East bloc, did not threaten Ireland with reprisals. President Dwight D. Eisenhower adopted a more liberal approach to East–West trade and Ireland followed suit, but Minister for External Affairs Frank Aiken still had problems with issuing visas to Eastern European officials or signing official trade agreements. The press in Ireland was generally hostile to the idea of trading with Communists. The *Irish Independent* and (Catholic) *Standard* regularly denounced business with the East on account of religious persecution behind the Iron Curtain. Catholic groups could be troublesome for the government. As a result, Aiken's position was that Irish officials should not deal with Eastern European officials but that private individuals were free to do whatever they wanted.[41]

On 23 February 1953, the Department of Finance produced a memorandum entitled 'Trading with countries under Communist rule'. It was very clear that any public controversy arising from '"buying from the Reds"' had to be avoided.[42] Stalin's death shortly later on 5 March led to an improvement of East–West relations and the beginnings of what went down in history as détente. Ireland, however, remained entrenched in its anti-Communism, especially with the new government led by John A. Costello (Fine Gael). The following year, a memorandum was prepared for discussion within the government in which public opinion's hostility towards trade with the East was stressed. It was recommended that the government should therefore not encourage such trade, but at the same time it would not 'interfere with present private trading relations'.[43]

On 20 March 1957, Éamon de Valera (Fianna Fáil) was back in power. Frank Aiken was reappointed as Minister for External Affairs, a position he would occupy until July 1969. The attitude towards trade with the East bloc changed a little. During a meeting of the Foreign Trade Committee in April, the representative of the DEA said that Aiken felt that Ireland's position should be revised and trade developed especially with Czechoslovakia, 'a highly industrialised country' with which 'Ireland had a complementary economy which indicated that there should be an opening for our agricultural produce'. The committee agreed with this and also with the fact that 'the present balance of trade [with Communist countries] is unsatisfactory'.[44] In June, it was decided that 'Government officials and State agencies should be authorised to enter into commercial contacts with official representatives and agencies of Czechoslovakia and Poland to explore trade possibilities'. However, care should be taken to avoid the mention of official trade agreements without government approval first.[45] Dublin remained cautious, but there was nonetheless some progress. Developing trade with East Germany was not mentioned.

However, in January 1959, the *Irish Times* reported that a trade agreement had been signed between the British and the East Germans. There had been no difficulties as it did not involve diplomatic relations, in other words, the Hallstein doctrine had not been breached. A representative of the KfA (Kammer für Außenhandel, East German Chamber of Foreign Trade) would take up residence in London. As for the West German government, it had been informed and had had no objections to it. Besides the British, the French, Dutch, Belgians, Luxembourgers and West Germans also had similar trade agreements. The *Irish Times* wrote that 'East Germany's economic existence, at least, has been recognized'.[46] The newspaper implied that time had come for Ireland to change its attitude. Indeed, its trade statistics with East Germany spoke volumes. For 1958, the total value of exports to the GDR was £20,090 while imports totalled £714,112.[47] The West Germany embassy in Dublin reported to the Foreign Office in Bonn that Irish exports to the Soviet-occupied Zone were quasi insignificant.[48] And yet unlike its British neighbour, Ireland would not sign a trade agreement with the GDR.

Nonetheless, it was high time to redress that balance all the more since in January 1963, Britain's negotiations to join the EEC were dealt a mortal blow by General Charles de Gaulle. The French president deemed that the British were not ready to enter. This also meant the end of Ireland's hopes as it simply could not enter the Community without Britain as its economy was too dependent on the British market.

There was perhaps an opportunity to develop trade with the GDR when an East German delegation stayed in Dublin between 5 and 7 May 1963. The reason for this visit was a small trade war that had developed between the two countries. Tony O'Reilly, the head of Bord Bainne (Irish Dairy Board), had travelled to the Leipzig Fair a year earlier to strike a deal for Irish butter exports to the GDR. The East Germans, however, had refused and this in turn had led to the Irish government implementing the Restriction of Imports Act which meant restricting the importation of East German products such as potash. The aim was to force East Berlin to import more Irish goods. As a result, East Berlin had put forward to buy 500 tons of butter.[49]

The East German delegation's visit had been arranged by Kurt Ticher in Dublin and the British Labour MP Ian Mikardo. Ticher was born in the German Empire in Thuringia, which subsequently became a region in the GDR, in 1899 and had emigrated to Ireland in 1925.[50] He had a firm in the capital which imported goods from behind the Iron Curtain, especially from the GDR, and was on very good terms with the East German authorities. Ticher was in touch with the East German trade mission in London and also lobbied for more trade with the GDR and talks between Dublin and East Berlin to officialise relations.[51] The KfA's visit was most important as it shed light on the present difficulties to develop trade links between the two countries and also in the decades to come.

In a nutshell, and according to the East German report, the difficulties that emerged were that the East German economy was a planned one and that therefore there was little room for unexpected changes and last-minute decisions. The Irish officials said that their government wanted to improve the country's export figures and that it had difficulties to export more to free-market countries because of existing economic conditions. Although it is not stated in the East German report, it seems clear that the Irish officials were alluding to the fact that Ireland was neither a member of the European Free Trade Association (EFTA), nor of the EEC and its customs union. Córas Tráchtála (Irish Export Board) and Bord Bainne had sent delegations to the Socialist countries, the officials continued, and representatives of the Socialist countries had sent delegations to Ireland, all this to develop commercial relations. Achieving a balance of trade with East Germany was a reasonable demand but from East Berlin's point of view, Ireland had 'only a very small range of goods for export (butter, meat, wool and hides)' in which it was interested. Moreover, the East German light industry and consumer-goods industry was planning to export massively to West Germany. Import of such goods was therefore not necessary.[52]

The East Germans badly needed export outlets as their country was heading for the cliffs. Between 1961 and 1964, total national investment reached 66,000 million marks but it generated a rise of national income of only 10,700 million marks. This was simply unsustainable. The GDR embarked upon the New Economic System (NES) in which officials had to show more entrepreneurial spirit. The GDR's domestic market being too small, production was to be oriented towards export.[53] The NES was rather positively, yet cautiously reported by the *Irish Farmers Journal*, as one of its journalists covered the 'annual agricultural exhibition [in the Leipzig Fair]' and wrote that the East Germans went 'to great pains in welcoming West Germans, foreign visitors and journalists'.[54] So it was that both the GDR and Ireland were at an economic crossroads at the beginning of the 1960s, Dublin wishing to shed protectionism and embrace liberalism and East Berlin injecting some (very moderate) capitalist principles into its planned economy. Their common point to increase income was to increase export, but between the two countries Ireland was at a disadvantage. Both national economies were not complementary and, with the exception of one year, Ireland would never be able to attain a fair balance of trade. Significantly, the *Irish Independent* published an article entitled 'E. Germany buys Irish butter' in which it reported that 'a feature of the order [worth £150,000] is that Ireland will be the sole country in Western Europe supplying butter to this market'.[55] The newspaper was obviously warming to the idea of trading with the Reds, which it had initially loudly denounced. It must have dawned on many a mind that it looked as if the GDR was there to stay. The building of the Wall had made sure of that impression.

The beginnings of change in Ireland: 1964

The year 1964 was arguably the year when Ireland decided to become far more proactive in its trade with the East bloc, years after Western countries and neutrals had done so. But it began cautiously. On 5 January, the Irish embassy in Bonn answered a query of Córas Tráchtála (Irish Export Board) regarding West Germany's commercial relations with East Germany and other Communist countries. The embassy explained that Ludwig Erhard's government wanted to expand commercial activities and had concluded long trade agreements with Poland, Romania, Hungary and Bulgaria. It had also been decided to open trade missions there. As far as the so-called inter-zonal (FRG–GDR) trade was concerned, it had increased by 7.6 per cent from 1962 to 1963.[56] Clearly, neither the Wall nor the Hallstein doctrine was an insurmountable barrier to trade and this was probably why

Córas Tráchtála had inquired in the first place. In March, the *Kerryman* announced that East Germany had purchased 500 tons of butter worth £165,000. The newspaper expressed its satisfaction and stressed that it was essential to develop 'up-to-date marketing methods'. It rightly commented: 'We seem to have learned the lesson rather late, but better late than never'.[57]

Other regional newspapers concurred with the *Kerryman*. The *Connacht Tribune* reassured its readers that it was quite acceptable to do business with Communist countries. After all, Ireland had always been on friendly terms with Czechoslovakia and victims of Stalinism were being rehabilitated there, even 'Archbishop Beran of Prague has been released from prison'.[58] This was of course meant to placate Catholic opinion. Josef Beran was indeed a figure of Catholic resistance in Czechoslovakia, had been imprisoned and would eventually die in exile in Rome.[59] The *Connacht Tribune* remarked that '[British Prime Minister] Sir Alex [*sic*] Douglas-Home is of opinion that it is better to deal with a fat, rather than a lean Communist and that the West, within limits, should help to keep the Communist belly full. Strategic goods are, of course, not for sale to Eastern European nations.'[60] There was clearly a shift in public opinion towards dealing with the East bloc. On 1 September, an official Polish Trade Mission Bureau, operating in conjunction with its counterpart in London, was opened in Dublin.[61]

This development certainly had not failed to catch the West German embassy's attention. In April, Ambassador Heinz von Trützschler reported to Bonn the increased contacts between Irish exporters and East bloc representatives and the current negotiations with the Czechoslovaks in Dublin. But there were more noticeable developments. Twelve Irish firms had signalled their intention to participate in the autumn session of the Leipzig Fair which was far more than in 1939 when only one firm had participated. On top of that, it was being envisaged to organise an Irish exhibition in Brünn in the province of Thuringia just after the Leipzig Fair. Von Trützschler had even worrying news. He explained that the Irish had shown very little interest in participating in the Frankfurt Fair in West Germany despite the repeated visits of Siegfried Rost, its director. The ambassador suggested that a stronger publicity campaign for Frankfurt should be launched in Ireland in view of the East bloc's efforts and mentioned that the Ministry of the Economy and the Federal Foreign Trade Information Office had been notified.[62] Von Trützschler ought not to have been surprised as Ireland's efforts to join the EEC were being thwarted by de Gaulle who refused British membership. It was therefore to be expected that some Irish businessmen were going to look elsewhere.

In August, the *Sunday Independent* reported that Irish Wool Weavers Ltd was set for the Leipzig Fair and that Ireland would be represented along with other Western and neutral countries such as Britain, France, the United States, the Netherlands, West Germany, Sweden and Switzerland.[63] In September, the *Irish Farmers Journal* announced that nine farmers had left for the GDR on a tour organised by the chairman of the Irish Wool Producers to study market possibilities and also Communist farming structure.[64] All this was of course a consequence of the KfA delegation's visit to Dublin the previous year. The Irish farmers' stay in the GDR turned out to be a revealing cultural experience. It might have been expected that the Irish had been led to visit showcase farms by the authorities, but their encounters with East German farmers were surprisingly frank and open. The Irish were not always impressed by the local infrastructure, techniques and quality of the animals, especially pigs, but the East German management admitted that there were problems. The Irish also found out that there was a serious shortage of wheat that had to be compensated with imports from the Soviet Union.[65] This was a pertinent observation. The East German agricultural sector was experiencing a very modest annual growth of only 0.3 per cent while the industry was going through a boom of 4.4 per cent.[66]

Was there nothing positive in the GDR then? There was. The Irish farmers had noticed that rural housing was poor 'but health and educational services, which are free, seem excellent'. They were genuinely impressed by the 'high standard of education among the farmers'.[67] This observation was also pertinent. The education of farmers had been seriously neglected since the beginnings of the Irish Free State in 1922.[68] It is estimated that in 1966 a mere 10 per cent of farmers got more than primary school education.[69] At that period, the Irish government embarked upon major reforms in education, and more and more people compared their standards with those of Western Europe.[70] Clearly, it happened with the East too. However, the Irish farmers were far from being impressed with 'the facilities for entertainment in the rural areas' and described 'the social picture ... on the whole ... [as] Cromwellian'. According to them, 'entertainment ... is generated in the home'.[71] What was implicitly stated in this article was that there might be opportunities to export Irish agricultural products owing to East German deficiencies and shortcomings. It was revealing that these Irish farmers had not condemned the Communist system outright and even pointed out its superiority in the fields of education and health. They were no longer afraid to incur the wrath of their local clergymen. The winds of change were blowing over Ireland in the 1960s.

Table 1.1 Ireland's imports from and exports to Communist countries, Jan.–Nov. 1965

	Imports	Exports
Bulgaria	£10,614	£55
Hungary	£102,900	£6,945
Poland	£2,514,492	£378,937
Romania	£119,552	£42
Czechoslovakia	£493,375	£205,481
Soviet Union	£1,109,157	£750,116
Eastern Germany	£1,045,808	£204,294
Albania	£41	—
Yugoslavia	£212,236	£5,789
North Korea	£13,542	—
China	£392,341	£3,818
Outer Mongolia	£12,072	—
North Vietnam	£89	£3,393
Cuba	£153,255	£12,623

Source: NAI, Dublin, DFA, 300 series, part I, 305/249, Dáil debates, 8 February 1966

In 1964, Ireland's exports from the GDR totalled £337,044 but it imported for a total value of £1,379,411.[72] Trade relations with the East simply failed to take off. In February 1966, during a debate in the Dáil, the Taoiseach was asked if the figures of export/import with Communist countries were known. An official report was then circulated and the information contained told its own tale (see Table 1.1).

Although these figures were simply dwarfed by those of trade with West Germany, £23,998,000 for imports and £11,810,000 for exports,[73] it was obvious that Ireland had a very serious problem with export and marketing. It had a negative balance of trade with all these countries, with the exception of North Vietnam.

Over two years later, on 31 May 1968, the Foreign Trade Committee met. Problems and a lack of unity between the ministries involved immediately surfaced. J. T. Godfrey, the representative of the Department of Industry and Commerce and also chairman of the meeting, broached the issue of the KfA's proposal to hold trade talks between the GDR and Ireland for 'purchases of goods by each country from the other'. Godfrey said that his Minister, George Colley, had agreed with it. Yet, Colley was of the opinion that the DEA was 'too restrictive' in this matter and reminded them that West German officials were involved in trade with East Germany. The representatives of the DEA countered by saying that their ministry 'considered that political considerations might be involved in the manner in which trade negotiations were conducted between East and West Germany' and that 'they were aware that West Germany took a very serious view of other countries entering into formal discussions with East Germany'.[74] The DEA's analysis was plainly wrong and in all likelihood the result of a strong desire not to upset the West Germans at a time when Ireland was applying for EEC membership and relying on their support. But in Bonn, Foreign Minister Willy Brandt was thinking of normalising the FRG's relations with Eastern Europe, including the GDR. Moreover, the United Kingdom had become the GDR's most important trade partner in the West after the FRG.[75] The Hallstein doctrine was not much of a problem for the British and the DEA's worries were simply not justified.

Repatriating volunteer Ryan

If trade between the two countries made only very slow progress, the process of diplomatic recognition was even slower. It was in fact the occasion of the repatriation of the remains of Frank Ryan that gave the final push to establishing formal diplomatic links on a *de jure* basis. Ryan had been a member of the Irish Republican Army (IRA) and organised volunteers to fight on the republican side during the Spanish Civil War (1936–39). Imprisoned and condemned to death by Franco's victorious forces, he was eventually handed over to the Germans in 1940 and sent to Berlin where he was reunited with another IRA man, Seán Russell. The Abwehr, the German military intelligence headed by Admiral Wilhelm Canaris, developed an interest in the IRA in conjunction with the invasion of Britain, 'Operation SEALION', although the exact mission of Ryan and Russell remains somewhat unclear. Later that year, both men were sent to Ireland aboard a submarine. When Russell died from a burst gastric ulcer during the voyage the mission was aborted.[76] Ryan returned to Germany where he was in touch with other Irish exiles who sympathised with the republican cause. One of them, Francis Stuart who made propaganda broadcasts to Ireland, admitted well after the war: 'Ryan was in a very ambiguous position; starting off fighting for the International Brigade [in Spain] and ending up as an adviser to the SS Colonel Veesenmayer, a Jew exterminator. I never liked Ryan, we really didn't get on ... He should have made up his mind what he was doing'. Ryan had not much to do in Berlin as the invasion of Britain never materialised. He died of pleurisy and pneumonia in June 1944 and was buried in Loschwitz cemetery in Dresden.[77]

Shortly before the end of the war, in March 1945, first attempts were made to repatriate his body to Ireland but the post-war situation made this impossible. Years later, in 1961, there was a new attempt but it failed because of the disagreements between the Irish Workers' League (IWL, Communists) and a combination consisting of the Irish government, the Ryan family, traditionalist IRA members and the Irish–German Society which promoted links between Ireland and West Germany. This combination objected to the possibility that the repatriation of Ryan's remains might serve 'to boost the cause of international Communism which he never favoured during his life'. As to the IWL, in 1961 it told the Sozialistische Einheitspartei Deutschlands (SED, Socialist Unity Party of Germany or Communist party) to have nothing to do with the 'pro-fascist' Irish–German Society which was in touch with Ryan's family.[78]

In July 1966, on the occasion of the 30th anniversary of the establishment of the Spanish Republic, the East German authorities invited veterans of the International Brigades to attend the ceremonies. Among the guests was Michael O'Riordan, the Irish Communist leader. The Spanish Civil War, in which 5,000 German Communists had participated, was among the founding myths of the East German State. Thirteen members of the Central Committee of the SED had fought in Spain.[79] On 26 July, the *Irish Times* published a photograph of O'Riordan and two other Irishmen, Donal O'Reilly and Frank Edwards, standing at Ryan's grave together with SED officials. Edwards delivered an oration.[80] Ryan was a man of legendary status within the history of Irish republicanism,[81] and going to his grave in Dresden was like a pilgrimage for Irish Communists visiting East Germany.[82]

But that summer O'Riordan arrived in East Berlin with a special request, the repatriation of Ryan's remains. On 20 July, he had a meeting with Hermann Axen, a member of the SED's Central Committee who was responsible for media and agitation and also specialised in international relations. O'Riordan explained that Ryan was an important personality from the Irish working class and although he had never been a member of the Irish Communist party, he had joined the Spanish Communist party. He emphasised that the repatriation of his remains would be of 'great significance for the political struggle' in Ireland. This was precisely what some feared in Dublin. Axen answered that the Central Committee agreed in principle. He then went into detail about the organisation of the repatriation and said that it would receive much coverage in the East German media. He even suggested that a Pioneer unit (youth organisation) in Dresden could be named after Ryan and that a Frank Ryan scholarship in the school of journalism in the

University of Leipzig could be envisaged for Irish students. There was also the possibility to twin the cities of Dresden and Dublin in order to develop closer relations between the GDR and Ireland, he continued. As to O'Riordan, he would write articles on Ireland for the East German press.[83] It was evident that the East German authorities sensed that there was possibly some good propaganda value here and perhaps an opportunity to get closer to a Western country. Shortly afterwards, in September, the plans were officially approved in East Berlin.[84]

At the end of 1966, O'Riordan published an article entitled 'Ein Ire in der DDR' (an Irishman in the GDR) in the *DDR-Revue* (no. 11/66). It was a blatant and not so subtle piece of propaganda highlighting the many achievements of the SED regime. The conclusion of the article centred on Ryan. O'Riordan wrote that he had been invited to attend the 30th anniversary of the establishment of the Spanish Republic and that he subsequently had gone to Ryan's grave in Dresden, a grave that was looked after so well by the locals. He described Ryan as 'an outstanding Irish nationalist, anti-imperialist and anti-fascist fighter'.[85] Trouble was now brewing.

Some international readers of the *DDR-Revue* reacted strongly to O'Riordan's depiction of Ryan. A letter from Israel to the editor-in-chief questioned Ryan's anti-fascist pedigree since he had accepted to cooperate with the Nazis against Britain during the war. To the reader's mind this was unacceptable no matter what Ryan had done in Spain.[86] Then a second letter arrived, this time from Britain. The reader explained that he had read that Ryan had fought in Spain but that he later had collaborated with the Nazis. Therefore, he asked the editor-in-chief if he could clarify matters.[87] All of a sudden, the repatriation of Ryan's remains became a very delicate issue for East Berlin as it could damage the country's so-called *Imagepflege*, that is to say the care the authorities were taking to project a good image of the GDR abroad. The East Germans were perfectly aware that Ryan had acted according to the old Irish republican motto 'England's difficulty is Ireland's opportunity'. This is confirmed in a Stasi report: 'When the Second World War broke out a new group of IRA leaders entertained the idea of seeking support in Berlin in accordance with the traditional Irish nationalist policy of establishing alliances with Great Britain's enemies. They were not pro-Nazi but they did not share Ryan's anti-fascism either.'[88]

The Central Committee of the SED now hesitated and asked the Stasi to carry out investigations into Ryan's exact role in Nazi Germany. Shortly afterwards Erich Mielke, a Spanish veteran himself,[89] was given a report on the case. The head of the Stasi understood at once the potential for international embarrassment. After all, here was a comrade who had cooperated with the Nazis, those same Nazis who had destroyed Guernica in April 1937. Mielke wrote on top of the report: 'To head of Main Department IX. Check if records available. Assign to sections in charge. Urgent'.[90] Department IX (investigations) dealt with issues that had political ramifications.

On 6 October 1967, Department IX handed in its report. The Stasi agents had found some documents in the Deutsches Zentralarchiv (German central archive) in Potsdam in the GDR. They related to the Nuremberg trials and the witness statement of Kurt Haller, a former Abwehr man who had worked with Edmund Veesenmayer. Veesenmayer had been in the SS and had been involved in Irish operations between 1940 and 1943. He had been condemned to twenty years' imprisonment in Nuremberg but had been released after six. At some stage he worked closely with Ryan and Russell.[91] Unfortunately for the Stasi, evidence of Ryan's activities was not forthcoming. The agents stated that 'the investigations and verifications aiming at establishing why Frank Ryan was to be sent to Ireland or if he used the possibility of being sent home to fight for his country against fascism were without result'. However, they were able to establish that he had 'died from pneumonia and pleurisy in the Dr Eugen Weidner Sanatorium in Dresden on 10 June 1944'. They added that it was also alleged that before 1945, people, including foreigners, had been treated in this particular sanatorium for venereal diseases, or '*unangenehme Krankheiten*' (unpleasant diseases) as they euphemistically wrote.[92] This explains why Veesenmayer wrongly believed that Ryan had died from such a disease.[93]

After due consideration the East German authorities took the decision to abandon plans to repatriate Ryan's remains to Ireland. From their point of view, it was certainly the wisest thing to do in order to avoid any international embarrassment. There is no evidence in the archives that they informed O'Riordan of their decision, although it seems very likely that they must have done so, perhaps informally during a meeting in East Berlin. As a result, Ryan's body remained in Dresden and his myth lived on. On 19 June 1968, the Northern Irish Communist Betty Sinclair was on a holiday in East Germany and visited Loschwitz cemetery. She wrote in her meticulously kept diary:

> This morning we all went to the grave of Frank Ryan ... We arrived about 8.00 AM. I said a few words of thanks for the care taken of the grave & the memory of this great Irishman. Cde [comerade] Czygie [?] replied and stated that the anti-fascist movement in the GDR would always have the grave as their care. Ryan, born in 1902, was buried on February 13, 1944 – such a short time before the end of the war! His movements from Spain are still a mystery.[94]

It certainly was not a mystery for the members of Central Committee of the SED and Erich Mielke.

Remarkably Frank Ryan had caught the imagination of an East German thriller writer called Karl Heinz Weber. In 1969, he wrote a manuscript that was clearly based on his life. The plot centres on an Irishman, James Stewart O'Daven, who had fought in the International Brigades in Spain and who had been taken prisoner by Franco's forces. In 1940, however, the Spaniards agree to hand him over to the Germans as Admiral Canaris believes he can be of some use in the planning of the invasion of Britain. But as 'Operation SEALION' has to be postponed, O'Daven is sent to the propaganda department in Berlin where he is employed in broadcasting to Ireland. But despite working for the Nazis, O'Daven remains a true-blooded Communist and finds a clever way to warn the British of German troop movements while speaking in Irish. When the Nazis discover what O'Daven is really up to, he is executed together with other Irishmen in February 1945. The plot thickens then as years later an Irish and an East German professor working on his case find out that the current Chancellor of West Germany, Kurt Georg Kiesinger (Christian-Democrat), had been a Nazi during the war. Stasi agents, who are the heroes in the book, try to solve the O'Daven mystery, being helped by the East German professor.

The plot is certainly well conceived and it is obvious that the book is strongly biased against the West German government. Weber tries to show that many former Nazis are present at the highest governmental levels in Bonn. Therefore, the book could be rapidly dismissed as a mere piece of East German propaganda except for the fact that it was revealed in 2012 by the magazine *Der Spiegel* that in the former West Germany twenty-five federal ministers, one Federal Chancellor (Kiesinger) and one Federal President (Walter Scheel) had been members of Nazi organisations.[95] It was little wonder that Weber's manuscript was sent for analysis to the Stasi before being published since Stasi agents were the heroes. The professionals were definitely impressed by Weber's work. Apart from a few technical details that needed revision, they deemed that it could be published as it was ideologically correct and wrote that 'the novel is loosely based on the Irishman Frank Ryan's life'.[96] It is not known how Weber got his information on Ryan. The book was eventually entitled *Auch Tote haben einen Schatten* (even the dead have shadows) and was published in 1975.[97] It was advertised in *Neues Deutschland* (the SED's mouthpiece), *Tribüne*, *Das Volk*, *BZ am Abend*, *Freie Presse* and *Börsenblatt* in the GDR.[98] It is interesting to notice that in 1976, the East German

Horizont wrote in a footnote that 'the leader of these Irish anti-fascists, IRA member Frank Ryan, was later abducted and transported to Germany by Nazi counter-intelligence and murdered'.[99] This was nowhere near the truth.

Tremendous East–West developments

Through the impetus given by Willy Brandt, the West German Social-Democratic Foreign Minister (1966–69) and then Chancellor (1969–74), things began to change on the Cold War chessboard. Brandt was in favour of normalising relations with Eastern Europe in general and East Germany in particular and began his *Ostpolitik* (eastern policy). The West Germans were one step short of recognising the GDR but relations were established, although not formally diplomatic, and the cumbersome Hallstein doctrine was jettisoned. After intense and complicated negotiations the two Germanys eventually signed the Basic Treaty in December 1972, recognising each other as sovereign states. This in turn led to the speedy recognition of the GDR by the West. For example, on 9 February 1973, London officially established diplomatic relations with East Berlin. The following year, on 4 September 1974, Washington did the same. Both the FRG and the GDR had also become full member states of the United Nations on 18 September 1973.[100] In the meantime, Washington and Moscow were making progress in the Strategic Arms Limitation Talks (SALT) and the Conference on Security and Cooperation in Europe (CSCE) began in Helsinki in July 1973 with the participation of thirty-five states including Ireland and the GDR. Détente flourished between East and West.

Parallel to these tremendous East–West developments, interest in Eastern Europe was seriously developing in Ireland. President Charles de Gaulle of France kept vetoing Britain's entry into the EEC and since Ireland's economic fate was ultimately tied to the British, it could not join either. Could therefore the East bloc not provide economic opportunities while waiting for eventual EC membership? This was the reasoning of G. Martin Wheeler of the Irish Exporters' Association in an article entitled 'Have more trade with Communists' published by the *Sunday Independent* in March 1967.[101] In July, the *Irish Times* published for the first time an advertisement for the international Leipzig Fair, the biannual fair in the ancient East German city.[102] In 1969, it was announced that Corás Tráchtála (Irish Export Board) was about to appoint a representative behind the Iron Curtain.[103] The *Irish Farmers Journal* wrote that pedigree lambs worth £5,000 were exported to East Germany.[104] In April 1970, Ireland signed its first trade agreement with an East bloc country, Bulgaria, although the signing was a very discreet affair.[105] In July 1971, a similar agreement with Romania was signed.[106]

However, nothing happened with the GDR. Obviously, Jack Lynch's government remained cautious as far as East Germany was concerned although caution was no longer necessary in view of the current East–West developments. What little trade there was, was still largely in favour of the East Germans. In July 1971, it was revealed in the Dáil that 'in the 14-month period ending on 31st May, 1971, imports from Eastern Germany amounted to £1,031,844 and total exports amounted to £28,692'. A deputy called it a 'ridiculous adverse balance of trade'.[107] In any case the Eastern European craze was only short-lived. At last, Ireland became a member of the EEC on 1 January 1973 and then turned its eyes fully on the continent, the Western half that is. Exploring trade with the East was relegated to the background.

The Irish government was of course analysing the rapidly developing East–West situation. On 31 March 1970, Ambassador Eamonn Kennedy wrote about the historic meeting between Chancellor Brandt and Willi Stoph, the Chairman of the East German Council of Ministers, at Erfurt in the GDR. He suggested that '[Ireland's] policy *vis-à-vis* East Germany might now take account of changes in West German attitudes, while we should, at the same time, let Bonn make the running'.[108] This was pragmatic and sound advice. Kennedy also pointed out that the Stoph–Brandt meeting reminiscent of the meetings between Taoiseach Seán Lemass and Northern Irish Prime Minister Terence O'Neill back in 1965. He wrote that the two Germanys 'might in the future exchange High Commissioners on Commonwealth lines, instead of Ambassadors, to indicate that they do not regard each other as foreign countries, but nevertheless, that they do recognise each other's existence as states'. We can take it, I think, that the Ulbricht regime would normally not accept such a compromise but they might have to do so under Russian pressure.[109]

Kennedy's remark on the Commonwealth was certainly a pertinent one as that had been the original arrangement between the Irish Free State and Britain. There was also going to be a similar arrangement between the GDR and the FRG as both countries would exchange representatives but not ambassadors. As will be seen in Chapter 3 some West German officials made comparisons between the Anglo-Irish situation on the one hand, and the West German–East German on the other hand. Their report was subsequently copied by a Stasi mole in Bonn and sent to East Berlin for further analysis. That way Walter Ulbricht knew what to possibly expect during talks with the West Germans. Kennedy's observation that Ulbricht might not like this idea but might be forced by the Soviets into accepting it was correct.

In fact, the East Germans had been preparing for such an eventuality. In 1967, SED–Central Committee member Albert Norden, who was a specialist on the question of German unity and also the chairman of the (East) German–British Friendship Society, had first mentioned the two-German nations theory,[110] which would allow East Berlin to reject out of hand Bonn's possible reunification initiatives. Clearly, Brandt's *Ostpolitik* was upsetting the SED regime. It should be mentioned here that initially the historic meetings between Lemass and O'Neill in 1965 had been positively commented upon by the East German Ministry of External Affairs as it believed it was a model for communication and for enhancing cooperation between the GDR and the FRG. Helmut Schmidt, who would become Chancellor of West Germany in 1974, also believed this and said so openly in a speech in Hamburg in March 1967, which was reported to Dublin by the Irish embassy.[111] But in the end, the Irish example was totally irrelevant.

But now the question of the recognition of the GDR was becoming an issue for the DEA, one that could not be easily ignored. On 29 November 1971, the Irish embassy in The Hague informed Dublin that the Dutch Parliament had just debated the recognition of the GDR. The Dutch foreign minister had stated that the right time would be when both the GDR and the FRG would be admitted to the United Nations and that 'while the Dutch Government generally supported Herr Brandt's East Policy it "was not tied hand and foot" to it'.[112] The Netherlands and the GDR officially entered into diplomatic relations on 5 January 1973. Dutch–East German relations developed rather quickly in a spirit of East–West cooperation.[113] Neutral Switzerland had eventually recognised the GDR on 20 December 1972.[114]

However, things were dragging with Ireland. In June 1971 during its 8th party conference, the SED reflected on the conception of a new foreign policy for the years between 1971 and 1975 owing to the rapidly evolving international situation. It was decided to develop relations between the GDR and Ireland in 1972.[115] The East Germans were clearly very eager, as they went as far as to draft an agreement document for official diplomatic relations between the two countries scheduled for 1973.[116] That was being too eager. In March 1973, talks between Irish and East Germans at the United Nations were inconclusive. The Department of Foreign Affairs (DFA, which had replaced the DEA) remained noncommittal on the question of exchanging ambassadors. The Irish permanent representative hinted that the DFA had limited means. The East German diplomat appeared not to be convinced by the excuse.[117]

In July 1973, the recently appointed Minister for Foreign Affairs, Dr Garret FitzGerald (Fine Gael) travelled to Helsinki for the Conference on Security and Cooperation in Europe (CSCE) where he had meetings with all his Eastern European counterparts except with the Bulgarian minister. He also had talks with Andrei Gromyko to explore the possibility of opening diplomatic relations with the Soviet Union, which the two countries eventually agreed to do shortly afterwards.[118] FitzGerald's meetings in the Finnish capital clearly showed Ireland's desire to normalise relations with the East bloc and they appeared to follow the diplomatic *élan* created by Brandt's *Ostpolitik*. FitzGerald also met East German Deputy Foreign Minister Oskar Fischer at the latter's request. He told Fischer that it was difficult for Ireland to formalise relations because of administrative problems but explained that it had already recognised the GDR when the Irish delegation voted in favour of the GDR's entry to the United Nations. It was this declaration of FitzGerald, taken down in the official protocol of the meeting by the East Germans that would constitute the only official document in the bilateral relations between the two countries for the years ahead. East Berlin made strenuous efforts to convince Dublin to officially establish relations with an exchange of ambassadors. Irish diplomats were approached notably during sessions of the United Nations. But East German efforts were not crowned with success.[119] It is stated in an undated East German document that subsequently contacts were established between the two embassies in London but that the Irish were delaying proceedings because they wanted to focus on their recently acquired EC membership and also 'because for the time being the Republic of Ireland does not see any possibility to accredit its ambassadors to Socialist states'.[120]

In February 1975, the Western European Desk of the Ministry of External Affairs in East Berlin analysed the current situation. It remarked that 'because Ireland is of relatively little significance within the group of capitalist states, there are no specific interests for the GDR to develop comprehensive official relations with Ireland'. From an economic point of view, there were only 'limited interests' for the GDR. The small balance of trade was very largely in favour of the GDR. Shannon Airport offered the possibility to establish a stopover for Interflug, the national airline, for flights to North and South America. For Ireland, the main point was to increase exports to the GDR. The Ministry of External Affairs believed that EC membership would restrict export possibilities for traditional Irish products such as beef and textiles and that therefore the East German market would be considered as a new outlet. Ireland had no political interests in developing relations with the GDR.[121] This assessment was realistic.

The following month, the East German Ambassador to the United Kingdom, Karl-Heinz Kern, met the Soviet Ambassador to Ireland, Anatoli S. Kaplin, in London. Kaplin made it clear that trade was Ireland's main motivation in establishing official relations with the Socialist states. He also named two factors which explained why Ireland remained hesitant, however. First, he said that there were 'right-wing forces in the Government that wish to prevent an improvement of the relations, and the powerful influence of the Catholic Church plays a role'. Second, he told Kern that the British were still putting pressure on the Irish not to do so.[122] Kaplin was definitely right concerning the British. Across the Irish Sea in London, Prime Minister Edward Heath's government was quite worried when it became known that the Soviets would open an embassy in Dublin. Espionage concerns were the reason as Soviet diplomats and pseudo diplomats would be free to travel between the two islands.[123] An East German embassy would only add more worries.

The East Germans kept reminding the Irish of their existence. The day Patrick Hillery became President of Ireland, on 3 December 1976, Erich Honecker, the new leader of the GDR, sent him a congratulatory telegram. A few lines on top of the document indicated that the context of the telegram was the opening of formal diplomatic relations.[124] This time, a reply came from Ireland, albeit twenty-seven days later, and Hillery briefly thanked the General Secretary of the SED.[125] It was brief but at least it was a reply unlike earlier in the Cold War when no reply would have been given. In that sense, it could be argued that there was some progress. Similar telegrams were sent from East Berlin in July 1977 when Jack Lynch became Taoiseach again and Michael O'Kennedy Minister for Foreign Affairs. Dublin's answer was a little bit quicker on these occasions.[126]

In March 1977, the East German Ministry of External Affairs wrote in a report that Ireland had had diplomatic relations with the Soviet Union since 1973 and with Czechoslovakia, Poland and Hungary since 1976. According to information received by the embassy in London, the Irish government had at present not much interest in the Socialist states and the little interest there was, was dictated by trade: 'In relation with the establishment of diplomatic relations with Czechoslovakia and Poland the Irish demanded a considerable increase of the trade volume. The trade volumes amount to £17 million with the USSR, £9 million with Poland and £6 million with Czechoslovakia. The GDR's trade volume with Ireland presently totals about £3 million and is constituted almost exclusively by GDR exports.'[127] In other words, Dublin had no immediate incentive to negotiate an exchange of ambassadors with East Berlin. Moreover the volume of trade between Ireland and the GDR more than paled by comparison to that between Ireland and the FRG. In 1976, Ireland imported goods from West Germany at a total value of £160,751,000, and exported goods to West Germany at a total value of £161,031,000.[128] The figures for the United Kingdom and the United States were even far more explicit. The Ministry of External Affairs' report was subsequently sent to the Stasi.

All this meant that Irish–East German bilateral relations in the 1970s were conducted on an ad hoc basis with no real guidance or direction. In August 1977, the Ministry of External Affairs in East Berlin wrote pessimistically that 'concerning the development of relations with the GDR no decision is to be expected from the Irish side in the near future. The Irish Ambassador in London told the East German Ambassador that the establishment of diplomatic relations is intended but cannot be scheduled yet. He hopes to be able to say something more concrete in September/October.'[129] Ireland remained the only Western European country not to have officialised its relations with the GDR, and Erich Honecker would have to wait. Then unexpectedly Frank Ryan's remains resurfaced.

'Corpse diplomacy'

On 28 June 1978 in London, the Irish embassy sent its East German colleagues a note explaining that Minister for Foreign Affairs Michael O'Kennedy had been asked by Frank Ryan's sister, Eilís, if his remains could be repatriated: 'In order to initiate the process, the Irish authorities would be grateful to have information from the German Democratic Republic on the procedures and regulations regarding the repatriation of the remains for transmission to Miss Eilís Ryan'.[130] This was Ireland's first ever official letter to East Berlin.[131]

Edgar Uher, an East German diplomat specialised in Irish affairs and HVA officer (the Stasi's foreign intelligence department) learned how it all began. In Dublin, some people had been giving thought to the repatriation. According to Uher, a meeting took place in the kitchen of a prominent Fianna Fáil family, the Andrews. Christopher Stephen 'Todd' Andrews had been a republican fighter during the Irish revolution (1916–23) and later a founding member of Fianna Fáil. His son David was a parliamentary secretary to the Minister of Foreign Affairs (1977–78) and subsequently a minister of state at the Department of

Foreign Affairs (1978–79). His son Niall was a deputy in the Dáil. Years later Uher was told about this meeting in the very same kitchen together with Ambassador Martin Bierbach and his wife on the occasion of Bierbach's presentation of credentials to the president of Ireland. Present at the first kitchen meeting were Todd Andrews, who had been a personal friend of Ryan, David Andrews, Michael O'Riordan and a few others. Todd Andrews wanted the remains to be repatriated. O'Riordan agreed and argued in favour of the repatriation on three counts: first for humanitarian reasons, second for family reasons and third in the interest of Irish–East German relations.[132]

In his unpublished memoir, Uher wrote the following:

> Todd Andrews was an old friend of Ryan. When nobody wanted to employ Ryan after he was released from jail in Ireland, Todd employed him. Andrews had two sons, David and Niall. Both had become Members of Parliament for Fianna Fáil and both had been asked by their father to use all their political influence to bring the body of his friend Ryan home. Of course, there had been talks about bringing Ryan home before. But this time it was serious. Niall Andrews promised to take the matter up with Charlie Haughey [then Minister for Health and Social Welfare, soon to be Taoiseach]. Something he did. Haughey, himself sympathetic to the Irishmen who fought on the Republican side during the Civil War and aware of Ryan's role, consented. The Irish Minister for Foreign Affairs, O'Kennedy, was asked to approach the East Germans.[133]

What happened then was a rather complicated bureaucratic process in East Berlin. Briefly, in September 1978 Uher was told that the SED had agreed with the repatriation. Initially, Ryan's activities in Nazi Germany still posed a problem – all the more since Erich Honecker had personally spent more than ten years in Nazi jails. Nobody wanted to incur the wrath of the SED leader. However, then came a coincidence that incited the SED to go ahead with it. O'Riordan was writing his book *Connolly Column: The Story of the Irishmen Who Fought for the Spanish Republic* which was to be published in the GDR (1979). In the preface, O'Riordan mentioned: 'To the memory of my father, who, because of the propaganda against the Spanish Republic in Ireland did not agree with my going to Spain, but who disagreed more with our "coming back and leaving your commander, Frank Ryan behind"'. This sentence impressed East Berlin and the book made it clear that Ryan had not collaborated with the Nazis. Uher was of the opinion that O'Riordan's conclusion was 'surely correct'. Ryans's body in the cemetery of Loschwitz in Dresden could be exhumed. Yet, the proceedings were not that straightforward as political interference came into play.

The East German Ministry of External Affairs then produced a draft of a decision for the Central Committee of the SED to sign. This was absolutely essential to get things moving as the party was in charge. This draft read: 'To promote the establishment of diplomatic relations between the GDR and Ireland, to fulfil a humanitarian task and to respond to a request from the Irish Communist party the mortal remains of Frank Ryan, presently at Loschwitz cemetery, should be exhumed and handed over to the demanding family of the deceased'. However, only a week later a perplexed Uher heard Kurt Nier, the Deputy Foreign Minister, thundering: 'You would not believe it ... but there are people in this house who want to establish diplomatic relations with a body. This is the height of folly! The GDR does not indulge in corpse diplomacy.' It subsequently transpired that there had been some tensions between Nier and someone at the International Relations Section of the Central Committee. The result was that the draft was revised so that it now read that Ryan's remains should be repatriated for humanitarian reasons and also to do the Communist Party of Ireland (CPI) a favour. Establishing diplomatic relations seemed no longer an objective.[134] And yet, 'corpse diplomacy' would precisely achieve that.

On 6 February 1979, the Ministry of External Affairs sent a two-page document to the International Relations Section of the Central Committee of the SED, outlining the proceedings to be adopted. The repatriation was approved and the necessary steps were being taken by the Ministry and the Committee of Anti-Fascist Resistance Fighters of the GDR. The decision to go ahead was justified on the grounds that Ryan had fought in Spain and 'until his death in 1944 he had been interned near Berlin and was buried in Dresden-Loschwitz'. The Berlin part was obviously not accurate. Then it was stated that Ryan's sister wanted the repatriation with military honours and participation of Spanish veterans. Moreover, 'the Irish embassy in London supports the proposal. The CPI is in favour of a worthy handing-over ceremony and points out to the positive effects for the image of the GDR in Ireland'.[135] On 13 February, the Central Committee officially approved the repatriation but the issue of Ryan's activities in Nazi Germany still lingered. The SED decided that the Committee of Anti-Fascist Resistance Fighters of the GDR and not the Ministry of External Affairs should be outwardly responsible for the event. Obviously, the party was trying to protect the state in case things went wrong. Also, it feared that the West Germans might try to manipulate the event to criticise East Berlin. Consequently, the decision was taken that the repatriation ceremony should not be given too much publicity.[136]

On 12 June, the Central Committee's International Relations Section informed Honecker that everything was set for 19 June. A deputy of the Dáil and an Irish television crew would come over, and also a small delegation of Irish anti-fascist fighters led by 'comrade Michael O'Riordan'. For the reburial ceremony in Ireland, someone of the GDR embassy in London would participate 'depending on the circumstances'.[137] The last phrase indicated that East Berlin remained wary of any possible incident. According to Uher, some on the Irish side got carried away as they remarked that Ryan's remains could be repatriated aboard an East German battleship. That was going too far for East Berlin.[138] On 19 June, the *Irish Times* announced on page 17: 'Military honours for Ryan at exhumation'. It was explained that the East German army, veterans of the International Brigades from Ireland, Germany, Britain and the United States, Michael O'Riordan and Niall Andrews would attend the ceremony and that 'Mr Niall Andrews, TD [Irish for Member of Parliament], son of Ryan's old friend, Dr C. S. Andrews, was at the centre of the recent work to secure his repatriation'.[139] The East German authorities knew nothing about Andrews's role at that point in time.[140]

The ceremony took place without any incident. Kurt Höfer of the Committee of Anti-Fascist Resistance Fighters of the GDR summed it up in a subsequent report. He had a 'friendly conversation' with Andrews on the way to Dresden. The Irishman appeared to be curious about the industrial, agricultural and social aspects of the country and was 'much impressed by the openness of the discussion and also by the hospitality and the honour shown to Frank Ryan'. He told Höfer about his father's friendship with Ryan and assured him that if the East German ambassador in London travelled to Dublin for the reburial ceremony, 'he would get plenty of impressions and much information on Ireland'.[141] It sounded as if Andrews was signalling an imminent breakthrough in Irish–East German relations. At Heidefriedhof cemetery, where many monuments commemorated the victims of fascism, representatives of the Ministry of External Affairs and the Central Committee of the SED were present as was a guard of honour of Spanish veterans. By contrast the East German army was absent as O'Riordan had been too late with his request. After a speech of a representative of the Committee of Anti-Fascist Resistance Fighters, which was much appreciated by the Irish delegation, Ryan's remains were officially handed over.

In the afternoon, the Irish delegation travelled to Ryan's former grave in Loschwitz. Then they were given a guided tour in the Army Museum where particular attention was paid to the anti-fascist struggle and the liberation by the Red Army. Later that day during the farewell dinner, Andrews profusely thanked the East Germans and 'voiced the expectation that the friendship between the two peoples would grow stronger'.[142] Again, it sounded as if official diplomatic relations were in the air. Höfer concluded his report by saying that the ceremony would have 'very valuable and positive political results'.[143] In this, he was not mistaken. According to Uher, Andrews had been told towards the end of the visit that East Berlin was interested in opening official diplomatic relations.[144] Things looked promising for the East Germans but they still had to be a little bit more patient.

On 20 June, Frank Ryan was finally home. The plane transporting his remains landed at Dublin Airport where his sister and nephew were waiting. This time, the event figured on the *Irish Times*' front page.[145] The next day, Ryan was laid to rest in Glasnevin cemetery in Dublin, the resting place for many Irish nationalists and republicans. It is quite remarkable that so many years after his death the memory of Frank Ryan was able to reunite the different and sometimes rival factions of Irish republicanism and the far left. Among those present were George Gilmore, a former IRA veteran who had co-founded the left-wing Republican Congress in 1934, Roddy Connolly, son of the Marxist James Connolly who had been one of the leaders of the Easter Rising in 1916, Ruairi Ó Brádaigh, leader of the Provisional Sinn Féin, Joe Cahill, one of the leading members of the Provisional IRA, Thomás Mac Giolla, leader of Sinn Féin/the Workers' Party, Michael O'Riordan, leader of the CPI, Bernadette Devlin, Socialist and republican activist, and Michael Mullins representing the Irish Transport and General Workers' Union (IGTWU).

In an uncanny way it was the same with the Germans: Heinz Knobbe, the East German Minister in London, represented the GDR, while Rudiger Lukowicz, the first secretary of the West German embassy in Dublin, represented the FRG. But also watching the ceremony from the sidelines was Helmut Clissmann.[146] Before the war, Clissmann had been in Ireland, trying to promote academic exchanges with Nazi Germany and to establish links between the IRA and German intelligence. During the war, he had been involved in intelligence activities concerning Ireland.[147] Todd Andrews and his two sons were of course also at the ceremony.[148]

In a report written by the Western European Department of the Ministry of External Affairs, it was stated that the whole event had been 'extremely effective in a foreign propaganda sense for the GDR'. After the ceremony, Knobbe met Secretary of State for Foreign Affairs David Andrews and the decision was taken to open diplomatic relations probably at the end of 1979.[149] 'Corpse diplomacy' had eventually paid off. The two men agreed on the idea of double accreditation. Andrews suggested that the Irish Ambassador in The Hague would also be accredited to East Germany. Knobbe thought of the East German Ambassador in London. But 1979 passed and nothing happened. Honecker was really intent on having official diplomatic relations with Ireland as it remained the last state in Western Europe, together with Monaco, Andorra and the Vatican,[150] not to have any with the GDR. On 14 May 1980, the SED leader was on his way to Cuba and the following telegram to Patrick Hillery was written on the occasion of the East German plane crossing Irish airspace: 'In flying over the territory of the Republic of Ireland, I would like to convey to you, dear Mr. President, my best regards. I am convinced that the maintenance of peace and the continuation of the process of détente are in the interests of our two states and peoples.' A second similar telegram was sent on the way back.[151] It sounded almost as if Honecker wanted to become Hillery's new best friend. But Hillery was certainly in no hurry since he thanked the East German leader for his kind greetings almost two months later on 7 July.[152]

By the autumn of 1980, East Berlin believed that once again nothing would materialise. But then, the unexpected at long last happened. At the United Nations, Minister for Foreign Affairs Brian Lenihan told his East German counterpart, Oskar Fischer: 'Let's have relations. We could do it next week.'[153] It must have taken the East Germans some time to get used to Irish ways. The option of double-accreditation in The Hague and London was now accepted. According to Edgar Uher, the East German leaders never had the intention of setting up an embassy in Dublin as the GDR's coffers were empty in the 1980s despite Soviet insistence that they should do so. In the mid-1970s, East Berlin would have insisted on an embassy. This decision financially suited the Irish as well.[154]

On 21 November 1980, a small article on *Neues Deutschland*'s front page announced the establishment of diplomatic relations between the GDR and Ireland.[155] The *Irish Times* had an equally small article but published on page seven.[156] It looked almost like a non-event. In the end, East German insistence on having official diplomatic relations was essentially conditioned by Erich Honecker's attitude and sense of prestige for there was nothing much the GDR could actually gain from them as trade remained small and mass tourism with a sudden influx of hard currency was a most unlikely scenario. Uher was correct when he wrote: 'the lack of relations with one European country, whether practically important for the GDR or not, was something nobody wanted to have to explain to Honecker, who took it quite personally not to be recognised'.[157] From an Irish point of view the GDR was simply not on top of the agenda. The bad, if not abysmal, balance of trade explained why Dublin was not particularly vigorous in its dealings with East Berlin.

After recognition, the two sides had to adapt to different styles of doing business and this could engender some intercultural clashes. Uher alludes to a certain carelessness or laid-back attitude of the Irish that was sometimes disconcerting for the Germans (East or West). On one particular occasion, Vice Foreign Minister Kurt Nier and Uher went to Iveagh House, the DFA's headquarters, which apparently knew nothing about their visit. On another occasion, Uher went there with Ambassador Martin Bierbach. They got stuck in a traffic jam and the ambassador, already nervous, blamed him for this delay. Uher answered that he could not predict the pattern of traffic in Dublin. They eventually arrived late at Iveagh House. Once inside, they found out that there was no reception committee and were simply told by a person who had a desk at the entrance to go up to the third floor. There, they waited for about thirty minutes until the Minister for Foreign Affairs arrived and simply said: 'It is a pleasure to meet you [meaning the East Germans specifically] as with von Lambsdorff the previous day it had all been so punctual'.[158] Otto von Lambsdorff was the West German Minister of the Economy. Bierbach was relieved. The last East German Ambassador to Ireland, Dr Joachim Mitdank, was positively impressed by the simplicity, openness and friendliness of the people he met.[159]

Minister O'Malley sees red

On 17 August 1977, the readers of the *Irish Times* could spot an advertisement for the Leipzig Fair. By now, they were used to the fair's logo and biannual publicity campaigns in Ireland. On this particular occasion, it was stated that the 'centrepiece of the display is the exhibition of high quality products of the GDR … Leipzig, the world trade metropolis, waits to welcome you!'.[160] It is not known whether Desmond O'Malley, the new Fianna Fáil Minister for Industry and Commerce, read the advertisement but he would certainly not go to Leipzig. Being perfectly aware that trade with the East bloc was not getting any better for his country, O'Malley saw red. He threatened to impose sanctions on East bloc imports as 'a policy of last resort' and said that the government would have 'to act more decisively' as 'the imbalance of trade has remained very severe … in spite of Ireland opening a number of embassies in these countries'. Córas Tráchtála's intensive efforts had not paid off. However, O'Malley diplomatically added that if the East showed goodwill and bought more Irish goods then he 'would defer action'.[161] His warning was taken seriously, at least by East Berlin. But Ireland's export problems to Eastern Europe would simply not go away and Taoiseach Jack Lynch's government would introduce some restrictions.

In Dublin, Kurt Ticher read the *Irish Times* article on O'Malley's threat and immediately informed the East German embassy in London, urging it to do something about it.[162] On 13 October, O'Malley reiterated his concerns in the Dáil, saying that the amount of money generated by exports to the East bloc was not worth the amount of money invested by Córas Tráchtála in trade promotion campaigns. The next day, the *Irish Times* published a pertinent article appropriately entitled 'Trying to knock an export hole through the iron curtain'. It began by stressing Córas Tráchtála's efforts such as opening a new office in Poland, replacing its officer in Moscow and 'mounting a trade display in Czechoslovakia'. There had been much 'euphoria' in Ireland when last December in Moscow the then Minister for Foreign Affairs, Dr Garret FitzGerald, had signed the Economic Cooperation Agreement. The Soviets had said that they would consider buying 10,000 tons of Irish beef. Unfortunately for the Irish, it never materialised. The newspaper rightly called it the 'beef sales flop' and gave a succinct summary of Ireland's seriously negative balance of trade with Eastern Europe in 1976. However, it also pertinently remarked that Irish trade with other parts of the world was proving far more lucrative, notably with Nigeria that 'is now a market much more valuable to Irish exporters than all of the Eastern bloc countries together, and this has been achieved after only about three years of effort, and at a fraction of the promotional cost'.[163] On 15 December, the *Irish Times* published the following government notice: 'Notice to Importers. Prohibition of imports of motor car tyres – The German Democratic Republic (commonly known as East Germany).'[164] Minister O'Malley had taken action.

What O'Malley could not have known is that Erich Honecker's government had taken his threat very seriously and that it had studied the possibility of increasing Irish imports. Indeed, since Honecker had replaced Ulbricht in 1971, there had been some noticeable improvements in the GDR's economy. Agriculture was modernised, in stark contrast to Poland's, and 'a high degree of agricultural self-sufficiency' was achieved.[165] This shut the door to possible Irish agricultural exports. Another problem for the Irish was that the GDR traded on very favourable terms with the FRG and 'as a result of agreements between the two Germanys there were no trade barriers or external tariffs;

hence the GDR was in practice a secret extra member of the European Economic Community (EEC)'.[166] This made Irish exports to the GDR more difficult. Despite the fact that the GDR was doing quite well especially when compared to other Communist countries, not everything was satisfying under Honecker's new economic regime as the major problem of foreign trade debt remained. But Bonn was so generous as to grant East Berlin very important loans in return for political gains such as improvement in human rights, visits of families between the two Germanys and so on. It should not be forgotten either that Bonn considered East German citizens as potential West German citizens.[167] Artificial economic respiration continued for East Berlin but it knew that it could not afford to lose export outlets in the West, including small Ireland on the periphery of Europe. But, in the Irish case, the difficulties soon became apparent.

Alerted to Irish concerns about trade conditions with Eastern Europe by Kurt Ticher, the East German embassy in London wrote a report in which it outlined the existing difficulties. According to the latest statistics at hand, the GDR exported goods to Ireland for a total value of 8,200,000 Valuta Mark (East German appellation for Deutsche Mark) in 1975 and 11,000,000 Valuta Mark in 1976. For 1977, the estimated figure was between 12,000,000–14,000,000 Valuta Mark. Potash remained the GDR's main export item but sales in farming equipment had really taken off. It was stated in the report that it was difficult to see how imports from Ireland, apart from textiles, could be increased. The import of fish might be a possibility. Yet, the import of more textiles was advised for 'symbolic' reasons.[168] The last comment was very revealing. Trade compatibility between the two countries was not there. It functioned from the GDR to Ireland but not the other way round. In March 1978, a Stasi agent reported to Main Directorate XVIII (protection of the national economy) a conversation he had had with a representative of O'Dwyer & Ticher Ltd (name blacked out) at the Leipzig Fair. Interestingly, the conversation was not about exporting Irish goods to the GDR, but about importing more East German products into Ireland.[169]

In June 1978, Valentine Heavy, the managing director of Bond International Ltd in Dublin which exclusively dealt with developing trade opportunities for Irish firms in Eastern Europe, acknowledged that Irish exports had been low but was convinced that a market for consumer goods would develop behind the Iron Curtain which could be exploited.[170] This assessment was far too optimistic. The reality was that national economies behind the Iron Curtain were stagnating and about to experience serious economic deterioration in the early 1980s.[171]

But Heavy did make a pertinent comparison between Ireland and the other Western European countries in their trade with the East bloc when he stressed that Ireland's trade deficit totalled '£48,733,000' while the West's favourable balance of trade reached '£5.5 billions'. As Heavy put it, 'other countries of Western Europe have learned to trade with the East'.[172] It was an explicit criticism of Córas Tráchtála's approach. It has been suggested that there might have been 'general competitive deficiencies in the Irish economic environment, such as inadequate infrastructure or excessive labour costs', which helps to explain why Irish exporters did not perform as well as other foreign exporters on the international market.[173]

In August 1979, the Ministry of External Affairs in East Berlin reflected on commercial relations between the two countries. It argued that 'as a result of the non-existence of diplomatic relations between the GDR and the Republic of Ireland, there is no legal basis at governmental level for the development of foreign trade relations'. There was no reason to complain about the GDR's export figures (see Table 1.2).

The major part of the GDR's exports to Ireland remained potash by far, followed by agricultural machinery, combine harvesters, motorcycles and tyres. The KfA (East German Chamber of Foreign Trade) in London operated as the middleman between the two countries as there was no East German commercial representation in Ireland. The Ministry was rather optimistic regarding exports and estimated that an increase of 10 per cent to 15 per cent, even of 20 per cent, could be achieved in the coming years.

However, there was a possible snag. The Ministry of External Affairs explained that the increase in exports was conditioned by the increase of imports from Ireland and admitted that until now these imports were 'totally insignificant' as compared to the GDR's exports. The few Irish goods consisted essentially of textiles and of a selection of foodstuffs. In the past, meat and butter had also been imported but because of the exceptionally high prices, it had to be discontinued.[174] This was bad news for Ireland as its main agricultural exports were precisely meat and butter. Moreover, as has been ascertained: 'Imports of Irish agricultural produce by countries other than the UK tended to be sporadic and were usually confined to specific requests for a particular commodity, often to compensate for a temporary fall-off in domestic supply'.[175] The Ministry of External Affairs' table shows a sharp decrease in 1977. Potash might well be the explanation for this (see Table 1.2). Indeed, Irish farmers began to use fertilisers on a large scale in the 1960s until the late 1970s. But when they were faced with economic difficulties, they tended to save money on production expenses.[176]

Table 1.2 **GDR's export figures to Ireland, 1975–79 in Valuta Mark (VM)**

1975	1976	1977	1978	Plan 1979	Contract obligation by 30/06/1979
VM8,700,000	VM18,100,000	VM14,000,000	VM14,500,000	VM16,000,000	VM10,100,000

Source: AA-PA, Berlin, MfAA, ZR 627/97, 'Information über den Stand der Außenhandelsbeziehungen der DDR zu Republik Irland', by MfA, 9 September 1979

The Ministry of External Affairs mentioned that the Irish government had imposed restrictive measures on East German imports on several occasions, notably concerning potash (1970–71) and tyres (1977 and 1978). It added that so far it could not see 'any real possibilities to significantly increase imports from Ireland'.[177] While this was true the ministry seemed to have missed the point that Desmond O'Malley's warning in 1977 did apparently not have drastic effects on the GDR's exports figures as shown in Table 1.2. It might perhaps have slowed down the increased rate of East German exports but it did not lead to a significant decrease. Therefore, the ministry had perhaps no reason to be seriously worried. In any case, it concluded its report by stressing that if diplomatic relations were established (rumours were then in the air), then the practicality of a governmental trade agreement should be explored. For Ireland, the development of trade would be the key factor in the establishment of formal diplomatic relations.[178]

Eventually, East Berlin did take the decision to buy more fish. In November 1979, the *Kerryman* reported that an East German ship was buying huge quantities of mackerel from Irish fishermen.[179] But simultaneously the East Germans stepped up their commercial activities in Ireland. In March 1983, the *Irish Farmers Journal* advertised a Fortschritt combine harvester, which, according to the advertisement, was a bestseller.[180] Tourism in the GDR seemed to have become an alternative. Readers of the *Irish Times* could find reports on East Berlin and Leipzig among others and their touristic and cultural attractions.[181] For Honecker's government, Western tourism meant an entry of much needed hard currency. But the GDR would not be overwhelmed by Irish mass tourism and nor could Dublin expect mass tourism from the GDR. Not even the Irish ambassador to the Netherlands and the GDR's visit to East Berlin in June 1985 led to an improvement in the burning trade issue.[182]

On several occasions, Dublin took commercial reprisals to incite East Berlin to buy Irish. In June 1986, Dr Garret FitzGerald's government restricted the import of East German iron and steel products.[183] But in the end successive Irish governments, even with the strenuous efforts of Córas Tráchtála and others, were never in a position to solve the trade incompatibility problem and the ever-lasting negative balance of trade. But part of the problem was that Irish businesspeople and farmers knew that the GDR was a cheaper source of imports. In June 1989, Ambassador Joachim Mitdank was on an official visit to Ireland. Again, the trade issue was discussed, but nothing new emerged.[184] Yet, there was something of a surprise. The East German embassy in London reported that in 1988, Ireland had exported goods for a total value of £8,400,000 and imported for a total value of £8,900,000.[185]

Ironically, a balance of trade had at long last been achieved just at a time when the GDR was entering the final phase of its life. The embassy rightly commented that there was a balance but 'at a very low level'.[186] However, only a year later, it was overwhelmingly in favour of the East Germans again. Not that it would do the bankrupt East German state much good. Perhaps appropriately, the final statistics were announced in the Dáil by Desmond O'Malley, who had returned as Minister for Industry and Commerce. He declared that 'total Irish trade with East Germany in 1989 amounted to only IR£13.2 million, of which Irish exports accounted for IR£4.4 million. In common with the other countries of Central and East Europe, East Germany has been a difficult market for Irish exporters. Lack of convertible currency has been a particular problem.'[187] In any case, trade with the GDR never came anywhere near trade with the FRG. In 1988, Ireland exported goods for a total value of £1,368,785,000 to the FRG and imported for a total value of £880,811,000.[188] In the end, Dublin never signed any official trade agreement with East Berlin.[189]

Irish perceptions of East Germany

The perceptions the two countries had of each other were often rather negative and coloured by political bias and also ignorance. Ireland was rabidly anti-Communist and the spearhead of anti-Communist crusades was the Catholic Church. In June 1947, Colonel Dan Bryan, head of the G2 (Irish military intelligence), reported that about 1,000 people were pro-Soviet in Ireland. He was not particularly worried, however.[190] The colonel was right not to. Communism simply never got a solid foothold in the country. In 1951, there were only 103 official party members. That same year, Michael O'Riordan stood as a candidate for the general election in the constituency of Dublin South West and got a meagre 295 votes, representing 0.7 per cent of the poll. Despite the fact that he posed no threat, O'Riordan had been vehemently opposed by the Catholic Church. The *Standard* put up posters warning the electorate not to vote for him: 'You Can't Vote for the Red O'Riordan' and even went as far as to publish the photographs and addresses of known Communists.[191] It was rather intimidating and as has been rightly stated: 'it required considerable courage to identify openly with the Communist movement in Dublin in these years'.[192] Years later, figures had not improved for the Irish Communists. For example, during the Dublin City Council local election (proportional representation) in June 1985 the four candidates of the CPI obtained a total of 388 first preference votes.[193] In Northern Ireland, Communist membership stood at about 1,000 members in 1945, according to the *Irish Times*.[194] During the local government election in Belfast, the CPI obtained 245 votes in 1985 and 175 in 1989, both figures representing 0.2 per cent of the electorate.[195] Edgar Uher comments humorously: 'There was a time I knew all the members'.[196]

The press in Ireland regularly highlighted the Red threat. In July 1949, the *Limerick Leader* reminded its readers that Patrick Pearse, the republican leader of the Easter Rising of April 1916, had warned against it.[197] In June 1950, the *Irish Times* published an article entitled 'No religious freedom in East Germany'.[198] In May 1953, the *Anglo-Celt* had an article entitled 'Death warning to priests in East Germany'.[199] In June, the *Irish Times* reported the East German workers' uprising on its front page,[200] followed a few days later by the title 'Russian reprisals in East Berlin'.[201] It is true that the Soviet repression of the uprising had been heavy-handed. In April 1959, the *Connacht Tribune* reported that Dr Browne, the Bishop of Galway, denounced the 'persecution of the Church in East Germany' in front of about 500 children.[202]

The building of the Wall in Berlin in August 1961 provided the newspapers with almost endless possibilities to denounce what they saw as the evil East German regime. In October, the *Irish Independent* ran as a headline 'The prison that is East Berlin'.[203] In November, the *Irish Times* published an article entitled 'East Germans fire on fleeing women'.[204] Clearly, the Wall damaged the East German government's reputation beyond repair, and this was a breeding ground for Western propaganda. Lectures for the public on the dangers of Communism were also given. In March 1963, the *Westmeath Examiner* announced a lecture by Fr Patrick Joy entitled 'The menace of Communism',[205] and in October 1965, the *Nenagh Guardian* reported that Nenagh Council had given a civic reception to 'Mr. Douglas Hyde, former well-known Communist and ex-editor of *The Daily Worker*, the British Communist newspaper'. He lectured on the theme 'Positive answers to Communism'.[206] Hyde had converted to Catholicism and rejected Communism in his book *I Believed: The Autobiography of a Former British Communist*, published in 1951.

Yet, things began to change gradually from the mid and end-1960s onwards, although certainly not to the extent of drastically changing the image the Irish had of the GDR and the East bloc. This was because of the development of détente and also, as seen, because some in Ireland believed that Eastern Europe could constitute a new possible outlet for exports. However, in May 1964, Seán Lemass reiterated in the

Dáil that 'passports issued in the Soviet-occupied zone of Germany were not acceptable here for identification purposes'.[207] The Taoiseach was serious and the following month the *Irish Times* reported that three East Germans who 'were refused entry into Ireland on Thursday because their travel documents were not in order, were flown out from Shannon to Amsterdam'.[208] In March 1966, the *Sunday Independent* and the *Irish Times* informed their readers in pure Cold-War fashion that a 'daring escape' of an East German family had happened at Shannon Airport. As the plane had made a stopover on its way to Cuba, the family had asked for political asylum and was quickly spirited away to the West German embassy in Dublin.[209] Such escapes were rather rare in Ireland.

The Irish authorities were willing to cooperate in these issues as the West German embassy had requested back in December 1958 as seen. That a supposedly neutral country was helping a prominent NATO member state does not come as a surprise. At the time of writing, the Edward Snowden affair has revealed that Sweden, another supposedly neutral, had helped the Americans in the monitoring of the Soviet Union since the end of the Second World War. Neutrals in Western Europe were actively pro-West. They had too much in common.[210] The Soviet invasion of Czechoslovakia in August 1968 was roundly condemned. Minister for External Affairs Frank Aiken demanded the immediate withdrawal of the 'aggressors',[211] and Brendan Corish, the leader of the Irish Labour Party, declared that 'the invasion showed the true nature of Russian imperialism'.[212]

Nonetheless, the early 1970s saw the timid beginnings of advertisements for tourism in the GDR. Détente was making good progress, the status of Berlin was redefined, East and West Germany admitted each other's rights to exist and a string of Western states recognised the GDR. In January 1970, the *Irish Times* praised the reconstruction of Dresden which had been levelled to the ground in an Allied bombing raid in February 1945. A large photograph showed the beauty of the city. It was no problem obtaining visas and the inhabitants of Dresden were particularly welcoming.[213] Berolina, the East German tourist office, cooperated with a travel agency called Abbey Travel in Dublin and advertisements to visit the GDR appeared from time to time in the *Irish Times*. The package holidays on offer were above all oriented towards an educated public, curious about local culture behind the Iron Curtain.[214]

Some trade-union members also had the opportunity to visit the GDR.[215] So did members of the Connolly Youth Movement, which was affiliated to the Communist Party of Ireland (CPI), and those of the Irish Democratic Youth Movement (IDYM), which was affiliated to

Sinn Féin/the Workers' Party (SF/WP). The journalist Henry McDonald had been a member of the IDYM. At the beginning of the 1980s, he travelled with the group to East Berlin to stay in an international youth camp under the supervision of the East German Communist youth movement, the Freie Deutsche Jugend (FDJ, free German youth) and, according to him, 'no doubt the Stasi's eyes and ears'. McDonald described the camp as 'a hive of hedonism and bed-hopping'. On one occasion, he asked an East German girl 'if she wondered what life was like on the western side of [the] border'. She did not answer lest McDonald should report her. He was then 'oblivious to the fact that we were in fact visiting a vast prison camp, a paranoid state, a society run by a self-serving and hypocritical elite who thought they knew what was best for the workers and peasants'. It was only after the collapse of the GDR that he realised what kind of regime had ruled the country and why the girl had not answered his question.[216]

The impressions of the few Irish travellers who went to the GDR varied. In December 1981, a group of them took exception to an article published in the *Irish Times* which described East Berlin as 'drab'. According to what they had seen, the city was anything but drab and they described the article as being full of Cold-War clichés. They claimed that 'the shops were full of goods, and jammed with shoppers'.[217] It might well have been the case that these Irish tourists had been taken to an Intershop where the finest of East German products and also Western consumer goods were for sale for hard currency. In the 1980s, the GDR's economic problems were becoming very acute. On the occasion of the 30th anniversary of the GDR in 1979 the *Irish Times* had mentioned 'an economy of shortages' and the 'widespread use of West German currency in East Germany to obtain goods and services'.[218] An Irishwoman appreciated the culture on offer in East Berlin, Weimar and Leipzig but complained about the rudeness of restaurant waiters and border guards.[219]

Several Irish artists exhibited their works or performed in the GDR. The painter and designer Robert Ballagh travelled to East Berlin where he had been invited by the Verband Bildender Künstler (VBK, association of visual artists). The VBK was an association of East German artists who made statements in their art on political and social issues. His visit coincided with the Youth Festival so that there was a particular festive mood in the city, including many cultural activities. He was particularly impressed by the VBK's organisation and wrote that 'the exhibition and symposium were presented in a totally professional manner with a level of expertise unfortunately uncommon here in Ireland'. All in all, Ballagh was pleasantly surprised with his stay in the GDR and admitted that his 'short experience contradicted most attitudes about the GDR that are prevalent in Ireland'. However, he pertinently remarked that his visit took place when many events were happening in the city and that 'my views must therefore be coloured. For that reason I feel I must plan a return visit in more normal times in order to develop a fuller picture of life in the GDR'.[220] Ballagh was right to remain cautious. The artist Bärbel Bohley was also a member of the VBK until she began to militate for civil rights in the GDR. She was consequently excluded from the VBK in 1983 and harassed by the Stasi.[221] Among those people and groups targeted for extensive surveillance operations by the Stasi were what the regime deemed to be 'critical artists'. Harassment and so-called 'disintegration plans' were implemented such as trying to implicate them by association with teenagers and lovers.[222] The good mood in East Berlin and the lofty ideals of the VBK masked certain realities.

The Sands family from Northern Ireland performed Irish traditional music in 1972 in the GDR. Colum Sands remembers: 'We went there in 1972 and people were asking us for news songs, songs about our situation. We were back the next year for a huge political song festival [Festival des Politischen Liedes]'. The Sands family became very popular.[223] *Neues Deutschland* wrote about them that they were 'almost regulars in Berlin. They sang about the dreams and struggles of their people for freedom, justice and peace'.[224] Jacqueline Maloney from County Cavan won three awards for her song 'To Your Harbour – To Your Shore' at the International Music Festival in Rostock.[225] Cormac O'Duffy's 'Dresden Requiem' was selected to be performed on the occasion of the 40th anniversary of the bombing of the city in 1945.[226] Yet, the number of Irish artistic/cultural visits was limited and was certainly not systematically reciprocated by East German ones.

Some Irish authors caught the attention of the East Germans. In December 1983, the author and journalist Breandan Ó hEithir wrote a rather negative book review of Anthony Bailey's *Along the Edge of the Forest: An Iron Curtain Journey*. To his mind Bailey was too critical of the East bloc regimes, describing 'every border guard who pops up to take his photograph … as if he were a member of a firing squad'. Ó hEithir also made the point that the recent exchange of eighty-three East German prisoners for West German money could be interpreted differently. He preferred to sit on the fence on this issue of buying humans: 'These prisoners are either "political" or "anti-social", depending on the colour of your own politics.'[227] It is extremely doubtful that Helmut Kohl, the West German Chancellor, would have agreed to buy East German antisocial elements. There is perhaps an explanation for Ó hEithir's lack of criticism here. He spoke German and was a member of the Ireland–GDR Friendship Society, which he had joined out of curiosity. His novel written in Irish, *Lig Sinn I gCathú*, published in 1976 and translated into English as *Lead Us into Temptation*, was later also translated into German, *Führe uns in Versuchung*, and published in East Germany in 1985. According to Damian Mac Con Uladh, 'his annual visits to the GDR were financed by the royalties (paid in non-convertible GDR marks) from the German translation of his novel'.[228] Ó hEithir seemed to have good reason for sitting on the fence.

A handful of Irish idealists settled in the GDR. Belfast-born Elizabeth Shaw left for the country in 1946. A Communist, she believed that the Soviet Union was building something new. A brilliant cartoonist, she made fine and witty caricatures of Western leaders for different East German newspapers like *Neues Deutschland*,[229] which helped to brighten the day in a society ruled by a rather humourless Communist regime during the period of high Stalinism.[230] She was taken aback by the uprising in June 1953 and then felt that not everybody in the GDR was clearly satisfied with what Walter Ulbricht was doing. Beside caricatures, Shaw also made illustrations for children's books. She believed in her ideals and stayed in the GDR until its demise. She was happy to have made that decision.[231]

Jack Mitchell, a Scotsman of Irish descent, was another such idealist. In the 1950s, he settled in the GDR where he did much to emphasise the cultural dimension of the working-class struggle. He lectured in literature in the Humboldt University in East Berlin and associated folk song with drama and also poetry. He was much involved in the political-song scene of the Oktoberklub in the East German capital and invited Irish and Scottish musicians to perform for the club's established political song festival.[232]

But not all idealists were convinced by what they experienced in East Germany. Cork-born Patrick Galvin was a playwright and poet inspired by Gaelic poetry. He was also much concerned by the poverty of his native city. In 1956, he was invited to perform in East Berlin and was introduced on East German television as 'an Irish folksinger'. He gave lectures on Irish folk music but did not really warm to the local political culture. On the contrary, he was put off by Ulbricht regime's aggression in promoting world peace and said that 'it was almost frightening'.[233] At a time when people were regularly marshalled into parading for peace, Galvin's comments were not surprising.[234]

There was also the creation of the Ireland–GDR Friendship Society in 1977 whose aim was to advertise in favour of the GDR by promoting all sorts of events. It only had around eighty-five members in the whole of Ireland between 1977 and 1979.[235] The CPI was not always on good terms with the society as it had had no role in setting it up despite the fact that the SED approved of it. A delegation of the Freie Deutsche Jugend (FDJ, Free German Youth) reported after a visit to Dublin that 'in the main the members [of the society] are young intellectuals, who are mostly sympathetic to Sinn Féin/[the Workers' Party]'. It would also appear that many members did not join out of ideological conviction but rather because they were curious. About two or three trips to the GDR took place every year and it is estimated that between 1978 and 1990 around 150 people participated. In the GDR, a sister organisation was set up in 1981, the DDR–Irland Freundschaftsgesellschaft, but it appears not to have been particularly active and nothing much was done to make Ireland known.[236] The DFA kept tabs on these Irish friendship societies with the GDR and the Soviet Union, and also on Irish delegations heading for East Berlin and Moscow. It sought to figure out who these Irish people were and why they went there.[237]

An age of discovery of the GDR by essentially the Irish cultural and intellectual elites seemed to be taking place. Nonetheless, it did not make the issues of human rights and religious freedom go away. The relations between the church, overwhelmingly Protestant, and the Communist and atheistic state were fraught with tensions and never developed harmoniously. The SED feared that the church could channel dissent and that committed Christians could form a threat. The party approached the religious issue in different ways, ranging from confrontation to subtle attempts to control it, and also infiltrating it with Stasi informers. However, the SED did not win that battle. The church provided a platform for dissent and supported 'oppositional cultures'.[238] In 1982, the executive secretary of the Irish School of Ecumenics, Reverend Raymond Kennedy, had the opportunity to visit the GDR and meet different religious representatives. A rabbi told him that the number of Jews kept declining. The vicar-general of the Catholic Bishop of Berlin explained how the state did everything not to arrange for religious education in schools while the Protestant Bishop of East Berlin accused the SED of wanting to turn the youth into atheists.[239]

Two years later the *Irish Times* wrote that the Evangelical Church (mainly Lutheran) in the GDR 'has taken a leading role in promoting the independent peace movement in East Germany'. This was not to the SED's liking and several young people from an ecumenical group had been arrested for opposing compulsory military service and criticising the armament policy of both NATO and the Warsaw Pact. Many had also been placed under house arrest and detained by the Stasi.[240] The *Irish Times* also reported on the fate of dissidents, opponents and reformers, like Wolf Biermann, a poet and singer who had been expelled from the GDR, and Professor Robert Havemann, an outspoken critic of the SED.[241] The *Irish Independent* reminded its readers that the shooting of fugitives still occurred from time to time.[242]

The Conference on Security and Cooperation in Europe (CSCE), in which Ireland and the GDR participated, led to the signing of the Helsinki Accords or Final Act in the summer of 1975. Included were agreements on human rights. In Ireland, the Workers' Party (WP), known until April 1982 as Sinn Féin/the Workers Party (SF/WP), was inspired by the CSCE and set up the Irish Committee for European Security and Cooperation. In reality, the Irish Committee simply represented Moscow's views on the armament issue.[243] It was much preoccupied by Ireland's neutrality and maintaining peace and cooperation. In August 1982, Seán Garland sent the DDR–Komitee für Europäische Sicherheit und Zusammenarbeit (GDR committee for European security and cooperation) an invitation to participate in a conference on peace and disarmament in Dublin in January 1983. Garland claimed to 'have developed a good relationship with the Irish Prime Minister, Charles J. Haughey' with whom discussions on holding the conference had been held. The event would focus on the role of neutral states, the creation of a nuclear-free Europe and 'the role of the mass media in the struggle for Peace, Security and Cooperation'. Human rights, a most delicate issue in the GDR, were however not on the agenda although Garland indicated that there would be room for other topics. Michael Mullen, the General Secretary of the Irish Transport and General Workers' Union (ITGWU) who was also the Irish Committee's Honorary President, would open the conference and it was expected that Haughey would make a speech. The East Germans accepted the invitation, ready to do everything for peace. But then the conference was cancelled as Mullen died suddenly.

It would appear that the subsequent relations between the Irish Committee for European Security and Cooperation and the East Germans were rather inconsistent. In May 1988, the Friedensrat (peace council) of the GDR wrote a report on the participation of Professor Stefan Doernberg in a conference in Dublin organised by the Irish Committee later that month. The Friendensrat was of the opinion that Doernberg should take this opportunity to meet members of the Irish Committee but also of the Irish Campaign for Nuclear Disarmament (CND). The talks should centre on activities in favour of peace. There was nothing on human rights. Interestingly, the Friedensrat complained that it had sent material and publications to the Irish Committee 'for several years' but that it had 'received hardly any publications or material containing information on activities of the peace movement despite several promises made'. It was suggested in the report that the Irish Council should confirm that it got the Friedenrat's material and that it should send documentation to East Berlin. There had been 'brief meetings' between East German and Irish representatives during international conferences.[244] But that was it.

The Irish press largely reported the dramatic events of 1989 when thousands of East German citizens fled to the West while other tens of thousands protested in the streets of Leipzig, East Berlin and Dresden. Some tried desperately to board trains heading for West Germany by way of Czechoslovakia and Hungary where the borders were now open. The *Irish Independent* spoke of a 'freedom express'.[245] The *Irish Farmers Journal* commented: 'Their system had failed to deliver to ordinary people. This stampede was the most dramatic evidence ever of that failure.'[246] Mikhail Gorbachev was urging Erich Honecker to implement reforms, but the ageing SED Secretary General had difficulties in accepting this. Public pressure mounted. On 17 October, the *Irish Times* reported on a monster protest march of 100,000 people through the streets of Leipzig.[247] Honecker wanted to send in the tanks but was dissuaded from doing so. There was no point in provoking a civil war.[248] Two days later, the *Irish Independent* announced in plain language that Honecker had been 'dumped'.[249]

The question now was whether the Wall would be able to withstand this tidal wave of popular discontent. The answer soon came. On 9 November, it fell. Thousands of West and East Berliners embraced each other. The *Irish Independent* had an appropriate title: 'Blitzkrieg on the Wall'.[250] On 3 October 1990, the day the two Germanys would be officially reunified, the *Irish Times* stated that 'two German teams will contest the women's World 15k road championship in Dublin' and that 'it will be the last opportunity for the Germans to compete as separate entities'.[251] And so it was that Ireland, the last country to have entered into diplomatic relations with the GDR in Europe, was also the last country to welcome a team from the GDR. One day in November, a Leipzig man told Irish journalist Fergus Pyle after the celebrations: '"The party is over … and now we must work, but with a hang-over"'.[252] Indeed, the former East Germany needed to be rebuilt and be incorporated into the former West Germany. An East–West mentality gap had to be overcome. It would be an arduous task. But that is another story.

The GDR's perceptions of the Northern Irish conflict

What about East Germany's views of Ireland and Northern Ireland? Predictably, the country's troubled relations with Britain were going to be a source of inspiration for the East German media. Britain was deemed to be a colonial and imperialist power and colonialism and imperialism were two concepts that were vehemently denounced by Marxism-Leninism. In 1956, the IRA launched a poorly planned offensive against the Northern Irish State with the aim of reunifying Ireland. It was called 'Operation HARVEST' and lasted until 1962 when it was abandoned as it was not supported. What it did harvest was an increased opposition to resist reunification by the unionist/Protestant population in Northern Ireland. On 16 December 1956, the front page title of *Neues Deutschland* read: 'British terror against Irish uprising'. It was explained that troops and police forces were used to suppress the 'freedom movement' and that 'patriots are being tortured'.[253] Perhaps it was a crude attempt to counterbalance some of the negative effects of the uprising of 1953 in East Berlin and the very recent one in October in Budapest, both crushed by the Soviet army. The treatment of the IRA by the East German press remained ambivalent though. Ten years later in 1966, the *Weltbühne*, a literary journal, described it as a 'terrorist organisation'.[254] In July 1969, when the Troubles were about to break out with the arrival of the British army in Belfast and Derry (Londonderry), *Horizont*, a weekly journal that dealt with international policy and economy, had a long article entitled 'Northern Ireland, the "white colony"' explaining British oppression and the Irish struggle for freedom.[255]

It is interesting here to say a few words on how the IRA was portrayed in popular East German encyclopaedias. In 1964, *Meyers Neues Lexikon* had the following definition:

> Irish Republican Army (IRA)
> Emerged in 1919 from the Irish Volunteers of the illegal Irish Republic. The IRA split during the signing of the Free State Treaty [*sic*] in 1921 into governmental troops and a left wing which, under leadership of de Valera until 1923, led a guerrilla warfare ['*Partisanenkrieg*'] for the establishment of a republic and the reunification with Northern Ireland. After de Valera's capitulation this group has continued its struggle with individual acts of terror especially in Northern Ireland until the present day and initiated in 1939 and especially in December 1956 large-scale operations. The IRA is illegal in Ireland and in Great Britain.[256]

Four years later in 1969, the definition had shortened quite a bit:

> Irish Republican Army (IRA)
> An illegal combat unit ['*Kampfverband*'] founded in 1919. Its bourgeois-nationalist remainder tried after 1923 to achieve the reunification of Ireland by guerrilla warfare ['*Partisanenaktionen*'] and acts of individual terror. It officially ceased its struggle in 1962.[257]

In 1986, the *BI Universallexikon* had this to say:

> Irish Republican Army IRA)
> Combat troops ['*Kampftruppe*'] set up by Irish patriots in the struggle for independence since 1916. It split during the setting up of the Irish Free State in 1921 into governmental troops and a left wing which fought against the Dominion status compromise until 1923. A remainder of the organisation continued its actions illegally especially in Northern Ireland and was isolated by the masses. It split in 1969 into an 'official' wing, which cooperated with other progressive forces in seeking political solutions, and a petty bourgeois/anarchist 'provisional' wing, which, through its sectarian insistence on acts of individual terror, gives the British authorities, and the extremist organisations of the Anglo-Scottish community, pretexts for suppressing the civil rights and workers' movement.[258]

Certainly, these definitions were not without ideological baggage. Wolfgang Döhnert, a former correspondent of the Allgemeiner Deutscher Nachrichtendienst (ADN, general German news agency from the GDR) in London, comments that the word '*Partisananaktionen*' had 'a positive connotation because it suggests a certain legitimacy'. Indeed, the word 'partisan' is positive in Marxist-Leninist jargon. Döhnert pertinently points to an inconsistency in the 1969 definition: 'So the phrase "*Partisanenaktionen und individueller Terror*" is in my opinion an obvious contradiction, because from the Marxist point of view "*Partisanenkrieg*" [a war of partisans] is part of legitimate defence against oppressors but "individueller Terror" [acts of individual terror] is rejected as a form of criminal action.'[259] The 1986 definition, however, leaves absolutely no doubt that the PIRA was rejected.

When British troops were deployed in Northern Ireland in August 1969, *Neues Deutschland* described them as occupiers.[260] The newspaper's title made absolutely no doubt whatsoever where its sympathy lay: 'London's colonial knout rules Northern Ireland'.[261] In 1970, a split occurred in the IRA. There were now two rival organisations: the Official IRA (OIRA), Marxist in outlook, and the Provisional IRA (PIRA), more traditional nationalist/republican. It was the PIRA that would fight the British army and the Royal Ulster Constabulary (RUC, Northern Irish police). Assassinations and bomb attacks became a daily routine in Northern Ireland. The PIRA and the OIRA feuded, fought against the British and the RUC and also against Protestant/loyalist paramilitaries like the Ulster Volunteer Force (UVF) and Ulster Defence Association (UDA). It was little wonder why *Neues Deutschland*'s correspondent, Werner Goldstein, wrote that the IRA was involved in an 'anarchist bombing terror' and all that it would achieve would be the deepening of the division between the Catholic/nationalist and Protestant/unionist communities. It would also play into the hands of the British army.[262] The last point remained to be seen. The British army could also be its own worst enemy as it made irreparable blunders.

On 1 February 1972, two days after Bloody Sunday when the British army killed fourteen unarmed civilians in Derry in extremely controversial circumstances, *Neues Deutschland* published a photograph of the soldiers in action. The title was: '"They shot although I had a white flag"'.[263] *Horizont*'s front page consisted of a large photograph, showing British soldiers and a terrified Northern Irish woman. The title was 'Bloodthirsty imperialism'.[264] Undoubtedly, the Troubles constituted first-rate material for propaganda purposes, but was it really propaganda in this particular case? Bloody Sunday had shaken Europe, East *and* West. The Irish embassy in Denmark, which was a NATO member state, reported that the independent daily quality newspaper *Information* had severely criticised the British.[265] A representative of the Danish radio and television informed the Irish ambassador confidentially that 'the British have complained that the news coverage is biased in [Ireland's] favour', but they were unsuccessful.[266] Wolfgang Döhnert makes a pertinent point when he posits whether ADN coverage of Paul Hill's ordeals, after he was unjustly accused by the British of bombing a pub in Guildford in November 1974 and tortured by them, would have constituted Cold War propaganda.[267]

The British government's decision to establish diplomatic relations with East Berlin in February 1973 did not have a softening impact on East German newspaper denunciations of British rule in Northern Ireland, although Irish republican violence was also roundly condemned. On 21 November 1974, two pubs in Birmingham in Britain were bombed killing twenty-one people. It is widely suspected that the PIRA carried out the attacks. Two days later *Neues Deutschland* and *Neue Zeit* announced that nineteen people had died. The *Berliner Zeitung* wrote that the Communist Party of Great Britain (CPGB) and the CPI had condemned the attacks as 'senseless acts of violence that can only play into the hands of far-right forces in Great Britain and Ireland'.[268] On 21 July 1976, the PIRA killed the British Ambassador in Dublin, Christopher Ewart-Biggs, and a British civil servant by blowing up their car. In the following days, the *Berliner Zeitung* reported that the assassination was condemned by 'leading representatives' of the CPGB and the CPI during a meeting in Belfast. Both parties issued a common declaration, condemning 'individual acts of terror'.[269]

Horizont severely condemned the PIRA. In 1976, Frithjof Schulze wrote that the Provisionals were 'increasingly of a Maoist and anti-Communist orientation'. There was of course no love lost between the GDR's Soviet ally and China. According to him, PIRA leaders accepted invitations issued by Maoist groups in Italy, West Germany and the United States. They were in touch with the 'anarchist Breton underground organisation FLB [Front de Libération de la Bretagne]' and also with similar groups in the Basque region in Spain. Unsurprisingly, Schulze praised the Marxist OIRA and explained that unlike the PIRA, the OIRA believed that the 'unity of action of all the revolutionary organisations with the working class and the [Irish Communist party] reunified since 1970 is the most important prerequisite for a successful struggle against imperialism in both parts of Ireland'. On 3 December 1974 on East German television, the General Secretary of the CPI, Michael O'Riordan (a former IRA man), had declared: 'There are no differences of opinion between the Official IRA and the CPI on basic questions'.[270] That would very soon change.

Reporting on the brutalities committed by the British army continued unabated. However, British army brutality was real. In January 1978, *Neues Deutschland* informed its readers that Britain had been condemned by the European Court of Human Rights in Strasbourg because of human rights abuses,[271] while in August the *Neue Weg* of Halle wrote about the dreadful detention conditions in the prison of Long Kesh (Maze Prison).[272] The hunger strikes of republican prisoners in Long Kesh led by PIRA member Bobby Sands in 1981 were widely reported by the East German press as they had been in the West. In the GDR, they provided *Neues Deutschland* with an opportunity to attack British imperialism in action. After Sands's death, the newspaper emphasised his working-class roots and described Long Kesh as a 'concentration camp'.[273] The term 'concentration camp' was too strong and certainly tactless bearing in mind recent German history. But this was Cold-War propaganda, the art of exaggeration.

Sands's death provoked a kind of duel between the West and East German media in which the Westerners came off the better. On 9 May 1981, Werner Castor from the West German radio declared that whether one considered the PIRA as a terrorist organisation or not, the way Sands's death was reported in the GDR raised questions, notably what was the GDR's position towards terrorism? Castor had noticed that *Neues Deutschland* was being inconsistent. On Tuesday, *Neues Deutschland* had written that 'the cause of the recent disturbances was a hunger strike of several members of the terrorist wing of the IRA in the Maze Prison, who had been sentenced by British special courts'. Yet, on Wednesday, the same newspaper wrote that Sands had been recently elected to the House of Commons in London as a member of the 'Irish resistance organisation, the Provisional IRA'. Castor commented that he supposed that on the one hand, the GDR wanted to distance itself from terrorism, as was the case with the Baader-Meinhof gang (Red Army Faction, RAF, in the FRG), but, on the other hand, it was not easy 'to simply dismiss the IRA as "counter-revolutionaries" like it had been done with terrorist organisations in West Germany'.

The *Berliner Zeitung* had written that 'state violence in Northern Ireland provoked pointless counter-violence of the IRA'. Castor believed that there was nothing wrong with this statement except that the *Berliner Zeitung* also claimed, wrongly, that the British government was only looking for a military solution to the Northern Irish conflict. Castor stressed that for the past twelve years the British had sought political solutions. Whether these solutions were good ones or not was another matter, he continued. At the end of the broadcast, Castor attacked East Germany by saying that what was described as 'state violence' in Northern Ireland was 'maintenance of security and order in the GDR'. Moreover, he pointed out, how could the GDR press write about London's anti-democratic repression of the Northern Irish when 'a prisoner, condemned for belonging to a terrorist organisation, has been elected Member of Parliament'?[274] Touché. The Stasi was in possession of a transcript of Castor's broadcast. But as Wolfgang Döhnert, the former correspondent of the ADN in charge of Ireland between 1971 and 1990, remembers: 'The nature of the news produced by the crisis in Northern Ireland served objectively the unmasking of the imperialist system with its shortcomings and crimes.'[275] In the end, views were conditioned by political background.

On 13 October 1984, the correspondent of *Neues Deutschland* in London, Reiner Oschmann, reported that a PIRA bomb attack on British Prime Minister Margaret Thatcher killed at least four people and wounded thirty others in the Grand Hotel in Brighton where the annual conference of the Conservative Party was taking place.[276] On 9 November 1987, the newspaper wrote about the PIRA attack in Enniskillen in Northern Ireland which killed eleven people and wounded dozens of others. Although the PIRA was not mentioned in the article (it would admit responsibility shortly afterwards) it would have been relatively easy to guess for those East Germans who had followed the events in Northern Ireland who the perpetrators were. It was mentioned that 'the explosion happened at a monument where hundreds of soldiers and civilians had gathered to remember those who fell during both world wars'.[277] Bearing in mind the very strong remembrance of the Second World War in Eastern Communist countries, this particular PIRA bomb attack cannot have failed to disturb politicians and people alike in the GDR.

It must also be noted that in the 1980s the Soviets had serious reservations about international terrorism. Contrary to what has been claimed by some politicians, journalists and propagandists in the West, Moscow was not pulling the strings of terrorist groups the world over. Under Mikhail Gorbachev (1985–91), there was a distinct dislike of such groups and the regimes that supported them like Colonel Gaddafi's Libya. It had also been the case under Leonid Brezhnev's leadership (1964–82) although the Soviets knew full well that some of the freedom fighters they supported in their cause of national liberation were actually terrorists, used terrorist methods or had the potential to become terrorists. Also, the Soviet leadership feared that their own country might become the target of terrorist attacks.[278] As will be shown, the Stasi was equally concerned by the possible security threat that the PIRA posed to its operations in the FRG and to the GDR itself. This means that the East German press was no longer describing Irish republicans as freedom fighters. East Berlin was also desperately looking for financial support from the West, essentially of course from the FRG. The country's economy was heading full steam towards the abyss. Now was not the time to upset the West with support for terrorists or freedom fighters.

The GDR television had a few broadcasts on the Troubles. In December 1977, an East German crew travelled to Belfast to shoot a documentary entitled 'Bringt die Folterer vor Gericht' (Bring the torturers to justice). The crew roundly condemned the behaviour of the British army which was portrayed as a brutal oppressor. A shot shows Harland and Wolf, the famous shipyard in the city, then a British helicopter and a British sniper taking up position while the journalist comments that the British army arrived for the first time in Northern Ireland in 1969 and that the province has been in flames ever since. He adds that before this the soldiers shot workers who struggled to have their wages increased. Clearly the message was that the army was at the service of the capitalist exploiters.

The East German television crew enters a nationalist ghetto in Belfast, probably the Falls Road, and the journalist says that 'the British army goes hunting' in that area. There is a meeting with Madge Davison of the CPI who speaks about the abuses of civil rights and the torturing and killing of Catholic prisoners. According to Davison, the British have violated the Helsinki Accords of 1975. As previously mentioned, it was true that in 1978 the European Court of Human Rights condemned the use of certain interrogation techniques by the British. Fr Denis Faul was also interviewed about these brutal methods. To drive home his point, Faul reads out testimonies of prisoners who were tortured. The rest of the documentary shows shots of Crumlin Road jail and interviews of people who were beaten up by the British. However, nothing is said about the PIRA's terrorist and murderous activities, except a brief comment made by the journalist, stating that the majority of the Northern Irish people condemns terrorists.[279]

The East German Evangelical Church was much interested in the Northern Irish conflict and more particularly in the Corrymeela Community experience. Corrymeela was a project aiming at opening dialogue between Christians of different denominations and promoting peace. It was located at Ballycastle in County Antrim and had been the brainchild of Ray Davey who as a British prisoner of war had been shocked by the destruction of Dresden.[280] This definitely formed a link between Northern Ireland and East Germany. Furthermore, the SED regime would not be opposed to contacts between the Evangelical Church and Corrymeela since it would complement its own commitment to world peace as it loudly claimed. In December 1981, the Evangelical Church in the province of Saxony invited Carol Walsh of Corrymeela to come to Magdeburg on the occasion of the World Day of Prayer. Walsh would not only talk about the current conditions in Northern Ireland but also participate in the preparation of exhibitions in various communities. She had already visited the GDR with a Northern Irish youth group during the previous summer. As to the church in Saxony, it had taken a close interest in the Troubles 'for many years' through its work with its own youth groups and contacts with Northern Irish youth groups and Corrymeela.[281]

During a study visit to the Irish School of Ecumenics in Dublin in October 1983 on behalf of the East German Evangelical Church, Walter Schulz and Martin Lange took the opportunity to travel to Belfast, the 'trouble area'. Their subsequent report made for interesting reading devoid of any Marxist-Leninist terminology and influences, and therefore contrasted with the reports East Germans read in their newspapers. It was objective and unbiased. They pointed out that there were 'extremist groups on both sides [who] have inwardly to a large extent freed themselves of their Churches'. It was not a religious conflict but a politico-nationalist one in which there were some religious aspects. Belfast was now ghettoised along so-called peace lines that separated Protestant/unionist and Catholic/nationalist communities. Because of the fighting, some firms had pulled out of the city, causing more and more unemployment. This in turn was 'a breeding-ground for extremist and terrorist activities. It is particularly bad for the young who let themselves be carried away by dangerous agitators to commit violent acts.' Much British money was pumped into Northern Ireland, creating a welfare state that Ireland could not afford. Life was cheaper in the North, which explained why so many Southern cars and lorries crossed the border every day.

Schulz and Lange wrote that 'the psychological effects of violence over a long period of time are considerable. Emotions become dulled. Sympathy for victims of the conflict has diminished. One lives with the tensions and hopes not to be affected personally. It is feared that effects on children are particularly strong.' What both men had certainly not expected was that despite the conflict, Anglo-Irish relations were far from being bad:

> What was surprising for us was a double observation. On the one hand, we experienced how closely connected Great Britain and Ireland were. The borders were totally open, including between Northern Ireland and the Republic. The road links were good. The economic relations were pronounced. On the other hand, there were latent and evident tensions. This was not very noticeable in Dublin. However, the Irish were fond of showing their guests signs of their struggle for independence. One imagined that the border crossing from South to North would be very bad. But for us there was no passport control.[282]

In this passage, Schulz and Lange had accurately described the complexity of Anglo-Irish–Northern Irish relations. Both men concluded that 'the situation in Northern Ireland appears to be hopeless. All attempts at political solutions have failed so far. The Churches are engaged in dialogue with one another, but they do not get anywhere with the extremist groups. It is known that the exponent of radical Protestantism, Reverend Paisley, originally a Presbyterian minister, has set up his own Church in which he was elected leading theologian for life.'[283]

Another rare East German who had the opportunity to travel in Northern Ireland and Ireland was the author Walter Kaufmann. Kaufmann was of Jewish origin and fled to Britain before the war. After the outbreak of the hostilities, the British authorities sent him to Australia.[284] It was there that he developed a strong interest in Ireland as he worked alongside Irish migrants. He later returned to Europe and settled in the GDR. After visits to Ireland, Kaufmann published a couple of books. In *Flammendes Irland; Wir lachen, weil wir weinen* (burning Ireland; we are laughing because we are crying) published in 1977,[285] he gives an account of his travels and meetings in the island with ordinary people but also with Michael O'Riordan and James Stewart, the Communist leaders. One gets the impression that Kaufmann is more inspired by the North. The pro-GDR/Marxist bias is not overbearing, but rather subtle. The PIRA is criticised as are the unionists generally described as far-right-wing people. The British army is certainly not depicted in favourable terms, nor is the British judiciary system. Northern Ireland has become a militarised society where the living and social conditions are very bad. There are references to the peace walls separating Catholics and Protestants. Unsurprisingly, Kaufmann makes the case that only the CPI and Communism can reunite the Northern Irish people, which will lead to reunification. There are many references to storytelling and meetings in pubs but no simplifications and generalisations.

The same year Kaufmann published another small book of about thirty pages called *Patrick*.[286] It was intended for children of more than 9 years of age and included illustrations by Angela Brunner and photographs by an Irishman called Brendan Murphy. The photographs show the British army in action in the streets of Belfast. The book is about the daily life of a young boy called Patrick, evolving in a violent environment. One of his friends is shot by a British soldier who mistakenly believes that the ketchup bottle he is carrying is a bomb. He is left on the street without any further attendance from the British. The soldier is not punished for the shooting. The book highlights everyday British imperialism and is a one-dimensional account of the Northern Irish conflict. Interestingly, it was used for teacher-training purposes in the pedagogical institute in Rochlitz in Saxony.[287] *Patrick* certainly served the needs of an educational system directed by Marxist-Leninist ideology.

East German perceptions of Ireland

Ireland figured quite regularly in different East German newspapers. The articles were mainly political and economic analyses of the country, including general presentations for the readers. If, of course, there was news relating to the current Cold War, then so much the better. In November 1960, *Neues Deutschland* published a small article entitled 'Ireland will not become a member of NATO', concerning Taoiseach Seán Lemass's recent declaration that there were no arguments in favour of Ireland joining a military alliance.[288] However, it did not explain that despite its neutrality the country favoured the West. In October 1970, the newspaper reported with much glee that US President Richard Nixon's welcome in Ireland had been rather controversial. Dublin was the last port of call of the president's European tour and he wanted to visit the graves of his Irish ancestors. He also met 'pro-American millionaires'. However, some people did not extend the famous Irish traditional welcome and protested against the war in Vietnam. One placard read: 'Wanted for murder: Nixon-killed 250,000 Vietnamese'.[289]

In July 1966, the Australian Rupert Lockwood published an article entitled 'Ireland today' in the *Weltbühne*, a weekly magazine that dealt with politics, arts and economy. Native English speakers were often employed to write about Ireland. Lockwood lambasted property developers and speculators that were destroying Georgian architecture in Dublin and was slightly amazed that it went unopposed by the people.[290] He was right about the property developers and speculators,[291] but it was also the case that some slums needed to be cleared, as he admitted. In October 1972, Günther Cwojdrak wrote a very positive review of Seán O'Casey's *Juno and the Paycock* performed in East Berlin. O'Casey, a left-wing playwright, was popular in the GDR. Cwojdrak emphasised the 'Irish struggle for independence against English rule' and the life of the 'Irish working-class family, the Boyles'.[292]

There were some religious contacts between the GDR and Ireland but it simply could not be compared to the situation between the GDR and for example the Netherlands where a very strong peace movement existed. Protestant parishes in the Netherlands established no fewer than 380 partnerships with Protestant parishes in the GDR.[293] Whereas Ireland was overwhelmingly Catholic, the GDR was in theory overwhelmingly Protestant. Unlike Protestants, Catholics did usually not play an active political role in East Germany.[294] The archives of the former Catholic Church in the GDR reveal that only a handful of priests travelled to Ireland to attend international meetings.[295]

There was definitely more contact between East German and Irish Protestants. Exchanges between clerics and lecture tours were envisaged, notably between the East German Evangelical Church and the Irish School of Ecumenics in Dublin. During a meeting at Croydon in England, Reverend Alan D. Falconer of the School met Reverend Christa Lewek of the Bund der Evangelischen Kirchen in der DDR (BEK, federation of the Evangelical Churches in the GDR). The idea to send East German students to Dublin was to be explored. Falconer was very positive about the Croydon meeting and wrote to Lewek: 'Croydon was an attempt to explore, among other things, the ways in which *détente* in the signatory states of the Helsinki Final Act [CSCE] may be pursued. Theological research is one through which understanding between our peoples and our churches may be furthered and strengthened.'[296] As seen, the East German Evangelical Church had definitely developed an interest in the Northern Irish conflict.

In October 1983, Walter Schulz, a member of the Regional Church Assembly, and Reverend Martin Lange were in Dublin on behalf of the BEK. The general idea was to reflect on developing contacts with the churches in the GDR. They visited the School of Ecumenics and were satisfied that it had a 'very good reputation'. They described their stay in Ireland as 'very informative' and found the atmosphere to be very friendly.[297] In August 1984, Dr Günter Krusche informed Falconer that he had been allowed to spend two weeks in Dublin in 1985. He put forward a series of lectures ranging from 'The situation of the Protestant Churches in the Socialist society' to 'The self-understanding of the pastor in an urban and secularised society'.[298]

On 21 November 1980, *Neues Deutschland* greeted the opening of diplomatic relations between Ireland and the GDR on its front page. Dr Franz Knipping, who was the newspaper's correspondent in London, wrote a substantial article on Ireland, emphasising its struggle against British imperialism but also its current economic problems. He pointed out that more and more US firms settled in the country, attracted by financial benefits, and that the CPI was the 'revolutionary vanguard' of the growing Irish working class.[299] The remark on the CPI was very far from being correct. Probably in conjunction with this event, *Horizont* published a major article entitled 'The Shannon legend' by Helga Knipping about the development of the town around the airport of the same name. It certainly was not all-round praise. For example, she wrote that placards informed the inhabitants that a library was going to the built, but that in fact money was still missing for its construction.

But Knipping's most critical remarks, perhaps, concerned the fate of Irishwomen. She remarked that shopping offered them 'the only opportunity for verbal communication as four out of five women are excluded from professional life'. Their lives were confined to their 'narrow familial circles'. Possibilities to use kindergartens were limited.[300] Her remark about Irishwomen needs to be somewhat qualified. It is true that in the GDR many women were employed, much more than in Ireland but also than in West Germany. In 1984, 50 per cent of the workforce in the GDR was female as compared to 39 per cent in the FRG. But they rarely occupied managerial positions. As far as kindergartens and crèches are concerned, there were plenty of them in the GDR owing to a shortage in workforce, thus a desire to employ more women. But the education provided for small children was questionable as there was a military and ideological side to it.[301]

Social problems in Ireland seemed to be a source of inspiration for the East Germans. In 1979, the GDR television broadcast a documentary entitled 'Insel des Abschieds' (island of the farewells). It was part of a series called 'Von Alltag im Westen' (about everyday life in the West). The poverty of the country was stressed. The documentary begins with a beautiful shot on an Irish landscape with sheep. There are also poor farmers with carts drawn by donkeys. Tin whistle music can be heard in the background. The journalist explains that emigration is part of the Irish way of life and that 'the tragedy began eight hundred years ago when the English turned their island into a colony'. According to him, the plundering of Ireland allowed Britain to become the first industrial nation in the world. The television crew travels to County Limerick and visits a small and visibly run-down farm. The journalist comments that farmer Paddy Creighton (?) first approved of joining the EEC in 1973. Today, the journalist continues, many small Irish farmers have disappeared. Creighton explains that only the big farmers have no reason to complain and that two of his children have emigrated to the United States and Britain.[302]

The television crew then travels north to Galway, while giving some details on the Great Irish Famine of 1845. Abandoned farms along the road are shown. In the harbour of Galway, the journalist says that fishing was a means of existence for many but that nowadays big EEC fishing trawlers are threatening their very existence. Irish fishermen are angry with French and Dutch fishermen. Inside a pub, a traditional music session is taking place. The journalist once again criticises the British by explaining that there was once a time when bards were hunted down by the English as they were the only people who reminded the Irish that Ireland existed. He then interviews Declan Bree of the Sligo/Leitrim Independent Socialist Organisation who explains that the Irish government is not good enough against unemployment. According to him, the Catholic Church is also bad, is always pro-British and does not really help the poor. He suggests that what Ireland needs perhaps is a Socialist government. There is a shot of factories and firms and the journalist denounces the West German *Konzern* which had disgracefully described Ireland as 'a country of cheap and willing workers'. The end of the documentary shows scenes of abject poverty in a Travellers' community. The journalist comments that there are about 75,000 Travellers in Ireland and that they are social outcasts. Some of them explain that they live on social welfare benefits.[303]

Was this documentary objective? There was a definite anti-British colonialist/imperialist bias. East German viewers were well aware and critical of the heavy ideological baggage of GDR television programmes.[304] Also, the number of Travellers would appear to be too high.[305] However, it was most definitely the case that the economic picture at the end of the 1970s and during the 1980s in Ireland was very far from being rosy. Furthermore, Ireland got a raw deal with the Common Fisheries Policy, a fact recognised by the European Union only in 2011.[306] The so-called Mansholt Plan, the rationalisation of agricultural production, was not fondly remembered in Ireland and was perceived by many as a stratagem to force '"inefficient" farmers' to retire.[307] There was certainly objectivity on these issues in the East German commentary.

After diplomatic relations had been established, meetings between Irish and East German politicians and diplomats began to take place on a regular enough basis. In February 1983, East German Ambassador Martin Bierbach met the Speaker of the Dáil, Tom Fitzpatrick, in Dublin. Bierbach said that the GDR was interested in developing parliamentary contacts between the Dáil and its East German counterpart, the Volkskammer, in the interest of peace. Fitzpatrick, who was also the chairman of the Irish group of the Inter Parliamentary Union (IPU), agreed but pointed out that the Dáil only had 'limited possibilities to develop inter-parliamentary contacts'.[308] A visit within the IPU framework eventually took place in September 1988 when an Irish delegation led by Speaker Seán Treacy visited East Berlin where they were welcomed by the Volkskammer's chairman, Horst Sindermann. Treacy later profusely thanked Sindermann for the GDR's 'generous hospitality' and spoke about 'a most enlightening experience'. He would look after the visit of an East German delegation to Ireland.[309]

This visit materialised a year later, in September 1989, when East German parliamentarians led by Manfred Scheler arrived in Dublin. They met Treacy but also other Irish politicians such as Denis Lyons, the Secretary of State for Tourism, and Michael O'Riordan. The East German report on the visit mentioned that 'on the whole the talks took place in a very friendly and open-minded atmosphere'. It was also noted that 'at all the meetings, the Irish put no provocative questions regarding the FRG's smear campaign against the GDR'. They also 'particularly praised the GDR's noteworthy initiatives for the creation of nuclear weapon-free zones in the world'.[310] The last remark was to be expected as Ireland had taken the initiative in the field of nuclear disarmament for many years, culminating in the signing of the Non-Proliferation

Treaty in Moscow in 1968.[311] It must have been one of the very last East German inter-parliamentary visits as the Wall came down in November.

Lastly, there were some academic contacts also. Professor Dorothea Siegmund-Schultze of the Department of Languages and Literature of the Martin Luther University of Halle-Wittenberg organised a series of conferences on Irish society and culture which ran from 1976 until the end of the GDR. Not only academics and students from Ireland and the GDR were invited to give papers but also notably from France, Britain, the FRG, Hungary and the Soviet Union. Among those who attended were Jack Mitchell (GDR), Anthony Coughlan (Trinity College, Dublin), Patrick Rafroidi (University of Lille, France), Maurice Goldring (University of Paris VIII), C. Desmond Greaves (Connolly Association, London), Maolsheachlainn Ó Caollaí (Gaelic League), Christopher J. Woods (Maynooth, Ireland) and Pronsias MacAonghusa (Arts Council of Ireland).

In September 1988, Irish Ambassador James Kirwan made a short speech to open the conference. He paid tribute to Siegmund-Schultze's efforts and donated a series of books on behalf of the Cultural Relations Committee of Ireland.[312] Siegmund-Schultze then edited the papers for publication in a series entitled *Irland; Gesellschaft und Kultur* (Ireland; society and culture). A handful of East German language assistants were sent to Irish universities.[313] But all in all academic exchanges remained very limited with the exception of the Ireland Conference in Halle. It has been claimed by Christopher Andrew and the KGB defector Oleg Gordievsky that the Stasi had an agent code-named 'Klavier' working as a lecturer in Ireland at the end of the 1980s. However, this 'Klavier' does not appear in the available Stasi material.[314]

Ménage à trois between the SED, the CPI and the WP

Finally, what about the relations between the Communist Party of Ireland (CPI) and the Sozialistische Einheitspartei Deutschlands (SED, Socialist Unity Party of Germany, or Communist party)? These relations were straightforward at the beginning and became more complicated towards the end of the GDR with the arrival of a new party in the Irish political ring, Sinn Féin/the Workers' Party (SF/WP), known as the Workers' Party (WP) from April 1982 onwards. The first contacts between Irish and East German Communists probably took place when a small Irish delegation travelled to East Berlin to participate in the World Festival of Youth in August 1951. The first formal meetings between the Irish and Northern Irish Communist parties and the SED took place in all likelihood at international conferences of Communist parties in

Moscow in 1957 and 1960.[315] On 31 May 1963, the Communist Party of Northern Ireland (CPNI) wrote to their comrades in East Berlin that they 'would welcome a message of greetings from your Party to us' on the occasion of the CPNI's thirtieth anniversary.[316] First Secretary Walter Ulbricht replied personally by sending his 'fraternal greetings' and wishing the CPNI good luck in their struggle.[317] In October 1967, Hermann Axen, a member of the SED's Central Committee, welcomed CPNI General Secretary Hugh Moore. Both men discussed, among other things, the deteriorating situation in Northern Ireland.[318]

The SED made sure not to forget the Communists south of the border. For instance, on 23 April 1965, Ulbricht sent a message of greetings and encouragement to the Irish Workers' Party (IWP), which was meeting for their fifth party conference in Dublin. Ulbricht stated that the SED and the IWP were involved in a 'common struggle … against West German imperialism'.[319] But attending Irish Communist meetings could sometimes lead to unexpected situations for East German journalists. Wolfgang Döhnert remembers covering probably the seventeenth party conference. When he and his colleague Werner Goldstein of *Neues Deutschland* entered a room to meet the Irish leaders, a handful of young comrades began to sing '*den wir fahren gegen Engel-land*' (we sail against England) a favourite song of the German navy during the Second World War. Both men were consternated, especially Goldstein who was Jewish and who survived the war thanks to Britain's hospitality. The two journalists immediately explained that 'we've got nothing to do with that!'. According to Döhnert: 'Michael [O'Riordan] remarked dryly and without any harshness in his voice or on his face: "Well, many young comrades still have to learn a lot from party education"'.[320]

On 14 March 1970, Ulbricht sent a congratulatory message to the Irish Communists on the occasion of the reunification of the CPNI and IWP into the CPI.[321] The event was greeted by *Neues Deutschland* and *Horizont*.[322] In January 1973, *Neues Deutschland* published on its front page a photograph of O'Riordan in discussion with Erich Honecker, the SED's new General Secretary. The meeting was described as having taken place in a 'warm atmosphere'.[323] This would precisely be *the* issue between the CPI and the SED until the end of the GDR in 1990, namely the maintenance of those existing good relations as the CPI was being challenged by the emergence of a new Moscow-oriented Communist party in Ireland, Sinn Féin/the Workers' Party (SF/WP). The political wing of the OIRA (Marxist) was Official Sinn Féin. At the beginning, the relations between the CPI and Official Sinn Féin were good. It should be noted that the OIRA, unlike the PIRA, had renounced violence in

Northern Ireland and was now fully committed to a left-wing political solution to the Troubles. The Officials had established some contacts with the Freie Deutsche Jugend (FDJ, free German youth) during the latter's visit to Ireland in May 1975. But, by 1976, the relations between the CPI and Official Sinn Féin had dramatically deteriorated because of a different approach to the conflict in Northern Ireland. The Officials appealed to the British government to introduce democratic reforms, but the CPI was far more radical as it demanded the immediate withdrawal of British troops and the reunification of Ireland. O'Riordan wanted the British out.[324]

However, there was another reason: the CPI feared competition.[325] A brief look at electoral results is hugely significant. During the general election (proportional representation) in Ireland in February 1973, O'Riordan only got 466 first preference votes out of 30,434 in the constituency of Dublin Central.[326] In June 1977, the CPI fielded two candidates for the 166 seats in the Dáil. It obtained a meagre 544 first preference votes. The figure more than paled by comparison with Fianna Fáil's 811,615. But it became a humiliation for the CPI to know that SF/WP led by Tomás Mac Giolla obtained 27,209 first votes.[327] The electoral humiliation continued unabated. In February 1987, the CPI fielded five candidates and got 725 first preference votes. But the Workers' Party (WP, which had replaced SF/WP in 1982) fielded 29 candidates and got 67,273 first preference votes, which represented four seats in the Dáil. Even the Democratic Socialist Party did better than the CPI and got 7,424 first preference votes and one seat.[328] Finally in 1989, the year the East bloc collapsed, the general election saw the CPI getting 342 first preference votes (for two candidates) and the WP, now led by Proinsias De Rossa, got 82,263 first preference votes, representing seven seats in the Dáil.[329] It was nothing short of a triumph for the WP and a complete rejection of the CPI.

On 9 June 1978, O'Riordan was in East Berlin where he had a meeting with representatives of the SED. He told them that 'the CPI opposes the terrorist group within the IRA', although he added that 'the CPI has personal contacts with individual leaders of the PIRA'. This could be problematic for the SED as so far the East German press had condemned the PIRA. Being an experienced politician and knowing what buttons to push, O'Riordan then moved to discredit the OIRA and declared: 'The leadership of the OIRA is in the hands of the Irish bourgeoisie, which supports direct elections for the EC parliament.' Bourgeoisie and EC were two upsetting words for the SED. Then O'Riordan tried to convince his hosts that his party was making some good progress: 'The CPI is developing well and is getting new members, especially young workers.'[330] This was very far from being the truth, considering the last general-election results. As for the Officials, they accused the CPI of adopting 'a policy of conditional support for the Provisionals ... a right-wing Nationalist organisation which is at times manipulated by the ultra-left'.[331] The SED could appreciate the complex divisions within Irish Communism.

But, if SF/WP, an orthodox Marxist party, wanted to establish links with the SED, could Erich Honecker's regime refuse? In August 1981, the Central Committee of the SED was well aware of the intense rivalry between the CPI and SF/WP and knew that the CPI did not want the SED to enter into official relations with SF/WP. The problem was that SF/WP's youth organisation, the Irish Democratic Youth Movement (IDYM), wanted to develop links with the SED's FDJ. Torn between this development and O'Riordan unquestionable loyalty, the SED eventually decided to maintain links with the IDYM although relatively discreetly.[332] However, there was an additional problem for the SED: the Soviets. In March 1982, presumably the KGB sent a report to the Stasi regarding the increasing popularity of SF/WP. The document itself was destroyed, but its surviving summary sheet indicates that the Stasi rated the Soviet report as 'average value' (see Table 3.18, summary sheet no. 54). In May, a second report was sent to the Stasi on the CPI and the party conference of SF/WP (now in fact the WP). This time the Stasi rated it as 'low value' (see Table 3.19, summary sheet no. 57). It would seem that the Soviets were applying some pressure on the East Germans to consider relations with the WP. That would soon be made very clear. But the SED did everything possible to avoid deterioration in its relations with the CPI. In March 1983, it was decided to confer the Stern der Völkerfreundschaft (star of friendship between the nations) on Seán Nolan on the occasion of his seventy-fifth birthday. The ceremony would take place during the SED delegation's visit to the CPI in Ireland.[333] The following year, Honecker congratulated James Stewart on his becoming general secretary of the CPI.[334] But then the Soviets interfered directly.

It had come to Moscow's attention that the WP was doing far better than the CPI and contacts were made in December 1983. It would appear that the WP was very interested in Moscow's coffers. In September 1986, it would send the Central Committee of the Communist Party of the Soviet Union (CPSU) a letter, asking for £1 million no less. This definitely contrasted with the CPI's Communist orthodoxy.[335] The CPI was also far more modest regarding financial matters as it asked the SED for a £300 subvention only to be able to attend a conference of Communist parties of the EC in Lisbon. The SED agreed to pay for the flight tickets.[336] On 7 February 1985, East German Ambassador Gerhard Lindner arrived at the Soviet embassy in Dublin for talks with Ambassador Alexei Nesterenko. This could be a difficult meeting. East German diplomat and HVA (East German foreign intelligence) officer Edgar Uher, who was present at the time, remembers that Nesterenko was 'cold arrogant and had no interest in getting a feel with the country he was posted to'.[337] Lindner asked him about bilateral relations and developing contacts in Ireland. Nesterenko had nothing good to say. According to him, Irish officials were not remotely interested and even avoided being too much in touch with the Soviet embassy. He believed they were reactionaries, influenced by US President Ronald Reagan and the Vatican.

Regarding the CPI, Nesterenko did not mince his words. It was only a 'very feeble force' which had no influence. This was due to strong anti-Communism in the country, driven by 'rightist and especially clerical forces'. But the CPI had also itself to blame. The Soviet ambassador explained to Lindner that the CPI was not present in grass-roots organisations within work places. It had partly isolated itself and was 'not disposed to cooperate with other progressive forces like SF/WP [WP] on the basis of compromises'. Although O'Riordan was a true Communist and that the CPI could be grateful to him, his replacement by James Stewart had been necessary and reflected a desire to become more dynamic and active. But, continued Nesterenko, the CPI's relations with the WP remained problematic. The Soviet Union had official contacts with the WP and 'sees in this party an important political force with which the embassy has to work'. Then he added that 'the other Socialist states, among which the GDR, should concentrate on SF/WP [WP] ... It has a stronger influence and is disposed to active contacts'.[338] Indeed, back in 1983, the CPSU had invited leading members of the WP to Moscow and Estonia.[339] What Nesterenko was telling Lindner in between the lines was to dump the CPI.

This was a very delicate matter for Lindner because as Uher justly writes O'Riordan was 'an old friend of the GDR'.[340] But Moscow had spoken. Lindner tried his best to see what could be done. Two days later, he met Stewart, O'Riordan and Eoin Ó Murchu, a member of the National Executive Committee of the CPI. First, he transmitted Erich Honecker and Hermann Axen's personal greetings to the party leadership. O'Riordan replied by stressing the 'traditional fraternal relations between the CPI and the SED'. The main theme of the CPI's conference was to figure out how its influence in the country could be increased, which was not that surprising bearing in mind the very poor electoral results. Clearly, Lindner did mention the possibility of establishing grass-roots organisations in the place of work as Nesterenko had pointed out because the East German report of the meeting stated: 'The formation of party grass-roots organisations in workplaces is, however, not intended for the future. The CPI would have had bad experiences with such grass-roots organisations in the past because their activities focused exclusively on economic matters. Furthermore, these grass-roots organisations would have frequently acted like independent decision-making committees including in cadre issues ("acted like a caucus").' This was why grass-roots organisations had been suppressed.[341] Basically, the CPI did not like what it did not control.

Stewart, O'Riordan and Ó Murchu told Lindner that together with the Ireland–GDR Friendship Society they would prepare activities for the fortieth anniversary of the GDR in 1989. According to them, the main political forces and the government would try to ignore it because of the country's neutrality in the Second World War and the widespread anti-Soviet feelings. This explanation did not sound very convincing and Lindner must have known it. Indeed, these political forces and the government had nothing to fear from a CPI that was in an electoral abyss. But then Stewart, O'Riordan and Ó Murchu brought up the very thorny question of relations with the WP. It was written in the East German report: 'On their initiative the Irish comrades spoke about the issue of the relationship with Sinn Féin/the Workers' Party [WP]. The CPI's relations with that party would not have improved; there would practically not be any cooperation in future. The request was reiterated to abstain from any relation with Sinn Féin now or in future.'[342] There was obviously no hope of the CPI and the WP being reconciled.

Things got all of a sudden more complicated for the SED when Seán Garland, the WP General Secretary, sent a letter to Honecker on 28 January 1986. It was an invitation to officialise relations between the two parties and it is difficult to avoid the feeling that it had been cleverly conceived. Straight away, Garland began by stating that back in December 1983 in Moscow, his party and the CPSU had been in agreement on 'many of the important and fundamental problems facing humanity' and that it had been decided that 'the two Parties would establish relations'. Honecker could possibly not ignore the Soviet aspect of the letter. Then Garland wrote that the WP wanted to establish relations with other Communist and worker parties in the world. The WP was 'active and growing throughout all Ireland'. It was true that the party's number of first preferences votes was increasing. Included in the letter were those magical sentences that people like Honecker loved to read: 'Alone among Irish political parties, the Workers' Party states that the enemy of Irish workers, the enemy of all workers in the world, is Anglo-American Imperialism.'

Garland then stressed his party's commitment to help freedom movements like the African National Congress (ANC) and the Palestine Liberation Organization (PLO) and also to help revolutionary movements in El Salvador and in Chile. He probably could not have known that the East Germans were training ANC and PLO members.[343] But did he know that Honecker's son-in-law was a Chilean who had fled the Pinochet regime? The letter ended with a request for a meeting between WP and SED members in either East Berlin or Moscow where Garland had been invited to attend the twenty-seventh congress of the CPSU. Also, Garland invited the SED to send a delegation to his party's annual conference.[344] Nowhere in the letter was the CPI mentioned and this must have caught Honecker and others' attention.

In London, Edgar Uher analysed the situation. He had just returned from the CPI's party conference in Belfast and found that the tensions between the CPI and the WP had even increased. Bearing in mind that Garland had been invited by Moscow, it was clear to his mind that the CPI massively resented this. In a report, he summed up what was going on and stressed that the CPI was becoming more realistic and that it had even acknowledged the efforts of the Ireland–GDR Friendship Society whereas before it had not disguised its hostility towards the society. Uher knew that the relations between O'Riordan and Nesterenko were 'frosty'. He wrote that the East German embassy in London, also accredited to Ireland, had so far not been involved with the WP because of the very good relations with the CPI. Having said this Uher and the embassy were perfectly aware that the WP had more influence than the CPI. The main problem between the two parties was the national question: the WP believed that reunification was not realistic while the CPI insisted on it.[345]

On 17 February 1986, the Central Committee of the SED informed Honecker on the latest developments. It was put forward that the ambassador should acknowledge Garland's letter and that the SED was willing to welcome him to East Berlin after the party's annual conference. Honecker agreed and instructions were sent to Lindner in London.[346] The ambassador, however, sent back a telegram with the following information. The CPI's annual conference had taken place and several decisions had been taken. Stewart was to go to the SED's party conference in East Berlin and O'Riordan to the CPSU's in Moscow. Ó Murchu was to go to the East German embassy in London to explain his party's position on relations with the WP. The CPI deemed that it was up to the SED to decide about its relations with other political parties and the CPI would not object. It respected the CPSU's decision to enter into relations with the WP but was not happy about it. If the SED decided to do the same, then the CPI would ask these relations to be 'at the lowest level possible'. Also, if it came to a meeting between the SED and the WP, the CPI asked for it to take place on the margin of the CPSU's party conference in Moscow and not in East Berlin.[347]

But the CPI had also very interesting information which it shared with the East Germans. It claimed to know that the WP imported arms for the OIRA from Iraq by way of middlemen in Rotterdam. Ó Murchu, who had been a member of the OIRA before he joined the CPI, had 'personal knowledge of this'. Furthermore, 'in order to raise funds large quantities of heroin (£1 million), also probably from Iraq, had been smuggled into Ireland'.[348] This was a very serious allegation. But was it true or was it part of a CPI mud-slinging operation? There seems to be no definitive answer but there are a couple of significant hints. Back in 1981, SF/WP realised that it badly needed money to run its electoral campaigns as the party was not able to financially compete with the political tenors, Fianna Fáil and Fine Gael.[349] This might help to explain why the party had asked for £1 million from the CPSU in September 1986. But also apparently OIRA members had travelled to Iraq in the early 1980s and had returned with gifts from Saddam Hussein's regime and contacts had been established with Saddam's party.[350]

If the above information was correct, then the SED leadership had to proceed extremely cautiously all the more since the GDR was increasingly in need of the West's cash in order to survive economically. Now was certainly not the time to upset the West with some dark intrigue in Ireland and Northern Ireland. Honecker sent a personal congratulatory message on Stewart's re-election as general secretary of the CPI.[351] But far more significantly, the SED chose to meet a WP delegation in Moscow and not in East Berlin, therefore granting the CPI's wish. The meeting between Bruno Mahlow and Seán Garland took place on 4 March 1986. Garland explained that his party had relations with the CPSU, the French and Italian Communist parties and even the Workers' Party of (North) Korea. On behalf of the Central Committee of the SED, Mahlow invited a delegation of the WP to visit the GDR after the SED's eleventh party conference (in the report, the word 'after', '*nach*', is underlined). He added: 'Further contacts should take place through the East German embassy in London which has been instructed to inform comrades of the Workers' Party on the domestic and foreign policies of the GDR and the preparations of the eleventh party conference of the SED'. Garland thanked Mahlow and put forward a meeting in June. The two men then discussed the international situation. Garland tried to impress Mahlow by pointing out that from the very beginning his party had condemned the independent trade union Solidarność (Solidarity) in Poland. He also said the WP might increase its deputies in the Dáil from four to seven.[352] Garland was not mistaken in his electoral predictions.

But the East Germans delayed things. In May, Lindner was in Dublin where he met Tomás Mac Giolla, the WP leader, informing the latter that unfortunately a meeting between his party and the SED had to be deferred until the autumn. Mac Giolla showed understanding,[353] but he would have to be patient as well. In November 1987, *Neues Deutschland* published an article entitled 'Happy birthday to Michael O'Riordan' on the occasion of his seventieth birthday. There was also his photograph. The article was in fact a reproduction of a personal letter sent by Erich Honecker and it could not have been more praiseworthy. For instance, there was the following passage: 'The Communists of the German Democratic Republic consider you to be an indefatigable and selfless fighter for the main interests of the working class and all the workers of your country, for peace, democracy and national independence. Your contributions are inseparably bound with the development of the Communist Party of Ireland.'[354] Neither Mac Giolla nor Garland had reached that level of praise yet in East Berlin.

However, the SED's opening of relations with the WP eventually did happen. In April 1988, an SED delegation travelled to Dublin to participate in the WP's annual congress.[355] There a message of greetings from Honecker was read, wishing the party 'every success in your discussions'.[356] In July, a WP leader, Proinsias De Rossa, went to the GDR and attended a disarmament conference during which Honecker made a speech.[357] Yet, the SED made sure that its privileged partner in Ireland remained the CPI. In March 1989, Honecker sent an invitation to attend the fortieth anniversary of the founding of the GDR to James Stewart, the party's leader.[358] Stewart replied that it was 'an honour for our party to attend the 40th Anniversary' and wrote that O'Riordan, now national chairman of the CPI, and Brian Campfield, who looked after Northern Ireland, would go to East Berlin.[359] A similar invitation was not sent to the WP. Incredibly, the East German leadership was not too worried about the increasing popular discontent at home that was shaking the GDR to its foundations. It did not accept Mikhail Gorbachev's perestroika and glasnost in the Soviet Union. As the SED's chief ideologist Kurt Hager put it: 'Would you feel obliged to change the wallpaper of your home if you neighbour did so?'[360] It could not have been more eloquently put.

The fortieth anniversary of the GDR in 1989 was a surrealistic event reported by the *Irish Times*. When Gorbachev landed in East

Berlin, he was welcomed by Honecker at Schönefeld Airport. The East German leader did not display too much warmth, but he certainly did display it eagerly when Nicolae Ceauşescu, the 'Genius of the Carpathians',[361] arrived from Romania. Youths shouted at Gorbachev: 'Help us, help us'. The Soviet leader answered: 'You should not panic'. Meanwhile, serious clashes occurred at the railway station of Dresden where thousands wanted to board trains going West.[362] At the massive official parade in East Berlin, cries of protest could be heard and protest banners could be read. Mieczysław Rakowski, the former Polish premier, asked Gorbachev if he understood German. Gorbachev replied: 'Enough to read what's written on the banners. They're talking about perestroika. They're talking about democracy and change. They're saying: Gorbachev, stay in our country.' Rakowski opined: 'If it's true that these are representatives of people from twenty-eight regions of the [GDR], it means the end.' Gorbachev briefly answered: 'I think you're right'.[363] Rakowski was right indeed, but it took East German leaders some time to realise that the end was nigh.

It happened abruptly. Before the Wall was breached on 9 November 1989, tens of thousands fled the country on foot, by car or by train. Images of desperate people trying to cross the Iron Curtain were broadcast all over the West. Although the WP supported Gorbachev's efforts at reform in the Soviet Union, the new party leader, Proinsias De Rossa, made reassuring statements in an article published in the *Irish People* on 17 November. He wrote: 'Much of the media coverage of events in Eastern Europe has been superficial and simplistic. What we are witnessing is not the collapse of socialism but birth pangs of a new, more democratic and stronger socialism.' As if that total misreading of the situation were not enough, he added: 'Right-wing politicians in this country are in no position to be smug about the exodus of people from the GDR. Proportionally more people have emigrated from Ireland in the past year than from the GDR.'[364] The party leader seemed to have forgotten that a wall and an iron curtain had been built to prevent East Germans from leaving the country *en masse*. Perhaps De Rossa had been carried away by a new political *élan* since at the recent general election in June, his party had obtained seven seats in the Dáil representing 82,263 first preference votes. The CPI under the leadership of James Stewart had obtained a miserable 342 votes.

Despite the events in Eastern Europe, the WP did not seem to forget that it needed cash. On 27 November, Mr Harrison and Mr McCann arrived in the East German embassy in London to have talks about developing business contacts with the GDR. They were welcomed by Herr Vorpahl. In fact, they had already broached this topic during a previous visit to East Berlin. It was a rather shady deal that consisted in replenishing the party's coffers. The idea was that an Irish firm, whose name was not disclosed by Harrison and McCann but that dealt with the construction sector, would be interested in importing large quantities of cement '(up to 200,000 tonnes) from the GDR into Ireland on a letter-of-credit basis'. This firm had already dealt with the GDR in the past. According to the East German report: 'At the same time it has been emphasised that under no circumstances can these transactions take place directly with the party and that interconnection through a commercial firm is necessary'. It would appear that the East Germans agreed with this plan as it was indicated in the report that for now the deals would concentrate on cement and, if everything was satisfactory, on chemicals and construction materials.[365]

Their visit coming only about two weeks after the end of the Berlin Wall, it was clear that Harrison and McCann were miles away from reality. Egon Krenz appeared to be too. He had replaced Honecker as General Secretary of the SED and on 25 October 1989, he sent a message of 'fraternal struggle greetings' on behalf of the Central Committee to the CPI which was about to begin its twentieth party conference. Krenz briefly mentioned their meeting at the fortieth anniversary of the GDR and wrote that the '[SED] will do everything in the future to guarantee peace and to defend the Socialist society of the GDR as a creation of the working people of our country'.[366] On 3 October 1990, Germany was reunified and the GDR absorbed into the FRG. The SED was for ever confined to the history books and Honecker fled to Moscow and eventually died in Chile in 1994.

In 1982, Reiner Oschmann, the correspondent of *Neues Deutschland* in London, travelled to Ireland to cover a CPI congress. About to return to Britain, he realised that he had forgotten his jacket and unexpectedly went back to his guesthouse only to find two men inside the bedroom he had just vacated, checking his paper basket. He wished them 'the best of luck' and rushed off.[367] The Irish authorities clearly kept a close eye on East German visitors. But what did East German intelligence think about Ireland and Northern Ireland?

Notes

1 T. Diedrich, 'Die DDR zwischen den Blöcken. Der Einfluss des Warschauer Paktes auf Staat, Militär und Gesellschaft der DDR', in T. Diedrich, W. Heinemann & C. F. Ostermann (eds.), *Der Warschauer Pakt: Von der Gründung bis zum Zusammenbruch, 1955 bis 1991* (Bonn: Bundeszentrale für politische Bildung, 2009), pp. 68–9.

2 G. FitzGerald, *Ireland in the World: Further Reflections* (Dublin: Liberties Press, 2006), pp. 124–5.
3 For this immediate post-war period, see I. McCabe, *A Diplomatic History of Ireland, 1948–49: The Republic, the Commonwealth and NATO* (Blackrock: Irish Academic Press, 1991).
4 D. Keogh, *Ireland and Europe, 1919–1948* (Dublin: Gill & Macmillan, 1988), p. 202.
5 *Ibid.*, pp. 203–5.
6 Skelly, *Irish Diplomacy at the United Nations, 1945–1965*, pp. 19, 149, 240–1, 243 and ch. 6, 'Swords into Plowshares: Ireland's Nuclear Non-proliferation Initiative', pp. 247–65.
7 J. Cooney, *John Charles McQuaid: Ruler of Catholic Ireland* (Dublin: O'Brien Press, 1999), see for example ch. 15 'Cold War Churchman, 1948–49', pp. 218–33.
8 Auswärtiges Amt-Politisches Archiv (archive of the German Foreign Office) (hereafter AA-PA), Berlin, B31, Bd. 60, West German embassy, Dublin, to Foreign Office, Bonn, 19 February 1953.
9 Dublin Diocesan Archive (hereafter DDA), XXIII/257/1/(1), 'Activities of O'Riordan Michael, Secretary, Irish Workers' Party, 37, Victoria St, South Circular Road, Dublin', by An Garda Siochána, 14, November 1967.
10 *Ibid.* A file entitled 'The papers of Archbishop John Charles McQuaid C.S.S.p., relating to Communists, 1940–1967' compiled by Mr Peter Sobielowski, contains 161 pages of archival references to Communist activities and shows the extent of surveillance operations by the Vigilance Committee under the control of Archbishop John Charles McQuaid. Included are reports provided by An Garda Siochána.
11 Dáil Éireann, vol. 127, 31 October 1951, 'questions and oral answers, Berlin Youth Rally', at http://debates.oireachtas.ie/dail/1951/10/31/00100.asp (accessed 22 September 2013).
12 A. Applebaum, *Iron Curtain: The Crushing of Eastern Europe* (London: Penguin, 2013), pp. 348–50.
13 National Archives of Ireland (hereafter NAI), Dublin, Department of Foreign Affairs (hereafter DFA), 300 series, part 1, 305/321, Department of Defence to DEA, 13 March 1957.
14 *Ibid.*, Department of Justice to DEA, 29 March 1957.
15 D. Mac Con Uladh, 'Poor Relations', p. 82, n. 44.
16 M. O'Driscoll, 'West Germany', in M. O'Driscoll, D. Keogh & J. aan de Wiel (eds.), *Ireland through European Eyes: Western Europe, the EEC and Ireland, 1945–1973* (Cork: Cork University Press, 2013), pp. 50, 56–7.
17 M. O'Driscoll, 'Hesitant Europeans, Self-Defeating Irredentists and Security Free-Riders? West German Assessments of Irish Foreign Policy during the Early Cold War, 1949–59', *Irish Studies in International Affairs*, vol. 21 (2010), pp. 89–104.
18 Wylie, *Ireland and the Cold War*, see ch. 4 'Cold War Diplomacy in the Case of East Germany', pp. 117–48, for quote, p. 129.

19 NAI, DFA, secretary's files, 2001/43/88, East German Ministry of External Affairs to DEA, 31 May 1965.
20 *Ibid.*, embassy series Rome, 1918, 'Recognition of States', Seán Murphy, DEA Secretary, to Irish embassy, Rome, 14 November 1956.
21 Mac Con Uladh, 'Poor Relations', p. 82.
22 *Ibid.*
23 M. Treacy, *The Communist Party of Ireland, 1921–2011: Vol. 1: 1921–1969* (Dublin: Brocaire Books, 2012), pp. 235–6. This very well-researched and informative book based on the recently made available files of the Communist Party of Ireland says, however, little on the relations between Ireland and the GDR or on the relations between the Communist parties of the two countries.
24 NAI, DFA, secretary's office, P series, P168, 'Report on Visit to the Federal Republic of Germany, September 3rd to 17th, 1954', by Conor Cruise O'Brien.
25 *Ibid.*, confidential reports, 313/10A, 'The Catholic Bishop of Berlin', by T. J. Kiernan, Irish Minister Plenipotentiary in Bonn, 28 July 1955.
26 *Ibid.*, embassy series Bonn, D/4, 'German Federal Government Policy in regard to the Pankow regime', by T. J. Kiernan, Irish Minister Plenipotentiary in Bonn, 28 July 1955.
27 *Ibid.*, confidential reports, 313/10A, 'The Soviet Sector of Berlin', by T. J. Kiernan, Irish Minister Plenipotentiary in Bonn, 10 August 1955.
28 *Ibid.*, 'Refugees from the Soviet Zone of Germany', by T. J. Kiernan, Irish Minister Plenipotentiary, 29 July 1955.
29 M. Fulbrook, *History of Germany, 1918–2000: The Divided Nation* (Malden, MA Oxford and Victoria: Blackwell, 2004), pp. 149–50, 158.
30 *Cork Examiner*, 8 January 1953.
31 Fulbrook, *History of Germany, 1918–2000*, p. 159.
32 M. Fulbrook, *Anatomy of a Dictatorship: Inside the GDR, 1949–1989* (Oxford: Oxford University Press, 1995), pp. 192–3.
33 NAI, DFA, secretary's files, 2001/43/88, 'Fear of economic breakdown in East Germany', July 1961 (no author mentioned).
34 *Ibid.*, embassy series Bonn, D/2/1, Ó Ceallaigh to Cornelius Cremin, DEA secretary, 19 August 1961.
35 Tony Geraghty, *Brixmis: The Untold Exploits of Britain's Most Daring Cold War Spy Mission* (London: HarperCollins, 1997), p. 267.
36 AA-PA, B31, Bd. 197, West German embassy, Dublin, to Foreign Office, Bonn, 5 December 1960.
37 NAI, DFA, 419/33/20, West German embassy, Dublin, to DEA, 31 December 1958.
38 *Ibid.*, embassy series Bonn, 14/13, Irish embassy to DEA, 22 October 1958.
39 O'Driscoll, 'West Germany', pp. 28–9.
40 Interview with Dr Joachim Mitdank, the last East German Ambassador to Ireland, Berlin, 12 January 2010.

41 Geiger, 'Trading with the Enemy: Ireland, the Cold War and East–West trade, 1945–55', pp. 122, 125, 126, 133–4, 135.
42 NAI, DFA, 300 series, part 1, 305/249, 'Trading with countries under Communist rule', by the Department of Finance, 23 February 1953.
43 *Ibid.*, 'Memorandum for discussion with Minister', 15 October 1954.
44 *Ibid.*, embassy series Bonn, 12/7I, 'Trade with Communist countries', by Foreign Trade Committee, 16 April 1957.
45 *Ibid.*, 300 series, part 1, 305/249, Department of the Taoiseach to DEA, 25 June 1957.
46 *Irish Times*, 26 January 1959.
47 Wylie, *Ireland and the Cold War*, nn. 62 and 84, p. 146.
48 AA-PA, B31, Bd. 128, West German embassy, Dublin, to Foreign Office, Bonn, 26 August 1959.
49 Mac Con Uladh, 'Poor Relations', p. 85.
50 Edgar Uher, 'Last rites: East Germany's deal for an Irish patriot's body', unpublished memoir in possession of the author (given by Mr Uher to the author on 13 December 2010), p. 28. Mr Uher is a former East German diplomat and one of the very few specialists on Irish affairs in the former GDR.
51 Mac Con Uladh, 'Poor Relations', p. 85.
52 AA-PA, Ministerium für Auswärtige Angelegenheiten (East German Ministry of External Affairs, hereafter referred to as MfAA), A13100, 'Bericht ueber die Reise der Kollegen Prescher und Schmidt von der Handelsvertretung Grossbritannien nach Irland am 5., 6. and 7. Mai 1963', written by Prescher, Prescher to Plaschke, 15 May 1963.
53 M. McCauley, *The German Democratic Republic since 1945* (New York: St. Martin's Press, 1983), pp. 107–16.
54 *Irish Farmers Journal*, 24 July 1965.
55 *Irish Independent*, 8 May 1963.
56 NAI, DFA, embassy series Bonn, 12/7I, Irish embassy Bonn to Córas Tráchtála, 5 January 1964.
57 *Kerryman*, 14 March 1964.
58 *Connacht Tribune*, 28 March 1964.
59 G. Weigel, *The Final Revolution: The Resistance Church and the Collapse of Communism* (Oxford: Oxford University Press, 2003), p. 65.
60 *Connacht Tribune*, 28 March 1964.
61 Janusz Skolimowski & Cezary Lusiński, *Ireland & Poland* (Dublin: Embassy of the Republic of Poland, 2001), p. 28.
62 AA-PA, B38-IIA1, Bd. 119, 119-4, West German embassy, Dublin, to Foreign Office, Bonn, 3 April 1964.
63 *Sunday Independent*, 16 August 1964.
64 *Irish Farmers Journal*, 26 September 1964.
65 *Ibid.*, 14 November 1964.
66 McCauley, *German Democratic Republic since 1945*, pp. 124–5.
67 *Irish Farmers Journal*, 14 November 1964.

68 Garvin, *Preventing the Future*, pp. 168–9, 194–5.
69 K. A. Kennedy, T. Giblin & D. McHugh, *The Economic Development of Ireland in the Twentieth Century* (London and New York: Routledge), p. 218.
70 T. Brown, *Ireland: A Social and Cultural History, 1922–2002* (London: Harper Perennial, 2004), pp. 237–8.
71 *Irish Farmers Journal*, 14 November 1964.
72 Wylie, *Ireland and the Cold War*, n. 84, p. 146.
73 *Statistical Abstract of Ireland, 1968* compiled by the Central Statistics Office, Dublin, p. 147.
74 *Ibid.*, Foreign Trade Committee report, 31 May 1968.
75 B. Becker, *Die DDR und Großbritannien 1945/49 bis 1973: Politische, wirtschaftliche und kulturelle Kontakte im Zeichen der Nichtanerkennungspolitik* (Bochum: Universitätsverlag Dr. N. Brockmeyer, 1991), p. 173.
76 M. H. Hull, *Irish Secrets: German Espionage in Wartime Ireland, 1939–1945* (Dublin: Irish Academic Press, 2003), pp. 40–1, 126–31, 134–8.
77 *Ibid.*, pp. 186–90.
78 Mac Con Uladh, 'Poor Relations', p. 80.
79 A. Krammer, 'The Cult of the Spanish Civil War in East Germany', *Journal of Contemporary History*, vol. 39, no. 4, special issue: Collective Memory (Oct. 2004), pp. 531–60.
80 Photograph published in the *Irish Times*, 26 July 1966, p. 12.
81 'Frank Ryan: A Revolutionary Life', by Fearghal McGarry, Queen's University, Belfast, at www.qub.ac.uk/sites/frankryan/InterpretativeResources/HistoricalContext/FrankRyanArevolutionarylife (accessed 31 July 2013).
82 Mac Con Uladh, 'Poor Relations', p. 80.
83 Stiftung Archiv der Parteien und Massenorganisationen der DDR im Bundesarchiv (Foundation Archives of Parties and Mass Organisations of the GDR in the Federal Archives), Berlin (hereafter SAPMO-BA), DY/30/12881, report on meeting between Axen and O'Riordan on 20 July 1966.
84 *Ibid.*, DY/30/J/IV2/3A/1375, 'Überführung der sterblichen Hülle des Spanienkämpfers und irischen Patrioten, Genossen Frank Ryan, nach Irland', 1 September 1966.
85 Bundesbeauftragte für die Unterlagen des Staatssicherheitsdienstes der ehemaligen Deutschen Demokratischen Republik (the Federal Commissioner for the Records of the State Security Service of the Former German Democratic Republic; archive of the former Stasi), Berlin (hereafter BStU), MfS-SdM, Nr. 1438, 'An Irishman in the DDR'.
86 *Ibid.*, 'An der Chefredakteur der DDR-Revue' (letter from Israel, no date).
87 *Ibid.*, 'Sehr geehrter Redakteur!' (letter from Chester), 1 January 1967.
88 *Ibid.*, 'Frank Ryan' (undated, but very probably written in 1967).

89 Krammer, 'Cult of the Spanish Civil War in East Germany', p. 538.
90 BStU, MfS-SdM, Nr. 1438, 'Überprüfung der sterblichen Hülle des auf dem Friedhof Dresden-Loschwitz beigesetzten Iren Frank Ryan nach Irland', 30 June 1967 (Mielke's marginalia on top of report, dated 12 July 1967).
91 Hull, *Irish Secrets*, pp. 131–2.
92 BStU, MfS-SdM, Nr. 1438, 'Bericht zu den Ermittlungen über den Iren Frank Ryan', 6 October 1967.
93 Hull, *Irish Secrets*, n. 183, p. 343.
94 Gilbert Library, Dublin, Communist Party of Ireland papers, Seán Nolan-Geoffrey Palmer Collection, Betty Sinclair diary, box 55, diary no. 1, 16/06/68–10/07/68, entry for 'Wednesday, 19/06/1968, Dresden-Leipzig'.
95 'Welle der Wahrheiten', *Der Spiegel*, 1/2012, at www.spiegel.de/spiegel/print/d-83422497.html (accessed 30 July 2013).
96 BStU, MfS-ZAIG, Nr. 26968, file re Stasi review of manuscript 'Auch Tote haben ihre Schatten'; the file also contains material on Frank Ryan.
97 Karl Heinz Weber, *Auch Tote haben einen Schatten* (Berlin: Militärverlag der Deutschen Demokratischen Republik, 1975), p. 316.
98 BStU, MfS-ZAIG, Nr. 26968, file re Stasi review of manuscript 'Auch Tote haben ihre Schatten'; the file also contains material on Frank Ryan.
99 *Horizont*, 1976, no. 2, p. 28, n. 2.
100 McCauley, *German Democratic Republic since 1945*, pp. 135–40, 187–91, 248–51.
101 *Sunday Independent*, 5 March 1967.
102 *Irish Times*, 21 July 1967.
103 *Ibid.*, 14 April 1969.
104 *Irish Farmers Journal*, 25 October 1969.
105 *Irish Times*, 27 April 1970.
106 *Ibid.*, 21 July 1971.
107 Dáil Eireann debates, Ceisteanna-Questions Oral Answers, 'Trade with East Germany', 29 July 1971, at http://debates.oireachtas.ie/dail/1971/07/29/00011.asp (accessed 27 September 2013).
108 NAI, DFA, 2001/43/202, Kennedy to Hugh McCann, DEA secretary, 31 March 1970.
109 *Ibid.*
110 H. Müller-Enbergs, Jan Wielgohs & D. Hoffmann, *Wer war wer in der DDR?* (Berlin: Christoph Links Verlag, 2001), DVD edition (2004), 'Albert Norden', p. 628.
111 Mac Con Uladh, 'Poor Relations', p. 83 and n. 50 (p. 83).
112 NAI, DFA, embassy series Bonn, D/3, Eoin MacWhite, Irish Ambassador to the Netherlands, to McCann, 29 November 1971.
113 J. Pekelder, 'Vom "Sowjetdeutschland" zum "rotten Preußen"; Niederländische Wahrnehmungen der DDR (1949–1973)', in Pfeil (ed.), *Die DDR und der Westen*, p. 305 and n. 43 (p. 305).

114 T. Steffen Gerber, 'Zwischen Neutralitätspolitik und Anlehnung an den Westen; Die Beziehungen zwischen der Schweiz und der DDR (1949–1972)', in U. Pfeil (ed.), *Die DDR und der Westen: Transnationale Beziehungen 1949–1989* (Berlin: Ch. Links Verlag, 2001), pp. 340–1, 347.
115 AA-PA, MfAA, C164/77, 'Jahresorientierung 1972 für die Entwicklung der Beziehungen zwischen der DDR und der Republik Irland', 1971.
116 *Ibid.*, C4461, 'Vereinbarung über die Herstellung diplomatischer Beziehungen zwischen der Deutschen Demokratischen Republik under der Republik Irland' (Vorschlag), 1973.
117 NAI, DFA, 2006 release, 2005/145/1403, Donal Clarke to Hugh McCann, DFA secretary, 16 March 1973.
118 G. FitzGerald, *Just Garret: Tales from the Political Front Line* (Dublin: Liberties Press, 2011), pp. 183–7.
119 Uher, 'Last rites', p. 9.
120 AA-PA, MfAA, C4460, 'Stand der Gespräche diplomatischer Beziehungen DDR–Irland', undated.
121 *Ibid.*, C4461, 'Zum Stand der Beziehungen zur Republik Irland', 19 February 1975.
122 *Ibid.*, C4463, 'Vermerk über ein Gespräch des Genossen Botschafters Kern mit dem Botschafter der UdSSR in der Republik Irland, Genossen Kaplin, am 20.03.75 in der DDR Botschaft [in London]'.
123 O'Halpin, 'Intelligence and Anglo-Irish relations, 1922–73', pp. 137, 148n. 29.
124 AA-PA, ZR629/97, Honecker to Hillery, 3 December 1976.
125 MfAA, Hillery to Honecker, 30 December 1976.
126 *Ibid.*, Oskar Fischer to Michael O'Kennedy, 5 July 1977, Willis Stoph to Jack Lynch, 6 July 1977, Lynch to Stoph, 22 July 1977; O'Kennedy to Fischer, 22 July 1977.
127 BStU, MfS-HAII, Nr. 35670, 'Zum Stand der Beziehungen DDR–Republik Irland', by MfAA, 22 March 1977.
128 *Statistical Abstract of Ireland, 1978* (Dublin: Central Statistics Office), p. 166.
129 BStU, MfS-HAII, Nr. 35670, 'Irische Außenpolitik nach dem Regierungswechsel' by MfAA, 17 August 1977.
130 Irish embassy in London to East German embassy, 28 June 1978, document in possession of the author (given by Edgar Uher).
131 Uher, 'Last rites', p. 10.
132 Interview with Edgar Uher, Berlin, 10 January 2010.
133 Uher, 'Last rites', p. 18.
134 *Ibid.*, pp. 9–14.
135 SAPMO-BA, DY/30/J/IV2/3A/3264, Fischer to Winkelmann, 6 February 1979.
136 Uher, 'Last rites', pp. 14–15.
137 SAPMO-BA, DY/30/12881, Winkelmann to Honecker, 12 June 1979.
138 Interview with Edgar Uher, Berlin, 10 January 2010.

139 *Irish Times*, 19 June 1979.
140 Uher, 'Last rites', p. 15.
141 SAPMO-BA, DY/30/12881, 'Überführung der sterblichen Überreste des ehemaligen irischen Interbrigadisten Frank Ryan am 18.6.79 Dresden', by Kurt Höfer, 20 June 1979.
142 *Ibid.*
143 *Ibid.*
144 Uher, 'Last rites', p. 17.
145 *Irish Times*, 21 June 1979.
146 *Ibid.*, 23 June 1979.
147 Hull, *Irish Secrets*, pp. 32–3.
148 *Irish Times*, 23 June 1979.
149 SAPMO-BA, DY/30/12881, 'Abschlußvermerk über die Überführung der sterblichen Überreste Ryan', MfAA, 26 June 1979.
150 Mac Con Uladh, 'Poor Relations', p. 81.
151 AA-PA, MfAA, ZR629/97, Honecker to Hillery, 14 May 1980 and 19 May 1980.
152 *Ibid.*, Bierbach to Plaschke, including Hillery's message, 8 July 1980.
153 Uher, 'Last rites', pp. 19–20.
154 *Ibid.*
155 *Neues Deutschland*, 21 November 1980 (SAPMO-BA).
156 *Irish Times*, 22 November 1980.
157 Uher, 'Last rites', p. 8.
158 Interview with Edgar Uher, Berlin, 11 January 2010.
159 J. Mitdank, *Die DDR zwischen Gründung, Aufstieg und Verkauf* (Berlin: NoRa, 2008), pp. 222–6.
160 *Irish Times*, 17 August 1977.
161 *Ibid.*, 24 August 1977.
162 SAPMO-BA, DL2/6679, Ticher to Haufe, including *Irish Times* article, 25 August 1977.
163 *Irish Times*, 14 October 1977.
164 *Ibid.*, 15 December 1977.
165 Fulbrook, *History of Germany, 1918–2000*, pp. 174–5.
166 *Ibid.*, p. 175.
167 *Ibid.*, pp. 175–6.
168 SAPMO-BA, DL2/6679, Haufe to Nebel, 'Republik Irland', 30 August 1977.
169 BStU, MfS-HAXVIII, no. 16817, 'Information über ein Gespräch mit Herrn XXX am Messestand der Firma O'Dwyer & Ticher Ltd, Dublin/Ireland', 13 March 1978.
170 *Irish Times*, 22 June 1978.
171 Fulbrook, *History of Germany, 1918–2000*, p. 176.
172 *Irish Times*, 22 June 1978.
173 Kennedy *et al.*, *Economic Development of Ireland in the Twentieth Century*, p. 243.

174 AA-PA, MfAA, ZR 627/97, 'Information über den Stand der Außenhandelsbeziehungen der DDR zur Republik Irland', by the MfA (Ministry of Foreign Trade), 9 August 1979.
175 Kennedy *et al.*, *Economic Development of Ireland in the Twentieth Century*, p. 209.
176 *Ibid.*, pp. 219–20.
177 AA-PA, MfAA, ZR 627/97, 'Information über den Stand der Außenhandelsbeziehungen der DDR zur Republik Irland', by the MfA (Ministry of Foreign Trade), 9 August 1979.
178 *Ibid.*, MfAA, ZR 627/97, 'Information über den Stand der Außenhandelsbeziehungen der DDR zur Republik Irland', by the MfA (Ministry of Foreign Trade), 9 August 1979.
179 *Kerryman*, 2 November 1979.
180 *Irish Farmers Journal*, 5 March 1983.
181 *Irish Times*, 3 December 1983 and 7 January 1984.
182 SAPMO-BA, DL2/6679, 'Vermerk über ein Gespräch Genosse J. Steyer/Herr K. W. Heaslip, Botschafter der Republik Irland, am 4.6.1985', 18 June 1985.
183 *Irish Times*, 20 June 1986.
184 SAPMO-BA, DL2/6679, Joachim Mitdank to Kurt Nier, representative of the MfAA in charge of relations with Western countries, 30 June 1989.
185 *Ibid.*, 'Handelsziffern Irland-DDR gemäß Unterstaatssekretär J. Swift am 29.06.1989', by East German embassy in London, 3 July 1989.
186 *Ibid.*
187 Dáil Éireann, vol. 398, 'Exports to East Germany', 22 May 1990, at www.oireachtas-debates.gov.ie (accessed 29 April 2009).
188 *Ireland, Statistical Abstract, 1990*, compiled by Central Statistics Office, Dublin, p. 166.
189 Mac Con Uladh, 'Poor Relations', p. 86.
190 NAI, secretary's office, A55I, 'Communist Group since 1945', 23 June 1947.
191 Treacy, *Communist Party of Ireland*, pp. 236–7.
192 M. Milotte, *Communism in Modern Ireland: The Pursuit of the Workers' Republic since 1916* (Dublin: Gill & Macmillan, 1984), p. 220.
193 'Irish Election Literature', local election results for Dublin City Council, at http://irishelectionliterature.wordpress.com/2011/07/21/1967-1974-19791985-1991-1999-2004-2009-local-election-results-for-dublin-city-council-and-dublin-county-council (accessed 20 February 2013).
194 *Irish Times*, 29 May 1946.
195 'Local Government Elections 1985–1989: Belfast', in Northern Ireland Elections, at www.ark.ac.uk/elections/85-89lgbelfast.htm (accessed 20 February 2013).
196 Interview with Edgar Uher, Berlin, 10 January 2010.
197 *Limerick Leader*, 9 July 1949.
198 *Irish Times*, 16 June 1950.

199 *Anglo-Celt*, 30 May 1953.
200 *Irish Times*, 17 June 1953.
201 *Ibid.*, 19 June 1953.
202 *Connacht Tribune*, 18 April 1959.
203 *Irish Independent*, 16 October 1961.
204 *Irish Times*, 13 November 1961.
205 *Westmeath Examiner*, 9 March 1963.
206 *Nenagh Guardian*, 30 October 1965.
207 *Irish Independent*, 28 May 1964.
208 *Irish Times*, 20 June 1964.
209 *Sunday Independent*, 6 March 1966; *Irish Times*, 7 March 1966.
210 *Svenska Dagbladet*, 6 December 2013, at www.presseurop.eu (accessed 6 December 2013).
211 *Irish Times*, 22 August 1968.
212 *Ibid.*, 26 August 1968.
213 *Ibid.*, 14 January 1970.
214 *Ibid.*, 19 April 1986 and 26 May 1987.
215 *Ibid.*, 15 July 1983.
216 H. McDonald, *Colours: Ireland – From Bombs to Boom* (Edinburgh and London: Mainstream Publishing, 2005), pp. 78–86.
217 *Irish Times*, 29 December 1981.
218 *Ibid.*, 6 October 1979.
219 *Ibid.*, 7 January 1984.
220 *Ibid.*, 4 July 1984.
221 Müller-Enbergs *et al.*, *Wer war wer in der DDR?*, 'Bohley, Bärbel', p. 88.
222 J. Gieseke, *Der Mielke-Konzern: Die Geschichte der Stasi, 1945–1990* (Munich: DVA, 2006), pp. 193–5.
223 'Hall of Fame – The Sands Family', by Geoff Harden, 7 July 2010, at www.culturenorthernireland.org/article/1608/hall-of-fame-the-sands-family (accessed 10 October 2013).
224 *Neues Deutschland*, 13 February 1980 in Zeitungsinformationssystem, Staatsbibliothek zu Berlin, Preußischer Kulturbesitz (hereafter ZEFYS/DDR-Presse), at http://zefys.staatsbibliothek-berlin.de/ddr-presse (accessed 11 October 2013).
225 *Anglo-Celt*, 27 July 1984.
226 *Irish Times*, 24 August 1984.
227 *Ibid.*, 10 December 1983.
228 Mac Con Uladh, 'Poor Relations', p. 78; 'Death of writer Breandan Ó hEithir in Dublin', *Irish Times*, 27 October 1990.
229 See for example *Neues Deutschland*, 1 February 1953, 5 February 1953 & 10 May 1953, among others (SAPMO-BA).
230 Applebaum, *Iron Curtain*, pp. 448–9.
231 E. Shaw, *Wie ich nach Berlin kam: 'Irish Berlin'* (Berlin: Aufbau Taschenbuch Verlag, 2000), pp. 76, 134–5, 173–6, 194, 231.

232 *Irish Times*, 5 June 1997.
233 *Ibid.*, 14 May 2011; *Neues Deutschland*, 12 September 1956 (ZEFYS/DDR-Presse).
234 Applebaum, *Iron Curtain*, p. 272.
235 Mac Con Uladh, 'Poor Relations', pp. 77–8.
236 *Ibid.*, pp. 77, 79.
237 E. Delaney, *An Accidental Diplomat: My Years in the Irish Foreign Service, 1985–1995* (Dublin: New Island, 2001), pp. 69–70.
238 Fulbrook, *Anatomy of a Dictatorship*, see ch. 4 'Render unto Caesar? The Pivotal Role of the Protestant Churches', pp. 87–125.
239 *Irish Times*, 3 September 1982.
240 *Ibid.*, 14 August 1984.
241 *Ibid.*, 1 December 1976.
242 *Irish Independent*, 21 May 1985.
243 Hanley & Millar, *Lost Revolution*, p. 462.
244 SAPMO-BA, DZ/22/21, Garland to DDR-Komitee für Europäische Sicherheit und Zusammenarbeit, 4 August 1982, GDR-Komitee to Irish Committee for European Security and Cooperation, 7 September 1982, Garland to GDR-Komitee, 3 November 1982 & report of Friedensrat, 4 May 1988.
245 *Irish Independent*, 5 October 1989.
246 *Irish Farmers Journal*, 21 October 1989.
247 *Irish Times*, 17 October 1989.
248 Gieseke, *Der Mielke-Konzern*, p. 257.
249 *Irish Independent*, 19 October 1989.
250 *Ibid.*, 11 November 1989.
251 *Irish Times*, 3 October 1990.
252 *Ibid.*, 6 November 1990.
253 *Neues Deutschland*, 16 December 1956 (SAPMO-BA).
254 *Weltbühne*, 20 July 1966, p. 912.
255 *Horizont*, July 1969 (SAPMO-BA).
256 'IRA', in *Meyers Neues Lexikon* (Leipzig: VEB Bibliographisches Institut, 1964), vol. 4. The author is most grateful to Wolfgang Döhnert (Berlin) for this information on East German encyclopaedias (in a letter to the author, 27 January 2010).
257 'IRA', in *Meyers Neues Lexikon* (Leipzig: VEB, Bibliographisches Institut, 1969), vol. 9.
258 'IRA', in *BI Universallexikon* (Leipzig: VEB, Bibliographisches Institut, 1986), vol. 3.
259 Wolfgang Döhnert (Berlin) in a letter to the author, 27 January 2010.
260 *Neues Deutschland*, 15 August 1969 (SAPMO-BA).
261 *Ibid.*, 22 August 1969 (SAPMO-BA).
262 Mac Con Uladh, 'The GDR and Northern Ireland', p. 98.
263 *Neues Deutschland*, 1 February 1972 (SAPMO-BA).
264 *Horizont*, February 1972 (SAPMO-BA).

265 NAI, DFA 2003/17/98, Irish embassy in Copenhagen to secretary of foreign affairs, 10 March 1972, including translation of article in *Information*, 7 March 1972.
266 *Ibid.*, Dillon to Hugh McCann, DFA secretary, 9 March 1972.
267 Wolfgang Döhnert (Berlin) in a letter to the author, 19 October 2009.
268 *Neues Deutschland*, 23 November 1974, *Neue Zeit*, 23 November 1974 & *Berliner Zeitung*, 23 November 1974 (ZEFYS/DDR-Presse).
269 *Berliner Zeitung*, 23 July 1976 (ZEFYS/DDR-Presse).
270 *Horizont*, 1976, no. 2, p. 28 (SAPMO-BA)
271 *Neues Deutschland*, 19 January 1978 (SAPMO-BA).
272 *Neue Weg*, 3 August 1978 (DO4/3512, SAPMO-BA).
273 *Neues Deutschland*, 6 May 1981 (ZEFYS/DDR-Presse). Besides articles in *Neues Deutschland*, see also *Berliner Zeitung* and *Neue Zeit*.
274 BStU, MfS-ZAIG, no. 11055, Stasi report (transcript) of Werner Castor's broadcast, 11 May 1981.
275 Letter from Wolfgang Döhnert (Berlin) to the author, 19 October 2009.
276 *Neues Deutschland*, 13/14 October 1984 (SAPMO-BA).
277 *Ibid.*, 9 November 1987 (SAPMO-BA).
278 C. Andrew & O. Gordievsky, *KGB: The Inside Story* (New York: HarperCollins, 1990), pp. 546–7, 632–3.
279 Deutsches Rundfunkarchiv, Potsdam-Babelsberg, 'Bringt die Folterer vor Gericht', 7 December 1977 by Fernsehen der DDR, 'Ein Bericht der Gruppe Dr. Katins'.
280 'The history of Corrymeela', the Corrymeela Community, at www.corrymeela.org/about-us/history-of-corrymeela.aspx (accessed 14 October 2013).
281 Evangelisches Zentralarchiv, Berlin (archives of the Evangelical Church in the former GDR), (hereafter EZA), 5096/11, 'Befürwortung', by Dr Krusche, 7 December 1981.
282 *Ibid.*, 'Bericht über den Konflikt in Nordirland', by Walter Schulz, 30 November 1983.
283 *Ibid.*
284 Müller-Enbergs *et al.*, *Wer war wer in der DDR?*, 'Walter Kaufmann', pp. 414–15.
285 W. Kaufmann, *Flammendes Irland: Wir lachen, weil wir weinen* (Rostock: MV/Taschenbuch, 2003), first published in 1977 in Leipzig by Brockhaus Verlag.
286 W. Kaufmann, *Patrick* (Berlin: Verlag Junge Welt, 1977).
287 This is clearly shown by stamps in the book (a copy is in possession of the author): 'Institut für Lehrerbildung "Clara Zetkin", Rochlitz'.
288 *Neues Deutschland*, 11 November 1960 (SAPMO-BA).
289 *Ibid.*, 5 October 1970 (SAPMO-BA).
290 *Weltbühne*, 20 July 1966, pp. 909–13 (SAPMO-BA).
291 D. Keogh, *Twentieth Century Ireland: Revolution and State Building* (Dublin: Gill & Macmillan, 2005), pp. 275–80.

292 *Weltbühne*, 17 October 1972, pp. 1323–6 (SAPMO-BA).
293 Pekelder, 'Vom "Sowjetdeutschland" zum "roten Preußen"', p. 305 and n. 43 (p. 305).
294 Fulbrook, *Anatomy of a Dictatorship*, pp. 88, 91.
295 Regionalarchiv Ordinarien Ost (ROO), Erfurt, Germany (archives of the Catholic Church in the former GDR), Vorsitzender/Sekretariat der BOK/BBK (Berliner Konferenz Europäischer Katholiken), K25, K32, K38, K44, K49, K75, K76 and K79 II. The archivist of the ROO, Dr Michael Matscha, told this author that a forty-year rule still applied to the consultation of certain documents. However, it is not likely that these documents contain significant information for this study. See also documents on religious issues contained in SAPMO-BA, notably files DO/4/4305, DO/4/4347 & DO/4/4604.
296 EZA, 5096/11, Falconer to Lewek, 10 February 1982.
297 *Ibid.*, 'Bericht über einen Dienstbesuch ... bei der Irish School of Ecumenics in Dublin/Irland durch Pastor Lange und OKR Schulz vom 25.10 bis 1.11.1983', by Schulz, 16 November 1983.
298 *Ibid.*, Krusche to Falconer, 26 August 1984.
299 *Neues Deutschland*, 21 November 1980 (SAPMO-BA).
300 *Horizont*, 1980, no. 7, pp. 16–17 (SAPMO-BA).
301 Fulbrook, *History of Germany, 1918–2000*, pp. 191–6.
302 Deutsches Rundfunkarchiv, Potsdam-Babelsberg, 'Insel des Abschieds', 6 November 1979, Fernsehen der DDR.
303 *Ibid.*, 'Insel des Abschieds', 6 November 1979, Fernsehen der DDR.
304 B. Stöver, *Der Kalte Krieg 1947–1991: Geschichte eines radikalen Zeitalters* (Bonn: Bundeszentrale für politische Bildung, 2007), pp. 272–3.
305 The exact number of Travellers for the year 1979 remains difficult to establish. In the census of 1996, the closest census to 1979 containing relevant figures, the number of Travellers is established at 10,891. Therefore, it seems unlikely that there were 75,000 Travellers in 1979 as stated by the East German television crew. See Central Statistics Office (CSO), 1996 Census, at www.cso.ie/en/media/csoie/releasespublications/documents/population/1996/travelcomm_1996.pdf, 'The demographic situation of the Traveller Community in April 1996', p. 237 (accessed 31 October 2013).
306 *Irish Times*, 24 September 2011.
307 'Impact of Agriculture Schemes and Payments on Aspects of Ireland's Heritage', by the Heritage Council, 1999, at www.heritagecouncil.ie/fileadmin/user_upload/Publications/Wildlife/Impact_of_Agriculture_Schemes_and_Payments_on_Aspects_of_Ireland.pdf (accessed 31 October 2013), see paragraph entitled 'The Mansholt Plan'.
308 SAPMO-BA, DA/1/15657, note written by Edgar Uher regarding meeting between Bierbach and Fitzpatrick, 28 February 1983.
309 *Ibid.*, DA/1/15846, Treacy to Sindermann, 13 September 1988; note on the Irish delegation's visit, 20 September 1988.

310 *Ibid.*, DA/1/15869, note regarding East German parliamentary delegation's visit to Ireland, 19 September 1989.
311 Skelly, *Irish Diplomacy at the United Nations, 1945–1965*, see ch. 6 'Swords into Plowshares: Ireland's Nuclear Non-proliferation Initiative', pp. 247–65, for Aiken, see p. 264.
312 D. Siegmund-Schultze (ed.), *Irland: Gesellschaft un Kultur*, VI (Halle: Martin-Luther-Universität Halle-Wittenberg, 1989/44, F92), p. 8.
313 Mac Con Uladh, 'Poor Relations', p. 86.
314 Christopher Andrew & Oleg Gordievsky cited in E. O'Halpin, *Defending Ireland: The Irish State and Its Enemies since 1922* (Oxford: Oxford University Press, 1999), p. 322 and n. 47. The author asked specifically for a search on 'Klavier' in the BStU (Stasi) archive in Berlin but no evidence was found.
315 Mac Con Uladh, 'Poor Relations', pp. 73–4.
316 SAPMO-BA, DY/30/IV/ A2/20/487, H. Moore to SED, 31 May 1963.
317 *Ibid.*, Ulbricht to CPNI, 13 June 1963.
318 *Ibid.*, note on meeting Axen-Moore, 26 October 1967.
319 *Ibid.*, Ulbricht to Irish Workers' Party, 23 April 1965.
320 Letter from Wolfgang Döhnert (Berlin) to the author, 19 October 2009.
321 SAPMO-BA, DY/30/IV/ A2/20/487, Ulbricht to CPI, 14 March 1970.
322 *Neues Deutschland*, 16 March 1970; *Horizont*, no. 14, 1970 (SAPMO-BA).
323 *Neues Deutschland*, 23 January 1973 (SAPMO-BA).
324 Mac Con Uladh, 'The GDR and Northern Ireland', pp. 98–9.
325 Mac Con Uladh, 'Poor Relations', pp. 75–6.
326 Dáil Éireann, *Election Results and Transfer of Votes in General Election* (February 1973) (Dublin: Stationery Office), p. 22.
327 Dáil Éireann, *Election Results and Transfer of Votes in General Election* (June 1977) (Dublin: Stationery Office), p. 54.
328 Dáil Éireann, *Election Results and Transfer of Votes in General Election* (February 1987) (Dublin: Stationery Office), pp. 55–6.
329 Dáil Éireann, *Election Results and Transfer of Votes in General Election* (June 1989) (Dublin: Stationery Office), pp. 54–5.
330 SAPMO-BA, DY/30/12881, note on discussion with Michael O'Riordan, 14 June 1978.
331 Mac Con Uladh, 'The GDR and Northern Ireland', p. 99.
332 SAPMO-BA, DY/24/11 5724 T2, Information on discussion regarding participation of international youth brigades from Ireland, 25 August 1981.
333 *Ibid.*, DY/30/12882, note on submission to the Politbüro, 9 March 1983.
334 *Ibid.*, DY/30/12880, Honecker to Stewart, 9 May 1984.
335 Mac Con Uladh, 'Poor Relations', pp. 75–6 and n. 19 (p. 76) (the letter was sent on 15 September 1986).
336 SAPMO-BA, DY/30/12883, James Stewart (CPI) to SED, 20 June 1989 & Sieber to Axen, 19 July 1989.
337 Uher, 'Last rites', p. 23.

338 SAPMO-BA, DY/30/12882, note on a conversation between Lindner and Nesterenko in Dublin, 9 February 1985, written by Edgar Uher.
339 Hanley & Millar, *Lost Revolution*, p. 462.
340 Uher, 'Last rites', p. 21.
341 SAPMO-BA, DY/30/12882, note on meeting between Lindner and representatives of CPI, 12 February 1986 (meeting took place on 9 February 1985).
342 *Ibid.*
343 Gieseke, *Der Mielke-Konzern*, pp. 239–40.
344 SAPMO-BA, DY/30/12882, Garland to Honecker, 28 January 1986.
345 *Ibid.*, Uher to Teutschbein, 4 February 1986.
346 *Ibid*, Central Committee to Honecker, 17 February 1986 & Sieber to Lindner, 19 February 1986.
347 *Ibid.*, Lindner to Sieber, 20 February 1986.
348 *Ibid.*
349 Hanley & Millar, *Lost Revolution*, p. 376.
350 *Ibid.*, p. 404.
351 SAPMO-BA, DY/30/12882, Honecker to Stewart, 24 February 1986.
352 *Ibid.*, note on a meeting between Mahlow and Garland in Moscow, 4 March 1986.
353 *Ibid.*, report on Lindner's trip to Ireland, 4 June 1986.
354 *Neues Deutschland*, 12 November 1987.
355 Mac Con Uladh, 'Poor Relations', p. 76.
356 Hanley & Millar, *Lost Revolution*, p. 487.
357 *Ibid.*, p. 489.
358 SAPMO-BA, DY/30/12883, Honecker to Stewart (draft, translation), March 1989.
359 *Ibid.*, Stewart to Honecker, 28 August 1989.
360 G. Dalos, *Der Vorhang geht auf: Das Ende der Diktaturen in Osteuropa* (Munich: Verlag C.H. Beck, 2010), p. 112.
361 *Ibid.*, p. 207.
362 *Irish Times*, 7 October 1989.
363 'Gorbachev on 1989', in *The Nation*, 28 October 2009, at www.thenation.com/article/gorbachev-1989 (accessed 20 May 2012).
364 Hanley & Millar, *Lost Revolution*, pp. 546–7.
365 SAPMO-BA, DL2/6679, note on discussion between Vorpahl and representatives of the Workers' Party, 28 November 1989.
366 *Ibid.*, DY/30/12883, Krenz to CPI, 25 October 1989.
367 Fax from Reiner Oschmann (Berlin) to the author, 21 June 2009.

Part II
Intelligence

2

Stasi history and sources

The archival legacy of the Stasi is more than impressive. There is a total of about 158 kilometres of archives. Included are 12 kilometres of index cards, representing about 39 million cards, and also over 15,000 sacks of torn and shredded documents of which about 440 sacks had been processed for reconstruction by October 2010. These 440 sacks represent an extra 950,000 pages. In addition, there are 1,440,000 photographs, microfilms and slides, 2,756 films and videos and about 31,300 audio recordings.[1] There should even be more, as the Stasi succeeded in destroying much material shortly after the end of the Berlin Wall.[2]

When the GDR collapsed in 1989–90, the Stasi shredded and incinerated much material, especially that concerning the Hauptverwaltung Aufklärung (HVA, main directorate of foreign intelligence). Nonetheless much has survived, notably the SIRA summary sheets. SIRA means System der Informationsrecherche der Aufklärung (information research system of the HVA). It was a computing system in which valuable documents were stored. Each document had a summary sheet meant for rapid consultation. When the writing was on the wall, the HVA destroyed the documents in electronic form but not their electronic summary sheets, believing that the code could not be cracked. That assessment was correct until 1998 when it was eventually cracked by Stephan Konopatzky working for the BStU, the archive of the former Stasi in Berlin.[3] Consequently, the SIRA summary sheets provide useful clues as to what information the original documents contained. The following is mentioned in these summary sheets: registration number of agents and sources, title of report, brief description, keywords, dates, assessment grade of the report and a few other items. There was definitely material about Ireland and Northern Ireland. Unfortunately, because of the destruction of documents, gaps appear in the history of the Stasi. Also, as far as Irish and Northern Irish issues are concerned it remains most difficult to reconstitute what is known as an 'intelligence cycle', namely 'planning and direction, collection, processing, analysis, and dissemination'.[4]

As the research for this book has established, the Stasi had some interest in Ireland, but far more in the terrorist conflict in Northern Ireland. To fully appreciate the variety of sources on which the information for this book is based and also the inherent problems of these sources, a few words must now be said on the nature of the documents available in the BStU. In March 1990, the West German television programme *Kontraste* filmed the destruction of the Stasi's electronic data, what appeared to be big round discs containing information on millions of citizens (victims and informers), spies, organisations and institutions. The data had been stored in the central computer of the Ministry of State Security in East Berlin. The *Kontraste* journalist commented dryly that the metal pieces of the discs would be turned into 'spoons and saucepans' and the plastic pieces into 'shopping bags'.[5]

How did it come to that? When the Wall fell on the night of 9 to 10 November 1989, it was clear that the GDR's days were numbered. Four days later, the chief of the Stasi, General Erich Mielke, made a pathetic appeal in the Volkskammer (the people's chamber, or parliament) and said: 'But I love all, really all people'. It did not sound particularly convincing. Soon, he ordered the destruction of some of the ministry's files. On 17 November, Hans Modrow, the last Communist Prime Minister, announced that the Stasi would now become the Amt für Nationale Sicherheit (AfNS, or Office of National Security). On 4 December in Erfurt, civil rights activists occupied the office of the AfNS to prevent further destruction of documents. In the following days, Citizens' Committees did the same elsewhere in the country. The AfNS's existence was brief, as the government dissolved it on 14 December.

On 15 January 1990, a huge crowd occupied the headquarters of the former Stasi in East Berlin, commonly known as 'die Zentrale' (the Centre). In this chaos, talks began between government officials and representatives of the Citizens' Committees, and it was eventually decided to destroy the Stasi's discs. Although some citizens were against this, a majority argued that it could not be known what kind of explosive information the discs might reveal. It was feared that in case of a quick reunification the West German secret services might use them for their own purposes. It also appeared that those who voted for the destruction wrongly believed that the material contained in the discs was still available in paper form.[6] This was a rather strange logic as there was not much point in destroying electronic documents and not their duplicates on paper.

But it also appeared that both East German *and* West German officials had some serious interest in the destruction of the discs. Old GDR elites did not want to be compromised while Bonn was afraid of embarrassing revelations and kept in mind the inner peace of a future reunified Germany.[7] In fact, the decision to destroy seemed to satisfy many. But that was not all. The HVA was allowed by the Citizens' Committees to dissolve itself and it grasped the opportunity with both hands to destroy many of its files. It managed to convince the citizens that it had nothing to do with internal repression in the GDR.[8] Much precious information was thus lost for ever. Jens Gieseke, an eminent specialist in the history of the Stasi, is right to quote Christopher Andrew, a leading expert in the field of intelligence studies: 'We don't know how much we don't know'. It is estimated that about a quarter of the Stasi material was either destroyed or disappeared, especially documents concerning foreign intelligence and topical cases. Yet, as Gieseke points out there are still remnants of HVA documents and there are two other sources, namely the HVA's index-card system of persons, also known by its pseudonym 'Rosenholz', and especially SIRA.[9] The SIRA system was operational from 1969 until 1990 and contained about 650,000 records when the GDR ceased to exist. Its purpose was to assist the HVA departments in charge of evaluation and analysis in their research and in their assessment of sources and also in making statistics.[10]

What about the Stasi's Irish files? As stated in the introduction to this book, research in the BStU unearthed a total of around 6,000 photocopies of original documents. The 6,000 total may sound impressive but everything is relative. British Professor Timothy Garton Ash's Stasi file is 325 pages long, while dissident songwriter Wolf Biermann's is 40,000.[11] Yet, the size is indicative of the interest the Stasi had in Ireland and Northern Ireland. It might very well be that it had even more material, bearing in mind the destruction of HVA files. There is definite evidence that some Irish material was torn to pieces by hand when the Stasi shredders had broken down in those frantic months of December 1989 and January 1990. File MfS-HAXXII, no. 19964, clearly shows that documents have been reconstructed, although in this particular file there was nothing secret as all documents were press despatches.[12]

It is striking that the reports and index cards on Ireland and Northern Ireland are essentially of an informative nature. In other words, it is more about what the Stasi *knew* about the situation in Ireland and Northern Ireland, and occasionally *how* it obtained the information, than what it actually *did* with the information obtained. Because of the lack of evidence regarding the exploitation of this information by the Stasi, it is pointless to indulge in long speculations unless logical deductions are feasible and credible. A last point must be made. Names of certain people that appear in files were blacked out by the BStU to protect their identity mainly because they are not relevant for the study under consideration or because they are not involved in or targeted by a particular Stasi operation.

The analysis of the Stasi documents for this book required careful reading and much attention, and there were pitfalls along the way. Open sources constitute a major part of the documents. The Stasi relied on many press articles to evaluate the evolving situation, especially in Northern Ireland. To get an impression of what it was particularly interested in attention had to be paid to the underlined passages in press cuttings. Also, now and again it typed in its own comments just under the article, the letters being almost of the same font and type size as those used in the article itself. Therefore, information could have gone easily unnoticed. Another pitfall, this one well known, is Stasi jargon. Reports and other documents are frequently riddled with jargon and also abbreviations, numbers and roman numerals. All needed to be explained. Fortunately, the BStU's remarkable website was of great help here by providing a list of abbreviations and explanations of Stasi terms.

Out of obvious security considerations the Stasi did not mention the name of the agent or source in the SIRA summary sheets. Only a registration number was mentioned and occasionally a code name. However, by looking up the registration number in the HVA index-card system F16 it is possible to get the person's name and also other details like date of birth, place of birth, address, profession, place of work, nationality, and party membership. In the HVA index-card system F22, the agent or source's code name is mentioned but there are no personal details. Also mentioned is the registration of files concerning the agent or source. The connection between F16 and F22 is the registration number. By so doing, the identity of several agents and sources could be established although not all of them.

But before embarking upon a detailed study of East German intelligence's assessments of Ireland and Northern Ireland, it is necessary to give a brief history of the Stasi and its organisation that might help to put things into context. On 8 February 1950, Minister of the Interior Dr Karl Steinhoff announced in the provisional parliament of the GDR that owing to recent acts of sabotage and destruction perpetrated by criminal elements directed by Anglo-American imperialists, a Ministerium für Staatssicherheit (MfS, Ministry of State Security, simply known as Stasi) would be created.[13] Steinhoff's allegations were not without foundation. After the end of the Second World War, the US

Democratic and Republican administrations had decided on policies of containment and liberation strategy to combat Communism in the world. In fact, a political planning staff had been set up in Washington in 1947, the aim of which was to prepare the downfall of Communist governments. Since the end of the 1940s, saboteurs from West Berlin and West Germany, like for instance the so-called Kampfgruppe gegen Unmenschlichkeit (KgU, combat group against inhumanity), had been targeting East German economic infrastructure. In the 1950s in West Germany, there were about 200 anti-Communist liberation groups who were ready to put into practice President Harry S. Truman's containment strategy. In the immediate post-war years there were also rumours that the Eastern part of Germany might be invaded by the West.[14]

In June 1948, the US National Security Council issued a directive defining the Central Intelligence Agency's (CIA) tasks in the unfolding Cold War: 'propaganda, economic warfare; preventive direct action, including sabotage, anti-sabotage, demolition and evacuation measures; subversion against hostile states, including assistance to underground resistance movements, guerrillas and refugee liberation groups, and support of indigenous anti-Communist elements in threatened countries of the free world'. The directive stressed that 'if [these activities were] uncovered the US Government can plausibly disclaim any responsibility for them'. As John Lewis Gaddis rightly comments: 'In short, American officials were to learn to lie'.[15] Markus Wolf, the legendary East German spymaster, wrote in his memoirs that the West was out to destroy the young GDR and he accused the Americans of being behind the uprising of 17 June 1953. He singled out the role played by Radio in the American Sector (RIAS), inciting people to revolt.[16] The East German leadership at the time attempted to show that Western agents provocateurs among others were deeply involved. Mary Fulbrook describes these attempts as 'somewhat far-fetched' and that the uprising was a very confused affair, be it the government's response or the demonstrators' coordination and actions. The events of June 1953 are still the object of different interpretations by German historians.[17]

Paranoia and fear of destabilisation of the GDR from within or without developed the Stasi into a fearsome secret police force, present at all levels of society. The East German regime was all too aware that the country had not been founded on democratic principles and freely endorsed by the people. At its beginnings, the Stasi numbered around 17,000 members; in 1961, around 20,000; in 1971, more than 45,500; in 1982, around 81,500; and in 1989, the last year of its existence, 91,015. But that was not all. The Stasi relied on a huge network of *inoffiziellen Mitarbeiter* (IM, unofficial collaborators, or informers) whose task it was to report on opponents to the regime and also on any behaviour considered devious. For example, people who wanted to leave the GDR, critical artists, 'reactionary clerical circles' and 'negative' groups of youths were targeted. These IMs generally had a written agreement with the Stasi. They either voluntarily agreed to work for it or were forced or were blackmailed into doing so. In the mid-1950s, there were between 20,000 and 30,000 IMs; in 1968, more or less 100,000; in 1975, around 180,000; and in 1988/1989 around 173,000. Of the IMs, 85–90 per cent were men. There were even IMs among the Protestant clergy. In the diocesan area of Thüringen, about 8 per cent of the clergy were IMs between 1969 and 1989.[18] The Stasi excelled at demoralisation techniques and psychological manipulation which allowed it to remain hidden in the background.[19] Clearly, there were airs of a police state in the GDR from very early onwards. The Stasi's most notorious prisons were Hohenschönhausen in East Berlin and Bautzen in Saxony. Between 1960 and 1989 there were about 110,000 political prisoners in the GDR. From the mid-1950s onwards, interrogation techniques became less violent and psychological torture was preferred.[20]

But the West, which proclaimed to be the standard-bearer of freedom and democracy, was certainly not above reproach. It is worth briefly recapping on the following facts. For example, the US authorities indulged in hunting down possible Communist sympathisers and spies during the era of McCarthyism and civil liberties were called into question.[21] Timothy Garton Ash, who as a British student in East Berlin was himself the target of a Stasi surveillance operation in 1980, writes that the United Kingdom's domestic secret service, MI5, kept files on British subjects that it did not trust, mostly people from the left.[22] In January 1972, the West German government introduced what went down in history as the so-called Radikalenerlass (anti-radical decree). This implied that any civil servant, from worker in a ministry to teacher in a school, could be dismissed if he/she were found to hold radical political views of the far left or the far right or if he/she belonged to any organisation deemed to be radical. People who wanted to apply for civil service jobs and who were believed to hold such views would not be appointed. This law was introduced by Social-Democratic Chancellor Willy Brandt at a period when terror actions of the Rote Armee Fraktion (RAF, Red Army Faction) were increasing. Over the years, about 1.4 million people were checked and about 1,110 were prevented from joining the public service.[23]

The examples above are not meant to attenuate the activities of the Stasi in any way by comparing them to those of Western intelligence activities.[24] But would it be an exaggeration to suggest that there were hints of Stasi-ism in the West? Moreover, at the time of writing, the Edward Snowden affair is in full swing. Snowden was a CIA operative who felt that the spying activities of the National Security Agency (NSA) went further than a bridge too far and that individual liberties of citizens were threatened. His subsequent revelations showed the unimaginable massive extent of the NSA's surveillance activities, all done to combat terrorism it was claimed. In Germany, the Snowden affair reminded people of the Stasi. Gotthold Schramm, a former Stasi agent and admirer of Snowden, declared: 'Compared to NSA surveillance today, what we did was like a children's game'. No doubt, though, that if the Stasi had had the technological know-how of the NSA it would also have used it. Hubertus Knabe, director of the Stasi prison memorial in Berlin, also admired Snowden's courage to speak out.[25] There is certainly plenty of food for thought here.

The Stasi was a complex organisation, divided into several directorates. Each of them had particular areas of expertise looked after by a *Hauptabteilung* (main department). For instance, Main Department III, abbreviated as HA-III, was in charge of radio and telecommunications intelligence, HA-VIII of arrests and observation, HA-XVIII of economic matters, HA-XX of civil organisations, church, cultural associations and so on, and HA-XXII of sabotage and terror attacks in possible enemy territory.[26] The Zentrale Auswertungs- und Informationsgruppe (ZAIG, central evaluation and information group) was, as its name suggests, in charge of evaluating received information. It was HA-XXII which analysed the activities of republican paramilitary groups in Northern Ireland, the ZAIG also providing analysis when needed. Within the Stasi, the HVA was in charge of spying abroad. If the Stasi had any contacts with Irishmen and women, then it would have been through HVA agents though, of course, HA-XXII and other departments might have their own contacts.

The HVA enjoyed a special aura: first, because the Ministry of State Security said that its work contributed to the stability of East–West relations and that its agents were *Kundschafter des Friedens* (scouts of peace) and, second, because of the myths surrounding its chief, Markus Wolf. Wolf was at the head of the HVA for years, and for years the West did not know what he looked like. He was the exceptionally gifted and almost mythical spymaster known as the 'man without a face' because it took Western intelligence agencies such a long time to identify him on a photograph. Unsurprisingly, the HVA's main target was West Germany but in 1971 its Department XII was set up to deal specifically with the North Atlantic Treaty Organization (NATO) and the European Community (EC). In 1973, Department XI saw the light and dealt with

North America, including military espionage on US troops based in West Germany. The military information the East Germans gathered was passed on to the KGB.[27] However, not everything was divulged to Moscow as Wolf claimed that he did not tell the Soviets 'the identity of my top moles or agents'.[28]

Heribert Hellenbroich, the former leader of the Bundesnachrichtendienst (BND, the West German federal intelligence agency for threats from abroad), believed that the HVA ranked fourth in the world's best intelligence agencies, after the Mossad, the CIA and the KGB but before the British, the French and the West Germans.[29] One of the HVA's master strokes was to infiltrate one of its agents into the West German Social Democratic Party (SPD). His name was Günter Guillaume and he managed to rise through the ranks and become Chancellor Brandt's personal assistant. The Stasi had also moles in West Germany's different intelligence services and police forces, and these moles provided information on the activities of members of the PIRA and the Irish National Liberation Army (INLA) in West Germany where they had embarked on a terrorist campaign directed against the soldiers of the British Army of the Rhine (BAOR) and British diplomatic personnel.

But what did East German intelligence know about Ireland and Northern Ireland?

Notes

1 'Die Arbeit der Stasi-Unterlagen Behörde' (DVD), made by the BStU (archive of the former Stasi), 2011. Chapter entitled 'Die Aktenbestände der BStU; Stand bis 31.12.2010' (PDF file).
2 Gieseke, *Der Mielke-Konzern*, pp. 18, 263.
3 H. Schwan & H. Heindrichs, *Das Spinnennetz; Stasi-Agenten im Westen: Die geheimen Akten der Rosenholz-Datei* (Munich: Knaur, 2005), p. 139.
4 L. K. Johnson, 'Governing in the Absence of Angels: On the Practice of Intelligence Accountability in the United States', in H. Born, L. K. Johnson & I. Leigh (eds.), *Who's Watching the Spies? Establishing Intelligence Service Accountability* (Washington, DC: Potomac, 2005), p. 61.
5 *Kontraste*, 13 March 1990, 'Vernichten oder aufbewahren? – Stasi-Akten als politische Zeitbombe', in *Auf den Spuren einer Diktatur*, a series of three DVDs produced by the Bundeszentrale für politische Bildung (bpb) and the Rundfunk Berlin-Brandenburg (rbb), 2nd edition, Berlin, 2005.
6 Gieseke, *Der Mielke-Konzern*, pp. 258–63.
7 *Ibid.*, p. 264.
8 H. Knabe, *West-Arbeit des MfS: Das Zusammenspiel von 'Aufklärung' und 'Abwehr'* (Berlin: Ch. Links Verlag, 1999), p. 133.
9 Gieseke, *Der Mielke-Konzern*, pp. 18, 206–7.

10 R. Engelmann, B. Florath, H. Heidemeyer, D. Münkel, A. Plozin & W. Süß, *Das MfS-Lexikon: Begriffe, Personen und Strukturen der Staatssicherheit der DDR* (Berlin: Ch. Links Verlag, 2011), pp. 272–3; H. Ziehm, 'Elektronische Datenträger', in Knabe, *West-Arbeit des MfS*, pp. 55–9.
11 Garton Ash, T., *The File: A Personal History* (London: Atlantic Books, 2009), p. 19.
12 BStU, MfS-HAXXII, no. 19964.
13 Gieseke, *Der Mielke-Konzern*, p. 23.
14 Stöver, *Der Kalte Krieg 1947–1991*, pp. 67, 69–72, 78.
15 J. L. Gaddis, *The Cold War: The Deals. The Spies. The Truth* (London: Penguin, 2007), pp. 162–3.
16 M. Wolf with A. McElvoy, *Man without a Face: The Autobiography of Communism's Greatest Spymaster* (New York: Public Affairs, 1997), p. 68.
17 Fulbrook, *Anatomy of a Dictatorship*, pp. 177–8, 183.
18 Gieseke, *Der Mielke-Konzern*, pp. 23, 71–2, 114–15, 155, 183, 193.
19 *Ibid.*, pp. 192–3.
20 *Ibid.*, pp. 182–3.
21 Gaddis, *The Cold War*, pp. 39–40, 46–7.
22 Garton Ash, *The File*, pp. 211–16.
23 'Berufsverbot für linke Gesinnung', at www.wdr.de, website of the Westdeutscher Rundfunk, 19 May 2006 (accessed 27 April 2010).
24 For a remarkable study on the Stasi's role in upholding the East German totalitarian regime, see G. Bruce's *The Firm: The Inside Story of the Stasi* (Oxford: Oxford University Press, 2010). Bruce made an in-depth study of the Stasi's activities in two localities in the GDR.
25 *Le Monde*, 21 October 2013; *Irish Times*, 5 July 2013.
26 Gieseke, *Der Mielke-Konzern*, pp. 104–6.
27 *Ibid.*, pp. 202–3, 209–10, 217–18.
28 Wolf & McElvoy, *Man without a Face*, pp. 14–15.
29 Gieseke, *Der Mielke-Konzern*, p. 202.

3

Keeping informed and spying on Ireland

A striking feature concerning the Irish and Northern Irish material uncovered in the BStU archive is that a substantial part of the 6,000 photocopies are press cuttings, overwhelmingly from the West German media. There were about 1,129 articles. The origin of some of them could not be identified. There are also a few cuttings from East German newspapers and magazines like *Neues Deutschland* and *Horizont*. All newspapers used were in the German language and the only newspaper from outside the FRG and the GDR was the Swiss *Neue Zürcher Zeitung*. The absence of English-language newspapers, which would have been relatively easy to obtain in the FRG or West Berlin, or even through the East German embassy in London, tends to indicate that HAXXII and the ZAIG (central evaluation and information group) were satisfied with the quality of information provided by the West German press. Of course, it should be borne in mind that the PIRA embarked on a terrorist campaign against the British Army of the Rhine (BAOR) in West Germany. So, there was plenty to read in West German newspapers. At first sight rather unexpected are some articles from *Bunte Illustrierte*, an illustrated newspaper specialised in royalty and stars, and *Bild-Zeitung*, the largest West German tabloid. There are also numerous dispatches from several news agencies like the West German Deutsche Presse-Agentur (DPA), the French Agence France-Presse (AFP) and the American Associated Press (AP).

The overwhelming majority of these articles, about 98 per cent, concern the conflict in Northern Ireland generally and the PIRA in particular. There was far less attention paid to Ireland because it was not considered to be politically significant among the countries in the West or deemed to be economically, financially and technologically of much interest. The press cuttings were occasionally organised into themes like for instance the kidnapping and killing of West German Consul Thomas Niedermayer in 1973, the kidnapping of Dutch businessman Tiede Herrema in 1975, the assassination of Lord Mountbatten in

1979, the hunger strikes of 1980–81, the death of Bobby Sands in 1981, the bombing of Harrods in London in 1983, the attempt to assassinate Prime Minister Margaret Thatcher in Brighton in 1984 and attacks on BAOR. All these events concerned the PIRA, but there were also articles on the INLA, Ulster Volunteer Force (UVF), Ulster Defence Association (UDA) and so on. Table 3.1 gives a precise survey of the press cuttings.

Table 3.1 Collecting press articles on Ireland and Northern Ireland

Newspaper & magazines	Number of articles & political orientation of newspaper/ magazine	Newspaper & magazines	Number of articles & political orientation of newspaper/ magazine
Der Abend (West Berlin)	20 (local)	*Neue Zürcher Zeitung* (Switzerland)	12 (Liberal)
Abendzeitung, 'AZ' (Munich)	1 (regional, tabloid, Liberal)	*Neues Deutschland* (GDR)	42 (Communist, official newspaper of the SED)
Arbeiterkampf (FRG)	3 (Communist)	*Nürnberger Nachrichten* (FRG)	13 (regional)
Bayernkurier (FRG)	1 (Christian Democrat)	*Quick* (FRG)	3 (illustrated magazine, Conservative)
Berliner Morgenpost (West Berlin)	48 (local, Conservative)	*Spandauer Volksblatt* (West Berlin)	11 (centre-left)
B.Z. (West Berlin)	64 (local, tabloid, Conservative)	*Der Spiegel* (FRG)	12 (magazine, centre-left)
Bild am Sonntag (FRG)	1 (Conservative)	*Stern* (FRG)	6 (left-Liberal)
Bild-Zeitung (FRG)	14 (tabloid, right-wing populist)	*Süddeutsche Zeitung* (FRG)	149 (left-Liberal)
Bunte Illustrierte (FRG)	1 (illustrated popular press)	*Tagesspiegel* (West Berlin)	243 (Liberal)
Darmstädter Echo (FRG)	1 (regional)	*Die Tageszeitung* (West Berlin)	33 (left)

Table 3.1 (Continued)

Newspaper & magazines	Number of articles & political orientation of newspaper/ magazine	Newspaper & magazines	Number of articles & political orientation of newspaper/ magazine
Deutsche Volkszeitung (FRG)	1 (Communist)	*Der Telegraf* (West Berlin)	1 (pro Social Democrat)
Frankfurter Allgemeine Zeitung (FRG)	163 (Conservative–Liberal)	*Unsere Zeit* (FRG)	5 (Communist)
Frankfurter Rundschau (FRG)	97 (left-Liberal)	*Das Volk* (GDR)	1 (Communist newspaper of the SED in Erfurt)
Freie Erde (GDR)	1 (SED newspaper for Brandenburg)	*Vorwärts* (FRG)	2 (newspaper of the German Social-Democratic Party, SPD)
Handelsblatt (FRG)	1 (economic, Liberal)	*Die Wahrheit* (West Berlin)	6 (Communist, financed by the SED)
Hannoversche Allgemeine Zeitung (FRG)	15 (regional)	*Die Welt* (FRG)	92 (Conservative)
Horizont (GDR, magazine)	27 (Communist)	*Welt am Sonntag* (FRG)	22 (Conservative)
Köln Stadt-Anzeiger (FRG)	7 (regional)	*Westdeutsche Allgemeine Zeitung* (FRG)	1 (regional)
Mannheimer Morgen (FRG)	1 (regional)	*Wochenpost* (GDR)	1 (Communist)
Neue Rheinzeitung (FRG)	3 (regional, independent)	*Die Zeit* (FRG)	4 (social-Liberal)
			Total: 1,129 press cuttings

Source: BStU, Berlin

What is interesting to notice is that the Stasi did not exclusively use newspapers whose political views were from the left or far left or in broad agreement with the regime in the GDR, quite the contrary even. The most often used newspapers were the *Tagesspiegel*, liberal, and the *Frankfurter Allgemeine Zeitung*, conservative–liberal, which was certainly no friend of the East German government. The West German media portrayed the Troubles as a terrorist conflict and not as a national war of liberation or an anti-colonialist struggle.

There is a common belief that intelligence services the world over are only interested in documents that are secret. Nothing could be further from the truth. According to Markus Wolf:

> we soon came to the conclusion that a careful reading of the press could often produce results far superior to secret reports of agents, and that our own analysts should draw independent conclusions from diverse sources in order to evaluate raw intelligence material … I also read a variety of West German newspapers and magazines, including the tabloid *Bild-Zeitung*, which, while lurid, often had better inside information on intelligence than its worthier rivals.[1]

What the East German spymaster wrote made sense. If good investigative journalists wrote highly informative articles, why neglect them? It should be pointed out that his approach was by no means original or innovative. In the last days of peace before the outbreak of the First World War, for instance, French intelligence complained that journalists were too well informed on France's mobilisation plans and that this was playing into the Germans' hands.[2] Once the articles were collected they were sent to the ZAIG for evaluation.[3] As Wolf remarked: 'Vast stretches of this work were very boring. Intelligence is essentially a banal trade of sifting through huge amounts of random information in a search for a single enlightening gem or illuminated link.'[4] But not only the ZAIG analysed such material.

Hauptabteilung (main department) XXII (HA-XXII) was in charge of watching international terrorists, liberation movements and so on. It was this department which kept a close eye on paramilitary organisations in Northern Ireland. It too collected press cuttings and filed them into different folders. One of these was entitled '*IRA, Medien* [media], *1989*, *no 59*'.[5] There was also HA-III in charge of radio and telecommunications intelligence.[6] HA-III had bases along the border with West Germany, extending into Czechoslovakia, and specialised in signal intelligence, known as SIGINT in intelligence jargon. It had two relay stations in Bonn located in the East German representation and the Soviet embassy, one in Cologne in the East German trade representation, and one in Düsseldorf also in a trade representation. This meant that much of West Germany was covered. The Stasi was therefore in a position to intercept communications from, among others, the BND (federal intelligence agency for threats from abroad) and its partners, Interpol, the Auswärtiges Amt (the West German Foreign Office) and also, from 1982 onwards, communications from the headquarters of BAOR.[7] As will be explained, the PIRA targeted British units based in West Germany. Therefore, it made perfect sense for HA-III to keep itself posted about what was going on in Northern Ireland. It closely collaborated with the HVA.[8]

But newspapers were not the only media source. HA-XXII also viewed or listened to reports of the Western radio and television. Receiving audio-visual Western media in East Berlin would not have been a problem since most East German citizens were able to view or listen to West German television and radio stations. A survey in various Stasi files shows that HA-XXII used the following West German and West Berlin media: ARD1, Bayerischer Rundfunk, SFB (Radio Free Berlin), SAT1, Südwestfunk Baden-Baden, ZDF, 100.6 (Berlin City Radio). There were also non-West German media: RIAS (Radio in the American Sector), RIAS TV, BBC, BBC-VT Agence France-Presse (AFP) and Associated Press (AP). Another important source was VT (Videotext, or teletex). Table 3.2 gives a precise survey of what was listened to or viewed about Northern Ireland (there is no item on Ireland).

It is to be noted that all these audio-visual media reports were compiled by HA-XXII between 1986 and 1989. This confirms that it took a rather late interest in the PIRA and the INLA. This time-frame

Table 3.2 Television and radio reports used by HAXXII, 1986–89

Name of media	No. of reports	Name of media	No. of reports
ARD1	13	RIAS TV	3
AFP	1	SAT1	6
AP	1	SFB	30
Bayerischer Rundfunk	1	Südwestfunk Baden-Baden	1
BBC	17	VT (Videotext)	48
BBC-VT	6	ZDF	26
RIAS	13	100,6	3
		TOTAL	169

Source: BStU, Berlin

does correspond to HA-XXII's reports and its demands for more information on Irish republicans as will be seen.

What was deemed to be relevant information was then sent to the directorate's *Lagezentrum* (situation centre) where the information was stored. HA-XXII kept a summary of all terrorist attacks throughout the world in a series of documents entitled *Aktuelle Medienmeldungen* (current news items). Table 3.3 provides a compilation of several Northern Irish examples.

Once HA-XXII was in possession of all relevant information concerning the activities of terrorist groups throughout the world for a given period, it developed a so-called *Lagefilm*, literally translated 'film of the situation', which was in fact a chronological factual summary of events: see Table 3.4.

Table 3.3 HA-XXII situation-centre, current news items

Media	Date & time	Title	Quote of news item
ARD [West German television channel]	09/11/1986, 16.00	'Bomb attacks in Dublin'	'Northern Irish paramilitaries placed four explosive devices in the Irish capital Dublin last Saturday. The Ulster Freedom Fighters [UFF] in Belfast claimed responsibility'
RIAS [Radio in the American Sector, West Berlin]	15/04/1987, 20.15	'Attempted bomb attacks by the IRA'	'The police in London defused a third letter bomb which, like the two previous ones, was addressed to an important governmental official'
SFB [Sender Freies Berlin; Radio Free Berlin]	09/05/1987, 04.00	'Bomb attack by the IRA'	'Nine people were killed during a serious incident in Northern Ireland'
ARD [West German television channel]	20/08/1988, 13.00	'Claiming responsibility for a bomb attack in Northern Ireland'	'The IRA has claimed responsibility for a bomb attack on a military bus in Northern Ireland. During the attack 7 British soldiers were killed and another 29 were wounded'

Table 3.3 (Continued)

Media	Date & time	Title	Quote of news item
SAT 1 [West German television]	13/03/1989, 09.00	'Regarding the situation in Northern Ireland'	'An explosive device of 675 kilos was defused 100 kilometres west from Belfast'
BBC	13/03/1989, 15.55	'Regarding the situation in Northern Ireland'	'A member of the security forces in Northern Ireland was wounded during an exchange of gunfire near Strabane'
BBC	13/03/1989, 16.00	'Regarding the situation in Northern Ireland'	'Members of the army defused a 15-kilo car bomb which had been hidden under the car of a member of the security forces in Maghera in County Londonderry'
100,6 [radio in West Berlin]	07/05/1989, 12.00	'Bomb attacks in Northern Ireland'	'Nine British soldiers were wounded last night during two bomb attacks in Northern Ireland. In two different places, bombs were detonated as soldiers were passing by. IRA terrorists claimed responsibility for the attacks'
ZDF [West German television channel]	26/10/1989, 21.45	'Attack on British soldiers in the Federal Republic of Germany'	'Two people were shot this night in Wildenraht near Mönchengladbach by unknown culprits. This crime took place at a petrol station near a base of the British army. The attackers were waiting in a parked car. As they saw their victims, they got out of their car and shot several times with an automatic rifle. A British soldier and his child were killed.

Media	Date & time	Title	Quote of news item
			The wife was seriously wounded. IRA terrorists are possibly responsible for this attack. The BKA [Bundeskriminalamt, West German federal criminal police] is investigating'

Source: BStU, Berlin

Table 3.4 Chronological factual summary: occurrence of international terror and violent events; working week of 22/08 to 28/08/1988

Serial number	Date	Place	Facts of the case	Hints about perpetrators/ claimed by perpetrators
373	—	—	—	—
374	24/08/1988	Northern Ireland/ Maghera	'Two policemen were slightly wounded during a car bomb explosion. The explosive device, which was hidden in a delivery van, was detonated as the squad car with the two policemen drove past'	IRA claimed the attack
375	25/08/1988	Afghanistan/ Kabul	'One person died and six others were wounded during a rocket attack on a residential area. Another terrorist attack claimed four lives'	Counter-revolutionary forces
376	26/08/1988	India	'Seven people were murdered in Punjab'	Probably Sikh extremists
377 etc…	—	—	—	—

Source: BStU, Berlin

By chronologically juxtaposing these events, the Stasi was able to figure out the trends of international terrorism either worldwide or in a particular region, and try to predict what possible developments might occur.

Besides media primary sources, the Stasi was interested in all kinds of literature about the conflict in Northern Ireland. HA-XX (state machinery, culture, church and underground) had a 295-page document entitled 'Statements by the Roman Catholic Bishops of Northern Ireland', ranging from 1981 until 1985. Among others it contained: 'Current Problems of Violence and of Social Justice, Irish Episcopal Conference, October 1981', 'Greenhills Conference, 25th January 1982, by His Eminence Cardinal Tomas O'Fiaich, Archbishop of Armagh', 'Statement Issued by Northern Catholic Bishops, July 4th 1983', 'Choices facing the Threatened Community, Justice or Violence, St. Anne's Cathedral, Belfast, Servite Priory, Benburb, April 3rd–4th 1984, by Bishop Dermot O'Mahony' and 'Peace: A Better way to Justice, Address for Eighteenth World Day of Peace, 1st January 1985, by Bishop Cahal B. Daly of Down and Connor'.[9] It is not known how the Stasi obtained these documents.

Of course, the terrorist activities of all paramilitary groups in Northern Ireland had caught the Stasi's attention and this quickly after the onset of the Troubles in 1969. As the East Germans had no agents or sources in Ulster (at least, this cannot be ascertained by the surviving documents) it became a question of acquiring good and reliable secondary sources which might inform them thoroughly and without taking risks. HA-XXII got hold of a West German book published in Bonn in 1976 entitled *Politik durch Gewalt; Guerilla und Terrorismus heute*, edited by Rolf Tophoven, a journalist specialising in terrorism. One of its contributors was the Dubliner Dermot Bradley, a reserve officer of the Irish army, who wrote a chapter called 'Die historischen Wurzeln der Guerilla und des Terrorismus in Nordirland' (the historic roots of guerrilla and terrorism in Northern Ireland).[10]

In 1977, HA-XXII acquired a copy of West German journalist Franz Wördemann's *Terrorismus* published in Munich and Zurich. This influential book mentioned all the republican and loyalist paramilitary groups and gave details on their structure and aims among others. Interestingly, Wördemann wrote about the PIRA that it had contacts with Palestinians, the Libyan government, Algeria, ETA and 'other European regional groups', but also with the 'IVth (Trotskyite) International in Brussels and individual groups of the "New Left" in European countries'.[11] That the PIRA had contacts with continental Trotskyites might sound rather surprising all the more since it was supposedly traditionally nationalist as opposed to the OIRA which was Marxist. Unfortunately, Wördemann did not include his source. But as Eunan O'Halpin pertinently explains:

> The patina of Marxist internationalism which was to be found in the speeches and statements of the Provisionals at conferences in Europe and elsewhere, while it put the wind up some intelligence and counter-terrorism analysts, was conspicuous by its absence in republican appeals to their key Irish-American audience. There, the Provisionals happily purveyed an unreconstructed, visceral anti-British rhetoric calculated to warm the heart of even the most fervent anti-Communist.[12]

It was a case of the PIRA being politically Janus-faced according to its needs.

Foreign books dealing with terrorism were translated by the Stasi into German. HA-XXII had a copy of Paul Barril's *Missions très spéciales* (very special missions) published in Paris in 1984. Barril had been an officer in an elite unit of the gendarmerie which dealt with terrorists. Chapter 19 of his book is an account of an incident which became known in France as '*Les Irlandais de Vincennes*' (the Irish of Vincennes). In 1982, Barril and his men arrested a group of three Irish people belonging to the INLA in an apartment in Vincennes near Paris. It subsequently transpired that the anti-terrorist unit had planted explosives and guns in the apartment which led to the release of the Irish in 1983.[13] In January 1989, the US Department of Defense in collaboration with the Department of State made public a document called 'Profile of Terrorist Organisations'. It included a message by George Bush, the Vice-President of the United States, to his fellow Americans and a preface by Frank C. Carlucci, Secretary of Defense. The document was over 200 pages and contained factual information on the main terrorist groups on every continent. The INLA and the PIRA were mentioned, but not their loyalist enemies. It landed on Lieutenant-General Gerhard Neiber's desk.[14] Neiber was one of Erich Mielke's four deputies and was responsible for several departments, including HA-XXII.[15]

The ZAIG had a copy of a brochure called 'Make Ireland a Nuclear Free Zone' published by the Irish CND (Campaign for Nuclear Disarmament) in Dublin. It dates from 1988 and contains different documents. One of them is the project of a bill of law entitled 'An act to establish in Ireland a nuclear free zone and to control the entry into the state's territory, airspace or territorial waters of aircraft or vessels equipped with nuclear, chemical or biological weapons or with nuclear propulsion systems'. It was claimed that 'some 12,000 foreign military aircraft overfly the Republic of Ireland each year, according to Irish government statistics... In all, 99% of overflying foreign military aircraft were from NATO countries (*Dáil Report* 15/12/87)'.[16] That the Irish CND had attracted the Stasi's attention was logical. During the 1980s a massive popular campaign for nuclear disarmament had developed throughout Western Europe in protest against the Reagan administration's decision, and the acceptance of NATO member states, to deploy cruise missiles. It was perceived as a serious escalation of the arms race between East and West.

In the Netherlands, for example, hundreds of thousands demonstrated against the installation of the missiles and they were supported by the churches. The Soviets identified the Netherlands as the 'weak link' in NATO. Consequently, the Stasi began infiltration and manipulation operations within the Dutch peace movement but they were not particularly successful, at least its attempt to steer the movement failed.[17] There is no reason to think, however, that the situation in Ireland was of particular interest to the Stasi as the Americans were not going to deploy cruise missiles in a neutral country. The evidence of this is an index card apparently created by the HVA on 23 February 1983. Apart from the title, 'Irish CND', and a very brief description, it provides no information whatsoever. There was not even a registration number.[18] The situation between Ireland and the Netherlands was utterly different.

The Stasi used some of these secondary sources to create information cards on the key players in the Northern Irish conflict. In an undated card created by HA-II (counter-espionage), it was stated that the IRA (no distinction between OIRA and PIRA) was a 'far-left group' which wanted to bring about the reunification of Ireland by terrorist means and 'a few members ... are in West Germany (mainly to buy arms)'. It was also stated that there were no 'far-right groups' in Ireland,[19] but here the Stasi would soon change its mind. It was essentially HA-XXII of course that kept the information on Northern Ireland updated. On 10 April 1984, it produced a chronology of the development of relations between Ireland and England. It was not devoid of mistakes, some rather comical. For instance, in 1366 the Statutes of Kilkenny were implemented in Ireland. These statutes were an attempt by the English to prevent their settlers from going native as they were in contact with Irish culture. The Stasi wrote: 'Contact with Iran is punishable for English people'. There were other such sloppy mistakes in this particular document.[20] They do not drastically affect the reader's understanding of the text but nonetheless coming from a very serious intelligence service with a great reputation for efficiency, they were rather surprising.

HA-XXII had index cards on two unionist groups. The first one was the Orange Order and the second one was the Democratic Unionist Party (DUP) under the leadership of Reverend Ian Paisley and his deputy Peter Robinson. While the Orange Order was described as being 'far-right Protestant', the DUP was 'far-right Protestant with a military orientation'. Both index cards were based on the same source, the *Deutsche Volkszeitung*,[21] which was a left-wing newspaper in West Germany financed by the East Germans.[22] This description, 'military orientation', was too vague and was wrong. In fact, the DUP did not claim to have official contacts with loyalist terrorists.

But the Stasi did not rely on open sources only. It also received information from its own sources and if deemed of value, it was sent to other units in charge of evaluation like the ZAIG. As previously explained, the HVA used to send its most valuable documents accompanied by a summary sheet, which contained details about the information in the document and its evaluation, to SIRA where they were electronically stored. Research for this book produced 160 summary sheets that include the names Ireland and Northern Ireland (recall that the original documents were destroyed but not their summary sheets). Not all the sheets are relevant as some only deal with the island and other Western countries generally speaking. But others do deal with Ireland and Northern Ireland on specific issues. It is worth giving comprehensive tables including the most relevant summary sheets so as to get a good general impression of what the Stasi knew.

A few words (not all) used in the summary sheets need to be explained beforehand. There are five assessment grades: *I* is very valuable, *II* is valuable, *III* is average value, *IV* is low value and *V* is without value. Concerning the sheets for this study, assessments were not systematic. Literally translated, '*Objekt-Hinweis*' means 'object-indication'. In lay terms it means that the contents of the document in question have at least something to do with a particular institution or person.[23] For simplicity's sake, not all German words (Stasi jargon) describing the contents of the summary sheets have been used. 'Note' simply indicates information of interest. The author has used a row of his own entitled 'keywords', that is words that appear in the original summary sheet and that give a general indication of what the original document was about (these original documents having been destroyed). Lastly, it should be noted that possibly the original documents of summary sheet number 4, but definitely of number 7 and number 11 were found in other archival sections of the BStU. There were obviously paper duplicates.

Table 3.5 SIRA summary sheets

Number	1	2	3	4
Reference of doc.	SE7000426	SE6905306	SE6901965	SE7003523
Sender	Registration number of sender: 1815/60	Registration number of sender: 1276/96	Registration number of sender: 1276/69	Registration number of sender: 3580/64
Source	n/a	n/a	n/a	n/a
Unit responsible for recording information	n/a	n/a	n/a	n/a
Number of pages	45	62	1?	46
Confidentiality level	1, very secret file	2, very confidential file	2, very confidential file	2, very confidential file
Entry date	18/09/1969	27/10/1969	29/10/1969	03/12//1969
Creation date	18/09/1969	27/10/1969	29/10/1969	03/12/1969
Keywords	EEC Council ministers; entry of Britain, Ireland, Denmark and Norway	EEC negotiations with Britain, Ireland, Denmark and Norway; agriculture; finance	EEC; entry of Britain, Ireland, Denmark and Norway; agricultural policy	Assessment of Council re entry of Britain, Ireland, Denmark and Norway
Assessment grade	n/a	n/a	n/a	n/a
Title	Report on 79th Council session, 15/09/1969	Opinion of European Commission for Council re Britain's, Ireland's, Denmark's and Norway's application	Opinion of European Commission for Council re Britain's, Ireland's, Denmark's and Norway's application	Opinion of European Commission for Council re Britain's, Ireland's, Denmark's and Norway's application
Object-indication	EEC	EC	EEC	EC
Note	n/a	n/a	n/a	n/a

Source: BStU, Berlin

Table 3.6 SIRA summary sheets

Number	5	6	7	8
Reference of doc.	SE7004929	SE7006387	SE7004899	SE7102956
Sender	Registration number of sender: 1606/68	Registration number of sender: 1606/68	Registration number of sender: 15905/60	HVA-XV [Dept. of Intelligence re Military Technology, Machine Construction and Air and Space]
Source	n/a	n/a	n/a	B, deemed reliable; registration number of source: XV/268/68; code name: 'Loewe' [Löwe]
Unit responsible for recording information	n/a	n/a	n/a	n/a
Number of pages	5	10	1?	31?
Confidentiality level	2, very confidential file	2, very confidential file	2, very confidential file	2, very confidential file
Entry date	01/07/1970	20/07/1970	05/08/1970	09/03/1971
Creation date	01/07/1970	20/07/1970	05/08/1970	01/06/1970
Keywords	EC; entry of Britain, Ireland, Denmark and Norway; industrial cooperation	EC; cooperation in foreign policy and commercial policy; IRA; development in Irish Parliament	Britain and Ireland's relations with West Germany and GDR; German question; recognition of GDR; assessment of East Policy [Willy Brandt's *Ostpolitik*]	Steel business; market analysis; Ireland – the market for BSC [British Steel Corporation] in the 1970 [title in English]

Table 3.6 (Continued)

Number	5	6	7	8
Assessment grade	n/a	n/a	n/a	III, AVERAGE VALUE
Title	Settlement re transitional periods for applicant countries	Report on best way and manner to reach progress re political union in perspective of EC enlargement	Thoughts of West German governmental circles on relations between Britain and Ireland, conclusions to be drawn for relations between West Germany and GDR	n/a
Object-indication	EC, EFTA	EC	n/a	British Steel Corporation (BSC)
Note	n/a	n/a	n/a	Sent to VEB [state-owned enterprise] Spurenmetalle Freiberg for information & to GDR Ministry for Mining, Metallurgy and Potassium in Berlin

Source: BStU, Berlin

Table 3.7 SIRA summary sheets

Number	9	10	11	12
Reference of doc.	SE7102065	SE7202596	SA7202810	SA7202878
Sender	Registration number of sender: 1719/69	HVA-XII (Dept. of Intelligence re NATO and EC)	HVA-II [Dept. of Intelligence re Parties, Organisations and Churches in West Germany]	HVA-XV [Dept. of Intelligence re Military Technology, Machine Construction and Air and Space]
Source	n/a	Registration number of source: XV/5485/60	Registration number of source: XV/750/66	Registration number of source: XV/4829/63
Unit responsible for recording information	n/a	n/a	HVA-VII [Dept. of Evaluation and Information], 'Moritz'	HVA-VII [Dept. of Evaluation and Information], 'Hans'
Number of pages	11	5	n/a	n/a
Confidentiality level	2, very confidential file	2, very confidential file	n/a	n/a
Entry date	18/05/1971	30/03/1972	19/08/1972	23/09/1972
Creation date	18/05/1971	30/03/1972	19/08/1972	23/09/1972
Keywords	EC; entry negotiations re Ireland	Belgium, assessment of crisis in Ireland and Northern Ireland	Energy policy; economic policy; raw materials; oil; Shell	Economic reunification of metal and steel industry in EEC; EC entry of Britain, Norway, Ireland and Denmark
Assessment grade	n/a	n/a	n/a	n/a

Table 3.7 (Continued)

Number	9	10	11	12
Title	EEC document no. 188 entry talks with Ireland	Assessment of development in Northern Ireland by the Belgian Foreign Ministry	Potential and structure of the energy industry of the countries entering the EC; Great Britain, Ireland, Denmark and Norway	Possible effects of EEC enlargement on the metal and steel industry of the Federal Republic of Germany
Object-indication	EC, Commonwealth	n/a	EC	EEC, EC
Note	n/a	n/a	n/a	n/a

Source: BStU, Berlin

Table 3.8 SIRA summary sheets

Number	13	14	15	16
Reference of doc.	SE7203607	SE7211131	SA7300500	SE7301020
Sender	HVA-I [Dept. of Intelligence re West German State]	HVA-XIII [Dept. of Intelligence re Fundamental Research]	HVA-XV [Dept. of Intelligence re Military Technology, Machine Construction and Air and Space]	HVA-I [Dept. of Intelligence re West German State]
Source	Registration number of source: XV/15905/60	Registration number of source: XV/1762/71; code name: 'Fichte'	Registration number of source: 1815/60	Registration number of source XV/15905/60
Unit responsible for recording information	n/a	n/a	HVA-VII [Dept. of Evaluation and Information], 'Lilo'	n/a
Number of pages	33	n/a	n/a	32
Confidentiality level	2, very confidential file	n/a	n/a	2, very confidential file
Entry date	12/10/1972	30/11/1972	15/02/1973	16/02/1973
Creation date	12/10/1972	26/02/1969	15/02/1973	16/02/1973
Keywords	West Germany; assessment of Ireland (opposition) IRA	Pumps; turbines; power station; Pigeon House [Poolbeg Generating Station, Dublin]	EC; differences in cooperation in foreign policy; Great Britain, Denmark, Ireland	West German foreign policy; assessment of Ireland, Catholic Church
Assessment grade	n/a	n/a	n/a	n/a

Table 3.8 (Continued)

Number	13	14	15	16
Title	Information Service of West German Foreign Office	n/a	The first ministerial Council of the enlarged EC and the differences that have appeared re the future functioning of this body	Information Service of West German Foreign Office
Object-indication	n/a	Pigeon House Ireland	EC	n/a
Note	n/a	Sent to power station construction	n/a	n/a

Source: BStU, Berlin

Table 3.9 SIRA summary sheets

Number	17	18	19	20
Reference of doc.	SE7304711	SE7301034	SE7302635	SE7400785
Sender	HVA-III [Dept. of Legally Covered Residences [embassies etc.], except USA and West Germany]	HVA-I [Dept. of Intelligence re West German State]	HVA-I [Dept. of Intelligence re West German State]	Soviet Union
Source	Registration number of source: 1093/67	Registration number of source: XV/15905/60	A, reliable, registration number of source: XV/2091/66	n/a
Unit responsible for recording information	n/a	n/a	n/a	n/a
Number of pages	2	8	7	2
Confidentiality level	2, very confidential file	2, very confidential file	2, very confidential file	2, very confidential
Entry date	10/04/1973	19/04/1973	28/04/1973	25/02/1974
Creation date	10/04/1973	19/04/1973	28/04/1973	25/02/1974
Keywords	Ireland; foreign policy; relations with Socialist countries	West German Foreign Office; assessment of Vatican, Britain and Northern Ireland	Northern Ireland; IRA; British government's crisis plan	Ireland; Britain
Assessment	n/a	n/a	n/a	n/a
Title	Explanations of Irish foreign minister re Ireland's policy towards the Socialist states	State of British relations with the Vatican, end January 1973	Northern Ireland, end February 1973	The Northern Irish problem
Object-indication	n/a	n/a	n/a	n/a
Note	n/a	n/a	n/a	n/a

Source: BStU, Berlin

Table 3.10 SIRA summary sheets

Number	21	22	23	24
Reference of doc.	SE7404963	SE7402606	SE7404315	SE7403954
Sender	HVA-I [Dept. of Intelligence re West German State]	Poland	HVA-I [Dept. of Intelligence re West German State]	HVA-XII [Dept. of Intelligence re NATO and EC]
Source	Registration number of source: XV/15905/60	n/a	Registration number of source: XV/6427/60	Registration number of source: XV/5485/60
Unit responsible for recording information	n/a	n/a	n/a	n/a
Number of pages	13	594	2	4
Confidentiality level	2, very confidential file	2, very confidential file	1, very secret file	2, very confidential file
Entry date	19/04/1974	10/05/1974	02/08/1974	20/08/1974
Creation date	19/04/1974	10/05/1974	02/08/1974	20/08/1974
Keywords	British economy and external trade; West Germany; Ireland; Northern Ireland	Assessment of EC's agricultural policy; production of meat, entry Britain Denmark and Ireland	Britain; secret service; Ireland; Northern Ireland; Greece; arms delivery	Britain; Ireland; Northern Ireland; domestic policy agreement
Assessment grade	n/a	n/a	n/a	n/a
Title	Great Britain's economic policy	The common beef and veal market [original title in English]	Northern Ireland, Federal Republic of Germany	Belgian assessment of situation in Northern Ireland
Object-indication	EC, Bundesverband der Deutschen Industrie (BDI)	EC	n/a	n/a
Note	n/a	n/a	n/a	n/a

Source: BStU, Berlin

Table 3.11 SIRA summary sheets

Number	25	26	27	28
Reference of doc.	SE7502079	SE7500281	SE7502394	SE7502316
Sender	n/a	HVA-XII [Dept. of Intelligence re NATO and EC]	HVA-XV [Dept. of Intelligence re Military Technology, Machine Construction and Air and Space]	HVA-XII [Dept. of Intelligence re NATO and EC]
Source	Registration number of source: XV/92/67	Registration number of source: XV/5485/60	Registration number of source: XV/483/68	Registration number of source: XV/5485/60
Unit responsible for recording information	n/a	n/a	n/a	n/a
Number of pages	15	6	49	5
Confidentiality level	2, very confidential file	2, very confidential file	2, very confidential file	2, very confidential file
Entry date	15/04/1975	17/04/1975	07/07/1975	08/1975
Creation date	15/04/1975	17/04/1975	07/07/1975	08/1975
Keywords	Aviation industry; development of project; financing; Shorts/Belfast	Ireland; domestic policy; party in government; foreign policy; relations with EC; attitude towards détente policy; negotiations with Britain	Ireland; population; economy; government; parliament; military policy; army; air force; civil defence	Britain; Ireland; Northern Ireland; elections; government

Table 3.11 (Continued)

Number	25	26	27	28
Assessment grade	n/a	n/a	n/a	n/a
Title	Development of an economical short-distance plane-Shorts/ Belfast project	Belgian assessment of Ireland's policy in 1974	Report on the situation in the West, special issue Ireland 1975	Belgian assessment of the Northern Ireland Constitutional Convention elections
Object-indication	n/a	EC	n/a	n/a
Note	n/a	n/a	n/a	n/a

Source: BStU, Berlin

Table 3.12 SIRA summary sheets

Number	29	30	31	32
Reference of doc.	SE7502709	SE7504697	SE7503281	SE7602793
Sender	HVA-I [Dept. of Intelligence re West German State]	HVA-XV [Dept. of Intelligence re Military Technology, Machine Construction and Air and Space]	HVA-I [Dept. of Intelligence re West German State]	HVA-I [Dept. of Intelligence re West German State]
Source	Registration number of source: XV/15905/60	Registration number of source: XV/92/67	Registration number of source: 13864/60	Registration number of source: XV/2091/66
Unit responsible for recording information	n/a	n/a	n/a	n/a
Number of pages	7	7	28	6
Confidentiality level	1, very secret file	2, very confidential file	1, very secret file	2, very confidential file
Entry date	22/09/1975	10/10/1975	06/11/1975	01/12/1975
Creation date	22/09/1975	10/10/1975	06/11/1975	01/12/1975
Keywords	EC; West Germany; Ireland, NATO measures; Middle-East policy	Ireland; European Investment Bank; telecommunications project	European political cooperation; MBFR [Mutual and Balanced Force Reductions] troop reductions; NATO; Warsaw Pact; Ireland; France	Ireland's presidency of EC Council of Ministers; West German assessment December 1975; economic political cooperation
Assessment grade	n/a	n/a	n/a	n/a

Table 3.12 (Continued)

Number	29	30	31	32
Title	Political assessment of Ireland's presidency in the EC during the first semester of 1975	Construction of telephone installations in Ireland	Western MBFR consultations	Ireland as a member of the EC, beginning December 1975
Object-indication	EEC, United Nations Organisation (UNO), NATO, European Parliament	European Investment Bank (EIB)	NATO, Warsaw Pact	EC, European Parliament
Note	n/a	n/a	n/a	n/a

Source: BStU, Berlin

Table 3.13 SIRA summary sheets

Number	33	34	35	36
Reference of doc.	SE7602313	SE7602310	SE7602307	SE7604786
Sender	HVA-SWT (technology and science sector)	HVA-I [Dept. of Intelligence re West German State]	HVA-SWT (technology and science sector)	HVA-XV [Dept. of Intelligence re Military Technology, Machine Construction and Air and Space]
Source	Registration number of source: XV/268/68	Registration number of source: 13864/60	Registration number of source: XV/268/68	Registration number of source: XV/268/68; code name: 'Loewe' [Löwe]
Unit responsible for recording information	n/a	n/a	n/a	n/a
Number of pages	18	18	20	n/a
Confidentiality level	2, very confidential file	1, very secret file	2, very confidential file	n/a
Entry date	27/02/1976	11/03/1976	24/03/1976	04/1976
Creation date	27/02/1976	11/03/1976	24/03/1976	n/a
Keywords	British economy; iron and steel industry; relations with Ireland; BSC [British Steel Corporation]	Ireland; domestic economic policy; security; terror; relations with EC, NATO, UN, West Germany, USSR, Czechoslovakia, GDR; Prime Minister Cosgrave	Iron and steel industry; BSC [British Steel Corporation]; external trade	Ireland; assessment of steel market

Table 3.13 (Continued)

Number	33	34	35	36
Assessment grade	n/a	n/a	n/a	n/a
Title	BSC London – commercial relations with the Republic of Ireland	Annual political report, 1975, Ireland	Assessment of the steel market of Northern Ireland and the Republic of Ireland and BSC export possibilities	n/a
Object-indication	n/a	EC, NATO, United Nations Organization (UNO)	n/a	n/a
Note	n/a	n/a	n/a	Sent to Metallurgy Business of the GDR, Berlin for information & to GDR Ministry for Mining, Metallurgy and Potassium in Berlin

Source: BStU, Berlin

Table 3.14 SIRA summary sheets

Number	37	38	39	40
Reference of doc.	SE7602762	SE7606095	SE7604050	SE7701349
Sender	HVA-XII [Dept. of Intelligence re NATO and EC]	Soviet Union	Hungary	HVA-I [Dept. of Intelligence re West German State]
Source	Registration number of source: XV/4705/63	n/a	n/a	A, reliable, registration number of source: XV/2227/73
Unit responsible for recording information	n/a	n/a	n/a	n/a
Number of pages	3	2	1	9
Confidentiality level	2, very confidential file	2, very confidential file	2, very confidential file	1, very secret file
Entry date	25/05/1976	02/11/1976	19/11/1976	17/02/1977
Creation date	25/05/1976	02/11/1976	19/11/1976	17/02/1977
Keywords	Ireland; Communist Party; Maoism	Ireland; domestic policy; Maoism; relations with China and Palestine	Socialist International; Ireland's entry; Social Democracy	EC; fishery policy; Northern Ireland; relations re West Germany and Ireland
Assessment grade	n/a	n/a	n/a	n/a
Title	Details for assessment of British and Irish Communist organisation	About the Irish party Sinn Féin	Meeting of bureau of the Socialist International on 23/10/1976	Relations between the Federal Republic of Germany and Ireland in relation with Irish President Hillery's visit to the Federal Republic of Germany from 06/02 until 11/02/1977
Object-indication	n/a	n/a	Socialist International (SI) Conference	EC
Note	n/a	n/a	n/a	n/a

Source: BStU, Berlin

Table 3.15 SIRA summary sheets

Number	41	42	43	44
Reference of doc.	SE7800848	SE7802355	SE7807329	SE7820896
Sender	HVA-XIII [Dept. of Intelligence re Fundamental Research]	HVA-III [Dept. of Legally Covered Residences [embassies etc.], except USA and West Germany]	Soviet Union	HVA-II [Dept. of Intelligence re Parties, Organisations and Churches in West Germany]
Source	B, deemed reliable, registration number of source: XV/4070/70	Registration number of source: 452/68	n/a	A, reliable, registration number of source: XV/2873/62
Unit responsible for recording information	n/a	n/a	n/a	n/a
Number of pages	15	3	2	9
Confidentiality level	2, very confidential file	2, very confidential file	2, very confidential file	2, very confidential file
Entry date	06/02/1978	21/03/1978	27/04/1978	09/1978
Creation date	06/02/1978	21/03/1978	27/04/1978	09/1978

Table 3.15 (Continued)

Number	41	42	43	44
Keywords	Economy; market analysis; chemical industry; raw material supply; manufacture of xylol in Britain, Ireland and the Netherlands, ammonia and xylol capacity of selected countries	Foreign policy; diplomacy; government; regarding establishment of diplomatic relations between the GDR and Ireland	Regarding the discovery of uranium deposits in Ireland	Liberal Party; contact; Report from [name blacked out] on activities of the Liberals in Ireland and Spain
Assessment grade	III, AVERAGE VALUE	III, AVERAGE VALUE	IV, LOW VALUE	III, AVERAGE VALUE
Title	n/a	n/a	n/a	n/a
Object-indication	EC	n/a	n/a	EC, Freie Demokratische Partei (FDP), European People's Party (EPP), Federation of Liberal and Democratic Parties in Europe, Friedrich Naumann Stiftung (FNS, West German Liberal think-tank)
Note	n/a	n/a	n/a	n/a

Source: BStU, Berlin

Table 3.16 SIRA summary sheets

Number	45	46	47	48
Reference of doc.	SE7903366	SE7906772	SE8004167	SE8022011
Sender	HVA-SWT [Science and Technology Sector]	HVA-I [Dept. of Intelligence re West German State]	HVA-III [Dept. of Legally Covered Residences [embassies etc.], except USA and West Germany]	n/a
Source	Registration number of source: XV/167/71; code name: 'Max'	A, reliable, registration number of source: XV/15905/60	A, reliable, registration number of source: XV/2962/78	n/a
Unit responsible for recording information	n/a	n/a	n/a	n/a
Number of pages	n/a	15	2	59
Confidentiality level	n/a	2, very confidential file	2, very confidential file	n/a
Entry date	28/03/1979	05/09/1979	23/06/1980	n/a
Creation date	n/a	05/09/1979	30/05/1980	n/a
Keywords	Ireland; electrical engineering; electronics; process control; propulsion	Terrorism; Conservative Party; IRA; Northern Ireland	Ireland; Northern Ireland; foreign policy; security; defence; army; Ireland's security and defence policy	Ideas of American Republican Party re foreign policy; Northern Ireland conflict

Table 3.16 (Continued)

Number	45	46	47	48
Assessment grade	n/a	III, AVERAGE VALUE	n/a	I, VERY VALUABLE [the document was assessed on 18/11/1980]
Title	n/a	n/a	n/a	n/a
Object-indication	n/a	n/a	NATO, EC	United Nations Organization (UNO), EC, Organization of the Petroleum Exporting Countries (OPEC)
Note	n/a	n/a	Sent to Soviet Union	Sent to Soviet Union

Source: BStU, Berlin

Table 3.17 SIRA summary sheets

Number	49	50	51	52
Reference of doc.	SE8100342	SE8103823	SE8104761	SE8105606
Sender	FFO [Frankfurt an der Oder], XV	HVA-XI [Dept. of Intelligence re North America and American Institutions in West Germany]	Soviet Union	HVA-I [Dept. of Intelligence re West German State]
Source	A, reliable; registration number of source: MfS/990/60; code name: 'Claus'	A, reliable, registration number of source XV/2171/73; code name: 'Weser'; GDR embassy in USA	n/a	A, reliable; registration number of source: XV/15905/60; code name: 'Adler'
Unit responsible for recording information	n/a	n/a	n/a	n/a
Number of pages	51	1	1	11
Confidentiality level	2, very confidential file	2, very confidential file	2, very confidential file	1, very secret file
Entry date	19/02/1981	25/05/1981	29/06/1981	21/07/1981
Creation date	26/01/1981	01/04/1981	06/06/1981	02/07/1981

Table 3.17 (Continued)

Number	49	50	51	52
Keywords	Economy; industry; investment; government; BDI [Bundesverband der Deutschen Industrie, Federal Association of German Industry, Cologne]; regarding studies of a BDI delegation into investment climate and the possibilities of industrial cooperation in Britain, Wales and Northern Ireland	Ireland;, Northern Ireland; Northern Ireland and US interests	Foreign policy; Margaret Thatcher; Charles Haughey; regarding the events in Northern Ireland	Northern Ireland; State; terror; Bobby Sands; IRA
Assessment grade	III, AVERAGE VALUE	III, AVERAGE VALUE	III, AVERAGE VALUE	III, AVERAGE VALUE
Title	n/a	n/a	n/a	n/a
Object-indication	BDI	n/a	n/a	n/a
Note	n/a	Sent to Soviet Union	n/a	Sent to Soviet Union

Source: BStU, Berlin

Table 3.18 SIRA summary sheets

Number	53	54	55	56
Reference of doc.	SE8122917	SE8201659	SE8201660	SE8203395
Sender	Soviet Union	Soviet Union	Soviet Union	HVA-III [Dept. of Legally Covered Residences [embassies etc.], except USA and West Germany]
Source	n/a	n/a	n/a	A, reliable; registration number of source: XV/175/75; code name: 'Eckart'; GDR embassy in Britain
Unit responsible for recording information	n/a	n/a	n/a	n/a
Number of pages	1	2	1	2
Confidentiality level	2, very confidential file	2, very confidential file	2, very confidential file	2, very confidential file
Entry date	15/12/1981	14/04/1982	14/04/1982	04/06/1982
Creation date	25/11/1981	17/03/1982	25/03/1982	04/05/1982
Keywords	Ireland; foreign policy; Regarding the relations between Britain and Ireland	Ireland; domestic policy; regarding the increasing popularity of Sinn Féin/the Workers' Party in Ireland	Ireland; government; foreign policy; regarding the foreign policy orientation of the new Irish government	Ireland; Northern Ireland; domestic politics; population; Catholic Church; armed forces; economy; terror; foreign policy; information regarding Northern Ireland, problems and perspectives
Assessment grade	III, AVERAGE VALUE	III, AVERAGE VALUE	IV, LOW VALUE	III, AVERAGE VALUE
Title	n/a	n/a	n/a	n/a
Object-indication	NATO, EC	n/a	EC	n/a
Note	n/a	n/a	n/a	Sent to Soviet Union

Source: BStU, Berlin

Table 3.19 SIRA summary sheets

Number	57	58	59	60
Reference of doc.	SE8203387	SE8205302	SE8224600	SE8303073
Sender	Soviet Union	HVA-III [Dept. of Legally Covered Residences [embassies etc.], except USA and West Germany]	Czechoslovakia	HVA-II [Dept. of Intelligence re Parties, Organisations and Churches in West Germany]
Source	n/a	A, reliable; registration number of source: XV/308/71; code name: ‘Norbert’; GDR embassy in India	n/a	A, reliable; registration number of source: XV/281/70; code name: ‘Dorn’
Unit responsible for recording information	n/a	n/a	n/a	n/a
Number of pages	2	3	4	1
Confidentiality level	2, very confidential file	1, very secret file	2, very confidential file	2, very confidential file
Entry date	04/06/1982	06/08/1982	11/02/1983	18/05/1983
Creation date	12/05/1982	29/06/1982	20/12/1982	01/04/1983

Table 3.19 (Continued)

Number	57	58	59	60
Keywords	Ireland; domestic politics; Communist Party; conference; regarding the conference of Sinn Féin/the Workers' Party	India; Indian evaluation of West Germany's, Ireland's and the EC's domestic and foreign policies	Ireland; Northern Ireland; NATO; regarding the Northern Irish issue, 25/11/1982	Ireland; foreign policy; domestic politics; industry; information of the West German embassy in Ireland dated 15/03/1983 re the annual conference of the Confederation of Irish Industry on 17/02/1983
Assessment grade	IV, LOW VALUE	III, AVERAGE VALUE	III, AVERAGE VALUE	III, AVERAGE VALUE
Title	n/a	n/a	n/a	n/a
Object-indication	n/a		NATO	n/a
Note	n/a	Sent to Soviet Union	n/a	Sent to Soviet Union

Source: BStU, Berlin

Table 3.20 SIRA summary sheets

Number	61	62	63	64
Reference of doc.	SE8307022	SE8332468	SE8404051	SE8404055
Sender	KMS [Karl Marx Stadt], nowadays Chemnitz], XV	Soviet Union	HVA-I [Dept. of Intelligence re West German State]	HVA-I [Dept. of Intelligence re West German State]
Source	A, reliable; registration number of source: XV/92/67; code name: 'Bettina'	n/a	A, reliable; registration number of source: XV/872/74; code name: 'Cello'; GDR representation in West Germany	A, reliable; registration number of source: XV/988/75; code name: 'Alfons'; GDR representation in West Germany
Unit responsible for recording information	n/a	n/a	n/a	n/a
Number of pages	6	2	4	4
Confidentiality level	2, very confidential file	2, very confidential file	2, very confidential file	2, very confidential file
Entry date	25/10/1983	09/01/1984	26/06/1984	11/07/1984
Creation date	01/07/1983	30/11/1983	05/06/1984	06/06/1984
Keywords	Extension of telephone network in Ireland	Regarding the talks between the prime ministers of Britain and Ireland	Ireland; Ronald Reagan; East–West relations; British attitudes to the	Security policy, foreign policy; East–West relations; regarding attitudes

Table 3.20 (Continued)

Number	61	62	63	64
			relations between the GDR and West Germany; regarding Reagan's behaviour in Ireland	of the CDU/ CSU [West German Christian Democrats] parliamentary leadership about Reagan's behaviour in Ireland and problems of permanent West German representation in the GDR
Assessment grade	IV, LOW VALUE	IV, LOW VALUE	III, AVERAGE VALUE	III, AVERAGE VALUE
Title	n/a	n/a	n/a	n/a
Object-indication	n/a	n/a	Western European Union (WEU)	CDU/CSU (Christian Democratic Union/ Christian Social Union)
Note	n/a	n/a	Sent to Soviet Union	Sent to Soviet Union

Source: BStU, Berlin

Table 3.21 SIRA summary sheets

Number	65	66	67	68
Reference of doc.	SE8431489	SE8432622	SE8502790	SE8531175
Sender	Soviet Union	Soviet Union	HVA-III [Dept. of Legally Covered Residences [embassies etc.], except USA and West Germany]	Soviet Union
Source	n/a	n/a	A, reliable; registration number of source: XV/1619/75; code name: 'Herbert'; GDR embassy in Sweden	n/a
Unit responsible for recording information	n/a	n/a	n/a	n/a
Number of pages	2	2	3	2
Confidentiality level	2, very confidential file	2, very confidential file	2, very confidential file	2, very confidential file
Entry date	08/08/1984	20/12/1984	18/04/1985	01/07/1985
Creation date	01/06/1984	01/11/1984	01/03/1985	01/06/1985

Table 3.21 (Continued)

Number	65	66	67	68
Keywords	Northern Ireland; Ireland; Britain; USA; conflict; differences; regarding some aspects of the Northern Irish problem	Ireland; Britain; foreign policy; regarding the results of the talks between the British and Irish heads of government	Ireland; France; foreign policy; East–West relations; Conference on Security and Cooperation in Europe (CSCE); regarding Irish and French positions at the Stockholm conference	Military cooperation; military strategy; northern flank; cooperation; NATO; regarding the activation of the military cooperation between the USA and Ireland
Assessment grade	III, AVERAGE VALUE	III, AVERAGE VALUE	III, AVERAGE VALUE	III, AVERAGE VALUE
Title	n/a	n/a	n/a	n/a
Object-indication	n/a	n/a	n/a	NATO
Note	n/a	n/a	Sent to Soviet Union	n/a

Source: BStU, Berlin

Table 3.22 SIRA summary sheets

Number	69	70	71	72
Reference of doc.	SA8572839	SE8601309	SE8690154	SE8730169
Sender	n/a	BLN [Berlin], XV	BLN [Berlin], XV	Soviet Union
Source	n/a	A, reliable; registration number of source: XV/2848/76; code name: 'Karl'	n/a	n/a
Unit responsible for recording information	HVA-VII [Dept. of Evaluation and Information], 'Sascha'	n/a	n/a	n/a
Number of pages	1	9	2	2
Confidentiality level	n/a	2, very confidential file	2, very confidential file	2, very confidential file
Entry date	20/12/1985	03/04/1986	13/06/1986	07/03/1987
Creation date	09/12/1985	01/02/1986	01/05/1986	01/02/1987
Keywords	Ireland; Northern Ireland; Britain; foreign policy; conflict settlement; agreement; regarding Anglo-Irish Agreement on Northern Ireland	Armed forces; nuclear weapons; telecommunications; regarding findings about military situation in Scotland, Northern Ireland and the Republic of Ireland	Ireland; domestic politics; armed forces; police; regime; police and military situation in Ireland	Ireland; domestic politics; government; crisis; regarding the government crisis in Ireland
Assessment grade	n/a	III, AVERAGE VALUE	n/a	III, AVERAGE VALUE
Title	n/a	n/a	n/a	n/a
Object-indication	n/a	n/a	n/a	n/a
Note	Sent to MfAA [GDR Ministry of External Affairs]	Sent to Soviet Union	n/a	n/a

Source: BStU, Berlin

Table 3.23 SIRA summary sheets

Number	73	74	75	76
Reference of doc.	SE8730755	SE8731602	SE8708873	SE8911173
Sender	Soviet Union	Soviet Union	NBG [Neubrandenburg], XV	HVA-VI [Dept. of Operational Tourist Traffic and 'Regime Issues']
Source	n/a	n/a	A, reliable; registration number of source: XV/6430/82; code name: 'Rosenberg'	A, reliable; registration number of source: XV/1586/87; code name: 'Aribert'; GDR embassy in Austria
Unit responsible for recording information	n/a	n/a	n/a	n/a
Number of pages	2	2	25	1
Confidentiality level	2, very confidential file	2, very confidential file	2, very confidential file	4, only for service use & open
Entry date	04/06/1987	07/11/1987	09/12/1987	19/05/1989
Creation date	01/05/1987	10/1987	11/1987	1989
Keywords	Ireland; United States; foreign policy; government; economy;	Ireland; United States; foreign policy; relations; cooperation;	Ireland; conjuncture; economy; main problem; regarding	Ireland; Austria; social contribution; cooperation; agreement

Table 3.23 (Continued)

Number	73	74	75	76
	East–West relations; regarding some aspects of the foreign policy orientation of the new Irish government	regarding the activities of the Americans in Northern Ireland	conjuncture analysis of Ireland in September 1987	on social security between Austria and Ireland
Assessment grade	III, AVERAGE VALUE	II, VALUABLE	n/a	III, AVERAGE VALUE
Title	n/a	n/a	n/a	n/a
Object-indication	EC	n/a	n/a	n/a
Note	n/a	n/a	n/a	n/a

Source: BStU, Berlin

After reading these 160 summary sheets, including in particular the 76 mentioned above in the SIRA tables, the following observations can be made. To begin with, who were hiding behind the code names and registration numbers of sources? The Stasi took all the necessary precautions to guarantee the protection of its officers, agents and sources. Two brief examples will suffice to illustrate this. Gabriele Gast, a high-ranking civil servant of the BND (the West German federal intelligence agency for threats from abroad), was working for the HVA. To protect this highly valuable source, the HVA gave her three code names, 'Gisela', 'Gerald' and 'Reinhard' to be used in different circumstances (Gisela being a female name, Gerald and Reinhard being male). Another important source was 'Friedrich'. At first sight, this code name would indicate a person, probably a man as it is a first name (Frederick in English). In fact, 'Friedrich' referred to information that was processed by HA-III (in charge of radio and telecommunications intelligence).[24]

However, research in the index-card systems (F16 and F22) of the HVA has made it possible to identify several individuals, but not all of them. 'Aribert', registration number XV/1586/87, was Rainer Frey. His file and index card indicate that he came from a working-class background, had served with distinction in the National People's Army (NVA) before he joined the HVA. He was also a member of the SED. He practised martial arts and was an OibE (*Offizier im besonderen Einsatz*; officer for special missions). Nothing indicates in the surviving documents of his file that he took a special interest in Ireland.[25] Frey worked for HVA section VI/A/2, responsible for preparing IMs (*inoffiziellen Mitarbeiter*, unofficial collaborators, or informers) to live in an operational area.[26] 'Weber', registration number XV/1508/75, but also XV/1093/62, was Siegfried Reichelt. He was a qualified engineer who had studied in Moscow. He was fluent in German, Czech, Russian and English.[27] Reichelt was at some point in time a member of HVA, SWT/AG1, a section that occasionally trained agents who would pose as scientific attachés working in the official residences of the GDR abroad (embassies, consulates etc.).[28]

'Schneider', registration number XV/192/73, was Hans Weber. Nothing much is known. He was born in Czechoslovakia during the war.[29] Like Reichelt, he worked for HVA SWT/AG1.[30] In contrast, much more is known about 'Anna', registration number XV/2873/62, who was very much a star agent in the HVA. She operated under the name Sonja Lüneburg, but her real name was Johanna Olbrich, born in Berlin.[31] Olbrich had been recruited in May 1962 and worked for HVA II/2 which targeted liberal and national groups in West Germany, especially the Freie Demokratische Partei (FDP, free democratic party, liberals). First, she became the secretary of an FDP Member of Parliament in the Bundestag, then secretary of the General-Secretary of the FDP and eventually she made it to secretary of the FDP Federal Minister of the Economy, Martin Bangemann.[32] This explains why she got information on Irish liberals in 1978 (see Table 3.15, summary sheet no. 44).

'Inge', registration number XV/2227/73, was Dagmar Kahlig-Scheffler.[33] She was a member of HVA I/3 which targeted the Foreign Office in Bonn, diplomats and the Bundesinstitut für ostwissenschaftliche und internationale Studien (federal institute for Eastern academic and international studies, BIOst). BIOst was based in Cologne and did research on the Soviet Union, Eastern Europe and China. Kahlig-Scheffler was a secretary in the chancellor's office. Between January 1976 and May 1977 she provided East Berlin with twenty-nine documents regarding, among others, persons working in the office, West Germany's preparations for the Conference on Security and Cooperation in Europe (CSCE) in Belgrade and information on the relationship between Chancellor Helmut Schmidt and US President Jimmy Carter. Her spying activities were short-lived as she was arrested in 1977.[34] Within this international context, it was not surprising that she obtained a document on the bilateral relations between West Germany and Ireland, the situation in Northern Ireland and the president of Ireland's forthcoming visit to West Germany (see Table 3.14, summary sheet no. 40).

Secretaries seemed to be a profession that the Western German security services needed to keep an eye on. 'Komtess', registration number XV/2091/66, was Helge Berger.[35] Berger had trained as a multilingual secretary in Paris when she was recruited by a so-called 'Romeo agent' in 1966. 'Romeo agents' were East German agents who targeted single or lonely women. Berger met one of them who posed as a British MI6 agent. The result was that she became a very important source of information for the HVA, notably in her postings in Paris, Warsaw and the Foreign Office in Bonn. She was eventually arrested in 1976, betrayed by a defector.[36] In his memoirs, Markus Wolf devoted a chapter to his 'Romeo agents' and wrote: 'When it began, I had no idea of the harvest it would bring for us. As far as I was concerned, it was the one instrument among many available to a cash-strapped and inexperienced intelligence service. The historical precedents were, however, promising.' Wolf mentioned that one great location for the HVA was the Alliance française in Paris: 'This establishment was a favourite recruiting ground for us, known as the secretaries' sandpit because [West German] government employees were sent there to learn

French'. 'Herbert' was sent to the city of love, met 'the nineteen-year-old Gerda' and performed wonders.[37] Indeed.

The next agent was perhaps the most unexpected. 'Walter', registration number XV/750/66, was Paul Gerhard Flämig. Flämig was a social-democratic Member of Parliament in the Bundestag. His index card and an additional document indicate that his recruitment by the HVA occurred in East Germany in 1967 and that he joined 'out of ideological reasons'.[38] Flämig worked for HVA II, which took a close interest in political parties, youth organisations and political associations in West Germany.[39] Besides being a member of the Bundestag, he was a member of the European Parliament and was involved in scientific and technological committees.[40] The document that he had transmitted to East Berlin in 1972 concerned energy policy and structure and included the names North Sea, Copenhagen, Western Europe, Norway, Great Britain and Ireland. It emanated from the European Parliament.[41]

The identity of 'Bettina', registration number XV/92/67, could not be established. The index card indicates that the person worked for BV Karl-Marx-Stadt (nowadays Chemnitz) XV and that he/she joined the HVA in February 1967.[42] BV stands for *Bezirksverwaltung*, a regional administrative unit of the Stasi which had responsibility for operations in a particular area in West Germany or West Berlin. This BV was responsible for gathering intelligence in the federal State of Nordrhein-Westfalen, especially the Rhineland area and Bonn. For example, it targeted the Ministry of the Interior, the Foreign Office School and the University of Bielefeld, but also the department of telecommunications of the Bundeswehr, the West German army.[43] This very likely explains where 'Bettina' laid his/her hands on a plan for the extension of the Irish telephone network in 1983 (see Table 3.20, summary no. 61). Incidentally, it can also be logically inferred from this that the West Germans had obtained the plan first. Edgar Uher, a former diplomat and HVA officer in the East German embassy in London, told this author:

> I remember that in '83 I brought a telephone directory back from Ireland which, as it was an original document and not yet in the files, was marked with a I (original not known, yet document of value). It was something that really made me laugh at the time as other material of much more interest got only II or III (there had been a school marking system for information obtained). It happened that I got a V (worst) for some pretty interesting stuff, but stuff not wanted, not demanded.[44]

Clearly, the HVA wanted to have the full picture of Ireland for some particular reason.

It is intriguing though that the HVA took an interest in Ireland's telephone network system in 1975 and in 1983 (see Table 3.12 and 3.20, summary sheets nos. 30 and 61 respectively). That an intelligence agency was eager to learn more about foreign technology goes without saying. It is also true that the East German authorities had decided in 1971 to partially restore the telephone links between East and West Berlin which had been severed for nineteen years, and that an automatic dialling system had been put in place between West Berlin and the GDR the year after.[45] Were they looking for some affordable technology? In this case it is very hard to see how East Germany could have benefited from Irish know-how. Indeed, the telephone system on the island was seriously outdated. In the 1960s, many phones dated from before the Second World War and only the well-off had them. It was not until the end of the 1980s that Ireland would eventually get a modern telephone system.[46]

Like 'Bettina', 'Hans Rosenberg', registration number XV/6430/82, also worked for a *Bezirksverwaltung*, BV Neubrandenburg XV. The index card is not very informative and the person's identity cannot be established.[47] This particular regional administrative unit was in charge of targeting institutions in the federal State of Schleswig-Holstein and West Berlin among others. It also targeted the trusteeship of inner-German trade relations.[48] This economic aspect might help to explain why 'Hans Rosenberg' had obtained a document on Ireland's economic conjuncture in 1987 (see Table 3.23, summary sheet no. 75). 'Korb', registration number XV/367/73, remains unidentified.[49] The individual worked for HVA XV/4 which targeted West German industries and banks, notably the Bundesvereinigung der Deutschen Industrie (BDI, federation of German industry).[50] This is the explanation why 'Korb' got a document from the BDI in 1979, dealing with the Western European transport system and road network in which Ireland was mentioned.[51] Interestingly 'Korb's' index card shows that he/she had been recruited in April 1973 and that his/her file was consulted by Stasi officer Werner Teske in September 1974. Teske was a member of the HVA but was not satisfied with his position within the Stasi. He kept secret material at home in order to possibly offer it to Western intelligence services. But it never came to that. After the successful defection of HVA member Werner Stiller to West Germany in 1979, the Stasi became suspicious of Teske and found the material he had taken home. Consequently, he was secretly sentenced to death and shot in the back of the neck in 1981. He was the last East German citizen to be executed.[52]

The identity of 'Max', registration number XV/167/71, could not be established.[53] It is known that he/she worked for HVA SWT/AG3, which was in charge of obtaining plans regarding military and encoding techniques although plans of a more general scientific nature were also sought notably in the field of electronics.[54] So it was that in 1979 'Max' obtained information on electrical engineering and electronics in Ireland (see Table 3.16, summary sheet no. 45). This individual must have been quite successful as he/she was due to be decorated by the Stasi with the medal of honour on the 40th anniversary of the GDR in October 1989. 'Herbert', registration number 1619/75, was recruited in 1975 and little else is known.[55] He/she was active in HVA III/A/2, which was in charge of the operational areas in Austria, Switzerland, Denmark, Norway, Sweden, Finland, Portugal and Spain.[56] 'Herbert' managed to obtain a document outlining the Irish and French positions at the Stockholm Conference of Confidence and Security Building Measures in 1985 (see Table 3.21, summary sheet no. 67). This conference was a follow-up to the Conference on Security and Cooperation in Europe (CSCE) which had taken place in Helsinki between 1973 and 1975.

'Karl', registration number XV/2848/76, remains nameless as well but it is known that he/she was a member of BV Berlin XV,[57] which targeted an impressive number of institutions in West Berlin like the Senate and the political parties, but also Western intelligence agencies and Allied political and military departments and offices.[58] That was why 'Karl' obtained information on the military situation in Ireland and Northern Ireland in 1986 (see Table 3.22, summary sheet no. 70). Also a member of BV Berlin XV was Inge Wucyna, alias 'Jutta', registration number XV/1815/60.[59] Wucyna was an employee in the finance department in the Senate of West Berlin and was a very productive agent.[60] In 1969, she obtained a report regarding the 79th EEC Council session about Ireland, Britain, Denmark and Norway's demand for EEC membership, and in 1973 another report on the first ministerial council of the enlarged European Community (EC) (see Tables 3.5 and 3.8, summary sheets nos. 1 and 15).

Who was 'Ahmed', registration number XV/2962/78? His/her index card is not particularly informative.[61] However, the following is known. According to Helmut Müller-Enbergs's research on the HVA, 'Ahmed' worked for HVA III/B/1, which looked after operations in the Middle East, including the Palestinian Liberation Organization (PLO). This individual was based in the East German embassy in Syria and was phenomenally productive. Between 1978 and 1989, his/her intelligence work produced no fewer than 2,022 pieces of information, 84 of which were very highly rated by East Berlin. 'Ahmed' also had access to certain circles in the West German Foreign Office in Bonn and to certain circles in the PLO.[62] It would seem that his/her information on Northern Ireland and Ireland's security and defence policy, which he/she obtained in 1980, came from NATO and the EC (see Table 3.16, summary sheet no. 47). 'Weser', registration number XV/2171/73,[63] worked for HVA XI, which targeted North America and US institutions in West Germany. He/she was an agent based in the East German embassy in Washington. In 1981, 'Weser' obtained information on Ireland and Northern Ireland in the United States and on US interests in Northern Ireland. The information was then transmitted to the Soviet Union (see Table 3.17, summary sheet no. 50). Incidentally, from 1980 onwards the KGB received approximately 250,000 pieces of information contained in the SIRA computing system.[64] Victor Cherkashin, a former KGB officer, describes the Stasi as 'consummate professionals, planning and executing [its] operations scrupulously'. According to him, of all the allied intelligence services of the KGB, 'the Stasi provided by far the best cooperation'.[65]

The agent hiding behind registration number XV/6427/60 (see Table 3.10, summary sheet no. 23) was Hagen Blau alias 'Merten'. His HVA index cards show that he had been recruited on 31 December 1959 when he was a young student in West Berlin and a member of the West German Social Democratic Party (SPD). Like 'Karl' he worked for BV Berlin XV.[66] But these were Blau's early days. In fact, he became a major asset for the HVA. His first code name had been 'Detlev', registration number XV/1507/59. Blau was a particularly successful agent and was managed by Lieutenant-General Werner Großmann, Markus Wolf's successor, no less. He was a civil servant in the Foreign Office and was very much au fait with Bonn's foreign policy. Blau had been trained to use a small camera, which had the size and look of a cigarette case, to take photographs of documents. In November 1971, he was transferred to the West German embassy in London where he would stay until 1975. He was extremely knowledgeable in the United Kingdom's negotiations to accede to the EC so much so that he was called 'Mr Europe' by his colleagues. Wolf was much impressed by Blau's activities and during the spy's time in London, the spymaster managed to meet him personally somewhere near East Berlin.[67] Blau's posting as a West German diplomat in Britain explains why he was able to send the HVA in August 1974 what looked to be a most interesting file containing the words 'Britain, secret service, Ireland, Northern Ireland, Greece and arms delivery'. Unfortunately, nothing more is known.

Another major asset for the HVA was Ludwig Pauli, registration number MfS 15905/60, code name 'Adler' (see Tables 3.6, 3.8–3.10, 3.12 and 3.16–3.17, summary sheets nos. 7, 13, 16, 18, 21, 29, 46 and 52). Like Blau, Pauli was a diplomat in the Foreign Office in Bonn. That the East Germans were most interested in targeting that particular institution was very obvious. Spies and sources within the Foreign Office would enable East Berlin to have more information on Bonn's foreign policy in the world and also information on West Germany generally speaking. In May 1978, Pauli was appointed to the West German consulate in Liverpool where he would stay until 1983.[68] From there, he sent two reports to the HVA regarding 'terrorism, the Conservative Party, the IRA and Northern Ireland' on 5 September 1979 and 'Northern Ireland, the State, terror, Bobby Sands and IRA' on 2 July 1981. Of course, Pauli had the perfect observation post as he was just across the water from Northern Ireland. But the information he gathered on the IRA did not seem to have impressed the Stasi headquarters since both documents got an 'average value (III)' assessment.

Klaus von Raussendorff, registration number MfS 13864/60, code name 'Brede', had been recruited in 1957 (see Tables 3.12–3.13, summary sheets nos. 31 and 34). He became convinced that Communism was the way forward and through initial contacts with the Free German Youth (FDJ) association of the SED, he accepted to work for the HVA. He became a diplomat in the West German Foreign Office and was a success story for the HVA. Von Raussendorff had much knowledge about the European integration process and the Western European Union (WEU), a think tank on security and defence issues. He was a prolific spy. Between 1973 and 1977, he took photographs of more than 250 documents, representing a total of about 5,000 pages.[69] It comes as no surprise that he had photographed a document entitled 'Western MBFR [Mutual and Balanced Force Reductions] consultations' in which Ireland's position on troop reductions in Europe was mentioned and another one entitled 'Annual political report, 1975, Ireland' that dealt with the country's relations with the EC, NATO and the East bloc countries.

The index card of 'Lorenz', registration number XV/4070/70, does not shed much light on his/her activities.[70] 'Lorenz' was active for HVA XIII/3, which looked after chemistry, chemistry technology and process engineering issues. He/she was a manager of a research and development agency based in Frankfurt am Main, West Germany.[71] That is why in 1978 'Lorenz' sent to East Berlin a document regarding the manufacture of xylol (xylene, hydrocarbons obtained from wood tar) in the Netherlands, Britain and Ireland (see Table 3.15, summary sheet no. 41). 'Löwe', registration number XV/268/68,[72] was active for HVA XV/2, which dealt with materials for armament, machines, transport and so on, also including metalworking companies.[73] This explains why he/she transmitted information on the Irish steel market in 1970 and 1976 to relevant metallurgic circles in the GDR (see Tables 3.6 and 3.13, summary sheets nos. 8 and 36 respectively). The index card for 'Fichte', registration number XV/1762/71,[74] leaves the identity of the agent or source in the dark and unfortunately does not reveal more on how he/she obtained the pump and turbine plans of Pigeon House, Poolbeg Generating Station, near Dublin in 1969. 'Fichte' was a member of HVA XIII, which dealt with fundamental research (see Table 3.8, summary sheet no. 14). 'Lorenz', 'Löwe' and 'Fichte' were cases of industrial espionage.

So it was that the HVA came into possession of economic and technological information on Ireland and Northern Ireland. There was nothing odd here despite the fact that neither Ireland nor Northern Ireland would have been considered to be leading industrial countries. According to Jens Gieseke, the HVA had a 'highly developed unofficial network' in the domain of industrial espionage. Gieseke further points out that 'economic espionage played a considerable role for the GDR' as it was essentially meant to make up for industrial shortcomings. The HVA would concentrate on wherever there was a crying need for the GDR and on what economic course the SED had decided upon.[75] Despite the fact that the World Bank ranked the GDR's economy twelfth in the world in 1984,[76] the GDR constantly needed to do a lot of catching up with the West. The partition of Germany had led to serious economic disruptions in the GDR.[77] It should not be forgotten either that in November 1949 the Western Allies had decided to set up the Coordinating Committee on Multilateral Export Controls (CoCom). The aim of CoCom was clear: to put on the embargo list any materials and technologies that would have helped the East to develop its own industries. Therefore, the setting up of a unit dealing with industrial espionage became a main priority for the East Germans. In 1951, the decision was taken to do so. The following year, this unit included six persons. By 1990, the Sektor Wissenschaftlich-Technische Aufklärung (SWT, scientific and technical intelligence sector) as the unit had become known within the HVA, numbered 500 persons.[78]

As previously mentioned, '*Objekt-Hinweis*' (object-indication) means that what is written in a document has at least something to do with a particular institution or person. It should be emphasised that this does not reveal with certainty where the spy or his/her source operated. For example, a document emanating from the EC in Brussels could very well have been obtained in the Foreign Office in Bonn. Yet, by simply adding up the amount of object-indications (institutions or persons) when available in the 160 SIRA summary sheets, it is possible to have some idea of where the HVA probably got most of its information on Ireland and Northern Ireland from.

It would appear that the European institutions in Brussels were by far the HVA's main source of information on Irish and Northern Irish affairs.

Table 3.24 Object-indications ('*Objekt-Hinweis*'); indications as to the probable origin of documents (based on the 160 SIRA summary-sheets regarding Ireland and Northern Ireland)

Object-indication	Number of times mentioned	Object-indication	Number of times mentioned
European Communities (EC)	71	Organization of the Petroleum Exporting Countries (OPEC)	1
North Atlantic Treaty Organisation (NATO)	10	Centre Energy Atomique (i.e. Commissariat à l'Energie atomique, France?)	1
European Free Trade Association (EFTA)	9	Pigeon House, Ireland	1
European Economic Community (EEC)	8	United States of America (no other details)	1
Commonwealth	8	US Army in Europe (USAEUR)	1
European Parliament	7	United Nations Security Council	1
Euratom	7	United Nations General Assembly	1
United Nations Organization (UNO)	6	Organization for African Unity (OAU)	1
Federation of German Industry (BDI)	5	South West African People's Organization (SWAPO)	1
Western European Union (WEU)	4	Budget Committee of the Bundestag	1
Organisation for Economic Cooperation and Development (OECD)	3	Bundestag	1
International Energy Agency (IEA)	3	Bundesamt für Verfassungsschutz (BfV, domestic intelligence service of the FRG)	1
International Monetary Fund (IMF)	3	European Commission	1
General Agreement on Tariffs and Trade (GATT)	2	Council of Europe	1

Table 3.24 (Continued)

Object-indication	Number of times mentioned	Object-indication	Number of times mentioned
European Investment Bank (EIB)	2	Free Democratic Party (FDP, German Liberals)	1
United Nations Conference on Trade and Development (UNCTAD)	2	European People's Party (EEP, Liberals in European Parliament)	1
Warsaw Pact	2	Federation of Liberal and Democratic Parties in Europe	1
BASF (chemical company)	2	Friedrich Naumann Stiftung (FNS, West German Liberal think-tank)	1
British Steel Corporation (BSC)	1	Christian Democratic Union (CDU, West German Conservatives))	1
Institute for Medical Statistics (Frankfurt?)	1	Christian Social Union (CSU, Bavarian Conservatives)	1
Gelsenberg Mineral Oil GmbH (Essen?)	1	Socialist International	1

Also noteworthy is that the East Germans had a mole in the Belgian civil service, very likely in the Foreign Ministry. The mole got documents on the situation in Ireland and Northern Ireland (1972–75) as analysed by the Belgians, in all likelihood based on reports emanating from their embassies in Dublin or London (see Tables 3.7 and 3.10–3.11, summary sheets nos. 10, 24, 26 and 28). His/her agent registration number was XV/5485/60 and his/her codename was 'Angestellter'. The index-card in F22 does not reveal the person's identity.[79] However, Rainer Rupp, Karl Rehbaum and Klaus Eichner, all former HVA members, write in their book that 'Angestellter' was 'a Belgian diplomat' who was particularly good at his/her job.[80]

Brussels was a main target for the HVA. HVA guideline 2/79 stipulated that 'vital leading committees of NATO and the EC are concentrated in Belgium'.[81] It might also be stated that the HVA did probably not target Ireland and Northern Ireland *specifically* but rather that it obtained information on these countries that came its way. There might be exceptions of course like for example the activities of Edgar Uher, registration number XV/175/75, code-named 'Eckart', who was a member of the East German diplomatic corps in London and also an officer of the HVA (see Table 3.18, summary sheet no. 56).

What about the assessment of the documents sent to East Berlin by the spies? Were they of quality? A close look at the summary sheets used here reveals that as far as Ireland and Northern Ireland were concerned, the material got many IIIs (average value) from the HVA's Department VII (evaluation and information). But one point should be stressed: the grading of the obtained information can be problematic to analyse. According to Edgar Uher:

> You surely find the school marking system funny, as it surely was, but the real serious thing was as follows. Information not wanted – either out of ignorance or, more often, as it conflicted with the politically wanted line – was simply ignored. You will have read that in the GDR (as surely in the other Socialist states) information on the situation on the ground in the country got filtered on its way to the leadership. The higher the information was handed to the better (in terms of what the leadership expected) it became. What I describe was basically the same mechanism on the intelligence side. And here I am sure that this was not specific to the GDR only, or even an issue during the Cold War only. It probably still is a general issue.[82]

Uher certainly made a pertinent remark. The invasion of Iraq in 2003 showed that intelligence reports were made to confirm what US President George W. Bush and British Prime Minister Tony Blair

Table 3.25 Assessment grades

Assessment grade	Of a total of 36 summary sheets that were given an assessment grade
I, very valuable	2
II, valuable	1
III, average value	27
IV, low value	6
V, without value	0

Table 3.26 Assessment grades of information coming from the Soviet Union

Assessment grade	Of a total of 13 summary sheets that were given to the HVA by the Soviet Union and that were given an assessment grade
I, very valuable	0
II, valuable	1
III, average value	8
IV, low value	4
V, without value	0

wanted to hear to proceed with the invasion, namely that Iraqi leader Saddam Hussein was in possession of weapons of mass destruction. Intelligence that pointed towards the contrary was ignored.[83] Therefore, it should be borne in mind that there is a chance that some of the following assessment grades are perhaps not entirely 'objective'.

The information the HVA received from the Soviet Union, presumably from the KGB, was clearly not of the finest quality either (see Table 3.26).

This would tend to confirm Markus Wolf's complaint that the Soviets were rather stingy when it came to sharing information with their allies with the result that they would often leave them in the dark. 'This was lamentably not out of character for the Soviets: For them, intelligence generally flowed in one direction only', Wolf wrote in his memoirs.[84] An HVA officer code-named 'Achim' seems to have specialised in Irish affairs since he/she assessed twenty documents between September 1978 and December 1984, followed by 'Elke' who analysed five between March 1978 and March 1987.

Lastly, a remark on the frequency of the 160 documents, the summary sheets of which were found in SIRA (see Table 3.27).

Table 3.27 Frequency of HVA documents, 1969–90

Year	Number of HVA documents	Year	Number of HVA documents
1969	11	1980	3
1970	16	1981	5
1971	12	1982	8
1972	6	1983	3
1973	15	1984	5
1974	13	1985	3
1975	18	1986	3
1976	16	1987	5
1977	4	1988	0
1978	9	1989	2
1979	3	1990	0

The HVA's interest in the island was at its highest from 1969 until 1976 inclusive, which was the period of the onset of the 'Troubles' in Northern Ireland. The 1970s, a period of détente and negotiations between East and West Germany that would lead to the signing of the Basic Treaty in 1972, witnessed a period of intense HVA activity. As Jens Gieseke puts it:

> From the viewpoint of the secret services, there were two main tasks during the period of *détente*. First, classic military and political–strategic espionage (as well as counterespionage) retained a high priority, whereas, second, the intensification of negotiations opened up a whole new field of operation ... the GDR still made a considerable effort in the field of international espionage (as in other fields), and would step up these efforts even more. Thanks to the long-term build-up of perspective [*sic*] agents, the information bases were considerable, giving rise to a correspondingly dense supply of information.[85]

In 1976 alone, an extra 600 people were recruited by the HVA. The recognition of the GDR by Western states meant that there was more intelligence work to be done.[86]

However, three points should be stressed in Ireland's case. First, far from all the documents between 1969 and 1976 dealt with the Northern Irish crisis and its wider repercussions. For instance, several dealt with Ireland's application to join the EC together with those of the United Kingdom, Denmark and Norway. It should be recalled that the HVA created a special unit to deal with EC affairs in 1971, Department XII.[87] Second, there is a clear discrepancy between the number of documents for the 1970s and that for the 1980s. This could have meant three things:

(1) that fewer officers, agents or unofficial collaborators (IMs) were available (or that some had been unmasked); (2), that fewer opportunities to obtain information presented themselves; or (3), that Ireland was simply not a priority on the HVA's agenda. Third, it is important to stress that SIRA is not the only source of available material and that in the 1980s the Stasi closely followed the unfolding situation in Northern Ireland all the more since Irish republicans were active in West Germany.

The following is a summary of the topics of the documents concerning Ireland that were stored in SIRA:

- Ireland's accession to the EEC and its subsequent participation;
- Ireland and the United Kingdom's relations with the FRG and GDR;
- steel business;
- Belgium's assessment of the crisis in Ireland and Northern Ireland, 1972;
- Ireland's energy policy;
- assessment of the Catholic Church;
- Report on Pigeon House (Poolbeg Generating Station, Dublin);
- Ireland's foreign policy and relations with Socialist countries;
- General assessment of Ireland, 1975;
- Irish Communists and Maoists;
- Relations between Ireland and the FRG, 1977;
- uranium deposits in Ireland, 1978;
- electrical engineering;
- Charles Haughey and Margaret Thatcher's talks about Northern Ireland;
- Confederation of Irish Industry meeting;
- extension of telephone network in Ireland;
- Ronald Reagan's visit to Ireland, 1984;
- activation of military cooperation with the United States, NATO, 1985;
- military situation in Ireland, 1986;
- governmental crisis, 1987;
- assessment of the Irish economy; and
- social security agreement between Austria and Ireland, 1989.

The electronic (SIRA) versions of these documents were destroyed, but some of their paper versions (two, possibly three) that had been stored elsewhere in the Stasi archive survived the shredders and incinerators and have been found.

The first document seems to date from the end of 1969, a stamp indicating 10 December, a time when Ireland was trying to become a member of the EC. It is entitled 'Information on the opinion of the EC Commission to the Council concerning Great Britain, Ireland, Denmark and Norway's applications for membership'. It appears to correspond with a report transmitted on 3 December 1969 located in the SIRA material; it is qualified as a 'very confidential file' (see Table 3.5, summary sheet no. 4). There was nothing said about Ireland in particular and this three-page document was a summary of what is called an 'opinion' in EC jargon, meaning a report. The European Commission had submitted this opinion to the Council of Ministers in Brussels. More precisely it was about what would happen in case of enlargement and what kind of economic problems might develop. The document was considered 'Top Secret' and its circulation was restricted in order to protect the source. A handwritten list of abbreviated names on top of the document indicates that it had been given to Hermann Axen, a specialist in international affairs and considered to be the brain of East German foreign policy, and Otto Winzer, the Foreign Minister.[88] The source was obviously not mentioned but it may well have been a member of the West German delegation in the EC or even a naive secretary in the Commission or Council's secretariat in Brussels who passed on information to a 'Romeo agent'. The HVA's interest in Western European integration was real. Besides the possibly valuable information it could obtain in Brussels, the GDR viewed with suspicion the development of the EC and, unlike other members of the COMECON (the East bloc's Council for Mutual Economic Assistance), it strongly argued against formal recognition of the EC and instead preferred bilateral agreements between individual member states of the COMECON and the EC. There was a logic to it. If the GDR negotiated bilateral agreements with individual Western countries, then diplomatic recognition might come about, but not if the GDR was simply included in the COMECON.[89]

Almost two years later, the HVA produced another report on European integration entitled 'Information on the European Communities' problems in foreign policy with the accession of Great Britain, Denmark, Norway and Ireland'. It was an analysis of how the enlargement of the Community would affect its relations with non-member states notably in the Mediterranean area, the Commonwealth and so on. The country of main concern was the United Kingdom and there was nothing specific about Ireland. Again, the report was 'Top secret'. The abbreviation of names added by hand on the document indicates that it was given to Axen, Winzer and Günter Mittag, the specialist in economic and industrial affairs of the SED's Central Committee.[90] It was also sent to Poland and Hungary.[91] But, that was not all. Also indicated is the abbreviation 'AG', which stood for *Arbeitsgruppe* (working group). It looked rather innocuous at first sight but was in fact calculated to be vague. In reality, 'AG' was the cover for the KGB *residentura* in East Berlin.[92] This meant that the HVA had transmitted this particular report to the Soviets and that it was deemed to be important.

On 5 August 1970, the HVA wrote a report entitled 'Information on the reflections of West German governmental circles on the relationship between Great Britain and the Republic of Ireland and the parallels to be drawn for the shaping of relations between the West German Federal Republic and the GDR'. A summary sheet in the SIRA material (see Table 3.6, summary sheet no. 7) shows that it had been classified as a 'very confidential file'. The list of abbreviated names indicates that this report had been given to the highest dignitaries of the regime, possibly including Walter Ulbricht, the First Secretary of the SED, but the abbreviation is unclear. It would have made sense if it had been transmitted to Ulbricht since he was battling for the international recognition of East Germany and that the FRG was opposing him, although by 1970 the international community was about to recognise the GDR.

If the first abbreviation is difficult to read, the second one is definitely Erich Honecker, the party's number two. It can therefore be very reasonably assumed that the first abbreviation on top of the list was indeed Ulbricht. After all, there was a strict hierarchy in the SED. Honecker was the Central Committee member in charge of security issues. He was also Secretary of the Nationale Verteidigungsrat (national council for defence) and would replace Ulbricht in May 1971. There were also Albert Norden, Central Committee member in charge of SED propaganda, Michael Kohl, Secretary of State for West German Questions in the Ministry of External Affairs, Axen, Winzer and the KGB *residentura* ('AG').[93] The HVA explained that during mid-May, 'West German governmental circles' had made an internal assessment of the relations between Great Britain and the Republic of Ireland to compare them with the relations between the GDR and the FRG. The following were their conclusions.

At first sight, the West Germans believed that the relations between Ireland and Britain could be used as a 'model' for the shaping of relations between the two Germanys. Concerning ordinary Irish and British citizens, Ireland and Britain were not foreign countries for each other despite being totally independent states. The British Ireland Act of 1949 did not consider the Republic of Ireland as a foreign country even though it was no longer a member of the British Commonwealth. Its citizens were not considered foreign nationals. However, since 1935,

British citizens had been considered foreigners in Ireland but had a special status as compared to others living in the country. The wording of the Act of 1949 could almost have been taken from a declaration of the West German government on its relations with the GDR. According to the West Germans, this Anglo-Irish legal arrangement was difficult to comprehend but it offered the practical possibility that 'the Irish in Great Britain and the British in the Republic of Ireland are broadly treated like nationals'. But the British went further than the Irish. For example, the Irish in Britain could opt for British passports, enter the diplomatic corps, vote and join the army. But in Ireland, there were certain limits imposed on British citizens, which had historic explanations. The Irish had fought hard to achieve independence and were not willing to renounce their distinctive outward features. The special position of British citizens in Ireland 'is still today a political hot potato'. But as the 'greater and stronger partner', the British could afford not to be too offended.[94]

The West Germans had paid attention to the economic relations too. The two countries had signed the Anglo-Irish Free Trade Area Agreement (AIFTAA) in 1965. The British pledged to abolish all their customs duties within half a year but the Irish would progressively abolish them until 1980. This was explained by the fact that Ireland represented only about 3 per cent to 4 per cent of the total of Britain's foreign trade. Half of all Irish imports came from Britain while about 70 per cent of all Irish exports went to Britain. This economic dependence explained why the Irish punt was coupled with pound sterling. The borders between the two states were very easy to cross for Irish and British citizens, easier than elsewhere in Western Europe. The West Germans described how despite Ireland's struggle for independence, everyday life between the two countries went on 'as if there had been no political separation'. The two governments were determined 'to preserve the close relations between the two States'. 'Even the conflict in Northern Ireland would not call into question the common basis of the practical integration of the citizens' everyday life', the West Germans added. The conclusion read:

> If one compared this special relationship between Britain and Ireland with the relations between the GDR and the Federal Republic, two differences would be striking in the opinion of these West German governmental circles. On the one hand, the same people live in the GDR and the Federal Republic and are not two different ethnic groups. But on the other hand, the ties of the common political and social system and of common life have been drastically broken during the past 25 years. That is why the special relationship between Great Britain and the Republic of Ireland will be able

> to function as an example, even though an imperfect one, for the shaping of relations between the GDR and the Federal Republic, if at least one part of the common economic, social and political foundation in the whole of Germany has been re-established and if both governments are interested in preserving this common foundation.[95]

The very last sentence in the report demanded discretion 'in the interest of the source's safety'. A few remarks come to mind. It was obvious that the West Germans had made this study as Willy Brandt's government was seeking better relations with East Germany. Indeed, the establishment of West German embassies in the Socialist countries was now only a question of time as was the normalisation of relations with East Germany without, however, exchanging ambassadors. These were the aims of Brandt's *Ostpolitik* (eastern policy). The Americans and the British were hoping that Bonn would be able to increase contacts between citizens of the FRG and the GDR while not formally recognising the East German State. They felt that if East Germany was recognised by the international community, then the Western Allies' presence in West Berlin might be seriously called into question.[96]

A last point of interest. On 14 May 1970, only about three months *before* the HVA submitted the said report to several SED leaders, the West German embassy in London had sent to the Foreign Office in Bonn a report entitled 'Relationship between Great Britain and the Republic of Ireland and the shaping of inter-German relations'. It is nowadays located in the Auswärtiges Amt-Politisches Archiv (AA-PA) in Berlin, the archive of the German Foreign Office. There are uncanny resemblances between the HVA and the West German reports. In fact, certain passages were almost identical with only minimal differences. For instance, here is the introductory paragraph of the West German embassy's report:

> West German embassy's report, 14 May 1970 (located in the AA-PA archive)
> At first sight the special relationship between Great Britain and the Republic of Ireland lends itself to a model for the shaping of inter-German relations. The two states, which are completely independent from each other legally speaking, are no 'foreign country' for each other practically in all questions that directly concern their citizens. In all the areas that traditionally play a special role in the national sentiment, Great Britain and the Republic of Ireland are also, however, two totally independent and sovereign states in their relationship. They exchange ambassadors and are side-by-side members of international organisations. Also, Ireland does not belong any longer to the Commonwealth.[97]

This is the HVA report:

> HVA's report, 5 August 1970 (located in the BStU archive)
> At first sight the special relationship between Great Britain and the Republic of Ireland would lend itself to a model for the shaping of inter-German relations, according to the assessment of West German governmental circles. The two states, which are completely independent from each other legally speaking, are no 'foreign country' for each other practically in all questions that directly concern their citizens. In all the areas that traditionally play a special role in the national sentiment, Great Britain and the Republic of Ireland are also, however, two totally independent and sovereign states in their relationship. They exchange ambassadors and are side-by-side members of international organisations. Also, Ireland does not belong any longer to the Commonwealth.[98]

There was obviously an East German mole in the Foreign Office in Bonn. The SIRA documents, and also the HVA F16 and F22 index-card systems,[99] provide the answer. The registration number of the sender, 15905/60 (see Table 3.6, summary sheet no. 7), indicates that this document had been transmitted to East Berlin by Ludwig Pauli, code-named 'Adler'. As stated, he worked in the Foreign Office.

For the West German government, which claimed to be the sole representative of the whole of Germany, the Irish–British relationship could constitute a model. If Bonn wanted to figure out what future relations with East Berlin could be like, it was pertinent to analyse the situation of other countries that were strongly related, yet separated. Ireland and Britain was a case in point. There is unfortunately no evidence to show how the East German government reacted to this Ireland–Britain comparison. However, one can hazard an educated guess. It is most unlikely that Ulbricht and Honecker would have agreed with it. As German reunification under a Communist regime was not on the cards, their efforts had been to obtain formal international recognition of the GDR. Their Germany was a different one. When Western countries began to recognise the legitimacy of the East German State in the early 1970s, at long last their aim had been achieved. The East German leadership would make sure that the GDR remained different. On 26 January 1973, one of the SED's main ideologists, Kurt Hager, explained that there was a different culture altogether in the GDR, thus rejecting the notion of a united German culture.[100] Dr Joachim Mitdank, the last East German ambassador to the United Kingdom and Ireland and who had previously been involved in the negotiations leading up to the Four Power Agreement on Berlin in 1972, told this author that the partition of Ireland was of no relevance to the partition of Germany.[101]

Those in Bonn who had conceived this comparison between Ireland and Britain to draw lessons for possible relations between East and West Germany had been rather naive because there was simply no way a man of Ulbricht's calibre would agree with it. The SED leadership might well make some concessions during negotiations with Brandt's government but not to the extent of imitating British–Irish relations. It was as easy to state now as it was back then. If Brandt and his team came up with some suggestions reminiscent of the arrangements between Dublin and London, the East Germans would have a prepared answer. The HVA had made sure of that. This document would have been of particular interest to Albert Norden who, as seen, was the first SED member to have spoken of two German nations in 1967. This theory had been created to justify the existence of the GDR and was meant to be an obstacle to German reunification.

On 23 August 1972, a report entitled 'Potential and structure of the energy industry of the countries entering the EC; Great Britain, Ireland, Denmark and Norway' was transmitted among others to Kurt Singhuber, the Minister for Ore Mining, Metallurgy and Potash,[102] Günter Mittag and also the KGB *residentura*. It had been written by 'Moritz' of HVA-VII (evaluation and information). It is recorded in SIRA (see Table 3.7, summary sheet no. 11). 'Moritz' explained that 'according to confidential internal information', a committee in charge of energy, research and atomic issues in the EC Parliament made an analysis of the power and structure of the energy industry of those countries about to join the EC. 'Moritz' wrote that Great Britain, Denmark, Norway (which would not join eventually) and Ireland's accession to the EC would significantly increase its energy potential. This in turn would affect the Socialist countries. For example, the gas and oil potential in the North Sea was mentioned. 'Moritz' then essentially wrote about Great Britain, Denmark and Norway. The paragraph on Ireland, by contrast, consisted only of a few lines:

> The primary energy sources are small and will have relatively little influence on the energy potential of the EC. The need for primary energy (1970 = 8 million tons of thermal units for coal) is met by 76% imports; the rest is met by the domestic production of peat (the annual extraction is 5 million tons) and also native hard coal and water power.
>
> The production of electricity occurs mainly in thermal power stations (87%) by means of water power. There are no nuclear energy stations and their construction is not planned in the foreseeable future.[103]

Ireland's energy resources were clearly not of a nature to attract the Stasi's attention.

These reports dating from the end of the 1960s and the beginning of the 1970s are among the most interesting ones in the surviving material. Between 1969 and 1979, the HVA produced about 8,500 reports in total that were sent to the GDR leadership, including the above-mentioned two, possibly three on Ireland. The overwhelming majority of them dealt with West Germany. For example, in 1974, 55 reports were written on the FRG, 31 on NATO, three on the United States, three on Belgium, three on Italy, one on Great Britain, one on France and one on Canada. It gives a clear idea of the HVA's main operational areas. As Jens Gieseke remarks, 'Reports regarding other individual Western nations in 1974 were, quantitatively, of comparatively little importance ... and in itself seldom of high operational value'.[104]

Interestingly, Gieseke points out that the language used by the HVA in these reports was 'extraordinarily objective' and not systematically impregnated by the 'official language regulations of the GDR'; in other words, by the predictable and biased Marxist-Leninist sentences like 'the "imperialist" and "aggressive" character of Western capitalism' and so on. Former HVA members claimed that their superiors had told them to avoid this, hence the objective character of their reports. Christopher Andrew, however, argues that intelligence services of the East bloc were not able to produce objective analyses of given situations for their respective leaderships because of their ideological bias. They invariably would exaggerate the aggressive nature of imperialist Western countries in accordance with Marxist-Leninist conceptions.[105] In the KGB's case, Andrew coined the witty expression 'ideological blinkers'.[106] If one considers the two, possibly three reports on Ireland – not many out of a total of about 8,500, it is true – it is quite clear that the language used by the HVA was indeed not burdened with ideological jargon and prejudice. But it might well have been different with the KGB of course.

To finish it must be emphasised that the Stasi files do contain other reports and documents on Ireland besides those mentioned in the SIRA material. These documents essentially constitute facts and general information. There is a general file, undated and untitled, which was created by the Zentraler Operativstab (ZOS, central operational staff). The ZOS was in charge of coordination assignments in preparation and realisation of central actions and safety missions. It also made overviews of relevant incidents and events for security policy. Unfortunately, there is nothing stated as to why the file was created in the first place. In any case, it contains nothing of a secret nature and is merely a collection of facts based on the following sources: the *Munzinger Archiv/Internationales Handbuch* (a West German publication specialising in factual information on countries and people), the *Taschenbuch des Öffentlichen Lebens* (a West German publication giving information on countries, embassies and so on), the *Herders Volkslexicon* (a West German publication on facts, countries and peoples) and *Horizont* (an East German publication on politics, international politics and economic matters).[107]

In 1983, HA-III (telecommunications) produced a small file almost exclusively based on West German press cuttings from newspapers like the *Süddeutsche Zeitung*, *Frankfurter Allgemeine Zeitung* and *Welt* and also a couple of East German publications, *Neues Deutschland* and *Horizont*.[108] In the mid-1980s, HA-VI (border controls, tourism) got a booklet from the GDR's state bank, containing specimens of Irish currency.[109] On 10 April 1986, HA-XXII/8 produced a chronology of facts regarding Anglo-Irish relations from the fourth century until 1918. It is not clear why it stopped at that precise year but its entry contained a serious error, not the first one: '1918: SINN FEIN Irish Members of Parliament elected in the British Parliament gather secretly in Dublin to set up the Irish national assembly and proclaim the independence of Northern Ireland'.[110] Another document seems to date from 1988 and is entitled 'Information material on Ireland and its capital Dublin'. It contains brief facts on the country's political system and parties, foreign policy, relations with the GDR and also the programmes of Michael O'Riordan's visit to East Berlin in September 1983 and of an Irish parliamentary delegation led by Speaker Seán Treacy in September 1988.[111] All in all there was not that much material on Ireland but again the SIRA tables do indicate that there had been more, some documents having gone up in smoke or in fragments.

This was the extent of East German espionage concerning Ireland. But the onset of the terrorist conflict in Northern Ireland, more generally known as the 'Troubles', in which the British army was massively involved, caught its attention. Serious monitoring took place.

Notes

1 Wolf & McElvoy, *Man without a Face*, pp. 51, 91.
2 D. Porch, *The French Secret Services: From the Dreyfus Affair to the Gulf War* (London: Macmillan, 1996), pp. 66–7.
3 BStU, MfS-ZAIG, nos. 10436, 10434, 10407, 10426, 10442, 10469, 28097, 10471, 10472 and 10444; ZAIG/1, no. 9553/1.
4 Wolf & McElvoy, *Man without a Face*, p. 110.
5 BStU, MfS-HA XXII, no. 18667, for press cuttings in IRA folder. See also nos. 6065/1 and 6065/2, for press cuttings on the events in Northern Ireland.
6 *Ibid.*, MfS-HA III, no. 16717.
7 A. Schmidt, '"Aufklärung" des Funkverkehrs und der Telefongespräche in

Westdeutschland-Die Hauptabteilung III', in Knabe, *West-Arbeit des MfS*, pp. 212–14, 218, 222, 223.

8 *Ibid.*, p. 213.

9 BStU, MfS-HA XX, no. 6819, 'Statements by the Roman Catholic Bishops of Northern Ireland', 1981–85.

10 *Ibid.*, MfS-HA XXII, no. 6065/19, copy of Bradley's 'Die historischen Wurzeln der Guerilla und des Terrorismus in Nordirland', 1976.

11 *Ibid.*, MfS-HA XXII, no. 1145/7, extract of Wördemann's *Terrorismus*, 1977.

12 O'Halpin, *Defending Ireland*, p. 312.

13 BStU, MfS-HA XXII, no. 1081, translation of Barril's book.

14 *Ibid.*, MfS-Sekr. Neiber, no. 3, 'Profile terroristischer Gruppen', 1 March 1989.

15 Gieseke, *Der Mielke-Konzern*, p. 319.

16 BStU, MfS-ZAIG, no. 6544, 'Make Ireland a Nuclear Free Zone', 1988.

17 B. de Graaf, 'Stasi in the Polder: The East German Ministry for State Security and the Netherlands, 1977–89', in B. de Graaf, B. de Jong & W. Platje (eds.), *Battleground Western Europe: Intelligence Operations in Germany and the Netherlands in the Twentieth Century* (Amsterdam: Het Spinhuis, 2007), pp. 196–204.

18 BStU, exact archival reference of this document is unknown. However, the title of this index card is 'Irish CND' and on the back of the card is mentioned 'HVA 23.2.83 II/1/1'.

19 *Ibid.*, MfS-HA II, no. 35670, 'Irland', no date but probably mid-1980s.

20 *Ibid.*, MfS-HA XXII/8, no. 17219, 'Zeittafel zur geschichtlichen Entwicklung der Beziehungen IRLAND/England und zu politischen Ereignissen', 10 April 1986.

21 *Ibid.*, MfS-HA XXII, no. 945, 'Organisation Oranje-Bünde'; 'Organisation Democratic Unionist Party', no date but both information cards based on the *Deutsche Volkszeitung*, 18 July 1986.

22 Frankfurter Allgemeine Zeitung, 9 October 2008.

23 The author is grateful to Mr Christian Schwack (BStU) for this information (e-mail exchange, 25 January 2013). For an explanation of the SIRA summary sheets, see Ziehm, 'Elektronische Datenträger', pp. 55–9.

24 Ziehm, 'Elektronische Datenträger', pp. 58–9.

25 BStU, F16/F22 HVA, Sira TdB 21, Rainer Frey, XV/1586/87, 'Aribert'.

26 H. Müller-Enbergs, *Hauptverwaltung A (HV A). Aufgaben – Strukturen – Quellen* (MfS Handbuch). (Hg. BStU. Berlin 2011), pp. 116–17, at www.nbn-resolving.org/urn:nbn:de:0292–9783942130158_010 (accessed 21 January 2013). Müller-Enbergs has written that 'Aribert's' name is Jürgen Karl. But the photocopies of the original documents show that the name is Rainer Frey.

27 BStU, F16/F22 HVA, Sira TdB 21, F16/HVA AK, Siegfried Reichelt, XV/1508/75; XV/1093/62, 'Weber'.

28 Müller-Enbergs, *Hauptverwaltung A (HV A). Aufgaben – Strukturen – Quellen*, pp. 200–1.
29 BStU, F16/F22 HVA, Sira TdB 21, Hans Weber, XV/192/73, 'Schneider'.
30 Müller-Enbergs, *Hauptverwaltung A (HV A). Aufgaben – Strukturen – Quellen*, p. 201.
31 BStU, F16/F22 HVA, Sira TdB 21, HA II/AKG-VSH, Johanna Olbrich, alias Sonja Lüneburg.
32 Müller-Enbergs, *Hauptverwaltung A (HV A). Aufgaben – Strukturen – Quellen*, pp. 64–5 (n. 273).
33 BStU, F16/F22 HVA, Sira TdB 21, Dagmar Kahlig-Scheffler, XV/2227/73, 'Inge'.
34 Müller-Enbergs, *Hauptverwaltung A (HV A). Aufgaben – Strukturen – Quellen*, pp. 51–3.
35 BStU, F16/F22 HVA, Sira TdB 21, Helge Berger, XV/2091/66, 'Komtess'.
36 J. Adams, *Historical Dictionary of German Intelligence* (Lanham: Scarecrow Press, 2009), pp. 29–30.
37 Wolf & McElvoy, *Man without a Face* (see ch. 8 'Spying for Love', pp. 135, 152–3).
38 BStU, F16/F22 HVA, Sira TdB 21, Paul Gerhard Flämig, XV/750/66, 'Walter'.
39 Müller-Enbergs, *Hauptverwaltung A (HV A). Aufgaben – Strukturen – Quellen*, pp. 61–2.
40 Adams, *Historical Dictionary of German Intelligence*, p. 109.
41 BStU, MfS, HV A/MD/2, SIRA-TDB 11, SE7207479, Eingangsdatum: 28.07.1972.
42 *Ibid.*, F22/HVA, Sira TdB 21, XV/92/67, 'Bettina'.
43 Müller-Enbergs, *Hauptverwaltung A (HV A). Aufgaben – Strukturen – Quellen*, pp. 291–4.
44 E-mail exchange between the author and Edgar Uher, 22 November 2012.
45 McCauley, *German Democratic Republic since 1945*, pp. 245, 247.
46 Garvin, *Preventing the Future*, pp. 141–3.
47 BStU, F22/HVA, Sira TdB 21, XV/6430/82, 'Hans Rosenberg'.
48 Müller-Enbergs, *Hauptverwaltung A (HV A). Aufgaben – Strukturen – Quellen*, pp. 301–4.
49 BStU, F22/HVA, Sira TdB 21, XV/367/73, 'Korb'.
50 Müller-Enbergs, *Hauptverwaltung A (HV A). Aufgaben – Strukturen – Quellen*, pp. 228–30.
51 BStU, MfS, HV A/MD/2, SIRA-TdB 11, SE7902787, Eingangsdatum: 20.02.1979.
52 Engelmann *et al.*, *Das MfS-Lexikon*, p. 297.
53 BStU, F22/HVA, Sira TdB 21, XV/167/71, 'Max'.
54 Müller-Enbergs, *Hauptverwaltung A (HV A). Aufgaben – Strukturen – Quellen*, pp. 202–4, n. 1053 (p. 203).
55 BStU, F22/HVA, Sira TdB 21, XV/1619/75, 'Herbert'.

56 Müller-Enbergs, *Hauptverwaltung A (HV A). Aufgaben – Strukturen – Quellen*, pp. 78–9.
57 BStU, F22/HVA, Sira TdB 21, XV/2848/76, 'Karl'.
58 Müller-Enbergs, *Hauptverwaltung A (HV A). Aufgaben – Strukturen – Quellen*, pp. 270–4.
59 BStU, F16/HVA, Sira TdB 21, XV/1815/60, 'Jutta'.
60 Müller-Enbergs, *Hauptverwaltung A (HV A). Aufgaben – Strukturen – Quellen*, pp. 270–4.
61 BStU, F22/HVA, Sira TdB 21, XV/2962/78, 'Ahmed'.
62 Müller-Enbergs, *Hauptverwaltung A (HV A). Aufgaben – Strukturen – Quellen*, pp. 81–2.
63 BStU, F22/HVA, Sira TdB 21, XV/2171/73, 'Weser'.
64 Schwan & Heindrichs, *Das Spinnennetz*, p. 141.
65 V. Cherkashin with G. Feifer, *Spy Handler: Memoir of a KGB Officer* (New York: Basic Books, 2005), p. 118.
66 BStU, F16/HVA, F22/HVA, Sira TdB 21, XV/6427/60, 'Merten'.
67 Schwan & Heindrichs, *Das Spinnennetz*, pp. 60–1, 64, 76–7, 134–6, 166–74.
68 *Ibid.*, pp. 8–9, 57–8, 59, 64, 183–5, 189–90.
69 *Ibid.*, pp. 26–7, 61–3, 64, 159–61.
70 BStU, F22/HVA, Sira TdB 21, XV/4070/70, 'Lorenz'.
71 Müller-Enbergs, *Hauptverwaltung A (HV A). Aufgaben – Strukturen – Quellen*, pp. 209–10.
72 BStU, F22/HVA, Sira TdB 21, XV/268/68, 'Löwe' ('Loewe').
73 Müller-Enbergs, *Hauptverwaltung A (HV A). Aufgaben – Strukturen – Quellen*, pp. 224–6.
74 BStU, F22/HVA, Sira TdB 21, XV/1762/71, 'Fichte'.
75 Gieseke, *Der Mielke-Konzern*, pp. 221–2. For the Stasi's technological and industrial espionage activities, see also Kristie Macrakis's *Seduced by Secrets: Inside the Stasi's Spy-Tech World* (New York: Cambridge University Press, 2008).
76 Fulbrook, *Anatomy of a Dictatorship*, p. 5.
77 G. Ebert & M. Leistner, 'Zu den Ergebnissen auf den Gebieten Militärtechnik, Metallurgie und Maschinenbau', in H. Müller, M. Süß & H. Vogel (eds.), *Die Industrie-spionage der DDR: Die wissenschaftlich-technische Aufklärung der HVA* (Berlin: edition ost, 2008), p. 69.
78 H. Vogel, 'Die Bedeutung der Wissenschaftlich-Technischen Aufklärung der DDR', in Müller, Süß & Vogel (eds.), *Die Industrie-spionage der DDR*, pp. 14–17.
79 BStU, F22/HVA, Sira TdB 21, XV/5485/60 (previously MfS 1206/59) 'Angestellter'.
80 R. Rupp, K. Rehbaum & K. Eichner, *Militärspionage: Die DDR-Aufklärung in NATO und Bundeswehr* (Berlin: edition ost, 2011), p. 137.
81 *Ibid.*, p. 27.

82 E-mail exchange between the author and Edgar Uher, 26 November 2012.
83 P. Gill, 'The Politicization of Intelligence: Lessons from the Invasion of Iraq', in H. Born, L. K. Johnson & I. Leigh (eds.), *Who's Watching the Spies? Establishing Intelligence Service Accountability* (Washington: Potomac Books, 2005), pp. 16–22.
84 Wolf & McElvoy, *Man without a Face*, p. 99.
85 Gieseke, 'East German Espionage in the Era of Détente', p. 408.
86 *Ibid.*, p. 401.
87 *Ibid.*
88 BStU, MfS-HVA, no. 154, 'Infromation über die Stellungnahme der EG-Kommission an der Rat zu den Beitrittsgesuchen Groβbritanniens, Irlands, Dänemarks und Norwegens', stamp-dated 10 December 1969. For biographical data, see Müller-Enbergs *et al.*, *Wer war Wer in der DDR?* 'Hermann Axen', p. 34; 'Otto Winzer', p. 923.
89 J. Wüstenhagen, 'RGW und EWG: Die DDR zwischen Ost- und Westintegration', in Pfeil (ed.), *Die DDR und der Westen*, p. 142.
90 Müller-Enbergs *et al.*, *Wer war wer in der DDR?*, 'Günter Mittag', p. 584.
91 BStU, MfS-HVA, no. 396, 'INFORMATION über Probleme der Außenbeziehungen der Europäischen Gemeinschaften, die sich mit dem Beitritt Großbritanniens, Dänemarks, Norwegens und Irlands stellen', 12 November 1971.
92 Gieseke, 'East German Espionage in the Era of Détente', p. 410.
93 Müller-Enbergs *et al.*, *Wer war wer in der DDR?*, 'Walter Ulbricht', p. 868, 'Erich Honecker', p. 373, 'Albert Norden', p. 628, Kohl, p. 452.
94 BStU, MfS-HVA, no. 169, 'INFORMATION über Überlegungen westdeutscher Regierungskreise, aus dem Verhältnis zwischen Großbritannien und der Republik Irland Parallelen für die Gestaltung der Beziehungen zwischen der westdeutschen Bundesrepublik und der DDR abzuleiten', 5 August 1970.
95 *Ibid.*
96 W. G. Gray, *Germany's Cold War: The Global Campaign to Isolate East Germany, 1949–1969* (Chapel Hill, NC and London: University of North Carolina Press, 2003), see ch. 8 'Of Two Minds: The Grand Coalition and the Problem of recognition', pp. 196–219, 208–9.
97 AA-PA, B38–IIA1, Bd. 318, 318–1, 'Verhältnis zwischen Grossbritannien und der Republik Irland und die Gestaltung innerdeutscher Beziehungen', West Germany embassy in London to Foreign Office in Bonn, 14 May 1970.
98 BStU, MfS-HVA, no. 169, 'Information über Überlegungen westdeutscher Regierungskreise…', 5 August 1970.
99 *Ibid.*, HVA index-card system F16, 15905/60, Ludwig Pauli; HVA index-card F22, 'Adler', 15905/60.
100 McCauley, *German Democratic Republic since 1945*, p. 244, 248.
101 Interview with Dr Joachim Mitdank, 12 January 2010, Berlin. See also Joachim Mitdank, *Die Berlin-Politik zwischen 17. Juni 1953, dem*

Viermächteabkommen und der Grenzöffnung 1989: Erinnerungen eines Diplmaten (Berlin: trafo, 2003).

102 Müller-Enbergs *et al.*, *Wer war wer in der DDR?*, 'Kurt Singhuber', p. 802.

103 BStU, MfS-HVA, no. 386, 'INFORMATION über die Potenzen und die Struktur der Energiewirtschaft der den Europäischen Gemeinschaften beitretenden länder Großbritannien, Irland, Dänemark und Norwegen', 23 August 1972.

104 Gieseke, 'East German Espionage in the Era of Détente', pp. 409–11.

105 *Ibid.*, pp. 413–14, 417–18.

106 Andrew & Gordievsky, *KGB*, p. 601.

107 BStU, MfS-ZOS, no. 2680, file on Ireland, untitled and undated.

108 *Ibid.*, MfS-HA III, no. 16717, file entitled 'Irland', no exact date but 1983.

109 *Ibid.*, MfS-HA VI, no. 5665, 'Kennzeichen von Banknoten und Münzen', no exact date but 1980s.

110 *Ibid.*, MfS-HA XXII, no. 17219, 'Zeittafel zur geschichtlichen Entwicklung der Beziehungen IRLAND/England und zu politischen Ereignissen', 10 April 1986.

111 *Ibid.*, MfS-ZOS, no. 2680, 'Informationsmaterial – Irland – Hauptstadt Dublin', no exact date but very likely 1988.

4

Northern Ireland in the *Zentralen Personendatenbank* (ZPDB)

Another important source is the ZPDB, which was a central data bank for persons who had caught the Stasi's attention. There are about sixty-five documents concerning Ireland and Northern Ireland, all of them in possession of HA-XXII (terrorism).[1] These documents are deemed '*Streng Vertraulich!*' (strictly confidential) and are not always easy to analyse as they are riddled with abbreviations. The Stasi used about 20,000 abbreviations which represent a mixture of German words and Stasi jargon.[2] In fact, the overwhelming majority of documents do not concern persons but activities of paramilitaries, almost exclusively the PIRA. These activities were factually dissected: the location and the occasion of the attack were mentioned, what arms or explosives were used, how many people died and were wounded, who claimed the attack and so on. Reading these brief dissections, it is hard to avoid the feeling that they are based on newspaper cuttings. This impression is soon confirmed when one discovers the source: '*Publikationsorgan NSA*'. NSA stands for '*nichtsozialistisches Ausland*', in other words, a publication from a non-Socialist country. The names of the newspapers are not given except on one occasion: 'SDZ', *Süddeutsche Zeitung*. In all likelihood, these ZPDB documents were only summaries of press cuttings and other media reports that the Stasi was collecting on Ireland and Northern Ireland. Forty-four relevant documents were created and indexed between 1 November 1984 and 2 August 1989. The sources of forty-three of them were Western media publications, representing about 98 per cent.

There is one exception, however. An intriguing document, the source of which seems to be exclusively Stasi (no further details given), shows that the Stasi learnt that someone in Belfast, presumably a PIRA member although this is not clearly stated, sent a letter on, probably, 29 February 1988 to a shipping company called SIA Line in Turku in Finland. It was written that attacks on ships and passengers would be carried out unless a ransom of 1.2 million Finnish marks was paid.

The Stasi indicated that the money had been paid. The report mentioned that the aim of this operation was 'to support the IRA'. The cover names of those involved have been blacked out by the BStU.[3] The cover name generally used by the PIRA, 'P. O'Neill', did in all likelihood not figure among them as the Stasi knew it. Moreover, it has not been blacked in other available documents.[4]

The ZPDB documents on Irish terrorist activities begin with the PIRA's attack on the Grand Hotel in Brighton, England, on 12 October 1984 during which Margaret Thatcher was nearly killed, to a PIRA attack in Hanover, West Germany, on 2 July 1989 during which a British soldier was shot dead and his wife and three children were wounded. Yet, there are several ZPDB documents on individuals. But no Irish Kim Philby emerges, at least this is not revealed in the surviving material. Nonetheless there are most interesting facts. A few files are on the IRA and several leading characters in the Northern Irish conflict. All of them are simply based on Western press cuttings and there is nothing to suggest any cloak-and-dagger moves to get information with the possible exception of the file on the IRA as it is based on a combination of press cuttings but also the work of an 'IM' ('*inoffiziellen Mitarbeiter*', unofficial collaborator or informer).

The IRA file dated 19/06/1989 found in the ZPDB deals with generalities. The IRA is described as being a 'far-left wing terrorist organisation' which uses 'illegal methods and propagates nationalism and terrorism'. The main part of the text explains that it came into existence in 1919 during the country's war of independence against Britain. In about 1969, the IRA took over the 'military defence' of the Catholic population in the ghettoes of Belfast and Derry. In 1970, a split occurred and the IRA had since been divided into two factions, the Official IRA (OIRA) and the Provisional IRA (PIRA). In December 1974, a splinter group named Irish National Liberation Army (INLA), politically represented by the Irish Republican Socialist Party (IRSP), broke away from the OIRA. Sinn Féin was the IRA's political wing. There would be contacts between the IRA, ETA, the RAF (Rote Armee Fraktion; Red Army Faction operating in West Germany) and NORAID (Northern Aid, an American fundraising organisation working in favour of Irish reunification). However, the IRA had been dealt severe blows by the British security services for the past few years. The ZPDB file claimed that potentially the IRA enjoyed a large measure of support among the Catholic population. This remark, written in 1989, was a hasty generalisation. It was also stated, correctly, that the IRA used the Republic of Ireland as a base of attack and a resting station. Its targets included the Northern Irish police (Royal Ulster Constabulary, RUC), the British army, enemy terrorist organisations, entrepreneurs and others. Most of its attacks occurred in Northern Ireland and Britain but 'spectacular actions' had also taken place in Western Europe.[5]

Then there are seven ZPDB files of individuals whose names are given. First, there is Gerry Adams. It is simply stated that he is the President of Sinn Féin, the political wing of the IRA (PIRA).[6] Second, there is Brendan McFarlane. The file erroneously states that he is 'probably a leading member of the INLA'. In fact, he was a member of the PIRA. It is also mentioned that he was arrested in Amsterdam in 1986 during an arms smuggle.[7] Third, there is Dominic McGlinchey (who would be shot dead in 1994). It is written, correctly, that he is 'probably the leader of the militant group, the INLA'.[8] Fourth, there is Patrick Joseph Magee. Almost nothing is written on him except that he is a member of the IRA (PIRA) and that his nickname is 'Chancer'.[9] In fact, Magee was the main PIRA man involved in the Brighton attack. Fifth, there was Peter Sherry. The file indicates that he is a member of the IRA (PIRA) and that he had 'allegedly been trained in a Libyan training camp'.[10] Relations between Colonel Muammar al-Gaddafi's Libya and the PIRA have been well documented.[11]

But the ZPDB files also contain two names of the Irish republicans' sworn enemies in Northern Ireland, the unionists and the loyalist terrorists. File number six is Reverend Ian Paisley's. It is mentioned that he is a member of the '*Evangelische Kirche*', which in Germany refers mostly to the Lutheran Church. This was rather a hasty generalisation because Paisley is indeed a Protestant but a Free Presbyterian and not a Lutheran. More curiously it is also explained that Paisley is the 'leader of the paramilitary Protestant organisation UEM in Northern Ireland'.[12] This is also mentioned in a document written by HA-XXII in October 1986, which is studied in detail below. According to this document, UEM stands for 'Ulster Ecclesia Militans'.[13] It remains most difficult to get more information regarding this UEM. An article in the *Irish Times* that deals with some Stasi connections with Ireland also describes it as standing for 'Ulster Ecclesia Militans',[14] but there are no further details.[15] In any case, the Stasi could easily have known that Paisley had a troubled relationship with paramilitaries. But like Adams's file, Paisley's is very far from being informative and useful. The same goes for the last file, number seven: Andy Tyrie of the Ulster Defence Association (UDA). It is stated that Tyrie is a member of the '*Evangelische Kirche*' and that he is the leader of the UDA.[16] However, nowhere is it mentioned that the UDA and the Ulster Volunteer Force (UVF) did not particularly like Paisley as the reverend and his followers had said on occasion that the UDA and the UVF were as bad as the PIRA. Paisley's relations with

Protestant terrorists (loyalists) remain ambiguous.[17] Loyalist leaders accused him of using them only when it suited him. Tyrie went as far as to write a play, *This Is It*, in which he portrayed how a young loyalist was duped by Paisley.[18]

A few remarks concerning the above. The Stasi obviously got the wrong information about Brendan McFarlane since it supposed he was a member of the INLA. By 1989, when McFarlane's file was created, it should have been very easy for HA-XXII not to have made this wrong supposition. McFarlane was a prominent member of the PIRA who had played a leading role with Bobby Sands during the PIRA prisoners' hunger strike in the Maze prison in Belfast in 1981, which had attracted worldwide attention. Simply reading the British and Irish newspapers, even West German ones, would have revealed that McFarlane belonged to the PIRA. This calls into question HA-XXII's efficiency in intelligence-gathering in the Northern Irish case. Regarding Ian Paisley, it was rather sloppy of the Stasi to write that he was a member of the '*Evangelische Kirche*', a broad-brush appellation. There were several Protestant churches in Northern Ireland that considerably differed in outlook. The remarks about McFarlane and especially Paisley might seem rather pedantic, but they are not. If the Stasi was to undertake operations in Northern Ireland, it might as well familiarise itself with the local situation, which is essential to success. The journalist Tim Weiner has described some of the CIA's disastrous operations throughout the world. One of the main reasons for the CIA's failures was frequently a very bad or a nonexistent knowledge of local cultures, societies and languages.[19] But the Stasi was impressively efficient in West Germany. So, what this tends to reveal is that Northern Ireland was not a top priority, even despite the fact that the terrorist conflict had serious consequences for Britain, arguably NATO's main member state in Europe. This lack of priority very likely explains this certain degree of sloppiness. Yet, as will be explained in Chapter 5, the Stasi definitely took a close interest in Irish terrorist activities in the FRG and obtained first-hand information.

There is also an interesting coincidence emerging here. There are seven Irishmen/Northern Irishmen mentioned above. But seven is also the number of Irish names the Stasi transmitted to the SOUD, the Russian acronym for System of Unified Registration of Data on the Enemy. These Irish and Northern Irish people fell under the category PK3 that is 'Members of terrorist organisations'.[20] The SOUD had been put forward by Yuri Andropov when he was head of the KGB. The idea was that all the secret services of the Eastern European countries would centralise names of people of interest to them. The Stasi was the most generous donator. By 1989, it had given 65,556 names.[21] It is over the top to consider Paisley a terrorist and the Stasi's information on him and the others was not exactly top secret, if it was *their* names that had been transmitted to the SOUD of course. Then again the Stasi did transmit Timothy Garton Ash's name to the SOUD. He was placed in category PK5 that is 'Persons who execute commissions for subversive activity against the states of the socialist community on behalf of hostile intelligence services, centres of political–ideological diversion, Zionist, hostile, émigré, clerical and other organisations'. Ultimately the SOUD failed as the secret services involved preferred to keep the best information to themselves.[22]

But there are more interesting files in the ZPDB than these seven persons. There are indeed files on four Irishmen, one Englishman or woman and one Austrian man or woman (the last two being involved with Irish republican terrorists). The first file simply records that the Irishman (PIRA) in question shot his way out of a court in Belfast; his name and his '*Rufname*' (name by which one is generally known) also figure but have been blacked out by the BStU.[23] The second file concerns a male member of the INLA. Not only did HA-XXII know his name and '*Rufname*' (blacked out) but also the numbers of his two false passports (blacked out), his two false names (blacked out) and his address in Belfast (blacked out). It is stated that he might be staying in West Germany and that he was planning attacks on British citizens and installations.[24] The third file is about a male member of the INLA and again HA-XXII knew his name and his '*Rufname*', the number of his false passport, his false name, his address in Belfast (all these details have been blacked out) and the facts that he might be staying in West Germany and was planning attacks on British citizens and installations.[25] It might very well be that these two INLA members were about to travel and operate together. The fourth file also deals with a male member of the INLA. HA-XXII knew his name and '*Rufname*', his address in Belfast and also the fact that he was undertaking a lecture tour in West Germany about the Irish question. He might be in touch with two particular individuals (all details blacked out).[26]

The fifth and sixth files are related and are the most interesting ones. File number five gives the details of an Austrian national. The gender is not written but the term '*Geburtsname*' is. It can be translated by name at birth or by maiden name. So, it is very likely that the person was a woman. The date of birth, name and '*Rufname*' have been blacked out. The exact address in Austria has also been blacked out, but not the town, Ferlach. It is stated that the person was preparing an arms transaction with an Englishman or woman (name blacked out).[27]

That it was the town of Ferlach would make sense in this context as it had a centuries-old tradition of gun making. File number six concerns an Englishman or woman, member of the PIRA. HA-XXII knew his/her name and '*Rufname*' (all blacked out) but the term '*Geburtsname*' is mentioned, again indicating that it was very likely a woman. The date of birth was also known (blacked out). It was the person who was about to contact the Austrian national with the aim of setting up the arms deal. The Austrian's name figures on this file (blacked out).[28] Both files reveal that the information came from a source abroad and that the Stasi seemed to have decided to watch the meeting between the Austrian and the Briton. Indeed, the term '*Op-int Kontakt*' (*OPerativ INTeressanter Kontakt*) is mentioned in both files. In Stasi jargon it means a person who was in touch with the Ministry of State Security and who had contacts with, or had possibilities to influence, a person or group which was of interest to the ministry.[29] There are no further indications or hints as to whom this '*Op-int Kontakt*' might have been.

However, one document reveals more on the Anglo (Irish)–Austrian meeting. Before studying this 23-page document in some detail, it must be stated that it appears in two different files, MfS/HA-XXII, no. 17219, and MfS/HA-XXII, no. 19156. The two documents are identical, one being a duplicate of the other. Also, this document appears to have been used in a study on the Stasi's operations in Britain.[30] It will now be commented on in the chronological order of its paragraphs as it is arguably the most interesting Stasi document on the conflict in Northern Ireland. It was written by HA-XXII/8 (terrorism, section 8 being in charge of international terrorism), dated 20 October 1986 and entitled '*Einschätzung zur extremistischen Organisation "Irish Republican Army-IRA"*' (evaluation of the extremist organisation Irish Republican Army-IRA).[31]

The first paragraph is called '*Entstehung und Entwicklung der Organisation*' (origin and development of the organisation) and it is not devoid of factual mistakes. The opening lines state that England had implemented a 'colonial policy' against Ireland since 1167 and that the English were responsible for starting the conflict. The Irish had been involved in a 'national liberation struggle', increasing in intensity as time passed by. The GDR being a Communist country, this particular interpretation conforms to a Marxist-Leninist interpretation of history. HA-XXII/8 wrote that 'petit-bourgeois nationalist Irish circles' founded Sinn Féin in 1910 and that it was inspired by Russian revolutionary developments. Sinn Féin was in fact founded in 1905 by Arthur Griffith who was not inspired by events in Russia but by the Austro-Hungarian political model, which he believed could be adopted for Anglo-Irish relations.[32] There were other such factual errors. A rather glaring spelling mistake was 'Eamon de Vatera' instead of de Valera.

What comes next is better. HA-XX/8 explained that the Troubles were the result of a combination of socio-economic factors and the discrimination of the minority, the nationalist/Catholic people, by the unionist/Protestant majority and the Royal Ulster Constabulary (RUC). HA-XXII/8 remarked that the IRA protected the minority against the attacks of the RUC, the British army and the loyalists. However, a split occurred in the IRA in 1970 and there had been two wings since: first, the Official IRA (OIRA) which abandoned the armed struggle and pursued its goal of establishing a 'democratic Socialist republic' by political means; second, the Provisional IRA (PIRA), also known as 'Provos' who fought for 'Christian Socialism without Socialists and Communists'. The PIRA's aims were to be achieved by 'armed struggle and terrorist methods'. Sinn Féin was described as being the 'political representative of the IRA [PIRA]'. Its President was Gerry Adams. HA-XXII/8 stated that from now on it would deal with the 'provisional wing' of the IRA (for clarity's sake the author uses the abbreviation PIRA throughout). The information contained in the document was based on 'unofficial information and official indications, including reports of Western media'.

Before moving on to the second paragraph, a last point should be mentioned. One of HA-XXII/8's sources of information on the IRA's history was *Nordirland*; *Probleme, Fakten, Hintergründe* (Northern Ireland; problems, facts, backgrounds) published by the East German journalist Christa Schaffmann in East Berlin in 1982. The evidence is all too obvious. In Schaffmann's book, there are the same factual and spelling mistakes, the same kind of terminology like '*Partisanenkrieg*' and especially the same sentences, which the Stasi had slightly changed with different turns of phrases or different nouns and adjectives. The following is but one example:

> –HA-XXII/8's report (1986):
> According to an action programme, this wing [OIRA] fights for a democratic, socialist republic in which the working class and its allies supervise the production, distribution and exchange methods.[33]
>
> – Schaffmann's book (1982):
> According to the action programme of October 1971, the official IRA fights for a democratic, socialist republic in which the working class and its allies supervise the production, distribution and exchange methods.[34]

HA-XXII/8 was guilty of plagiarism here. The beginning of the next paragraph was also inspired by Schaffmann's book, notably the passage on the SAS (Special Air Service, a British elite force). Of course, it could be argued that the Stasi simply needed an open source to provide the historical background and that there was no need for elaborate intelligence actions here. But with all due respect to Schaffmann, it would have been very easy for the Stasi to simply pick up the latest book on the IRA available in an Irish or British bookshop. The chances are that it would have been far more informative. All things considered, there was a rather dilettante approach in writing this part of the report.

The second paragraph is entitled '*Erkenntnisse zu Angriffsrichtungen, angewandte Mittel und Methoden der "IRA"*' (findings about the PIRA's targets, resources and methods). It was stated that the Northern Irish conflict had airs of a civil war and that the British security forces had interned more than 5,000 people between 1971 and 1976 after the introduction of internment without trial. The SAS had inflicted serious casualties on the PIRA. Therefore, the Irish republicans had abandoned their traditional organisation consisting of brigades, companies and so on and had come up with a far more effective organisation, the Active Service Unit (ASU). ASUs were small cells of three to five people, making it very difficult for the security forces to neutralise them. HA-XXII/8 listed the PIRA's targets: leading British and Northern Irish politicians, officers and soldiers of the British army, British and Northern Irish entrepreneurs but also people of the Catholic/nationalist minority. 'Order and security in the Catholic ghettoes' had to be maintained. Criminals, after repeated warnings, could be kneecapped (shooting through the knees). HA-XXII/8 indicated that 'members of Protestant paramilitary organisations, especially of the Ulster Defence Regiment (UDR) and the Ulster Defence Association (UDA)' were also targets. The problem here in the report is that the UDR was not a Protestant paramilitary organisation but a British infantry regiment, overwhelmingly composed of Northern Irish Protestants, whose aim was to protect lives and property. Again, this mistake could have been easily avoided. Mentioning the Ulster Volunteer Force (UVF) instead would have been appropriate.

According to HA-XXII/8, the PIRA's activities were an excuse for the British authorities to increase repressive countermeasures. Since 1974, the PIRA had spread its operations to Britain by attacking army installations, cinemas, subways and others. The aim of this was to attract international publicity. Its most spectacular attack happened on 12 October 1984 when it nearly killed Margaret Thatcher in Brighton. HA-XXII/8 commented that this bomb attack was subsequently used by the British 'to calumny the PIRA in a comprehensive Western media campaign and to manipulate public opinion in favour of reintroducing the death penalty for murderers in Great Britain'. Between 1978 and

1980, the PIRA attacked British army personnel and installations and diplomats in West Germany and the Netherlands. The Republic of Ireland was used by the PIRA as a 'rest base' and for 'logistical purposes'. Most of the PIRA's 'modern war material' came from the United States. This last piece of information was most definitely correct as Sean Boyne's meticulous study of gun-running operations to Ireland shows.[35]

HA-XXII/8 gave some details on hunger strikes, notably Bobby Sands's case. It explained that they were part of the traditional strategy of the Irish republican movement. In 1981, Sands went on hunger strike in jail, followed by other republican prisoners, in order to obtain the status of political prisoner. He died after sixty-six days. A total of ten men eventually died and the Thatcher government did not give in. HA-XXII/8 added that there were no indications to suggest that after 1980–81, there had been 'solidarity hunger strikes' among the PIRA/INLA prisoners for prisoners of other Western European terrorist organisations with similar demands, as had been the case in 1985 with RAF detainees. In 1982–83, the British introduced the 'supergrass' system. This was an incitement for PIRA members to betray their comrades in return for a new life and money. It was partially successful and the PIRA retaliated by kidnapping relatives of the supergrasses and threatening to kill them, which they did in some cases.

The third paragraph is most interesting: '*Nationale und internationale Verbindungen der "IRA"*' (national and international links of the PIRA). It begins with a brief explanation of how the INLA saw the light. On 8 December 1974, Seamus Costello broke away from the OIRA and set up the Irish National Liberation Army (INLA) whose political wing was the Irish Republican Socialist Party (IRSP). Costello was subsequently killed allegedly by 'former comrades in arms of the OIRA'. This was correct. The IRSP would only have around 1,000 members who were not particularly politically active. It was believed that Dominic McGlinchey had been the leader of the INLA since 1982. HA-XXII/8 wrote that there were 'visibly close contacts' between the PIRA and the INLA (this was indeed known to be the case).[36] These contacts became obvious during the coordination of the hunger strikes and escapes from jail in 1980–81.

In 1984, Western media reported about the 'alleged knowledge of enemy security services' of the INLA's financial sources and armament supplies in the Middle East. The finger was pointed at Libya where, 'allegedly', members of the PIRA, the INLA and even Protestant terrorist organisations had received military training in camps. The report read: 'In XXII/8 there is no confirmed operational evidence at hand'. Moreover, XXII/8 continued, there had been 'no clear evidence' until now that the PIRA had contacts with extremist groups in Britain such as the Scottish National Liberation Army (SNLA). It was deemed by 'unofficial' sources that the efforts of other terrorist groups to coordinate activities with the PIRA had failed because the PIRA's leadership was 'marked by fanatical Irish nationalism'.

Regarding continental connections HA-XXII/8 explained the following:

> On account of the same characterised nationalist–ideological basic attitudes there are contacts between the 'IRA' and the terrorist organisation 'ETA' in the Spanish Basque country. Indications of coordinated actions are not known.
>
> Western mass media have repeatedly reported on the knowledge of enemy intelligence organisations regarding alleged contacts of the 'RAF' and the 'Revolutionary Cells' with the 'IRA'.
>
> - Jean [Jan] Carl RASPE [RAF] in 1971 is said to have travelled to Great Britain in order to establish contacts with the 'IRA'.
>
> Furthermore, it was reported that a meeting with FRG, Italian, Arab, Japanese, French and Dutch representatives of terrorist groups is supposed to have taken place in Belfast in 1979. On that occasion agreements were supposedly reached between representatives of the 'IRA' and from the FRG concerning joint attacks on members of the British Army of the Rhine [BAOR].
>
> According to unofficial information, however, the so-called second generation of the 'RAF' undertook to make contact with the 'IRA', but it was only attempts and no viable contacts came about.[37]

It is most important to stress here that HA-XXII/8 clearly indicated that contacts between the PIRA and the RAF and this international meeting of terrorists in Belfast were *supposed* to have taken place, and that it did *not* possess information that confirmed this.[38]

HA-XXII/8 wrote in its report that according to 'reliable operational information', enemy security organisations deemed that members and installations of BAOR would be the targets of terrorist attacks and additional security measures would be taken. In another paragraph, it was stated: 'Operational knowledge regarding the Revolutionary Cells in the Federal Republic of Germany rules out that there are contacts with the PIRA'. HA-XXII/8 also wrote that NORAID (Northern Aid), which was a 'support committee' of American citizens of Irish descent, was particularly supportive of the PIRA. It would appear that their fundraising activities were worth millions, which provided the PIRA and the INLA with weapons. Then there was some sensational intelligence:

> According to available information, the arms trade and transport from the USA to Northern Ireland is steered, i.e. controlled by the CIA. Western mass media reported in 1983 among other years that such CIA activities became known through surveillance measures of the FBI.[39]

This was astounding to say the very least. It cannot be credible that the CIA was playing its part to undermine Britain, Washington's most reliable ally in Western Europe. What was in all likelihood meant here was that the CIA had in fact infiltrated PIRA gun-running operations and by so doing was able to manipulate the PIRA. There is no definitive answer, at least not found in archives in Berlin and Dublin. But it would seem that very strange things do happen in the murky world of gun-running. Apparently, during the 1980s the FBI made a deal with a notorious gangster called James 'Whitey' Bulger who was involved in getting weapons for the PIRA. The deal was that the FBI would not interfere in the PIRA business provided Bulger gave information on the Mafia in New England. Joe Cahill, who commanded the PIRA in Belfast, was at the heart of the plot and travelled to Boston to get weapons. On one occasion an FBI agent went as far as to provide explosives for the PIRA.[40] So, what this comes down to is that the FBI, or at least some of its agents, had conceived a rather devious operation to weaken the Mafia but at the expense of the US's British allies.

Paragraph four is called '*Maßnahmen gegnerischer Organe*' (measures taken by enemy organisations). At once, HA-XXII/8 stated:

> The ruling British circles have until now sought to bring under their control the totality of Ireland. Their economic interests and NATO's increasing military interest because of the geographic location of the island are main factors in this.
>
> The sending of troops by Great Britain in 1969 has secured these supremacist claims until now.[41]

Of course, this view is open to personal interpretation but there can be no doubt that both the PIRA and the INLA would have strongly agreed with HA-XXII/8. It might be relevant to remark here that as recently as 1974 some British Conservative politicians still believed that Ireland constituted a weak link in British defence.[42] In 1972, HA-XXII/8 continued, the British government abolished the Northern Irish government and dissolved Northern Ireland's Parliament, 'Storemont [Stormont]'. Direct rule from London was imposed. HA-XXII/8 explained that the Protestants' historic prejudices and fears of the Catholics were manipulated and that they were not prepared to grant the Catholic minority equal social and political rights. Two men among the Northern Irish population played a leading role,

Ian Paisley and Andy Tyrie. HA-XXII/8 added that 'the division of the Northern Irish working class and other employed classes was successful through massive ideological manipulation'. It went on to give several examples of exceptional measures taken by the British to combat the PIRA like internment without trial in 1971 and the denial of the status of political prisoner in 1976. Some of these measures circumvented existing British law.

HA-XXII/8 wrote that there would be around 4,000 PIRA prisoners in Northern Irish jails at that time. They were condemned to very long imprisonment sentences, in some cases over one hundred years. The PIRA had already attacked some of the judges because of this 'arbitrary justice'. According to information at HA-XXII/8's disposal, it could be stated that a number of persons had been imprisoned without any evidence that they were members of the PIRA or the INLA or that they had been involved in terrorist activities. They had confessed under torture.[43] It may be recalled here that on 18 January 1978, the European Court of Human Rights in Strasbourg found that the British army used controversial interrogation techniques in Northern Ireland.[44]

HA-XXII/8 pointed out that unlike in Spain, there was no evidence to suggest that there were 'death squads' operating among the British army and police against the PIRA, although it happened frequently that security forces 'chased persons and shot them'.[45] This issue of British army and RUC death squads or their shoot-to-kill policy remains controversial and serious hints point that this was indeed the case.[46] In the 1970s, Peter Wright, a former MI5 senior intelligence officer, had devised a plan to tap the Irish telephone network system using the British embassy in Dublin to gain vital knowledge on the PIRA. Although MI5 agreed, the British Foreign Office did not. Wright went on to suggest the 'planting [of] booby-trapped detonators on the Provisionals' but MI5 refused and told him: 'That's murder'.[47] HA-XXII/8 explained that the 'British ruling circles and the Northern Irish reactionary forces' invested much money and material to fight the PIRA. Special units were being trained similar to the West German anti-terrorist unit, the GSG9. But, 'it is alleged that forces of these special units also train fighters of the Protestant paramilitary groups'.[48] This was an allusion to the accusation that some British security forces worked with the Ulster Defence Association (UDA), the Ulster Volunteer Force (UVF) and others. It is known as 'collusion', and it was founded. In 1990, the Stevens inquiry found that the security forces did leak out information to loyalist terrorist groups. Some of these loyalists had made it public that in choosing their victims for assassination, they relied on information provided by these forces.[49]

HA-XXII/8 stated in its report that the security forces in Northern Ireland cooperated more and more closely with those of NATO countries, and surveillance of and search for terrorists were taking place via Interpol. It then mentioned an interesting technique that the British secret services used to get sources of information:

> Under the pretext of so-called lucky-dip holidays for Irish people done by computers, the British secret service has attempted several times to enlist them in southern European host countries as information sources. Obviously, the British secret service was helped by the respective secret services of these countries.[50]

HA-XXII/8 remarked that since 1984, Margaret Thatcher's government had been putting pressure on the British mass media to prevent it from giving information on the PIRA's struggle and the police's repressive measures. Such 'censorship' led to a public scandal involving the British Broadcasting Corporation (BBC) in August 1985. 'On the other hand, the media is being used time and again to influence public opinion, especially conservative social classes, against the PIRA', it continued.

HA-XXII/8 then turned its attention to some individual members of the PIRA and gun-running activities. It explained that international cooperation had led to arrests of some individuals and the discovery of arms transports. A detailed account was given of how eventually Patrick Joseph Magee, who was involved in the bombing of the Grand Hotel in Brighton on 12 October 1984, had been identified. Magee's fingerprints had been found on the hotel's registration document. Scotland Yard had mounted a surveillance operation on Peter Sherry who had, 'allegedly', been trained twice in Libya. This operation had led Scotland Yard to Magee who, after meeting Sherry in Carlisle, had driven to Glasgow. On 22 June 1985, the police had arrested a PIRA team in an apartment in Glasgow and a timetable for a bombing campaign had been discovered. HA-XXII/8 gave several examples of gun-running operations that had gone wrong for the PIRA. On 13 August 1983 in Le Havre in France, arms, including 'magazines for Soviet Kalashnikovs', had been discovered in a van. Two Frenchmen and one Irishman had been arrested. There was more: 'On 29/09/1984, the Irish navy brought in an Irish cutter named *Marita Ann* which had 7 tons of American war material on board. Allegedly, an American type KH-11 satellite was used and monitored a Canadian ship and the transfer of the cargo 240 km off the Irish coast. Five persons were arrested.'[51]

Interestingly, in his seminal study of MI5 published in 2009, Christopher Andrew devotes a long passage to the *Marita Ann* affair. He explains that MI5 got wind of the PIRA's gun-running operation a few months before it was due to take place and mounted a surveillance operation 'originally codenamed CARDOON'. Basing himself on MI5 documents, Andrew writes: 'In the early hours of 28 September ... an R[oyal] A[ir] F[orce] Nimrod observed arms being transferred to the *Marita Ann* from an American trawler which had crossed the Atlantic with its port of registration painted out ... When the *Marita Ann* was intercepted by the Irish naval vessel *Emer*, its crew initially believed they had been boarded by a fisheries protection vessel and shouted, "We have no salmon on board!".'[52] There is here no reference to an 'American type KH-11 satellite' and a 'Canadian ship'.

HA-XXII/8 wrote that in May 1985 in Boston, eight PIRA arm buyers had been arrested by the FBI and on 16 January 1986, three Irishmen had been arrested in Amsterdam as they were in charge of a container with weapons and ammunition. But the report also contains some very interesting information on an arms deal in Austria:

> According to unofficial information the meeting between PIRA member
>
> - [name blacked out], born in 1959 (no further details) and Austrian gunsmith
> - [name and address blacked out], Ferlach, in preparation or realisation of an arms deal was under the control of the security service of Karuten [Kärnten, in Austria].
>
> [Blacked out] travelled from the Federal Republic of Germany to Ferlach and subsequently travelled to Italy.
>
> The preliminary information sent by the Federal Ministry of the Interior in Vienna to the Italian authorities shows that there was an international exchange of information regarding these findings.[53]

The Stasi had obtained first-hand information. It must be added here that it had soon found out more details about the PIRA member in question as the ZPDB file, written on 14 November 1986 (as mentioned above), reveals the name (blacked out) of the individual and also the fact that he/she was English (probably a woman). The last sentence of the above extract tends to indicate that the Stasi had a source within the Austrian Ministry, or at the receiving end in Italy. According to Austrian journalists Kurt and Max Tozzer, the Stasi had spies in the country and they were 'particularly industrious and able'. In 2000, it became publicly known that there had been one spy in the Ministry of the Interior and two in the police headquarters in Vienna among other places. During the Cold War, arms had been smuggled into Austria by the Americans, British and Soviets to support their respective allies.[54]

It should also be noted that an arms scandal rocked Ireland in 1970. Some members of the Irish government might have been involved in smuggling weapons for the PIRA. It would seem that these arms originated from Vienna.[55] The West German embassy reported to Bonn at the time that initially Taoiseach Jack Lynch had said that they came from Czechoslovakia but that on 9 May he had told the Dáil that this was not so: 'I think they were transferred from Frankfurt to Vienna, but there was no mention of Czechoslovakia in this transaction'.[56] Interestingly, only a few days before, on 1 May at 3 PM, the Irish embassy in Bonn had phoned the West German authorities to inform them that about 5 tons of armament had been bought for the IRA in the Federal Republic and that they would 'possibly be shipped from Frankfurt Airport or the Port of Hamburg to Ireland in the coming days'. Mr Swift of the embassy asked that customs should be notified, which was done.[57] Obviously, the Irish government had reliable intelligence.

Before finishing the study of HA-XXII/8's document of 20 October 1986, the Austrian episode leads to the following question: was the Stasi involved in providing arms to the OIRA, PIRA or the INLA? Some authors have asserted that this had been the case. In his impressive history of the IRA, Ed Moloney writes that PIRA member Brian Keenan was said to have had contacts with the East bloc, especially with the Stasi, but that concrete evidence to support this is not forthcoming. Keenan was often described as the tough Marxist within the PIRA. As Moloney points out it was in fact the OIRA that got support from the Soviet Union and the East bloc: 'The Officials received cash, guns, and other aid both from East Berlin and from Moscow but no new evidence has ever been produced to indicate that the Provisionals enjoyed such generosity'.[58] As to Keenan, he wrote that he 'got his real political inspiration from the neocolonial struggles of South and Central America rather than from the dull orthodoxy of Eastern Europe'.[59] His name, however, is not mentioned in the surviving Stasi material. There is one index card with the name Brian Keenan but it concerns an Irishman who had been kidnapped by Islamic Jihad in Beirut in 1986.[60] In an authoritative study of the OIRA and the Workers' Party, Brian Hanley and Scott Millar write that 'by 1979 East German sources had also produced a shipment of new weapons, which were brought into Ireland by truck'.[61]

It can be stated here that in the 6,000 photocopies of original Stasi documents concerning Ireland and Northern Ireland, not a single sheet proves or even hints that the Stasi directly helped the OIRA, PIRA or INLA by providing either finance or armament. Therefore, as far as East Germany is concerned the said assertions cannot be confirmed. An important point must be emphasised though. This is not to say that it is absolutely certain that the Stasi did not do it, but based on the evidence of the surviving written material it simply cannot be proved. The Stasi was like a bureaucratic monster, recording every single operational detail and result. It would be inconceivable that no written trace would have existed. Of course, there is the possibility that all incriminating evidence met its fate in the incinerators when it became clear that the regime's days were numbered.

The fifth and last paragraph is the conclusion: '*Operative Schlußfolgerungen*' (operational conclusions). HA-XXII/8 predicted that the PIRA would continue its struggle against the British army, the RUC and members of Protestant paramilitary organisations because the 'political and military interests of the ruling British circles in Northern Ireland' meant that the British intended to stay. The PIRA had a very long experience in fighting and had a good structure. It used the territory of the Republic of Ireland as a base. HA-XXII/8 added that there was an important potential of support and sympathy among the Catholic population. It is not known how HA-XXII/8 had assessed this last point but it was very questionable. In any case, it wrote that the British government was pressuring the Irish government into taking more action regarding the border which was easy to cross for the PIRA. There was also increasing cooperation between the security services of NATO member states. However, the British strategy of 'drying up the breeding ground' for the PIRA in the Catholic community in Northern Ireland was hampered by the fact that the social-economic conditions kept deteriorating. In certain counties in Northern Ireland, unemployment among the Catholic minority reached levels of between 30 per cent and 60 per cent. HA-XXII/8's assessment was certainly realistic as unemployment could drive some to join the PIRA.

So, all things considered, what interest was the PIRA for the Stasi and the GDR? HA-XXII/8 stated that so far the PIRA had not 'developed hostile plans and intentions against the GDR' and had not 'misused' East German territory. HA-XXII/8 believed that 'no such activities are to be expected in the foreseeable future'. It was also satisfied that the PIRA had 'no contacts with persons from the GDR'. Concerning the 'so-called "Anti-imperialistic Western European Front"', the PIRA was not likely to join it soon 'since it does not identify with the political motives of the "RAF" and the "AD" [Action Directe, French terrorist group]'. Having said this, there was the possibility that it might use 'specific logistical support' of the RAF and the AD in order to attack 'British representatives and military installations'. It was decided that HA-XXII/8 would continue to closely watch and analyse PIRA activities and figure out if there was any danger to the GDR. HA-XXII/8 wrote:

> The compilation of the hostile-target file concerning the 'IRA' [PIRA], registration number XV 5414/85, is to be continued and all operational findings on terrorist activities and developmental trends are to be documented in the process of operational assessment of the situation/annual planning of work.[62]

A hostile-target file ('*Feindobjektakte*') in Stasi jargon meant an association, group, institution and so on outside the GDR against which the Stasi took action.[63] It did not necessarily mean that the Stasi was opposed to the PIRA but simply that its activities had caught its attention and that they had to be assessed in relation to the GDR. In his meticulous study of the Stasi's operations in the West, Hubertus Knabe has included a list of such associations, institutions and groups which the Stasi established in October 1988. The PIRA is number 90 and is defined as an 'Irish terrorist organisation', being watched by Department XXII.[64]

A few remarks come to mind. Clearly, according to this document at least, the GDR was not a base for the PIRA and there were no contacts with East Germans. If this had been the case, the report would undoubtedly have stated this. But, this interpretation poses a problem. Markus Wolf himself wrote in his memoirs in 1997:

> Until 1979, [Department XXII] had been relatively small, but the decision to widen our dealings with 'forces involved in armed struggle', as we put it, meant that it had to grow fast. Within a few years, it had more than eight hundred employees, although I believe only about twenty of them knew about the direct contacts with terrorist groups. It is now known that these contacts included the Irish Republican Army [IRA], the Basque separatist movement, ETA, and Carlos the Jackal. I did not know of these connections at the time and indeed I never met Carlos or other international terrorist stars.[65]

Whether or not Wolf did not know anything about connections with terrorists cannot be assessed here and is not the object of this book. However, his denying has been hotly contested.[66] But what the above extract could imply is that the author of the HA-XXII/8 report, a Captain Sell, did not know about direct contacts with the PIRA when he wrote it, or even that contacts with the PIRA began *after* October 1986 (when the report was written). After all, the Stasi was an arcane world where information did not reach everybody's eyes and ears, secrecy being paramount. The same goes for all intelligence services. Former KGB officer Victor Cherkashin writes: 'That was how the system worked. Intelligence information was so compartmentalized that we didn't tell even people who were involved unless there was a need for them to know.'[67] But as will be shown in the following chapter, a Stasi document written on 25 September 1989 very likely proves that there was no direct contact with the PIRA or support from the Stasi, and that consequently Wolf was most certainly wrong concerning contacts with the PIRA.

Overall, the ZPDB documents show that HA-XXII was able to obtain some very good information on Irish republicans. This was confirmed when the PIRA and INLA began their continental campaign against BAOR. The Stasi found out essential information thanks notably to its agents and moles deep inside the West German security organisations.

Notes

1 BStU, MfS-HA XXII, no. 19156, this file contains all the ZPDB documents.
2 www.bstu.bund.de, website of the Bundesbeauftragte für die Unterlagen des Staatssicherheitsdienstes der ehemaligen Deutschen Demokratischen Republik archive, Berlin (Stasi archive, website hereafter referred to as www.bstu.bund.de), 'Abkürzungsverzeichnis: Häufig verwendete Abkürzungen und Begriffe des Ministeriums für Staatssicherheit', by Klaus Richter (*et al.*), p. 3 (accessed on 6 May 2010).
3 BStU, MfS-HA XXII, 19156, doc. no. 228900108X, written on 19 January 1989.
4 *Ibid.*, doc. no. 2289001119, written on 19 January 1989.
5 *Ibid.*, doc. no. 2289007238, written on 11 June 1989.
6 *Ibid.*, doc. no. 2289007529, written on 17 July 1989.
7 *Ibid.*, doc. no. 2289007537, written on 17 July 1989.
8 *Ibid.*, doc. no. 2289007545, written on 17 July 1989.
9 *Ibid.*, doc. no. 228900757X, written on 17 July 1989.
10 *Ibid.*, doc. no. 2289007588, written on 17 July 1989.
11 See Moloney, *Secret History of the IRA*.
12 BStU, MfS-HA XXII, no. 19156, doc. no. 2289007553, written on 17 July 1989.
13 *Ibid.*, MfS-HA XXII, no. 17219, 20 October 1986.
14 'Stasi's IRA files suggest CIA link', by Denis Staunton, *Irish Times*, 29 June 1996.
15 This UEM does not appear in Steve Bruce's authoritative study on Paisley and his followers (*God Save Ulster: The Religion and Politics of Paisleyism* (Oxford: Oxford University Press, 1986)).
16 BStU, MfS-HA XXII, no. 19156, doc. no. 2289007561, written on 17 July 1989.
17 Bruce, *God Save Ulster*, pp. 78–9, 142 (and n. 19), p. 109.
18 H. McDonald & J. Cusack, *UDA: Inside the Heart of Loyalist Terror* (Dublin: Penguin Ireland, 2004), pp. 120, 134.

19 T. Weiner, *Legacy of Ashes: The History of the CIA* (London: Penguin, 2008), see for example pp. 281, 430–1.
20 M. Tantzscher, 'Datentransfers nach Moskau', in Knabe, *West-Arbeit des MfS*, pp. 292–3.
21 *Ibid.*, p. 292.
22 Garton Ash, *The File*, pp. 185–6.
23 BStU, MfS-HA XXII, no. 19156, doc. no. 2281002061, written on 11 August 1981.
24 *Ibid.*, doc. no. 2283000457, written on 13 January 1983. There are eight pages in this file. At first they appear to concern three different people but the same doc. no. tends to indicate that it is about a single person.
25 *Ibid.*, doc. no. 2283000422, written on 13 January 1983. There are six pages in this file. At first they appear to concern two different people but the same doc. no. tends to indicate that it is about a single person.
26 *Ibid.*, doc. no. 2283000393, written on 14 January 1983.
27 *Ibid.*, MfS-HA XXII, no. 19156, doc. no. 2286009414, written on 6 November 1986.
28 *Ibid.*, doc. no. 2286009422, written on 14 November 1986.
29 The author is grateful to Mr Christian Schwack of the BStU for this information. E-mail exchange of 13 April 2011.
30 Glees, *The Stasi Files*, pp. 135–8. In his pioneering work on the Stasi's activities in Britain, Glees gives as an example 'of material on the IRA' the document of 20 October 1986, written by HA-XXII/8, contained in file no. 17219. However, in Glees's version it is only three pages long while the original document is about twenty-three pages. Also, the translation of this document by the author differs substantially from the translation given in Glees's groundbreaking book.
31 BStU, MfS-HA XXII, no. 19156 and no. 17219, 20 October 1986 (identical documents), '*Einschätzung zur extremistischen Organisation "Irish Republican Army-IRA"*'.
32 aan de Wiel, *Irish Factor, 1899–1919*, pp. 90–1.
33 BStU, MfS-HA XXII, no. 19156 and no. 17219 (identical documents), 20 October 1986, '*Einschätzung zur extremistischen Organisation "Irish Republican Army-IRA"*'.
34 Christa Schaffmann, *Nordirland: Probleme, Fakten, Hintergründe* (Berlin: Dietz Verlag, 1982), p. 36.
35 S. Boyne, *Gunrunners: The Covert Arms Trail to Ireland* (Dublin: O'Brien Press, 2006), pp. 431–8.
36 T. P. Coogan, *The IRA* (London: HarperCollins, 1993), first published in 1970, p. 569.
37 BStU, MfS-HA XXII, no. 19156 and no. 17219 (identical documents), 20 October 1986, '*Einschätzung zur extremistischen Organisation "Irish Republican Army-IRA"*'.
38 It would appear that this author's translation differs considerably from Anthony Glees's in *The Stasi Files*, p. 137.

39 BStU, MfS-HA XXII, no. 19156 and no. 17219 (identical documents), 20 October 1986, '*Einschätzung zur extremistischen Organisation "Irish Republican Army-IRA"*'.
40 '"Whitey" Bulger and the FBI deal that opened up Boston to the IRA', by E. Moloney, *Irish Times*, 23 February 2013. Moloney writes about Kevin Cullen and Shelley Murphy's *Whitey Bulger: America's Most Wanted Gangster and the Manhunt that Brought Him to Justice* (New York: W.W. Norton, 2013).
41 BStU, MfS-HA XXII, no. 19156 & no. 17219 (identical documents), 20 October 1986, '*Einschätzung zur extremistischen Organisation 'Irish Republican Army-IRA"*.
42 S. Hartley, *The Irish Question as a Problem in British Foreign Policy, 1914–1918* (Basingstoke: Macmillan, 1987), p. 198.
43 BStU, MfS-HA XXII, no. 19156 & no. 17219 (identical documents), 20 October 1986, '*Einschätzung zur extremistischen Organisation "Irish Republican Army-IRA"*'.
44 Coogan, *The IRA*, pp. 545, 548, 546–7. For the Special Air Service's controversial actions in Northern Ireland and Ireland, see also Fr Raymond Murray's in-depth investigation, *The SAS in Ireland* (Cork: Mercier Press, 1990).
45 BStU, MfS-HA XXII, no. 19156 and no. 17219 (identical documents), 20 October 1986, '*Einschätzung zur extremistischen Organisation "Irish Republican Army-IRA"*'.
46 O'Halpin, *Defending Ireland*, pp. 336–7.
47 P. Wright with P. Greengrass, *Spy Catcher: The Candid Autobiography of a Senior Intelligence Officer* (New York: Viking Penguin, 1987), pp. 358–9.
48 BStU, MfS-HA XXII, no. 19156 and no. 17219 (identical documents), 20 October 1986, '*Einschätzung zur extremistischen Organisation "Irish Republican Army-IRA"*'.
49 O'Halpin, *Defending Ireland*, pp. 334–5.
50 BStU, MfS-HA XXII, no. 19156 and no. 17219 (identical documents), 20 October 1986, '*Einschätzung zur extremistischen Organisation "Irish Republican Army-IRA"*'.
51 *Ibid.*
52 Andrew, *Defence of the Realm*, pp. 703–4.
53 BStU, MfS-HA XXII, no. 19156 and no. 17219 (identical documents), 20 October 1986, '*Einschätzung zur extremistischen Organisation "Irish Republican Army-IRA"*'.
54 K. Tozzer & M. Tozzer, *Das Netz der Schattenmänner: Geheimdienste in Österreich* (Wien: Holzhausen Verlag, 2003), pp. 125, 131, 181–92, 203–5.
55 Boyne, *Gunrunners*, see ch. 2, 'The Gun Dealer and the Arms Crisis', pp. 52–88 and p. 67, for reference to Vienna, and p. 431 for reference to Austria.

56 AA-PA, B20-200, Bd. 1825, Mr Hamburger, West German embassy in Dublin, to Bonn, 12 May 1970.
57 *Ibid.*, B31, Bd. 376, Henatsch, V3, to Referat I A 5 im Hause, 4 May 1970, phone call made on 1 May 1970 at 3 p.m.
58 Moloney, *Secret History of the IRA*, p. 137.
59 *Ibid.*
60 BStU, HA XXII/VSH (AR2), index card regarding Brian Keenan.
61 Hanley & Millar, *Lost Revolution*, p. 404.
62 BStU, MfS-HA XXII, no. 19156 & no. 17219 (identical documents), 20 October 1986, '*Einschätzung zur extremistischen Organisation "Irish Republican Army-IRA"*'.
63 Definition of '*Feindobjekt*' found in the alphabetical list of abbreviations ('*MfS Abkürzungen von A–Z*') at the BStU website, www.bstu.bund.de (accessed 5 July 2010).
64 Knabe, *West-Arbeit des MfS*, p. 440.
65 Wolf & McElvoy, *Man without a Face*, p. 303.
66 See for example J. O. Koehler, *Stasi: The Untold Story of the East German Secret Police* (Boulder, CO: Westview Press, 1999), pp. 400–1. While there are some very good investigative qualities to this book, it is plagued by a very obvious anti-left and pro-American Republican Party bias.
67 Cherkashin with Feifer, *Spy Handler*, p. 17.

5

Watching the PIRA, the INLA and BAOR, 1970s–1980s

What was the impact of the Northern Irish crisis, or the 'Troubles', beginning in August 1969 with the arrival of the British army in Belfast and Derry (Londonderry), on the course of the Cold War? It remains difficult to give an exact estimation as not all archives have been disclosed be they in the East or the West. But there was most definitely a serious strategic impact as released documents show beyond any doubt. The Irish, the British, the North Atlantic Treaty Organization (NATO), the US Central Intelligence Agency (CIA), the Foreign Military Intelligence of the Soviet Army General Staff (GRU), the Soviet Committee for State Security (KGB), the Intelligence Department of the East German National People's Army (NVA) and the Stasi knew that the Northern Irish conflict was depleting the British defences of Northern West Germany, right on the front line of a possible East–West conflict. Moreover, HA-XXII closely watched the development of the PIRA's continental campaign against the British Army of the Rhine (BAOR), which began in 1973 as the HVA recorded two PIRA attacks that year, one in Mönchengladbach and another one in Hanover.[1] The Stasi's sources were not only West German media reports but also moles within the West German intelligence and security agencies.

On 7 March 1971, the Irish Ambassador to West Germany, Paul Keating, arrived in a village near Hanover, not that far from the Iron Curtain. He was welcomed to a 'small informal supper' by the Irish Honorary Consul in the city, Dr Grünzig. But Keating was not the only guest. The other one was Major-General Jack Harman, commander of the British 1st Armoured Division in West Germany. This immediately begs the question why such an important British general had decided to discreetly meet Ireland's ambassador at that particular juncture. It would seem rather improbable that this was a purely personal initiative.

According to Keating, Harman had roots in Cork, 'of what might be called a Southern Unionist family'. Therefore, he had 'no particular sympathy for the Northern variety'. Harman explained that units under his command were regularly sent to Northern Ireland for tours of duty. It appeared that not many of his men had much of an idea of what was going on in the troubled province. According to the general, 'briefing poses great difficulties [and] the rotation of troops also imposes strains on the British command in [West] Germany'. The number of Irish recruits, north or south of the border, for the British army was declining, he said. Several of his friends, including Lieutenant-General Ian Freeland who was 'a particularly close friend of his' had served in Northern Ireland.[2] Freeland had been appointed the first general-officer-commanding in Northern Ireland in 1969 and his relatively short command proved to be controversial, notably one of his orders that 'all civilians seen carrying firearms or using firearms in any way whatsoever are liable to be shot without warning'.[3]

Harman said that his solution to the crisis would be 'a united Ireland arrived at in about twenty years' time'. The problem was how to reach that objective, as he put it. Keating suggested that Dublin and London had to show goodwill and 'a desire to reach a settlement with the minimum of violence'. He added that 'it was a pity that the relations between the troops and the Catholics had deteriorated and attributed this to General Freeland being led astray by provocateurs to start on arms searches'. Without hesitation Harman agreed and remarked that 'the arms collected were very small in number and of no military importance'. Keating felt that the General was ready to jettison the unionists if necessary 'in the interests of close Anglo-Irish relations'. The conclusion of his report read:

> Basically, I would say [Harman's] feeling now about Irish affairs is one of frustration because of the unsettling effect they are having on his command and on recruitment. Also, I feel that he is conscious that the Irish affair is causing ill will for Britain in many circles in [West] Germany. This situation will not, of course, persist if assassinations and atrocities are committed or appear to be committed by so-called nationalists.[4]

The Irish ambassador was right here. The PIRA and INLA's continental campaign against BAOR and British diplomatic personnel and interests would not go down well in West German public opinion. The Troubles were forcing the British to withdraw troops from West Germany and redeploy them in Northern Ireland; not to the point of totally depleting NATO defences against a possible Warsaw Pact attack of course, but sufficiently enough to come to West Germany's attention and to cause some worries in NATO circles.

In August, Keating went to the Foreign Office in Bonn to deliver a copy of Taoiseach Jack Lynch's telegram to British Prime Minister

Edward Heath regarding the Northern Irish conflict. There, he handed the telegram to the acting desk officer in charge of Irish affairs, Mr Weill:

> [Weill] received it with interest and said it would be brought at once to the attention of the Secretary of State and of the Minister. This was a matter under study at the moment because while the [West] German Government had little freedom of manoeuvre vis-à-vis the British Government which was not only a prospective EEC partner but a present ally and a negotiating member of the four-power group deciding the future of Berlin, nonetheless it had a [*sic*] interest in the matter because any further British troops to be sent to the North [Northern Ireland] must be withdrawn from the defences of [West] Germany.[5]

As the FRG would be at the very centre of a possible East–West war, it was easily understandable that Bonn was paying attention to British troop movements.

But the West Germans were not the only ones to worry. On 26 July 1971, NATO's Military Committee met and considered the developing situation. The British member, Commodore J. Pertwee, announced that the Second Battalion of the Queen's Regiment was to be sent to Northern Ireland on 3 August 'to assist in maintaining order'. Pertwee admitted that this would 'temporarily increase the number of BAOR units in Northern Ireland to five' but the battalion 'should be back in BAOR by 31 August'.[6] However, on 16 September, NATO's Military Committee met again and this time General Sir Victor FitzGeorge-Balfour informed his colleagues that the 2nd Battalion of the Queen's Regiment 'would return to its normal situation in [West] Germany on 16 and 17 September 1971'.[7] Clearly, there had been some delays, which to anybody present at the meeting should not have come as a surprise if they had simply switched on their radios or televisions or read their newspapers and kept informed of the evolution of the Troubles.

In February 1972, a few days after Bloody Sunday when the British army killed fourteen unarmed civil-rights protestors in Derry, a very angry crowd ransacked the British embassy in Dublin. In West Germany, the *Stuttgarter Zeitung* ran as a headline '25,000 Irish attack British embassy'. The newspaper wrote that in West Berlin two British cars were blown up. The windows of the BBC and Reuters offices in the city had been smashed and a protest action took place in front of the British general-consulate. Eight people were being detained.[8] The British had difficulties in bringing the Northern Irish situation under control. There were now 21,000 soldiers in the province.

The British felt that they had to say something to reassure their allies. On 16 June, the NATO Council (civilian) met and the chairman welcomed Sir Geoffrey Jackson, the former British Ambassador to Uruguay who was going to talk about urban guerrilla problems. No doubt, Jackson had observed at close quarters the guerrilla techniques of the Tupamaros in Uruguay. In the course of his briefing, he claimed that 'the defeat of an underground movement presupposed that the terrorist had to be driven underground and that the local population's grievances should be redressed, thus ensuring that when the terrorist emerged he would be a nuisance rather than a hero'. According to him, 'this was precisely what was being successfully done in Northern Ireland'.[9] Jackson's statement was miles away from reality. This was precisely what the British were not doing. It was events like the Falls Curfew, internment without trial and Bloody Sunday that were making the PIRA stronger as resentment within the nationalist/Catholic minority grew stronger.

Jackson's briefing was followed by a discussion. The Greek representative, P. A. Cavalierato, remarked: 'whether or not these movements were supported and financed by international Communism, members of the Alliance should realise the dangers which they could create and the profits which could be derived from by international Communism'. Jackson replied that 'although no definite proof of overall [Communist] co-ordination or control had ever been given a number of isolated pieces of evidence added up to a suggestive whole'.[10] Neither Jackson nor Cavalierato could have known how right they were at that moment as the KGB was about to launch 'Operation SPLASH', a gun-running operation for the OIRA.

On 27 July 1972, perhaps a slightly embarrassed Lieutenant-General FitzGeorge-Balfour explained to his colleagues in NATO's Military Council that 'unfortunately' additional BAOR units would be sent to Northern Ireland and that it was not possible to say for how long. He added that 'the United Kingdom Authorities had taken into account the implications for NATO but events had dictated priority towards firm action in Northern Ireland'.[11] NATO was however not entirely persuaded by the British argument that BAOR units in Northern Ireland could be re-sent to West Germany in '72 hours' in case of a Warsaw Pact attack. Supreme Headquarters Allied Powers Europe (SHAPE) noted that the British First Corps in the Northern Army Group (NORTHAG) was lacking 'nearly one-third of its major combat units'. SHAPE believed that further delays would occur.[12]

But not only British generals and Irish diplomats knew what was going on. So did BAOR soldiers on the ground. A BBC documentary shown on television in 2012 made this crystal clear. As the famous British military historian Max Hastings said, Northern Ireland became 'the major commitment of the British army' and 'units based in [West] Germany ... would train in [West] Germany, and then one morning they all climb into the planes and wave goodbye to the families'. Lieutenant Antony Beevor, who would later become another famous historian, served with the 11th Hussars between 1966 and 1971. He declared to the BBC that the Allied armies in West Germany would have no chance against a Warsaw Pact offensive and that the most they could do was 'to fight a delaying action' during which the threat of nuclear weapons might deter the Soviets.

And was Northern Ireland a key factor in the weak resistance that BAOR would oppose to a Warsaw Pact offensive? The answer is a definite yes. Captain Christopher Renwick, who served with 16th/5th Lancers between 1975 and 1986, put it eloquently to the BBC: 'We didn't really have a snowball's chance in hell stopping the Soviet Union ... The disadvantages were first that an awful lot of personnel that comprised the force that would do the fighting were actually somewhere else. They were in Northern Ireland.'[13] And the more Northern Ireland would be destabilised, the more BAOR soldiers would probably have to leave, thus weakening NATO's defence. It is true that in the 1960s the Warsaw Pact was supremely confident of sweeping away NATO resistance and even believed that it could reach Lyon, deep inside French territory, in nine days' time.[14] However, it should also be noted that during the second half of the 1970s, the Soviets began to increasingly fear NATO's technological advances.[15] This might mean that the impact of the Northern Irish crisis on NATO defence would gradually become less preoccupying for the West, if the West was fully aware of its technological superiority of course.

The Americans also knew the problem that the Northern Irish conflict posed for West Germany's defence, and not only through NATO meetings. On 1 August 1977, the CIA wrote a report entitled 'The Balance of Forces in Central Europe'. A passage highlighted a possible weakness: 'The three British divisions in NATO's Northern Army Group (NORTHAG) also could deploy forward with most of their essential support, although at reduced strength. [footnote at bottom of page: "The British divisions initially would be short about five combat battalions that are located in Northern Ireland. These units would require at least 72 hours to return to Germany"].'[16] Seventy-two hours sounded like a long time to try to come back and stem the Warsaw Pact advance. Obviously, by 1977, the nature of the problem still had not changed.

On the other side of the Iron Curtain the East Germans were perfectly aware of what was going on. In March 1972, the Intelligence

Department of the NVA (national people's army) wrote that 'an additional main task for the [British] armed forces is presently the suppression of the civil rights movement in Northern Ireland'. It had come to its attention that the British army was experiencing some recruiting difficulties (there was no conscription in the United Kingdom). It noted that the 'volunteer reserve in Northern Ireland', the Ulster Defence Regiment, had been temporarily activated and comprised '6,700 men'.[17] The NVA's assessment was correct as General Harman had told Ambassador Keating about these difficulties the previous year.

But what the Irish, British, Americans, NATO, CIA and not even the East Germans knew is that in the meantime Moscow had decided to get involved directly in Northern Ireland. The former correspondent of the *Allgemeinen Deutschen Nachrichtendienst* (ADN/the East German news service) Wolfgang Döhnert, who was based in London and also covered events in Ireland, remembers a meeting with Michael O'Riordan, the Irish Communist leader, probably during the 17th congress of the party. Döhnert asked him 'off the record' if there were contacts between the Irish Communists and the IRA. O'Riordan remained 'unperturbed' and answered that 'there were no contacts between the party and that organisation ... A few individual party members may, perhaps, have connections, "but we neither approve nor disapprove them"'.[18] It was a cautious answer, yet not a straightforward denial.

According to documents revealed by Boris Yeltsin, the late President of the Russian Federation, in his book *The View from the Kremlin* published in 1994, on 6 November 1969, O'Riordan had sent a letter to the Central Committee of the Communist Party of the Soviet Union (CPSU) in which he requested '2,000 assault rifles (7.62 mm) and 500 rounds of ammunition for each; 150 hand-held machine guns (9 mm) and 1,000 rounds of ammunition for each'. He explained to the Soviets that 'there has always existed more or less good relations between the IRA and the Irish Communists. We not only conduct a number of public and anti-imperialist activities together, but for more than a year a secret mechanism for consultations between the leadership of the IRA and the Joint Council of the Irish Workers' Party and the Communist Party of Northern Ireland has existed and is operating.' It was all for civil rights and the struggle for independence, he continued. In his letter, he stated that two members of the IRA, Cathal Goulding and Seamus Costello, had approached him to obtain arms from the Soviet Union. O'Riordan suggested that 'the weapons may be delivered to Ireland on a tugboat, which will be run by a small select and reliable crew consisting of IRA members'.[19]

It looked too ambitious. It is hard to see how the Soviets would have been in a position to smuggle 2,000 assault rifles undetected into Ireland. Moreover it was problematic because if the Soviet-made rifles were intercepted by the British, Moscow would be in a very compromising position. The fact that only 500 rounds of ammunition were required for each rifle was not particularly realistic because the IRA would quickly run out of ammunition against the British army in case of a full-scale war. Seamus Costello too had approached the Soviets at their embassy in London and asked for arms. His request was rejected, however.[20]

The timing of O'Riordan's letter was not coincidental. Since August 1969, British soldiers had been in action on the streets of Belfast and Derry and two months before that, in June, O'Riordan had been in Moscow to participate in a conference of Communist parties. Soviet leader Leonid Brezhnev had then reiterated that it was the duty of the Communist bloc to support liberation movements struggling against imperialist forces. The situation in Ireland had not been mentioned specifically during the conference.[21] Yet, the Irish Communist leader could reasonably infer from Brezhnev's words that the Northern Irish crisis definitely constituted an anti-imperialist struggle, hence his asking for support. Moreover, O'Riordan was probably in Moscow's good books as he had agreed with the recent Soviet invasion of Czechoslovakia, unlike the Political Committee of his own party and other parties in the world. He represented the pro-Soviet faction within the Irish Workers' Party.[22]

As could have been expected, the Soviets pointed out to O'Riordan that it was a delicate matter. The sending of arms would provide opponents with the excuse that the IRA was acting 'on orders from Moscow' if the arms were intercepted or if it became known. Nevertheless, they did not turn down the request out of hand and between January 1970 and August 1972, Yuri Andropov, then head of the KGB and later leader of the Soviet Union, thought it over and O'Riordan was kept informed. The main issues were that the arms should not be Soviet made and that their provenance should not be known. O'Riordan should be able 'to guarantee the necessary conspiracy in shipping the weapons and preserving the secrecy of the source of their supply'. On 3 July 1972, O'Riordan wrote reassuringly to the Central Committee of the CPSU: 'As soon as you have made a political decision, I will take absolutely no part in the transport operation, and my role will only involve transferring the technical information about this to Seamus Costello. The shipment and all other operations will be carried out by members of the official IRA, who will not know anything about how this military material appeared or where it was obtained.'[23]

Eventually, on 21 August, Andropov informed the Central Committee: 'The KGB may organize and conduct such an operation ... A plan for conducting the operation is attached'. The operation was code-named 'SPLASH' and was a model of ingenuity. The Soviets had sent a vessel called *Reduktor* to explore the shoals of Stanton some 90 kilometres off the Northern Irish coast. The idea was to submerge bundles of weapons to a depth of about 40 metres. These bundles would be 'marked as experimental underwater exploration equipment that is to be submerged at a certain point in the Atlantic and then allowed to self-destruct'. In Murmansk, KGB officers would load the weapons 'including 2 machine guns, 70 automatic rifles, and 10 Walther pistols ... and 41,600 cartridges', all 'packed into 14 bundles, each weighing 81.5 kilograms'. To make sure that the weapons' provenance could not be traced back, they were all of German made and lubricated with West German oil. The packaging to wrap the weapons would be acquired abroad by the KGB.

Then, a ship with a KGB crew would set sail from Murmansk and head for the shoals of Stanton. Once there, the bundles would be submerged and the Soviet ship would immediately leave the area. Two or three hours later, a fishing vessel manned by 'friends' (OIRA members) would arrive and find a 'marker (a buoy of the type ordinarily used by fishermen of all countries to indicate nets below; in this case of Japanese or Finnish make)'. The Irish crew, not informed as to the contents of the packages, would then raise the bundles and sail to an Irish port from where the weapons would be carried to safe locations, as guaranteed by O'Riordan. The whole idea here was to avoid direct contact between the KGB crew and the Irish. Andropov added that 'in order to work out the details of the organizational matters connected with OPERATION SPLASH, a meeting has been planned with Comrade O'Riordan outside the territory of the Soviet Union'.[24]

Boris Yeltsin wrote that he did not know if the weapons were successfully delivered.[25] When asked about 'Operation SPLASH', two former OIRA members did not know either. As to O'Riordan, he said that he was not involved.[26] Another source indicates that the arms were collected by Seamus Costello. He had bought a trawler but strangely could not remember the name of the ship. Consequently, Goulding asked a man called Mick Ryan to take his car and drive to a harbour on the west coast where it was located and find out its name. The next day, Costello and Ryan arrived at a pub in Leeson Street in Dublin to meet O'Riordan, but Ryan had to remain outside. Years later, Ryan declared that, had the Soviets delivered the weapons, he would have known it. But this operation was top secret and many from the IRA command were left in the dark.[27]

It would seem that there can be very little doubt that the weapons were delivered. Vasili Mitrokhin, a former KGB archivist who defected to Britain with six cases full of documents in 1992, brought along written evidence with him that it was the case. According to Christopher Andrew, some of the arms were probably used during the internal feuding between the OIRA, the PIRA and the INLA, and the Soviets delivered other arms shipments to the OIRA in similar fashion.[28] It should be recalled here that not only O'Riordan was accused of gun-running operations for Irish republicans but that serious allegations were also made against two Fianna Fáil cabinet ministers, Charles Haughey and Neil Blaney. While charges against the latter were dropped, the former had to stand trial but was eventually acquitted. It was a scandal that rocked the nation during the so-called arms trial in 1970.[29] MI5 did not find out about 'Operation SPLASH' until Mitrokhin arrived.[30]

Boris Shtern, a former Soviet journalist, claimed that in 1971, he had been on board a Soviet trawler that delivered a crate to two Irishmen. A KGB man was involved. Although he did not know what the crate contained, Shtern believed it was weapons.[31] A former British soldier remembers how in July 1973 he came under attack: 'There was an almighty bang, followed by what I took to be complete silence. That silence was, of course, my own ears reacting to the concussion of an explosion, created by the warhead of a Russian made RPG-7 (rocket propelled grenade) hitting the large extractor fan above our heads.'[32] Clearly, Soviet arms were around in Northern Ireland. However, RPGs were not part of the package the KGB had delivered to Costello since those weapons were German made. Also, it remains difficult to trace the exact provenance of this Soviet armament. For example, did it come directly from the Soviet Union or through a third party, like Libya? Andropov was most concerned with the issue of traceability. Therefore, it seems most unlikely that the Soviets sent their RPGs directly to Northern Ireland.

But why had it taken the Soviets so long to take the decision to send arms to the IRA, now OIRA, and why did they do it at that particular moment in time during the second half of 1972? As explained above, there was the risk of being discovered which could be extremely embarrassing all the more since current East–West talks in Europe were about to lead to the holding of the Conference on Security and Cooperation in Europe (CSCE) in Helsinki in a bid to foster détente. But clearly the opportunity to contribute to the destabilisation of the United Kingdom had eventually proved to be too enticing for the Soviets. Indeed, more and more British soldiers kept pouring into Northern Ireland. In 1969, there were 7,952 soldiers, but by 1972 there were 21,776. London was well aware of the possible escalation of the conflict. In a Green Paper published in 1972, Ted Heath's government declared 'that Northern Ireland should not offer a base for any external threat to the security of the United Kingdom'.[33] The Soviets begged to differ.

In November 1972, the GRU, the Foreign Military Intelligence of the Soviet Army General Staff, sent to the NVA's Intelligence Department a report outlining the weakening of British defences in West Germany. The GRU's report was an assessment of BAOR between 16 August and 15 September 1972. In other words, it corresponds to the moment when Andropov took the decision to send arms to Northern Ireland. Was it a mere coincidence? That would appear unlikely. It is well known that there was no love lost between the KGB and the GRU. But on this particular occasion, Andropov must have considered all the information at his disposal to make his decision: the British were in trouble and this was weakening their position in West Germany. Now was the time to move.

The GRU's report was entitled 'Deployment of Units of the 1st Army Corps of the British Army of the Rhine in Northern Ireland'. The Soviets explained that the British were pouring more and more troops into the troubled province 'from 8,000 men (01.01.1971) to 21,000 (01.09.1972)' and gave details concerning the specificities of the regiments like reconnaissance, medium self-propelled artillery, anti-aircraft and so on. A tour of duty generally lasted four months and heavy equipment was generally left behind in West Germany. British soldiers also 'get a special training (among others street fighting, use of teargas, extinguishing fires, street patrolling) in the SENNELAGER training area'. The GRU's conclusion was a logical outcome:

> The personnel ready for combat of the British Army of the Rhine is being reduced by 15% regarding armoured forces, by 21.5% regarding infantry and by 33% regarding artillery brigade on account of the deployment of units of the 1st Army Corps in Northern Ireland. As a result the combat readiness of the British army in the FRG is considerably affected.[34]

Although there is no evidence that Andropov read this particular report, in all likelihood it made him make up his mind about sending weapons to the OIRA. Perhaps he had already reached his decision to go ahead with 'Operation SPLASH' by that time. The Red Army and the NVA knew what degree of resistance to expect if it came down to a full-scale offensive in northern West Germany. It is to be noted that the sending of British units to Northern Ireland was an open secret. Back in October 1969, the *Limburgsch Dagblad*, a Dutch newspaper from just across the border, published an article entitled 'Rhine Army ready for action in Northern Ireland'. It was explained that 'units ... have begun practising the controlling of riots and the performance of security operations'.[35] The Northern Irish conflict lingered on with no end in sight. In February 1975, the GRU notified the NVA's Intelligence Department that it still disrupted BAOR's organisation.[36]

Another potential source of arms supply behind the Iron Curtain was Czechoslovakia. The PIRA made contact with a firm in Prague called Omnipol. In 1971, Omnipol sold arms to the Irish republicans but they were intercepted at Schiphol Airport in Amsterdam. The British secret service had infiltrated the gun-running operation. In 1972, however, Omnipol refused to do business with the PIRA. It is suspected that on this occasion the British had conducted a so-called 'sting operation' (a deceptive operation meant to arrest people committing criminal acts red-handed).[37] In July 1973 during the CSCE in Helsinki, Dr Garret FitzGerald, the Irish Minister for Foreign Affairs, had a meeting late in the evening with the Czechoslovak minister in the latter's embassy. After the other guests had gone, FitzGerald broached the burning issue:

> When the guests left, I raised the attempt to smuggle Czechoslovak arms to the IRA through Amsterdam several years earlier. I was told that the Czechoslovak government had been very upset by this affair; the arms had been sold to a dealer with whom they had had a good relationship for the preceding two years and were intended for the Middle East. They had terminated their relationship with him in view of what had happened.[38]

The Czechoslovaks honestly admitted that they had been involved in this affair, although they claimed that it had been unintentionally so.

Interestingly, in a special National Intelligence Estimate the CIA and other US intelligence agencies wrote that 'the Provisional Irish Republican Army (PIRA) received brief Soviet propaganda support in 1971, and the Czechoslovaks may have provided it with arms in the same year. But two years later the group was described by the KGB as a "criminal terrorist" organization, and there are currently no direct Soviet contacts with it.'[39] It would appear that the CIA had not found out about 'Operation SPLASH'. But where did the CIA find out that the KGB had labelled the PIRA a '"criminal terrorist" organization?' There is no answer, but Andropov was apparently not too fond of the PIRA and its methods. In his study of the KGB, Christopher Andrew writes that by the mid-1980s Moscow 'became concerned by the adverse publicity caused by terrorists' use of Soviet weapons'.[40] Adverse publicity remained Moscow's overriding concern.

On 14 January 1976, the NATO Council met and considered a document entitled 'Half-Yearly Review of Subversive and Intelligence Activities', which had been prepared by NATO's Special Committee. The review dealt with the activities of national Communist parties. It showed that 'except in Italy, Communist parties in Western Europe had not been able to strengthen their positions and that many of them received covert financial support from the Soviet Bloc'. A. R. Menzies, the representative of Canada, argued that 'the Soviet Union was continuing the ideological struggle and that although it denied all responsibility for terrorism, Carlos [the Jackal] had spent several years in Moscow'.

Sir John Killick, the British representative, stressed his country's intransigent position towards terrorism but had a more discerning view. He said: 'With respect to terrorism in Northern Ireland … it was regrettable that a large proportion of the IRA's finances came from United States sources'.[41] Killick was right and this was soon confirmed by the Special Committee. On 17 November, it met again and submitted its second 'Half-Yearly Review of Subversive and Intelligence Activities'. It was stated that the United States and Canada were a source of money and weapons for 'Irish republican and Protestant extremists' respectively. The Special Committee also reported that 'Soviet Bloc countries and certain Arab countries (Iraq, Libya, People's Republic of Yemen) continue to support Palestinian extremists' and that 'in the United Kingdom, Iraqi and Libyan intelligence services, based on their missions, have been active in support of terrorists'.[42]

On 10 February 1977, the NATO Military Committee devoted a large part of its agenda to the situation in Northern Ireland. Major-General P. J. H. Leng, the director of Military Operations in the British Ministry of Defence, briefed the committee on the latest developments. He said that that 'co-operation with the government in the South [Ireland] was steadily growing and improving' although 'co-operation was a politically sensitive issue for the [Irish] and therefore entailed an understandable measure of deliberate caution on their part lest the active PIRA campaign spread into the South'. Leng also explained that the IRA was now divided. The OIRA was 'overtly Marxist' but had renounced military campaigns and therefore was 'not of principal concern in [British] military operations'. However, the PIRA 'had … increasingly become a neo-Marxist organisation whose ultimate objective was the violent over-throw of all existing Government, North and South, and to establish a Marxist regime in their stead'. Leng added that 'there was no evidence to date which indicated that either Soviet or

Warsaw Pact countries were taking part in that campaign'.[43] It would appear that British and NATO intelligence did not get wind of the KGB's 'Operation SPLASH'.

As seen, the NVA's Intelligence Department was aware of BAOR's weakness. According to General Werner Großmann, who had replaced Markus Wolf in 1986 as leader of the HVA: 'Virtually all areas of the adversary's military policy, development of armed forces, armament projects etc were no secrets for the military intelligence of the HVA'. The reality was that the HVA had disposed of 'solid sources' within NATO since the mid-1960s. One of them, Rainer Rupp, points out that only NATO's nuclear targets and its General Defence Plan were not known. As he writes, 'NATO ... represented for the HVA an open book'.[44] The mass of documents available for this study definitely indicates that the Stasi analysed the development of the 'Troubles'. Were the East Germans going to exploit the Northern Irish conflict in some way or another?

Bloody Sunday on 30 January 1972 had immediate effects on West Berlin. West Germany itself was at the time reeling from the terrorist attacks of far-left groups notably the Rote Armee Fraktion (RAF, Red Army Faction) with which the Stasi had dealings.[45] On 2 February, a bomb exploded at the British Berlin Yacht Club, killing a 66-year-old West Berliner who worked for the British forces. Both the *Telegraf* and the *Tagesspiegel* explained that this act of terrorism was related to the British army's intervention in Derry.[46] On 4 February, the *Neue Rheinzeitung* informed its readers that the criminal police in West Berlin had arrested two men aged 21 and 22 for possession of explosives. It was alleged that one of them had gone to Belfast in the summer of 1971 and had had contacts with the IRA. The newspaper stated that it was not possible to say yet if the two men were involved in the attack on the British Berlin Yacht Club.[47] In fact, the people involved were Verena Becker, Harald Sommerfeld, Inge Viett and Günter Räther, more commonly known as Willi Räther.

Räther was of particular interest to HA-XXII. He was a former GDR citizen who had served in the NVA border guards with the rank of *Unterfeldwebel* (roughly sergeant). In 1964, he defected to the West and managed to cross the Iron Curtain. In the early 1970s, he became a member of Schwarze Hilfe (Black Help), a far-left group, and cooperated with the Tupamaros of West Berlin, a far-left group who had initiated a bombing campaign in the city at the end of the 1960s. At the beginning of 1972, Räther left Schwarze Hilfe for the Bewegung 2. Juni (movement of the 2nd of June), which was an anarchist terrorist group and ally of the RAF. He was eventually arrested in 1973. Apart from the fact that the bomb attack had been carried out as a reprisal for Bloody Sunday, nothing indicates in his Stasi file that he had had any contacts with the PIRA or OIRA or had even set foot in Ireland or Northern Ireland. The closest he came to the island was when he worked on a freighter and arrived in Scotland in 1965. The Stasi mounted a surveillance operation of Räther but it was rapidly abandoned as his case did not offer any interesting prospects. This operation was code-named 'Feldwebel'[48] and had nothing to do with the PIRA or OIRA as seems to have been suggested.[49] The Bewegung 2. Juni's bomb attack on the British Berlin Yacht Club had been some kind of solidarity act with the Irish republicans, a deed not uncommon among terrorist groups.

The Stasi's Department HA-IX (investigations), was in possession of 118 photographs of the British army in action in Belfast and Derry. There is no date, but they probably are from the early 1970s. The first photographs show the prison of Long Kesh from the outside. But far more interesting is the fact that British soldiers were photographed at close range while on patrol in the streets of Belfast. Even more striking are photographs taken from *inside* the Palace Barracks in Holywood in County Down. One picture shows a soldier probably sitting in his room with a shirt hanging from a clothes hanger in the background. The soldiers were identified as belonging to the 1st Battalion of the Parachute Regiment and the 7th Battalion of the Ulster Defence Regiment (UDR). There follows a series of eight photographs of the 2nd Battalion of the Royal Regiment of Fusiliers, also taken from *inside* North Street, 'the military headquarters responsible for the Catholic district of Belfast' as HA-IX indicated. The photographs show a British unit preparing to go on patrol, the faces of the men easily recognisable (blacked out).

This does raise the issue of security at Holywood and North Street because it would seem rather inconceivable that an officer or non-commissioned officer would have allowed photographs to be taken inside a barracks with the OIRA and PIRA around. But who had taken the photographs? It appears most unlikely that journalists would have been granted full access to army bases in a conflict zone, or that an East German agent disguised as a British soldier had managed this feat somehow. In fact, it appears more likely that a soldier had taken them. There are two reasons for this. First, the photographs do not appear to have been taken secretly. Second, the photograph of the soldier sitting in his room tends to indicate that the photographer was familiar with the place. Besides, there are two other photographs of a soldier holding his submachine gun, taken at extremely close range, almost on top of the gun. It must be stressed that this explanation is speculation. It remains a complete mystery how the photographs eventually landed in HA-IX's archive in East Berlin. The remainder of the photographs show Catholic and Protestant areas surrounded by barricades and barbed wire. There are also several shots taken at night, showing a British patrol lining up men against the wall. Again, all this was taken at very close range.[50]

It must be noted though that in 1976 the East German *Horizont* published a photograph taken at relatively close range by Marianne Fröbus (East German?), showing a man lined up against a wall by a British soldier.[51] The following year, *Horizont* published an article written by the correspondent of the Soviet *Izvestia* in Britain, Oleg Vassiliev, which included a photograph of a British soldier checking a woman's handbag. This one had been taken at a very close range (there was no source provided, but was it Vassiliev?).[52] Clearly the British army did not prevent photographs from being taken, but in these two cases they had been taken *outside* the barracks and posed no security threat. But the use of photographs by intelligence services could sometimes have unforeseen and strange outcomes (see Figures 5.1–5.13). In 1975, for example, BRIXMIS, the British military mission to the Soviet forces in East Germany, had managed to take photographs of Soviet aircraft during daring and risky missions. Much to its amazement and disgust, some of them were published in US aviation magazines shortly afterwards. The British were not able to find out who the leak was.[53]

Figure 5.1 Long Kesh, detail view (source: MfS-HA IX, no. 2451)

Figure 5.2 Belfast, Catholic area, near Shankill Road (source: MfS-HA IX, no. 2451)

Figure 5.3 Holywood, near Belfast, Palace Barracks (1st Battalion of the Parachute Regiment) (7th Battalion Ulster Defence Regiment) (source: MfS-HA IX, no. 2451)

Figure 5.4 Holywood, near Belfast, Palace Barracks (1st Battalion of the Parachute Regiment) (7th Battalion Ulster Defence Regiment) (source: MfS-HA IX, no. 2451)

Figure 5.5 Belfast, North Street, military headquarters responsible for the Catholic area of Belfast (source: MfS-HA IX, no. 2451)

Figure 5.6 Belfast, North Street, military headquarters responsible for the Catholic area of Belfast (source: MfS-HA IX, no. 2451)

Figure 5.7 Belfast, North Street, military headquarters responsible for the Catholic area of Belfast (source: MfS-HA IX, no. 2451)

Figure 5.8 Belfast, North Street, military headquarters responsible for the Catholic area of Belfast (source: MfS-HA IX, no. 2451)

Figure 5.9 Belfast, North Street, military headquarters responsible for the Catholic area of Belfast (source: MfS-HA IX, no. 2451)

Figure 5.10 Belfast, Falls Road, soldiers preparing a roadblock (source: MfS-HA IX, no. 2451)

Figure 5.11 Belfast, near docks, checkpoints (source: MfS-HA IX, no. 2451)

Figure 5.12 Checkpoints (source: MfS-HA IX, no. 2451)

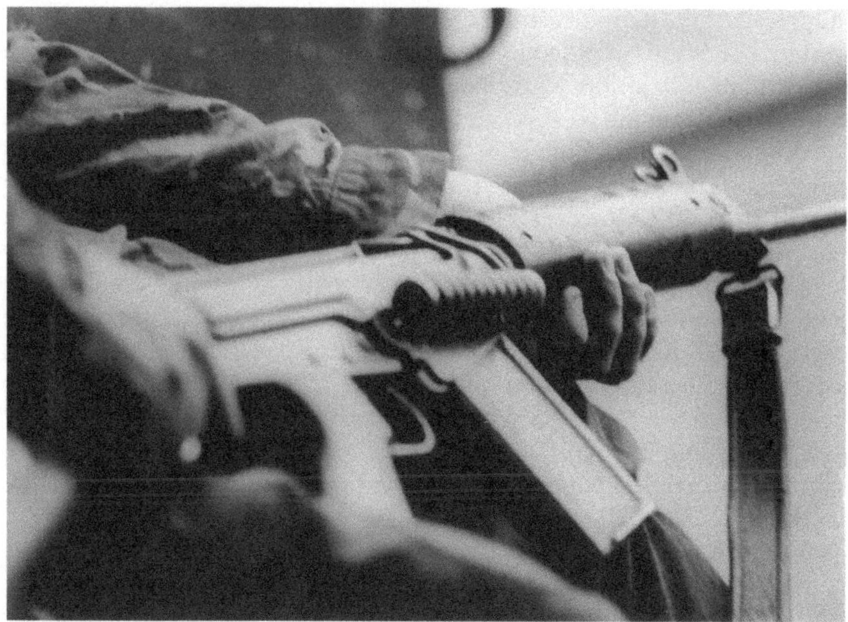

Figure 5.13 Fear – and English arguments (source: MfS-HA IX, no. 2451)

In November 1979, Major Lemme sent an 8-page document to General Gerhard Neiber, one of Erich Mielke's deputies. It was entitled 'Stance on International Terrorism' and represented the GDR's attitude towards terrorist activities throughout the world. The PIRA was included under the heading 'regional, autonomist/separatist movements'. Some of the document was in fact the draft of a speech meant to be read by a representative of the GDR's Ministry of the Interior at a UN meeting on criminality. The Stasi was asked to revise it and so it did. It suggested stressing that 'as a form of struggle to reach political aims, terrorism is entirely alien to our ideology'. It was added though that East Germany opposed any attempt at discrediting armed struggles of peoples against colonial and racist forces of oppression by defining them 'as a manifestation of international terrorism'.[54]

The issue of the Stasi's contacts with various terrorists groups has been hotly debated. When the change of regime was occurring in East Germany, many documents were destroyed by the Ministry of State Security.[55] However, definite links between the Stasi and terrorism have now been established and Markus Wolf frankly admitted this. In his memoirs, he wrote that in 1979 Mielke had ordered a study entitled 'On Activities of Representatives of the Palestinian Liberation Movement and Other International Terrorists and Their Attempts to Involve the GDR in the Preparations for Acts of Violence in the Countries of Western Europe'. Wolf explained that 'the proximity and ease of access to West Berlin were extremely useful to them'. However, the report stressed: 'Those activities from the territory of the GDR will result in political risks and jeopardize our national security interests'.[56] This statement was predictable when one bears in mind that at the end of the 1970s, the GDR had at long last achieved its ambition to be diplomatically recognised by Western countries. Therefore, if it transpired that it was involved in backing terrorists, those same diplomatic relations might well be broken off. According to Wolf, 'Mielke was terrified that our Palestinian connection would become public'. The Stasi was divided on the issue of terrorism.[57]

Yet, it is now known that the Stasi did train members of various terrorist groups (or what it might have considered to be anti-imperialist and colonialist liberation movements) and members of friendly security services in third-world and under-developed countries like Mozambique and Nicaragua for example. Over a thousand fighters from the African National Congress (ANC) were trained in Teterow in the northern part of the country while in 1980–81, eighty-one Palestinians were drilled on how to fight against Israel. Many Arab terrorists especially were able to use the GDR as a rest base or a transit country without any interference from the Stasi or the East German authorities. According to Jens Gieseke, between 1970 and 1989 almost 1,900 people from fifteen different states were trained although their numbers were reduced in the 1980s, possibly because of financial considerations.[58]

The KGB too had an ambivalent approach to terrorism. As shown, it only became reluctantly involved with the OIRA during 'Operation SPLASH'. It has been claimed that 'a worldwide web of terror' could 'be traced back to the Soviet Union'. However, since the disintegration of the Soviet Union, evidence has come to light that the KGB did try to control terrorist groups but that its influence was certainly not as important as was initially believed. Eunan O'Halpin, an expert in Irish intelligence, rightly remarks that some terrorists might well have been in touch with the Soviets and their allies but that did not mean that they were 'Russian pawns in the Cold War game'. They played an opportunistic game with the Soviets and essentially had their 'own agendas'. O'Halpin continues: 'in fact there is evidence that by the mid-1980s the Soviets were almost as alarmed by Qadhafi [Gaddafi] as was the West'.[59] Gaddafi sought a rapprochement with the Soviet Union. Back in 1973, MI6 got wind that a shipment of arms for the PIRA would be transported from Libya. The British warned the Irish and both monitored the *Claudia*'s journey from Tripoli until Dungarvan Bay where the Irish navy boarded the ship, arrested the PIRA members, including their leader Joe Cahill, and confiscated the arms which were mostly Soviet made.[60]

Worth mentioning in relation to gun-running operations originating from behind the Iron Curtain for terrorists in the West is an episode which involves the Romanian Department of State Security, far better known as the Securitate. Sometime in 1980 (no exact date), the Venezuelan-born international terrorist Carlos the 'Jackal' was invited to Bucharest to meet representatives of the Securitate. The connection between Carlos and the Romanians had been established by Kamal Youssef al-Issawi, also known as 'Ali', a member of the PFLP (Popular Front for the Liberation of Palestine). Carlos' partner, Magdalena Kopp, who was a member of the West German Revolutionary Cells, travelled first to the city to prepare the meeting. What the Securitate wanted from Carlos was that he silence Radio Free Europe (RFE) in Munich which broadcast propaganda about Romania. But, according to Kopp, cooperation between the Securitate and Carlos developed up to the point that it benefited ETA and the PIRA:

> Our contacts with the Romanians were an opportunity for ETA and the IRA to acquire a larger amount of weapons. I was not present for the consignment for ETA. However, I partly witnessed the one for the IRA. A French couple with a small child operated as couriers. Their names and the registration number of their camper van, equipped with double panels, were given to the Romanian authorities so that they were able to enter and leave the country without any problem. The meeting with the couple took place in a house on the outskirts of Bucharest where the weapons were kept. They did not know that we got the weapons from the Securitate. They also did not know that the caretaker, who was continually dragging his feet in the garden with his broom, was a Securitate man. They were simply satisfied that they got what they wanted.[61]

Although Kopp makes no distinction between the PIRA and OIRA, it was in all likelihood the Provisionals, as the OIRA had declared a ceasefire and had no need to get many weapons.[62]

Bucharest's involvement in providing arms to Western terrorist groups was revealed in spectacular fashion. In 1978, Lieutenant-General Ion Mihai Pacepa of the Departamentul de Informatii Externe (DIE, department of external information, or Romanian foreign intelligence) defected to the United States. In 1987, he published a sensational book on Nicolae Ceauşescu's regime, notably portraying its shady relations with the PLO. According to Pacepa's revelations, Western Communists were being trained in sabotage and guerrilla techniques in Romania, and neighbouring Tito's Yugoslavia had contacts with the Italian Red Brigades.[63]

But was the PIRA really not aware that these weapons came from the Securitate, as Kopp writes? There is no answer here. What is known is that a Romanian agent within the PLO, a Palestinian called Hani al-Hassan code-named 'Annette', provided the DIE with many weapons of Western make which he had acquired in Lebanon or obtained from the PLO's contacts with the Red Brigades in Italy, the RAF, the Japanese Red Army (JRA) and other terrorist groups.[64] It has been said that the PIRA set up an arms deals with the PLO in the 1970s and that the first contacts between the two terrorist groups had taken place in the early 1970s in Colonel Gaddafi's Libya.[65] The first contacts between representatives of the PIRA, Joe Cahill and Denis McInerney, and the Libyan Intelligence Service took place in Warsaw in 1972.[66] Ceauşescu and Gaddafi got on well, calling each other 'brother'.[67] In 1987, the *Eskund* in Tripoli harbour was loaded with, among others, 1,000 AK47 automatic rifles made in Romania. They were meant for the PIRA.[68] The ship was eventually intercepted by the French customs.

A last remark must be made on the Romanian connection. Magdalena Kopp states that it was the Securitate that was watching the whole operation for the PIRA, involving French nationals. But could it rather have been the DIE? In his memoirs, Pacepa mentioned that the DIE used 'French professional terrorists who had been given asylum in Romania and were regularly used ... for drug smuggling and terrorism'.[69] Were all these French nationals a mere coincidence? Then again, the DIE was as good as destroyed after Pacepa's defection in 1978, so it cannot be excluded that the Securitate had taken over.

Back in East Berlin Erich Mielke changed his attitude towards the use of international terrorists some time during the 1980s. Markus Wolf remembered that his idea was that they could be used as 'behind-the-lines guerrilla forces for sabotage against the West'. Wolf believed it was a 'harebrained idea' and sarcastically commented: 'We could hardly control someone like Carlos inside East Germany in peacetime, so how would he prove dependable or even useful in the chaos of war?' The HVA spymaster felt that 'Mielke was really driven by a sense of inferiority towards both the West and the Soviet Union ... He wanted to become internationally significant – even if it meant becoming entangled with organizations like the PLO or the Red Army Faction.'[70] Wolf's assertion that Carlos could not be controlled is confirmed by Magdalena Kopp who wrote that Carlos had no time for '"East German bureaucrats" who, he believed, were even "counter-revolutionaries"'. The East Germans feared that they too could become targets for the 'Jackal'. By the mid-1980s, however, Carlos and his group were no longer welcome in East Berlin and elsewhere in the East bloc.[71] They were too well known and too unpredictable, and did not fit into the Soviet Union's new perestroika and glasnost. The Stasi's greatest apprehension was that the West might find out that Carlos and his associates were moving around in the GDR. In May 1984, HA-III (telecommunications) reported the bad news that indeed the West knew Carlos was in East Berlin and elsewhere in Eastern Europe.[72]

Besides Wolf's psychological explanation of Mielke's sudden interest in using terrorist groups against NATO countries, there might be another one relating to the change that had taken place in the course of the Cold War. Since 1981, an aggressive US president, Ronald Reagan, had been determined to do away with Communism once and for all. The Soviets and their allies felt that the world was a few steps closer to war, which would help to explain Mielke's decision. That there was a definite new interest shown by the Stasi in the terrorist activities of the PIRA and the INLA from the mid until end of the 1980s is proven by the amount of press cuttings collected by HA-XXII.[73] Moreover, regarding the IRA (no distinction made between the OIRA and the PIRA) the decision was apparently taken in 1988 to use an IMB (unofficial collaborator of the counter intelligence service in contact with the enemy), which presupposes that there was some kind of a link with the Irish republicans or that the building of links might be envisaged.

Interestingly, the IRA with only one IMB was at the lower end whereas Abu Nidal, the leader of the Palestinian Fatah group, was at the higher end with six IMBs. The Carlos group had five, the Palestinian Liberation Organization (PLO) also five, the Japanese Red Army three and ETA (the Basque Liberation Movement) two.[74] This does not necessarily mean that HA-XXII had not much interest in the IRA: it could simply have been a question of a lack of opportunities arising to have IMBs in place. What this IMB assigned to the IRA did is totally unknown. It should also be stressed that despite the term 'enemy', the Stasi did not regard the IRA and indeed the other terrorist groups mentioned above as enemies. The Stasi categorised them as '*Feindobjekt*' (hostile target) as it had to be absolutely sure first that they did not pose any threat to the GDR, hence the term IMB. According to Edgar Uher, a former HVA officer dealing with Ireland and Britain:

> That IMB thing in 1988 is intriguing. It would be a departure from the line, but I remember (from my then French days) that there was some nervousness over 'early detection of aggression plans'. It had become a major issue but was – as I learned later on – mainly introduced by the Soviets who somehow had been convinced of some imminent aggression. So it might fit into this picture.[75]

If the PIRA could be used somehow against the British during hostilities in Europe, it was an option worth exploring. It sounded difficult, though. In any case, nothing more is known on this IMB and it should be stressed that this decision was taken the year before the Wall fell. So, he/she cannot have done much.

In his autobiography, Wolf admitted that the GDR was involved in supporting several terrorist groups like the PLO. He pointed out though that the Americans were not above reproach either as they were involved in supporting similar groups in South and Central America for instance. His conclusion was that 'many of these unholy alliances were, on both sides, the tragic product of the Cold War'.[76] It would be difficult not to agree with the spymaster's remark. The East bloc alone was certainly not to blame. As seen in Chapter 4, Wolf claimed that the Stasi was in touch with the IRA, ETA and Carlos. The problem is, however, that Wolf's successor at the HVA, Werner Großmann, told *Irish Times* journalist Denis Staunton in 1995 that the Stasi 'concentrated almost exclusively on the German-speaking world and had little interest in countries such as Britain and Ireland'. According to Großmann: 'We didn't get involved with people like the IRA either. We left that to the KGB.'[77] Interestingly, Wolf mentioned the IRA only once in his chapter on terrorism and did not expand on it unlike the PLO, RAF, Carlos and others. The INLA is not mentioned at all.[78] After examining the available material for this study, it looks likely that Wolf's memory was not correct regarding the IRA. But he did write that his HVA was not responsible for contacts with terrorists but that HA-XXII was.[79] As far as this study is concerned, what Wolf claimed is certainly proved by the amount of documents on the PIRA and the INLA that emanated from HA-XXII and not from the HVA.

As we have seen, it has been asserted that the OIRA had received arms and cash from East Germany. In their outstanding study of the INLA Henry McDonald and Jack Holland have written that 'between late 1984 and 1986 the INLA held a series of meetings with representatives of al-Fatah and other Arab sympathisers in Prague,

East Berlin, Warsaw and Tunisia'. In the Czechoslovak capital, the PLO had an office from where it could organise arms shipments for various international terrorist groups. Apparently, the PLO was free to move around the city without being bothered by the local security services. But this was not the case in Warsaw and East Berlin. The Stasi continuously watched the PLO, and negotiations could only take place secretly. According to McDonald and Holland's research, a route was created to smuggle small-calibre weapons. An INLA-member would go to Prague to meet a 'PLO F18' man in a flat in downtown Prague. Once an agreement had been reached, the INLA member would return to the West but not directly from Czechoslovakia. He would travel to East Berlin where he was provided with 'a twelve-hour visa', and there was even 'a diplomatic car to escort him'. Then, the INLA man was told that he could collect the arms 'in a car parked in West Berlin'. From West Berlin he would drive to France.[80]

These weapons were only very small calibre compared to the following consignment in 1986. McDonald and Holland have stated that a deal worth £70,000 was struck by the INLA with the PLO in Prague. It included 'a hundred light anti-tank weapons', 'forty AK47 rifles, three 12.5 mm machine guns, and two 80 mm mortars'. Of course, the previous route via Berlin was not adequate for this particular shipment and instead it was decided to transport the weapons into East Germany and then bring them to the Polish port of Szczecin on the Baltic Sea. There, they would be loaded on a ship bound for Cyprus. From Cyprus, they would go to France, and from France they would be smuggled into Ireland. But suddenly things went wrong. First, the Stasi did not allow the shipment to cross into the GDR and it took weeks for the operation to resume. Then, the French police eventually arrested the INLA men 'as they were getting ready to move detonators for remote-controlled bombs'.[81] In the end, the weapons never reached Ireland.[82]

Unfortunately, McDonald and Holland have not given any source for their information on this particular INLA–PLO connection. In the acknowledgements of their book, it is stated: 'It is inevitable and understandable that the majority of those who helped and guided us in our research for this work prefer to remain anonymous'. While on the one hand, this is indeed perfectly understandable in the shady world of terrorism on the other hand, it also means that it cannot be verified. There is no written proof of this in the surviving documents in the Stasi archive. There can be no doubt whatsoever that the vast bureaucratic machine that was the Stasi would have recorded this. Of course, evidence might well have been destroyed but there is simply no way of knowing.

A few additional remarks must be made here. F18 was the group in charge of intelligence in Fatah, the wing of the PLO controlled by Yasser Arafat. It was Rudolf Raabe, a member of the Revolutionary Cells and the Westdeutsches Irlandsolidaritätskomitee (WISK, West German Ireland solidarity committee) of which more later, who put the INLA in touch with F18.[83] That the Stasi was continuously shadowing these terrorists and others, and also that it had initially prevented the shipment of weapons from transiting through East Germany despite the fact that it came from neighbouring Czechoslovakia, a fellow Warsaw Pact member, was probably due to the fact that it did not want these weapons to compromise the GDR in any way. Wolf wrote about this fear of being compromised. If true, this affair definitely shows that the East Germans were reluctant to get involved. This is confirmed by another story. In 1980, Carlos and his right-hand man, the West German Johannes Weinrich, who had been instrumental in founding the Revolutionary Cells, arrived in East Berlin from Aden (South Yemen) via Moscow. Their suitcases were full of weapons and the Stasi confiscated the whole lot. The East Germans had not been warned by their Soviet allies. Weinrich emphatically told the Stasi that the Soviets had agreed with this shipment for ETA, apparently to be used in the fight to liberate El Salvador. Eventually, the Stasi took the decision to hand back the weapons which were subsequently collected by two ETA members in a garage in East Berlin.[84] At the end of the day, the Stasi files do not shed any light on this INLA–PLO connection.

What is certain though is that HA-XXII possessed information about attacks by the PIRA and the INLA on British army personnel based in West Germany. In August 1978, the PIRA targeted BAOR again. Several bombs were detonated but nobody was killed. It was clear though that the PIRA did not have the means for a long-term campaign on the continent but it was proud to announce that it was able 'to strike at British imperialism anywhere at any time'. In 1979, the PIRA killed the British ambassador to the Netherlands and a member of his staff in The Hague. In Brussels, the terrorists killed a Belgian banker whom they wrongly believed was the British minister to NATO. A BAOR base in Dortmund was also targeted but the attack resulted only in slight structural damage. In Brussels again they blew up a bandstand where the British army was about to perform injuring eighteen people. MI5 learned that the PIRA leadership was still not satisfied. In 1980, the terrorists killed a British officer at Bielefeld in West Germany. A few other BAOR personnel were targeted in West Germany and also a British EEC commissioner in Brussels, but there was no loss of life. Christopher Andrew writes that MI5 believed a change of strategy then occurred within the PIRA leadership, 'stemming from the fear that further operations might compromise the propaganda success on the continent of Sinn Féin's campaign to exploit sympathy for the hunger strikers. There were no further PIRA attacks on British targets on the continent until 1987.'[85]

In August 1979, the *Spiegel* published an article with an English title: 'Dublin Connection'. The question put was: 'Do West German terrorists cooperate with the IRA?'. According to the magazine, the security services believed that there were clues pointing in that direction. The Irish authorities, within the larger framework of Interpol, were perfectly aware of this and kept an eye out for suspicious West German 'tourists'. The *Spiegel* wrote that Rudolf Raabe was supposedly at least for four months with the INLA in Dublin where he was also in touch with other West Germans. According to the Bundeskriminalamt (BKA, West German federal criminal office), these people had gone to Dublin to avoid arrest at home. Obviously, the magazine continued, the Revolutionary Cells had enjoyed hospitality in Ireland in the same way they had showed hospitality towards PIRA members through one of the Rote Hilfe (Red Help, far-left) groups in Wiesbaden, for instance. It was said that the PIRA had been assisted by West Germans in their attack on the BAOR base in Dortmund.[86]

The *Spiegel* had information that four presumed members of the Revolutionary Cells from Frankfurt am Main, Rudolf Schindler, Sabine Eckle, Christian Gauger and Sonja Suder, had probably gone to Ireland incognito. A police investigator had dryly commented: 'They want to enjoy a bit of visual instruction in Northern Ireland'. West German investigators had been tipped off by their British colleagues that the PIRA intended to extent its operations to the continent with the support of West German radicals. Interestingly, the *Spiegel* wrote about the RAF's attempt to assassinate Alexander Haig, NATO's US supreme commander, in June 1979. According to investigators, the intended target might in fact well have been British General Jack Harman as the techniques used in the attack were reminiscent of the 'IRA or another Irish group'.[87] Ironically, Harman was in favour of Irish reunification, as we have seen. It was a fact that the PIRA's struggle in Northern Ireland had caught the attention of some far-left radicals in West Germany. Magdalena Kopp, who became a member of the Revolutionary Cells in the 1970s, believed that the state was becoming increasingly more right-wing and that some action had to be taken against it. Like ETA in Spain or the Black Panthers in the United States, the PIRA was a model.[88]

The Stasi had followed the developments of the PIRA's renewed continental campaign; the first attacks had occurred in 1973 and had been noted by the HVA. The ZAIG (central evaluation and information group) got hold of West German newspapers, including tabloids, whose articles reported on the attacks between 1978 and 1980. The most interesting article was perhaps one in the *Frankfurter Rundschau*: 'Red Army Faction allegedly helps the IRA'. A high-ranking PIRA member stated that his group was supported in West Germany by remnants of the Baader-Meinhof group (RAF) who provided accommodation and documents and who also transported weapons and ammunition. The PIRA member claimed that an international meeting of revolutionaries had taken place in the summer of 1979 in Belfast during which it had been agreed between the Irish and the West Germans to attack BAOR soldiers.[89] Was this public boasting in old Irish Republican Brotherhood (IRB)/Fenian style of a previous age meant to worry the British, or was it serious? As explained in Chapter 4 regarding the ZPDB (central data bank for persons), in October 1986 HA-XXII/8 had written that this meeting was supposed to have taken place.

At the beginning of the 1980s (no precise date), HA-XXII compiled a file containing the names, dates of birth and nationality of five men who were all PIRA members. They were: Joseph Patrick Doherty (20/01/1955), Angelo Fusco (02/09/1956), Paul Patrick Magee (30/01/1948), Anthony Gerard Sloan (15/06/1954) and Gerard Sloan (21/04/1953). It was rather scant information to say the least. HA-XXII wrote on all sheets: 'The MfS [Stasi] has no further details'.[90] All these men had in fact escaped from Crumlin Road Gaol in Belfast in June 1981.

Also in the early 1980s, HA-XXII produced a report entitled 'Most Important Foreign Extremist and Terror Organisations and Groups'. It wrote that the PIRA and Sinn Féin were both struggling for an independent Irish state and the reunification of Ireland. Interestingly, it pointed out, rightly, that the PIRA's terror tactics did not benefit from the 'unanimous support of Irish Catholics and the Irish Republican movement'. In 1970, a split occurred within the IRA and Sinn Féin and there were now two wings: the Official IRA (OIRA) that favoured 'first and foremost' a political solution to the Northern Irish crisis and that approved of violent methods only to defend the population against reprisals, and the Provisional IRA (PIRA) that favoured 'terrorist methods'. It remained difficult to give a strength assessment of the PIRA as there was 'conflicting information'. The number of members was in between 300 to 600 to which could be added '3,000 [PIRA] sympathisers who are willing to provide asylum, protection, transport etc. to PIRA members'. HA-XXII explained that the PIRA leadership was the Army Council, which consisted of seven persons.

It was stated in the report that in the 1970s, the structure of the PIRA was deeply reorganised. The Irish republicans had decided to abandon the classic military organisation based on battalions and so on and replace it with a cell structure (Active Service Unit, ASU). In each cell there was 'a maximum of 8 persons of whom only two have contacts with other cells operating in the same area'. 'There is a high degree of conspiratorial means in the PIRA', HA-XXII continued. According to what one of the PIRA leaders had said, recruitment of volunteers was done 'so thoroughly that only about 2 out of 13 candidates are selected'. Before they became members of a cell, these volunteers had to undergo 'a compulsory training'. Small groups of volunteers, males and females, were sent 'abroad for "special training"'. Unfortunately, HA-XXII did not give more details on this particular aspect. PIRA volunteers were taught how to handle explosives and how to shoot. They were also taught how to behave if they were interrogated by the enemy and 'members of cells are advised to operate under false names and not to live in areas that are known to be hideouts for republicans'.

HA-XXII wrote that in 1971, the PIRA had produced a 'programme of demands' that would lead to the end of the conflict in Northern Ireland. According to 'T. Kogan' [Tim Pat Coogan], author of *The IRA*, this programme was still on the PIRA's agenda today. It consisted in ending 'the campaign of violence directed against the Irish people, introducing free elections to build a parliament in Ulster whose activities could constitute a first step in the setting up of a new government in Northern Ireland, liberating all Irish political prisoners and compensating all those who suffer from English violence'. Of course, the main objective remained the reunification of Ireland, which could be attained with a '"revolutionary guerrilla warfare" focused first of all on forcing the English to withdraw from Northern Ireland and by so doing to create the political conditions for the reunification of the northern and southern parts of the country'. HA-XXII stressed that Margaret Thatcher's government claimed that the PIRA had a '"Marxist" orientation' but that this was rejected by the PIRA leadership.

HA-XXII remarked that 'recently the attacking methods of the PIRA had become more varied and more precise'. Since 1978–79, the PIRA had been using remote-control explosive devices and the number of people killed by this method was significant: 29 out of 86 in 1979. The targets were 'businessmen, off-duty soldiers of the "Ulster Defence Regiment", English soldiers, prison officers and influential personalities'. Until 1978, the PIRA operated exclusively in Ireland and in Great Britain but that year it attacked BAOR in West Germany, HA-XXII explained. This trend to broaden the front to the European continent became more pronounced in 1979 when the PIRA killed the British ambassador in The Hague and also killed a Belgian financier in a case of mistaken identity. In 1980, three British soldiers were shot in West Germany.[91]

Still at the beginning of the 1980s, HA-XXII paid very close attention to the activities of the Westdeutsches Irlandsolidaritätskomitee (WISK, West German Ireland solidarity committee) based in Oberursel in the region of Hesse, north-west of Frankfurt am Main. The WISK was an organisation run by Irishmen living in the FRG whose objective was to alert the West German population's attention to British oppression in Northern Ireland and the republican cause. It had been founded in 1971 and had initially supported the OIRA, but in 1975 there was a change of heart. The WISK announced in the *Starry Plough*, the Irish Republican Socialist Party's mouthpiece (the IRSP was the INLA's political wing), that it was now 'in complete agreement with the policies and objectives of the IRSP'. The *Starry Plough* added about the WISK: '[They are] one of the major support groups in Europe for Civil Rights and National Liberation in Ireland. During the course of the past few years, they have arranged numerous speaking tours in Western Europe for members of the Sinn Féin Ard Chomhairle [National Executive] and have given significant financial support to that organisation.'[92]

It was hardly surprising that the WISK had caught the attention of the West German press. In 1977, the *Welt* published an article entitled 'United front: IRA and German terrorists'. It explained that 'Irish bombers want to build a united front with the Baader/Meinhof bandits [RAF]'. It was based on the Palestinians' strategy to internationalise terrorism. According to the *Welt*, the West German security services had indications of 'direct contacts between violent German groups and members of the so-called Provisional IRA'. The newspaper reported about the WISK's activities in Oberursel and mentioned that it cooperated with the Gesellschaft für Völkerfreundschaft (society for friendship between the peoples) in Cologne, which was a radical far-left group, and also with the Vereinigten Linken (united left) based in Mülheim an der Ruhr.[93]

One initiative of the WISK was particularly memorable. In 1975, it invited IRSP member Peter Pringle, PIRA member Séamus Loughran and People's Democracy member Fintan Vallely to tour Western Europe. The trio went to Austria, Belgium, the Netherlands and Switzerland. But it was in Osnabrück in West Germany, home of a British army barracks (later attacked by the PIRA in 1980, 1989 and 1996), where a most embarrassing moment occurred for the city's mayor. He welcomed the three men in rather great pomp and even gave them records of the

Osnabrück symphony orchestra. As protocol would dictate, but no doubt publicity needs also, the trio presented the mayor with a copy of *The Battle of the Bogside*. It was apparently only then that he became aware of what politics they represented.[94] One member of the WISK was Rudolf Raabe who was also a member of the Revolutionary Cells, as seen.[95] The WISK was not the only support group for Irish republicans in Western Europe. In the Netherlands, for instance, the Ierland Komitee Nederland (Ireland committee, Netherlands) was founded in 1975 and supported the PIRA. It had a publication entitled *Ierland Bulletin* which lasted for twenty-five years and it even organised a visit to the Netherlands for a representative of Provisional Sinn Féin.[96] There was also the H-Blok/Armagh Komitee (H-block/Armagh committee) which lasted from 1968 until 1985 and supported republican detainees in prisons like Long Kesh.[97]

On 18 February 1981, HA-XXII reported that the BKA (federal criminal office in West Germany) had recently learned that 'members of the terrorist organisation "Provisional Irish Republican Army (PIRA)" detained in the "Maze-Prison" in Northern Ireland will start a hunger strike on the first of March 1981'.[98] The information proved to be correct as PIRA and INLA prisoners led by Bobby Sands defied Margaret Thatcher, claiming Special Category Status for paramilitary prisoners. Ten prisoners, including Sands, eventually died. HA-XXII wrote that the BKA expected that the WISK would take this opportunity to indulge in numerous pro-Irish republican activities. The BKA also estimated that 'the WISK will take advantage of the present hunger strikes of a total of 52 (count on 17/02/1981) sympathisers and members of terrorist organisations in the FRG and West Berlin detained in FRG prisons, to propagate the planned hunger strike of the Irish terrorists as a "solidarity action"'.[99] Certainly, this idea of expressing solidarity between different terrorist groups was a fact. In 1985, the RAF named its team that killed West German industrialist Ernst Zimmermann 'Patsy O'Hara'.[100] O'Hara was one of the ten republicans who died with Sands.

The BKA could base its assessment on a precedent. In 1979, the WISK had organised a major conference on the Northern Irish crisis and the situation in the H-blocks. The H-blocks were cells in the Maze prison where PIRA and INLA prisoners were detained (also loyalist/Protestant prisoners of the UVF and the UDA). That year, the republican prisoners had decided to begin a 'dirty protest' after the British authorities had decided to treat them as ordinary criminals and force them to wear prison uniforms, thus not considering them as combatants or prisoners of war. This protest consisted in smearing the walls of the cells with their own excrement. At the University of Frankfurt am Main, more than a thousand people had attended a conference where members of the INLA and Sinn Féin had spoken.[101] The BKA's assessment was right. Soon HA-XXII came into possession of a 30-page document published by the WISK entitled *Irisch-republikanische Gefangene im Hungerstreik; Zum Kampf der irischen Gefangenen im H-Block/Long Kesh und im Frauenknast Armagh* (Irish republican prisoners on hunger strike; to the struggle of the Irish prisoners in the H-block/Long Kesh and in the female nick in Armagh). The document was made up of several articles and letters written by republican prisoners, describing their detention conditions and struggle against the prison and British authorities.[102] The WISK sold or rented out other material like for example an Ireland calendar, a video about the supergrass (informer) system, a book entitled *Missing Pieces* about the Irishwomen's movement and 'didactic materials' on Northern Ireland. A complete list of publications and other items was available in *Revolutionärer Zorn*, the mouthpiece of the Revolutionary Cells.[103]

Time had come to target the WISK. In July, the Stasi prepared a 28-page report on its activities. According to its findings, it was not an organisation in the classical sense since it 'did not have a regular membership'. It was in fact a 'lose union of persons who are themselves members of far-left organisations or with which they sympathise'. Its managing committee was based in Oberursel. The WISK's aims were to organise press conferences and exhibitions and also to distribute pamphlets about the conflict in Northern Ireland. It remained difficult to ascertain to what extent it maintained 'direct or indirect contacts' with the PIRA and the INLA although the stay of four PIRA members in the operational area (mainly around Frankfurt am Main) in November 1980 indicated that it did have direct contacts. These PIRA members had come over to participate in 'solidarity demonstrations in favour of imprisoned Irish republicans'. They had travelled from Frankfurt to Bochum, Bremen, Hamburg and Heidelberg.

With the beginning of the hunger strikes in 1981 the WISK stepped up its activities. There was a strong cooperation with the 'Anti-H-Block Committee', founded by a West German citizen born in Northern Ireland, Frank Gallagher. Again, this cooperation mainly involved disseminating propaganda material and organising demonstrations. The Stasi wrote that the objectives of the leaders of the two organisations were to establish parallels 'between the detention conditions and prisons in Northern Ireland and those in the FRG, and also between the aims of Irish republicans and those of far-left organisations in the FRG and West Berlin'. The Stasi deemed that it was obvious that their overall objective was 'to strengthen their presence in the far-left spheres of the operational area [West Germany]'. 'Terrorist circles in the FRG and West Berlin' should be strongly mobilised for what the two organisations have described as their 'common struggle against the inhumane detention conditions'.[104] The Stasi estimated that the WISK and the Anti-H-Block Committee managed to mobilise anything between 60 and 600 persons, mostly coming from far-left circles, for their protest actions. The rather low figure could be explained by the fact that these protest actions were 'being prepared at short notice and spontaneously'. It was known that the WISK particularly supported the activities of the Revolutionary Cells and had undertaken protest actions in November/December 1980 at a court in Frankfurt where three Revolutionary Cell-members were being tried, Sybille Straub, Sylvia Herzinger and Hermann Feiling.

The Stasi then took a close interest in those persons who had attended several of the activities organised by the WISK and the Anti-H-Block Committee. On 22 November 1980 at 8.30 p.m., an event had been organised in Dornbusch House in Frankfurt. There were four people that caught the Stasi's attention (all names blacked out by the BStU) but none of them appeared in its records although one had been the object of a surveillance operation mounted by the West German State Criminal Office (LKA) of Hessen. On 26 November, there had been a 'solidarity event' organised in the Martin Luther King House in Hamburg. No fewer than twenty-two persons landed in the Stasi's books. But there was more: thirteen were already recorded by various departments. Eight were in HA-XXII's records, one in *Bezirksverwaltung* (BV, regional administrative unit) Schwerin, one in HA-II (counter-espionage), one in BV Rostock, one in HA-PS/AKG (protection of persons/evaluation and control group) and one in the HVA. Finally, there had been a non-authorised protest action on 16 April 1981 at 10.50 p.m. in Frankfurt. The Stasi focused on five persons, two of them being already recorded by HA-XXII. HA-VI (border control/tourism) had on record another three persons, including one who had paid a visit to an East German citizen in Karl-Marx-Stadt (today Chemnitz).[105] The WISK and the Anti-H-Block Committee in all likelihood knew that they were under surveillance, but not by West German security services only.

The end of the 28-page report was composed of two rather long attachments that dealt with two leading members of the WISK and the Anti-H-Block Committee in Frankfurt am Main. Although the names have been blacked out, the second attachment seems to refer to Frank Gallagher since it is mentioned that the person was born in Northern Ireland but was a West German citizen. The details the Stasi had gathered were impressive: the type of car the person was driving, including the registration number, the activities the person was involved in, the type of propaganda material the West German police had confiscated, the fact that the person was under surveillance for terrorist activities by the LKA in the federal State of Hessen, the number of a bank account in the Frankfurter Volksbank and above all the contacts the person had. All the names of the contacts and their addresses, their telephone numbers, their cars (including registration numbers) and their political affiliation (mostly Communists and members of the Revolutionary Cells) were known. All names in the document have been blacked out except one, Sabine Eckle, who was already recorded in the ZPDB (central data bank for persons).[106] As seen, back in 1979 the *Spiegel* had written that she might have gone to Dublin incognito together with three other members of the Revolutionary Cells. It looked as if the Stasi had rounded up the whole network, or at least the most important cogs in the machinery. It was mentioned in the end of the file that the persons were not in the Stasi's records. They were now.

On 17 September 1981, HA-XXII received information about the WISK from an informer working in the Springer media group. Axel Springer was a West German press baron and an implacable foe of the East German regime so much so that he had his headquarters built in West Berlin, only a few metres from the Wall to make sure the Communists got his message from the neon lights on top of the building. The informer reported that the 'far-left ... WISK is in possession of an internal American textbook on the training of anti-terrorist specialists'. This book, supposedly containing the latest knowledge about anti-terrorist fighting techniques, 'was translated by people from the WISK into German and was sold for 35 Deutsche Mark in the Technical University of West Berlin'.[107]

On 24 November 1981, the INLA began its continental campaign against the British. It was short-lived and ineffective. It took place in West Germany and the target that day was the British consulate in Hamburg. The bomb, planted in front of the building, failed to detonate. Twenty-four hours later it was the turn of the headquarters of the 7th Signals Regiment of BAOR in Herford in North Rhine-Westphalia to be attacked. This time the bomb did explode but caused only slight structural damage. Two days later, the West German police stopped a speeding car and arrested two people: the driver, Heinz-Joachim Stemler, who belonged to the Revolutionary Cells, and a passenger found in possession of a false passport for INLA member Michael Plunkett, then living in Paris.[108] It would seem reasonable to conclude that there were contacts between the INLA and the Revolutionary Cells and that possibly the Irish terrorists were using logistics provided by their West German friends.

Despite a lull in their campaigns, the PIRA and INLA were still very active in the FRG. On 19 October 1982, Colonel Linow of HA-II (counter-espionage) transmitted a report to his colleague Colonel Schenk of the same department. It concerned a planned attack on an important British person somewhere in Western Europe by the INLA. It was said that two INLA members were currently in West Germany to prepare the attack. This information had been transmitted by the BKA to the Ministry of the Interior in Bonn. The chances were that a telecommunication between the BKA and the ministry had been intercepted by the Stasi since the information originated from HA-III (telecommunications).[109] For the time being, it remained rather vague but it was going to become more precise. A few days later, on 26 October, Linow had more news from HA-III. This time, the BKA had learned from a 'reliable source' the identity of the two INLA members in question: names (blacked out), dates of birth (blacked out) and place of residence, Belfast. A description of the two individuals was also included. HA-XII (central information/data bank) did not have them on record.[110]

It was time for the specialists on terrorism, HA-XXII, to step in. On 20 November, they reported that the British Services Security Organisation in West Germany (BSSO, led by MI5) based in Cologne had transmitted the following information to the BKA. Two INLA members (names blacked out) were travelling with fake passports (numbers blacked out) respectively issued in Belfast on 1 July 1982 and 2 August 1982. One had an additional fake passport (all details blacked out). According to this information, they would be in the FRG 'to carry out "spectacular actions"'. There was other information concerning a third INLA member (name, date of birth and address blacked out) who was supposedly already in West Germany on a lecture tour regarding the Irish question. HA-XXII added that enemy intelligence services did not exclude that the two INLA members would meet the third one. Since the beginning of November, the BKA had been investigating the alleged planned attacks and had checked the activities of a West German citizen (name and date of birth blacked out), living in the city of Bergisch-Gladbach in North Rhine-Westphalia. The person's telephone number (blacked out) was provided and had been found by enemy intelligence services in a suspected French INLA courier's (name blacked out) writing pad. This courier would already have left Paris for Cologne by train on 30 October. HA-XXII wrote that enemy intelligence services had mounted a surveillance operation but that there had been no result so far and that HA-XII (central information/data bank) did not have any of the said persons in its records.[111]

Paris seemed to have become the place where the INLA dealt with the PLO to acquire weapons. The INLA was helped by a Frenchman called Bernard Jégat.[112] Jégat was an idealist and also believed in Ireland's cause, but he would later denounce Plunkett to Captain Paul Barril, wrongly believing that Plunkett had participated in an anti-Semitic terrorist attack on the restaurant Goldenberg in the Rue des Rosiers in Paris in 1982.[113] Was Jégat the courier? Barril, as we have seen, was an officer in an anti-terrorist unit. He suspected INLA member Jim Kerr, who lived in Switzerland with a German woman of the Revolutionary Cells and who regularly travelled to Paris to meet INLA and IRA people, of being in touch with a Swiss national called Bruno Bréguet who was a member of Carlos the Jackal's group. The meeting between Kerr and Bréguet would have happened in Paris at the end of January 1982. Bréguet was arrested the following month together with Magdalena Kopp (Revolutionary Cells), Carlos's wife. Kerr was also eventually arrested by the Swiss security services.[114]

Clearly, HA-XXII had a mole within the BKA that was providing very good information. From the 1970s onwards, the Bundesnachrichtendienst (BND, the West German federal intelligence agency for threats from abroad) had been very seriously infiltrated by the Stasi. It was the same with the Bundesamt für Verfassungsschutz (BfV, the West German federal office for the protection of the constitution, counter-intelligence) and the Military Counter-Intelligence Service.[115] The BSSO had a rather poor opinion of the way the West German security agencies were organised in a decentralised way, reflecting West Germany's federal political structure.[116] One document of HA-XXII about a PIRA attack on a BAOR base in Mönchengladbach (see below) emanated from the BfV as '*Verfassungsschutzbericht*' (report of the protection of the constitution) is indicated in handwriting on top of it.[117]

The situation within the BKA was not any different. Former HVA chief Werner Großmann quotes Rainer Engberding, the head of the BKA, as saying: 'The intelligence services of the GDR had so seriously penetrated our counter-intelligence that we were actually able to unmask [agents] only because chance came our way or a problem within the opposite side occurred or the opponent had decided to allow us to do so.'[118] Unfortunately, there is no way of checking in the BND, BfV or BKA archives if these security services possessed evidence on links between the Stasi, the PIRA and the INLA. As Wolfgang Krieger points out: 'The ... BND ... has yet to declassify a single page from its files'.[119] In the end, it would seem that the INLA did not carry out any attack in West Germany or elsewhere on the continent.[120]

But two Irishmen and one Irishwoman who were connected with the INLA and its political wing, the IRSP, were soon in trouble. On 9 August 1982, a terrorist attack in the Rue des Rosiers, the Jewish district in Paris, killed six people. An anti-terrorist unit set up by President François Mitterrand looked for the perpetrators and on 28 August arrested Michael Plunkett, Mary Reid and Stephen King in an apartment in Vincennes in the Parisian suburbs. Captain Paul Barril was involved. The arrests were hailed as a great victory against international terrorism. But then things began to go awfully wrong for the French authorities. The Irish claimed they were totally innocent (years later it was found that Abu Nidal had been responsible for the attack) and that the French anti-terrorist squad had planted evidence in their apartment. This political–terrorist saga became known as *Les Irlandais de Vincennes*, or the Vincennes Three. The court case against the Irish collapsed and they were released from custody in 1983.

HA-XXII followed the court case and managed to get hold of a written common statement in French by Plunkett, Reid and King after they had been declared innocent. Their statement was translated into German. The trio wished to stay in France despite everything that had happened as they believed they would not be able to lead a normal life free of political persecution in Ireland. HA-XXII had also obtained three individual written statements in French. King outlined his militancy in the IRSP and complained about the intrigues of the Irish Special Branch in Dublin, which he described as a 'political police'. Reid explained that she had first joined Official Sinn Féin and later the IRSP. She claimed that the Ulster Defence Regiment (UDR, British army) had detonated a bomb in front of her parents' house. As she did not trust the Irish Special Criminal Court and Special Branch, she asked for political asylum in France. Plunkett wrote that he had been a member of the Communist Party of Ireland (CPI) for a short period and then joined Official Sinn Féin. In 1974, he was one of the founding members of the IRSP. He too claimed that he was harassed by the Special Branch and that he was a target for the Special Air Service (SAS, British elite force). Therefore, he wanted to be allowed to live in France.[121] The Stasi was building a database on Irish republicans.

The Stasi obtained information about supposed planned attacks by the PIRA in West Germany in 1983. Again, its information originated from within enemy intelligence services. This time, it was believed that the PIRA was about to target a British general. As a result, security measures to protect the commander of the 1st British tank division based at Verden in Lower Saxony were increased.[122] Eventually, no attack took place. In August 1985, HA-XXII reported that the BKA, probably informed by one of the British intelligence services, had learned that the PIRA might use a new detonator for its bomb attacks, a radio-controlled 'infrared garage-opener'.[123] For the Stasi, every detail about Irish terrorists could help. The following month, HA-XXII found out that in a disco in Osterholz-Schrambeck in Lower Saxony a US soldier had been approached by a West German citizen who had asked him if he could provide the PIRA with arms belonging to the US forces. The soldier pretended to accept but informed his superiors. Consequently, a surveillance operation was mounted for subsequent meetings between the soldier and the West German. However, the Stasi source had not managed to know anything more about the outcome of this operation.[124] That the PIRA had decided to target the US army as a source of armament was not unusual. Back in the 1970s, security at US marine base Camp Lejeune in North Carolina was not exactly a model of efficiency and the terrorists acquired M-16 rifles there. George Harrison, a US gun-runner and PIRA supporter, remembered: 'We used to meet the Marines at a gas station in New Jersey ... There would be two or three of them on each occasion. They were not gangsters, just guys making a couple of bucks'.[125] So, why not West Germany also?

Discos seemed to have become dangerous places with unusual activities. On 5 April 1986, a bomb exploded in the La Belle disco in West Berlin, a favourite place among US soldiers. Three people were killed, including two US NCOs, and dozens were wounded. President Ronald Reagan did not take long to decide to bomb Tripoli and Bengasi as the Americans believed Colonel Muammar Gaddafi had ordered the attack. Relations between the United States and Libya had been degenerating for some time. On 15 April, the United States Air Force (USAF) carried out the bombing raids. The Stasi had been aware of the Libyan preparations to bomb the disco.[126] On 2 June, HA-XXII/8 got information from a source in the West that it was thought that the Libyans were about to initiate reprisal actions in Western Europe in the coming summer. In order not to become a target by the West, the Libyans were thinking of using Palestinians. It was known that they had also approached the Armenian Secret Army for the Liberation of Armenia (ASALA) and the Japanese Red Army (JRA) and that the two groups had refused to cooperate with them.

HA-XXII/8 wrote in its report that Gaddafi had set up a Revolutionary Committee in 1977 to protect his revolution and eliminate his opponents. On 2 March 1985, he had declared that he was willing to help all terrorists in European countries in which some of his opponents resided. He had 'especially mentioned the Baader-Meinhoff group [RAF], the

IRA and the Red Brigades [Italy]'.[127] It was known that the PIRA had received support from Gaddafi who provided them with arms. Several gun-running expeditions between Libya and Ireland had taken place since 1985.[128] However, the PIRA was certainly not going to be involved in attacks against the US army on behalf of Gaddafi as it drew non-negligible support from certain Irish-American circles. If these circles ever found out that the Irish republicans were involved, it would have catastrophic consequences. In October 1987, Gaddafi would provide 150 tons of armament to the PIRA, much of it made in the East bloc. But the ship transporting the arms, the *Eskund*, was watched by the Royal Air Force (RAF) and eventually intercepted by the French navy off Brittany. A traitor had tipped off the British.[129]

On 22 September 1986, HA-XXII/8 produced a document entitled 'Survey of Terrorist Activities of the IRA-1986'. It was a simple factual and chronological account but one that contained a rather stunning revelation. Indeed, the entry for 16 January 1986 states: 'Bomb attack on car of GDR soldiers – 1 dead, 1 wounded'.[130] It seems rather astonishing that the PIRA would have done so, or even killed West German soldiers. They had nothing to do with the Northern Irish conflict and such an act could only generate counterproductive publicity. It may well have been that HA-XXII/8 had written down the wrong perpetrators or victims, or even that there had been a sloppy mistake in the compilation of this particular document. As we have seen, sloppiness did occur although this would have been particularly sloppy. But perhaps the PIRA did carry out this attack by mistake. There is no definitive answer. HA-XXII continued to develop its knowledge of the Irish republicans. That year, it also acquired a small book written by John J. O'Connell entitled *Irish Terrorism: A Problem of British Design*, which had been published by the Defense Technical Information Centre in collaboration with the University of Los Angeles. A large part of the book was translated into German.[131]

Shortly afterwards a most intriguing episode took place. On 10 November 1986, a man (name blacked out by the BStU), holder of an Irish passport delivered at Bonn, was stopped by the East German border guards at Schönefeld Airport in East Berlin. He had been in the GDR before in 1984 to visit the Leipzig Fair as an independent trader but was not known by HA-XII (central information/data bank). This time he came from Beirut via Vienna. Except for the fact that the individual was in possession of 115 watches, 160 audio tapes and three Arabic typewriters, he was also in possession of a certain number of passports, notably ten fake blank Iraqi ones and a Lebanese one for Palestinians. The name on the Lebanese passport was not known by

HA-XXII. Apparently, these passports were meant to be given to an Arab individual in West Berlin. But besides the Irish passport the man had another Irish one, bearing the same name and a serial number starting with the letter J. The individual was currently being questioned by HA-IX (investigations) and so far no connection with an extremist group or political organisation had been established.[132]

Or was there not? The very same day General Willi Damm of HA-X (international relations) sent a 'top secret' letter to Lieutenant-Colonel Krasa, the Chief of Cabinet of the Czechoslovak Minister for the Interior in Prague. The heading of the letter was '*Aktion TERROR*'. '*Aktion TERROR*' was an initiative between all secret services of the Eastern European countries to exchange information about known terrorists.[133] Damm's letter began with a bit of sloppiness. He informed Krasa that the attached document contained information on the 'Iranian passports' used by the PIRA. It was most unlikely that the PIRA would use Iranian passports as they would not have been particularly discreet. In the most revealing attached document, the mistake became very obvious. The Stasi explained that it got more information on the Irish passports –indeed Irish, not Iranian – during an operation within the Austrian secret service. It was believed that they were used by the PIRA as it had been in possession of one hundred Irish passports since 1984. They had been stolen from the British desk in the Department of Foreign Affairs (DFA) in Dublin, and they started with the letter J:

> These passports would have the serial numbers J620701 to J620800. From this series, the following numbers have been seized again:
> J620701, J620763, J620723, J620727, J620768, J620780,
> J62076. (incomplete), J620788, J620795, J620797.[134]

In other words, when that individual was arrested by the East German border guards at Schönefeld Airport, the Stasi immediately knew that the chances were he was a PIRA member. This episode confirms that passport security in Ireland was not the best. In the 1980s, a certain number of blank passports had been stolen from the Passport Office. Two crew members of the *Eskund* arrested by the French were found to be in possession of these stolen passports. The thing became supremely embarrassing when it was revealed during the so-called 'Irangate' enquiry that Robert Macfarlane (and other US officials), Reagan's National Security adviser, had travelled to Iran on a fake Irish passport.[135] This problem seems to be persistent. In 2010, it was revealed that the Israelis had forged Irish passports for one of their operations.[136] A year later it was the turn of a Russian diplomat in Dublin to be involved in the forgery of Irish passports.[137]

As far as Schönefeld Airport was concerned, it was much frequented by international terrorists. Markus Wolf wrote:

> One way in which our ministry could slightly limit the activities of these [terrorist] groups was by controlling what they brought in and out of the country in their luggage. Like anyone else entering the country, these groups passed through screening at the airport and were usually found to be carrying or transporting weapons. It was decided by border control that they should be allowed to carry the guns, since going armed was clearly second nature to them.[138]

Wolf's statement is rather curious. How could the Stasi 'slightly limit' the activities of terrorists by allowing them to carry their guns? Obviously, the Stasi and those in control must have known that they were not for use on East German territory. In May 1982, Johannes Weinrich of the Revolutionary Cells arrived at the airport with no fewer than 25 kilograms of explosives in his suitcases. The Stasi temporarily confiscated the suitcases but Weinrich assured them that he would not use the explosives himself but give them to a liberation movement. The result was that they were handed back to him although the Stasi knew well that he had a target in mind. On 16 August 1983, the cultural institution Maison de France in West Berlin was blown up, killing one person and wounding twenty-one.[139] It should be recalled here that the Stasi had sent the names of seven Irish persons to the SOUD (see Chapter 4).

With all these PIRA activities – and also those of other international terrorist groups – it was on the cards that HA-XXII drew up a working plan for 1987 which consisted in gaining information on the 'AD [Action directe, France], CCC [Cellules Communistes combattantes, Belgium], ETA [Spain], IRA [Northern Ireland] [and the] Red Brigades [Italy]'. The report mentioned that 'all possibilities are to be used to identify further members [of these groups], to figure out relations with the GDR and to prevent possible dangers'. Everything was to be undertaken to obtain 'comprehensive information'.[140] HA-XXII not only focused on groups outside Europe such as the ANC and the PLO but also on groups in Western Europe, in other words, in NATO territory. For instance, the RAF had tried to kill US General Alexander Haig, NATO's supreme commander, on 25 June 1979. On 31 August 1981, the same RAF detonated a bomb at the US air force base at Ramstein and on 15 September it almost succeeded in killing US General Frederick Kroesen.[141] On 11 December 1984, the CCC inflicted considerable damage to a NATO pipeline in Belgium. A similar action happened in Spain a week later.[142]

There had been some cooperation between far-left terrorist groups, notably the RAF, CCC and AD that were anti-US and anti-NATO. In January 1985, the RAF and the AD had issued a joint-communiqué entitled 'The unity of revolutionaries in Western Europe'. Shortly afterwards, their words turned into deeds. On 25 January, the AD killed French General René Audran and on 1 February, the RAF killed Ernst Zimmermann, an important chairman of West German industrial federations. The actions of the two terrorist groups had been coordinated. The RAF had also contacts with the CCC for logistical purposes.[143] On 8 August 1985, the RAF and the AD attacked the US Rhein-Main airbase in Frankfurt am Main, killing two people and wounding over twenty. The Stasi had contacts with the RAF and some of its members even got some military training in the GDR, notably in the handling of anti-tank rocket launchers although the East Germans had been initially reluctant to become involved. They were more interested in gaining knowledge on international terrorism rather than actively supporting a terrorist struggle against the West German State. East Berlin and the RAF's political interests did not coincide.[144] The Stasi did not direct the RAF and the terrorists insisted on their autonomy. Cooperation between them declined from 1984.[145]

Therefore the significance of the fact that the Stasi had decided to take a closer interest in Western European terrorist groups besides the RAF should not be exaggerated, but clearly these groups did attract its attention as might have been expected from an intelligence service. The absence of systematic common targets could be a problem between the PIRA and continental far-left terrorist groups. The PIRA would never attack US bases and interests in Western Europe as this would very obviously alienate the important Irish-American community where it had some support as previously explained. The following example clearly illustrates this. In order to stress the unity between revolutionaries in Western Europe, the RAF unit that assassinated Ernst Zimmermann was called 'Patsy O'Hara', an INLA member who died on a hunger strike alongside PIRA member Bobby Sands in May 1981.[146] The PIRA, however, strongly disapproved of it. Groups like the PIRA and ETA were involved in essentially nationalist struggles and would not have much in common with the more ideologically driven RAF, CCC, AD and Red Brigades, who, incidentally, did not always agree with one another. In the end, this unity of revolutionaries collapsed,[147] if it ever had solidly materialised in the first place. And yet, there were contacts between some continental groups and the PIRA as HA-XXII was about to state. But in the meantime, HA-XXII had concluded that there were 'no indications of security risks and other hazards for the GDR and its allies emanating from the activities of the IRA'. The compiling of a '*Feindobjektakte*' (hostile-target file, see Chapter 4) on the PIRA was to continue 'with priority given to analysis'.[148]

In 1987, the PIRA resumed its continental campaign against the British. On 23 March, it detonated a bomb at the headquarters of BAOR at Mönchengladbach-Rheindahlen, injuring four Britons and twenty-seven West German officers and their wives who were in the middle of a party.[149] The next day, HA-XXII analysed the situation. It wrote that the PIRA had claimed the attack and that it had been responsible in the past for other such attacks, notably the shooting and killing of Colonel Marc Coe in 1980. It had more interesting information:

> Furthermore, [the IRA] was also active in the whole of Western Europe. So it was that on 16.01.86 the 'IRA' tried to ship arms (a container with arms and ammunition) in Amsterdam, which was prevented by the police.
>
> Activities of the 'IRA' in conjunction with other effective terrorist groups could be proved. There is confirmed information that it cooperated with the Carlos group in France (1980–1982) and that there are contacts with members of the 'Revolutionary Cells' in the FRG.[150]

There are no further indications concerning the source of this 'confirmed information'. It was of course not astonishing that the PIRA's attacks were massively covered by the West German media. The *Berliner Morgenpost* wrote that 'among the victims of the attack in Rheindahlen near Mönchengladbach there is also a major-general of the Bundeswehr [West German army]'. The *Tagesspiegel* explained that the aim of the attack was BAOR but that most of the wounded were Germans.[151] Northern Ireland suddenly seemed to be in the FRG's backyard.

One of HA-XXII's Western adversaries, the CIA, also analysed the latest PIRA bomb attack on BAOR in a so-called 'terrorism review' written on 9 April, which was much the same technique used by the Stasi. The CIA had information that the Irish republicans might have a base in the Netherlands:

> The PIRA reportedly has connections with radicals in the Netherlands who have helped with operations in West Germany. A man using an Irish passport bought the car used in the bombing in The Hague, registering the car in the Netherlands.
>
> The attack demonstrates the PIRA's renewed ability to attack British targets outside Northern Ireland, although geographic and logistic problems make such attacks difficult to mount on a routine basis.[152]

It remained to be seen if the PIRA would have difficulties in mounting attacks 'on a routine basis'. As will be explained shortly, in

September 1988, the Soviets would reach a different and it would seem more accurate conclusion regarding the PIRA's abilities. The Stasi too was aware of the Dutch connection.

On 20 April, Colonel Kempe from HA-X (international relations) sent top secret information to his colleague in Prague, Colonel Krasa. This information consisted of three reports, two concerning the PIRA. It was stated in the first report that the Stasi had 'further indications on the activities of enemy state security units' regarding the bombing at Mönchengladbach. The terrorist unit of the BKA had taken over the investigation and a special commission ('SOKO') based at the police headquarters of Mönchengladbach led by BKA member Karl-Heinz Pähler had learned from the Dutch security services that the Irishman X (name blacked out) had bought the car used for the bombing. However, he had also bought a blue Opel Ascona 1600 (registration number blacked out) on 26 January 1987. It was supposed that the Irishman was still in possession of the car. The West German police had been ordered to look for it and to arrest its occupants. In the second report, a Stasi source within the BKA indicated that the PIRA was possibly preparing an attack on the British embassy in Luxembourg on 19 April 1987. On 8 April, the BKA had warned the security services in the United Kingdom and Luxembourg through Interpol.[153] Obviously, the information came one day late since Kempe sent his information to Krasa on 20 April, but in the end there was no PIRA attack on the embassy.

In the meantime, HA-XXII decided to take a closer interest in the relations between the PIRA and the Carlos group and apparently found some very relevant information. According to its intelligence, an Irishman from the south-east of Ireland might have been the middleman between the PIRA and the Venezuelan terrorist. Besides his date of birth, his address and his passport number – and a passport photograph – the following is also mentioned on his Stasi index card: '[X] is a member of the Irish terrorist organisation "IRA". Through him contacts between the "Carlos" group and the "IRA" were supposed to be established. On account of the present crisis within the "IRA" – according to the "Carlos" group – the group has renounced further activation of the contact at this point in time'.[154] The BStU sent this author a photocopy of the original Stasi document without any blacked-out passages. The Stasi's source for this information was clearly a member of the Carlos group. However, further research on possible links between the Carlos group and the PIRA, and also on 'X', produced no results in the BStU.[155]

Carlos had stayed in East Berlin on several occasions – although his relationship with the East Germans appears to have been tense, as seen.

He had abandoned his job as a Spanish teacher in 1972 to concentrate on the Palestinian struggle against Israel. He travelled between London and Paris and while in the French capital he became a member of Mohamed Boudia's group. Boudia was the leader of the European section of the Popular Front of for the Liberation of Palestine (PFLP). He was working in a theatre called Théâtre de l'Ouest Parisien and was closely in touch with other terrorist groups like the Japanese Red Army (JRA), the RAF and also the PIRA.[156] Little is known about Carlos's contacts with the PIRA, however. It might very well be that he first met PIRA members through Boudia but that cannot be established. It would seem though that he had far more contacts with ETA, especially through one of the members of his group, Johannes Weinrich, who was also a member of the Revolutionary Cells.[157] According to Magdalena Kopp, the Carlos group had no precise aim and agenda but did have contacts with different 'Western European guerrilla groups' and Eastern European and Arab intelligence services.[158]

The PIRA resumed its continental offensive and targeted BAOR personnel in the Netherlands, close to the West German border. On 1 May 1988, a British soldier was shot dead in Roermond, and two others were killed in a car bomb in Nieuw Bergen. HA-XXII followed the matter by reading the *Frankfurter Allgemeine Zeitung*, the *Berliner Morgenpost* and the *Welt*. A spokesman of the Dutch police stressed that there were no border controls at certain crossings with West Germany and Belgium, while some Dutch press reports speculated that the RAF could have been involved in the attacks or at least provided logistical support for the PIRA. However, according to experts in London, the PIRA did not cooperate with the RAF as it considered the West German terrorists to be unreliable. Yet, the same experts conceded that the PIRA had been 'rather successful' in West Germany.[159]

There was no effective way of stopping the PIRA. On 13 July, a bomb exploded at the Glamorgan barracks in Duisburg in the FRG, wounding nine soldiers. The *Zeit* remarked that the PIRA terrorists used the open borders between the Netherlands and West Germany for their hit-and-run attacks, and that they were helped by some Irish migrants living in the Netherlands and also by the Ierland Komitee Nederland (Ireland committee, Netherlands), which had been founded in 1975 and supported the Irish republicans, as seen. The British Foreign Office had unsuccessfully tried to discredit the committee by accusing it of being involved in dealing with explosives in Northern Ireland. In this particular press article, HA-XXII underlined the paragraph that gave a brief summary of PIRA attacks on the continent and wrote in the margin: 'FRG, Belgium, NL [Netherlands]'.[160] Clearly, the PIRA's operational area had caught its attention. On 5 August, a bomb exploded at a BAOR barracks in Düsseldorf, wounding about four soldiers. The *Welt* explained that the BKA believed the PIRA member had transported the bomb on his/her bicycle. In this article, HA-XXII highlighted the fact that the PIRA used the name 'P. O'Neill' to claim attacks when writing to the press.[161] On 12 August, off-duty Warrant Officer Richard Heakin was shot dead in Ostend in Belgium as he was travelling back to England to join his family. HA-XXII read the *Tagesspiegel*'s report and underlined how and where the attack took place and what method was used.[162]

The Western security services did have some successes against the PIRA though. The same month, HA-XXII intercepted two telexes from the American Associated Press (AP) and the West German Deutsche Presse-Agentur (DPA) that announced the arrest on the Dutch–West German border of possibly two PIRA-members. The two men were arrested in Waldfeucht, after leaving the Netherlands and were found to be in possession of two pistols and two automatic rifles. There was a BAOR barracks in Waldfeucht. A short time later, HA-XXII read in the *Welt* and learned from the ARD (West German television channel) that the two men in question were Terence McGeough and Thomas Hanratty. McGeough was wanted in the United States for arms smuggling and in Britain for attempted murder. The two men were not in HA-XXII's records.[163]

Unsurprisingly, the PIRA attacks caused strains between the West German population living near British barracks and BAOR personnel. The *Welt* published an article entitled 'The invisible enemy scares the neighbours' which was noticed by HA-XXII. The newspaper wrote that civilians feared that they could become the victims of terrorist activities simply by living close to British army installations. There were about 150,000 British soldiers including relatives in West Germany. A spokesman for the Bundeswehr stated in Bonn that common service within NATO between the Bundeswehr and BAOR would 'continue as normally as possible'.[164] This was precisely what the PIRA wanted, to create havoc.

Some time (no precise date) during the second semester of 1988, an information sheet on the PIRA was created, probably by HA-XXII. It was rather informative of how the Stasi perceived the Irish republican terrorists. Under the heading 'Character', it was stated: 'International terrorism'. Under the heading 'Categorisation', it was stated: 'No subversive activities against the GDR; as a result of effective terror and acts of violence, dangers to the GDR and its allies can develop'. Under the heading 'Processing or control form', it was stated:

'Operational-analytical control'. It was explained under the heading 'Brief assessment' that Western mass media suspected that the PIRA had sympathisers in Western European countries. But, 'information that the [PIRA] cooperated with the 'RAF' was not gathered'. It had come to the Stasi's attention that the PIRA had increased its activities in 1987–88 and it estimated that taking into account British political and military interests in Northern Ireland, the PIRA would continue to target members of the British army, the Northern Irish police and Protestant paramilitaries. Under the heading 'Assignment for 1989', it was mentioned in pure Stasi jargon: 'Continuation of the operational–analytical assessment of the developing situation regarding the guarantee of current standby information'. In plain English, this probably meant that information on the PIRA would continue to be assessed. But it was the last heading that caught the eye 'IM [unofficial collaborator] use'. There was nothing written after this heading which suggests that no IM was employed in connection with the PIRA.[165]

In another document (post 30 August 1988), which contained some of the same passages just studied, there was extra information on the PIRA and the GDR: 'In the operational control of the [PIRA] so far, no indications have been found concerning hostile activities against the GDR and its allies, the use of territory of the Socialist countries for logistical purposes or existing contacts in the GDR'.[166] This in all likelihood shows that the Stasi was not actively supporting, cooperating or liaising with the PIRA unlike with other groups such as the PLO and the ANC. The mention of 'use of territory' and 'existing contacts in the GDR' reflected the fear of seeing the GDR compromised within the international community if contacts with terrorists were to be proved. For example, it is known that in 1979 the Stasi offered asylum to RAF members who wished to cease their terrorist activities. Ten of them crossed the Iron Curtain. But from 1984 onwards, as previously stated, the Stasi and the RAF no longer actively worked together. The East Germans made former RAF terrorists staying in the GDR change their identity and their place of residence several times lest they should be recognised. One of them was even forced to undergo plastic surgery.[167] Moreover, as will be seen shortly, HA-XXII/8 deemed that some of the PIRA's activities in West Germany might endanger the Stasi's own operations.

In September 1988, HA-XXII received a document from the Soviet Union entitled 'The [PIRA] changes its tactics'. It had been translated into German. Although the authors were not mentioned, it seems reasonable to assume that it was the KGB. It was stated that after having analysed the PIRA's activities against the British army in Northern Ireland and in several Western European countries, experts had reached the following conclusions. The PIRA disposed of an intelligence network, operational possibilities and financial means that enabled it to carry out specific 'terrorist actions' over a long period of time. Its leadership found it necessary to take into account political factors and public opinion while carrying out terrorist attacks. It could not be excluded that the PIRA would not only attack military but also civilian targets which 'symbolise the imperialist nature of the British Crown. This possibility is proved by the strengthening of the Northern Irish terrorists' relations with extremist organisations in the Near East for whom these "symbolic objects" are the most important thing.' According to the experts, the PIRA was successful in penetrating the British secret services which, in turn, could lead to a hardening attitude of Margaret Thatcher in the fight against terrorism.[168] The KGB had probably passed on this information to the Stasi within the SOUD or '*Aktion TERROR*' network.

A few weeks later, on 4 November, HA-XXII/8 produced a report entitled 'Information on the activities of the 'Irish Republican Army' (IRA) [PIRA]'. Marginalia on the report indicates that it had been transmitted to Werner Großmann's HVA. It had been decided that the HVA would be used to watch the activities of the PIRA in West Germany and West Berlin. HA-XXII/8 explained that the PIRA had a range of armament at its disposal like mortars, hand grenades, firearms and so on. In the past, the PIRA attacked British army units in Northern Ireland but since 1986 also in the Netherlands, Belgium and West Germany. There were three aspects that HA-XXII/8 singled out. First, barracks and other installations of the British army in Northern Ireland were 'real fortresses' and were generally located next to densely populated areas. Attacks on these fortresses often caused civilian casualties. But, British installations in the Netherlands, Belgium and West Germany were not that heavily protected which provided the PIRA with better chances of success. Second, 'immigrants of Irish or Northern Irish origin in these countries are very likely used for logistical purposes [by the PIRA]'. Third, actions in these countries gave the PIRA more publicity as 'it is working on the assumption that a killed British soldier in Western Europe will catch more attention in world public opinion than a killed Protestant policeman in Northern Ireland'. HA-XXII/8 had just stated the cynical truth.

HA-XXII concluded its report by saying that August 1989 would mark the twentieth anniversary of the British army's intervention in Northern Ireland and that the PIRA would step up its activities. Consequently, 'increased terrorist activities of the [PIRA] against installations and members of the British army in Northern Ireland, Great Britain, the FRG, Belgium and the Netherlands' were to be expected. The last two lines of the report read: 'GDR connections of the [PIRA] have so far not been established in the control and watching of this power potential ['*Kräftepotential*']'.[169] Trying to decipher Stasi jargon and using logic, this sentence implied that until now the Stasi had not used or cooperated with the PIRA. If the Stasi was in touch with the PIRA, HA-XXII, the department specialising in terrorism par excellence, would have stated this.

The term '*Kräftepotential*' is rather difficult to translate into English, hence the literal translation. But in this case, the meaning is rather straightforward. The term is not only used for the PIRA but also for other various groups like environmentalists, dissidents and so on. *Kräfte* (powers) is here a synonym for persons or a group while *Potential* refers to the possible strength of the group. What it roughly describes is the capability of a particular group.[170] It is also interesting to notice the choice of words used by HA-XXII. It spoke of '*terrorist* [author's italics] activities'. In other words, it did not regard the PIRA as an 'ideological partner' as has been claimed.[171] Surely, if it did, it would have used a more ideologically correct term such as 'anti-imperialist freedom fighter' or something along those lines. Operating in the very ideologically jargon-conscious environment that was East Germany, the Stasi would not have used the adjective 'terrorist' to describe the PIRA if it did not think the PIRA was a terrorist group. If some sort of cooperation with the PIRA was to be envisaged, then the prime motivation would be sheer opportunism and not ideological identification: the Stasi would regard the PIRA as a useful tool to weaken the United Kingdom, a most important NATO member, and the PIRA in turn would rely on logistical aid from East Germany to achieve its objectives.

On 29 November, HA-XXII/8 issued a report called 'Measures for further treatment of the "Irish Republican Army" (IRA) [PIRA]'. It was a follow-up to the previous one. A large extract is warranted:

> Regarding the further control and surveillance of this power-potential [PIRA] the following measures are suggested:
>
> 1) Concerning the collection of information on existing relations of Irish citizens with the GDR, it is necessary to get an overview of these persons' travels in the GDR. To that effect, it is essential to begin a special investigation within HA-VI [border controls, tourism]. Simultaneously, the travels of GDR citizens to Ireland and Northern Ireland must also be checked.
>
> In this connection, it must be checked within HA-II/AGA [counter-espionage/study group for foreigners living in the GDR] and HA-VII [counter-espionage in relation to the Ministry of the Interior and the People's Police] to what extent there is information concerning Irish citizens residing in the GDR.

2) To be in a position to obtain information on possible [PIRA] targets in the FRG and West Berlin, the acquisition of an overview of BAOR and other British armed forces' bases is indispensable.

   It must be checked within the HVA to what extent there is knowledge regarding this issue.
3) As information must be acquired, the available unofficial structures [Stasi network] are to be used to obtain information on areas where Irish students and workers are concentrated, especially in places where BAOR is based in the FRG and West Berlin.
4) The analytical reviewing of all accessible information and clues, Western publications included, will be continued.
5) After the suggested measures have been carried out, the results will be summarised in a report on the situation and on that basis further measures will be determined.[172]

If it was suspected that the PIRA and other republican groups were helped by some Irish migrants and students in West Germany and West Berlin, then it made sense for the Stasi to target them to see if useful intelligence could be obtained. In Munich alone, there were 6,000 Irish migrants.[173] But citizens of the FRG were probably not excluded either. HA-XXII already knew about the activities of the WISK near Frankfurt. It now remained to be seen what the results of this Stasi operation would be.

Two undated documents, but written in either 1988 or 1989 (the most recent dates mentioned being respectively March 1988 and August 1988) shed more light on this presumed cooperation between different terrorist groups in Western Europe. In the first document it is stated:

> The [PIRA] claimed responsibility for the bomb attack on the officers' mess of the British Army of the Rhine in Mönchengladbach on 23.3.87. In this context, until now there has been no evidence whatsoever of a cooperation between the 'AD', 'RAF' and [PIRA] within the framework of a so-called 'Western European guerrilla' as deduced by enemy counter-intelligence services. It cannot be excluded, however, that during actions in the FRG the [PIRA] resorts to logistical support of the 'RAF'. Confirmed information is available that between 1980 and 1982, the [PIRA] cooperated with the 'Carlos' group in France and had contacts with members of the 'Revolutionary Cells' in the FRG. Regarding the planning of an attack in Gibraltar in March 1988, which was foiled by the British anti-terrorist unit 'SAS' by shooting dead in cold blood the 3 suspected terrorists, it is assumed that they cooperated with the Basque terrorist organisation 'ETA'.[174]

The information on the Revolutionary Cells is interesting as back on 20 October 1986 (see the 23-page document studied in detail in Chapter 4) HA-XXII/8 had written that 'Operational knowledge regarding the Revolutionary Cells in the Federal Republic of Germany rules out that there are contacts with the PIRA'.[175] Clearly, the Stasi's knowledge was evolving.

In the second document, it is stated: 'It was suspected particularly by Western mass media that the [PIRA] had sympathisers at its disposal in ... [the FRG, the Netherlands and Belgium]. Information that the [PIRA] collaborates with the "RAF" was not gathered'.[176] Another document of interest, the exact references of which are missing but which emanated from the Zentrale Materialablage (ZMA, central information bank of the departments) was an index card concerning the INLA created on 10 August 1979. On it is written: 'Allegedly close contacts with the Baader-Meinhof group [RAF]'.[177] Unfortunately, there are no other details.

The year that would see the end of the GDR was 1989. Soviet leader Mikhail Gorbachev's perestroika and glasnost reforms were having tremendous effects within the Soviet Union. But in East Germany, the old leaders, the 'concrete heads' as Markus Wolf and others called them,[178] would not budge an inch. This frame of mind is actually reflected in the way the Stasi conducted its intelligence-gathering. It was simply business as usual. Erich Mielke was himself one of those 'concrete heads', perhaps even a reinforced concrete head in his case. Instead of concentrating on what was happening in Moscow and predicting the immediate future for the GDR, the Stasi went on with its repression in East Germany, its spying activities in West Germany, but also with its analysis of the evolving situation in Northern Ireland until the very end.

On 16 February, HA-XXII learned from the *Tageszeitung* that four PIRA sympathisers belonging to the Irisch-Republikanische Solidaritätsbewegung (Irish republican solidarity movement) had been arrested in Frankfurt by the West German police. Their apartments had been searched because they had been accused of having put up about one thousand posters with the inscription 'Maggie Thatcher – wanted for murder' as the British prime minister's visit to the city was approaching. A member called Gallagher had said that two other members had been arrested at the border-crossing (presumably the Dutch–West German border) near Aachen.[179] On 20 February, HA-XXII/8 asked HA-VI (border controls and tourism) to begin a 'special investigation' about Irish and Northern Irish citizens who had travelled in the GDR.[180]

In the meantime, Department IX (infiltration of enemy intelligence agencies) of the HVA had completed an investigation into the PIRA's activities in West Germany and neighbouring countries, which it transmitted to HA-XXII in April. The file was classified as 'top secret' and protection for the sources was required as some of the information came from moles within the BKA. The report listed every known PIRA attack from the bombing of the British headquarters in Mönchengladbach on 15 August 1973 until the killing of a British soldier in Ostend on 12 August 1988. Some entries in the report included a wealth of details like for example the brand of cars used in attacks, the car registration numbers, the quality of explosives, the origin of the detonators, the origin of the weapons and ammunition, banknotes in different currencies (West German, Belgian, US, Irish, Egyptian and Greek among others) and so on.

The HVA found out that the British citizen Michael John Tite, who rented a car from a company in Mainz on 29 August 1988, was in fact Terence McGeough who was arrested together with Thomas Hanratty on the Dutch–West German border as previously explained. A key belonging to McGeogh was attributed to an apartment in Malmö in Sweden, which was subsequently searched by the local authorities on 8 September 1988. Different forms of identification were found: one British passport, one US passport and a press identification card.[181] Through the infiltration of the BKA, the Stasi had also obtained McGeough's exact address in Northern Ireland – or at least the one he gave to the BKA. As to Hanratty, he appeared to have no fixed abode.[182] HA-XXII was able to appreciate some of the PIRA's organisational skills and network in Western Europe.

In April, HA-XXII got wind of a possible meeting planned for May Day in Berlin. Its source was a mole within the BfV. Apparently, according to information transmitted by Italian security services to the BfV, sympathisers of different 'terrorist organisations' in Western Europe were planning an 'international meeting' in West Berlin on 1 May. Not only far-left radicals would participate but also 'sympathisers of the [PIRA], the RAF, ETA, the Red Brigades and the AD'. The meeting was to be secret and meant to compare the objectives of the different groups involved and coordinate actions. An extract of the original BfV report was mentioned in HA-XXII's report: 'the meeting in Berlin would be the first real attempt to internationalise the revolutionary struggle as planned by the European far-left movement'. The source was deemed to be 'reliable'. So far, the BfV in West Berlin was not in a position to confirm the planned meeting.[183] It is not known whether it eventually took place.

In the summer of 1989, HA-XXII got more information on the current PIRA campaign in West Germany. On 19 June, the Irish republicans bombed the Quebec barracks at Osnabrück. Nobody was killed but the explosion had caused considerable damage. Through 'reliable connections ... in enemy security services' the Stasi obtained more details on the way the PIRA had operated in this particular attack and how the West Germans were organising their investigation.[184] On 2 July, Corporal Steven Smith was killed by a bomb as he got in his car in Hanover. His wife and his three children who were standing nearby were injured. A second car bomb was defused after the area had been evacuated.[185]

HA-XXII's source about the most recent developments was a mole in the BKA in Wiesbaden. The BKA estimated that the PIRA would continue with its attacks on BAOR. PIRA members in charge of logistics operated from the Netherlands. On 10 July, the Dutch police had met BKA members and given them a sketch on which border crossings in the region of Bad Bentheim had been marked. This sketch had been found by the Dutch during a round-up of a PIRA arms cache in the Netherlands back in 1986. It was believed that these border crossings were used by Irish republicans. HA-XXII further learned that a search operation was planned between the Dutch–West German border crossings at Oeding and Nordhorn between 13 July and 15 August, especially concentrating on periods outside regular traffic hours. The operation was code-named 'HARFE' (harp). The security level at BAOR installations was increased, including urban areas where families of soldiers resided. The HVA, HA-II and HA-XXII were all informed of these developments. But that was not all.

On 13 July, the LKA in Düsseldorf, tipped off by the British authorities, in turn informed other police departments that the chances of another PIRA attack some time during 13 to 16 July were particularly high as Margaret Thatcher was visiting Paris. The PIRA would use the opportunity to get more publicity. However, it was not possible to say what targets the Irish terrorists had in mind, but BAOR was now on alarm level 'keen wind amber'. Again the HVA, HA-II and HA-XXII were informed.[186] It is not known whether or not the Stasi sent agents to that particular Dutch–West German border area. In the event, no attack took place during the period in question. Instead, the PIRA suffered a setback. On 18 July, the *Tagesspiegel* reported that the French had arrested three PIRA members in the east of the country. According to informed circles in Paris, the three were planning an attack against BAOR.[187] But, it did not deter the PIRA which was about to embark upon another spree of attacks and killings.

Peter Morré, a former West German prosecutor who was active in cases against the PIRA, wrote about his experiences in joint cooperation between the West German and Dutch security forces between 1978 and 2000, especially concerning the period 1987–90. The following is based on his reminiscences and offers a most interesting insight on PIRA operations against BAOR. In all, twelve people were killed: one in Belgium, five in the Netherlands and six in West Germany. First, the PIRA sent 'lone assassins', but from 1980 onwards it sent Active Service Units (ASUs) which usually stayed on the continent for a period of about six months. Their aim was 'to kill as many British personnel as possible', explains Morré.

The PIRA members had fake identities and used the Netherlands as a base of attack on BAOR. There were several reasons for this. English was widely spoken in the Netherlands, life was not too expensive and the country was also a rest base for many BAOR soldiers on leave. Furthermore, there were not many border checks between the Netherlands and West Germany. For example, Dutch and West German prosecutors believed that all the PIRA attacks on BAOR in 1988 were carried out by an ASU based in Geleen near Maastricht in the Netherlands. It was the BKA that dealt with the PIRA, assisted for a while by local police forces and also by BAOR's Special Investigation Branch (SIB). Morré remembers that 'direct contacts were established with the Royal Ulster Constabulary (RUC) in Belfast'. The BSSO was also involved and provided information on suspects.

However, not everything ran smoothly, says the former prosecutor. Dutch and West German security agencies believed that the British had several informers within the PIRA's ASUs and possessed knowledge that they did not share with them. Had they done so, it would have led to a more efficient cooperation. As Morré rightly observes: 'Not being fully informed by the other parties is practically inherent to multilateral investigations and intelligence cooperation'.[188] In October 1989, for instance, it was announced by the West German press that the British security services had suffered a most serious setback. The PIRA had managed to obtain top secret documents regarding a network of informers that the British used in their fight against the PIRA. Apparently without the knowledge of the West German security services, British military intelligence had begun work on this network within the Irish community in the FRG back in 1979. HA-XXII learned about this most relevant development in the intelligence world by reading the *Süddeutsche Zeitung* and the *Kölner Stadt-Anzeiger*.[189]

Yet, Morré stresses that there was some excellent collaboration. For example, a PIRA missile attack on a Royal Air Force base near the Dutch border was thwarted. There was also good collaboration between Dutch, West German and Belgian prosecutors. In the late 1980s, a Dutch police unit became attached to the BKA. It was discovered that several of the cars that were used by the PIRA to carry out its attack against the British forces' Joint Headquarters in Rheindahlen near Mönchengladbach had been acquired in the Netherlands. Morré says that the BKA had an 'IRA subdivision'.[190] In 1988, British officers of the G5 (investigations) made more than fifty liaison visits to colleagues of continental security and intelligence services in order to coordinate actions against Irish terrorists. The G5 concluded: 'Most if not all of these liaisons have stated that they look to the Security Service [MI5] to take a lead on Irish terrorist matters and to play a co-ordinating role in determining the response to specific threats.'[191]

The PIRA continued its attacks during the summer of 1989. On 30 July, shots were fired from a van at the Barker barracks at Paderborn, but nobody was killed. On 28 August in Hanover, a soldier discovered a bomb under his car and it was defused. On 1 September, two soldiers came under fire near the York barracks in Münster, one of them seriously wounded. On 7 September, Heidi Hazell, a West German woman married to a British soldier, was shot dead in her car. The West German press reacted immediately. The magazine *Quick* wrote '*Tod den Engländern*' (death to the English).[192] The *Zeit* followed with '*Belfast liegt im Münsterland*' (Belfast lies in the region of Münster).[193] The magazine *Stern* managed to get an interview with 'Sean', the PIRA member responsible for activities abroad. He stated that Hazell's death was a mistake that definitely damaged the cause. But it was believed she had been a member of the Women's Royal Army Corps. To the question if there were going to be more attacks in the FRG, 'Sean' answered 'Yes, I am sorry' and explained that there was no way that British soldiers could kill and torture in Belfast and Derry and then go to West Germany to recuperate. He added: 'They will hear from us everywhere'.[194] It turned out to be the case. On 26 October, the PIRA killed a Royal Air Force non-commissioned officer and his 6-month-old baby, wounding his wife, at a car park of a fast-food restaurant in Wildenrath.[195]

That these PIRA activities seriously worried the BKA, LKA, the Dutch police and the British security services was obviously not surprising. But what was perhaps surprising is that they worried HA-XXII/8 too. What if PIRA activities endangered Stasi operations and GDR installations in West Germany? On 25 September 1989, HA-XXII/8 produced a report, summing up the latest PIRA attacks. It was entitled 'Need for information about the activities of the IRA in operational area [West Germany]'. HA-XXII/8 asked for more information regarding the following issues:

- Location of the bases of the British armed forces in the FRG and West Berlin.
- Situation of the military installations and also residential areas of the bases.

– To what extent are installations of the GDR or other socialist states located near military installations/residences of the British armed forces?
– What hazards exist for our installations?
– Areas of concentration of Irish students and workers in particular in locations where there are [British] bases.
– Relations/contacts of the [PIRA] or its political wing 'Sinn Féin' in the FRG and West Berlin.
– What recruiting possibilities the [PIRA] has in the FRG and West Berlin?
– What persons/groups are being used by the [PIRA] for logistical purposes?[196]

The KGB had surveillance teams around US NATO bases (and no doubt British and French as well),[197] and so had the East Germans.

HA-I (counter-intelligence within the NVA and the border guards) had created an impressive handbook on seventy British infantry and tank regiments and battalions which, at some stage, were based in West Germany. There was nothing top secret as the information was factual. It concerned the historic background of these units, their insignia and, above all, where they had been based in the FRG and abroad. It was obvious proof that they were being monitored. For example, about the Royal Scots Dragoon Guards (Carabineers and Greys), HA-I noted that they were successively based in Osnabrück in the FRG (1977), Catterick in the UK (1977–78), Belize (1978–79), Belfast (1979–80), Paderborn in the FRG (1980–83), Fallingbostel in the FRG (1983) and Sennelager in the FRG (1984). There were also several units with an Irish background: the Queen's Royal Irish Hussars, the 5th Royal Inniskilling Dragoon Guards, the 1st Battalion of the Irish Guards, the 1st Battalion of the Royal Irish Rangers and the 2nd Battalion of the Irish Rangers. HA-I reported nothing special about these Irish-British units.[198] By 1960, the Intelligence Department of the NVA had managed to infiltrate some of the British bases in the FRG. It even managed to take photographs within Royal Air Force bases like for instance at Wildenrath.[199]

From an East German perspective, Irish republican attacks on BAOR were not particularly welcome. If, say, an HVA or an HA-I unit was monitoring a British base, would a PIRA attack not jeopardise it by attracting unwanted attention on the area? Indeed, back in July, HA-I had been informed of possible PIRA attacks. A reliable source had reported to East Berlin that the BKA had warned that the PIRA could resume its bombing campaign and that members of the West German fire brigade and rescue units had to take extra precautions like observing the immediate surroundings of the place where an attack had occurred, reporting suspicious activities to the police, and cooperating closely with the military police and the police. The source had mentioned that there was some unease among members of the fire brigade as they deemed that the Anglo-Irish conflict was not their concern. It was demanded from the British to impose order and they were deemed to be fully responsible for doing so.[200] Too many terrorist activities around BAOR bases could end up upsetting East German intelligence. When Johannes Weinrich of the Carlos group told the Stasi that it should attack NATO bases in the FRG, the conversation got heated and a Stasi officer told him he was a 'political nutcase'.[201] It was also clear that the Stasi's investigation into Irish people living in West Germany had not yielded its fruits yet or was still not being implemented.

But this particular document dated 25 September 1989 is most significant. Indeed, it was written about one and a half months before the fall of the Berlin Wall and the subsequent speedy demise of the GDR. Again, the same questions were put concerning the Irish migrant community and possible links with the PIRA, the risk that PIRA actions endangered Stasi operations near BAOR installations, the possible contacts the PIRA and Sinn Féin had in West Germany and West Berlin and so on. It was obvious that the Stasi still had no answers to these questions and that it began to take an active interest in the PIRA only towards the end of East Germany's existence. Therefore, it can be very reasonably assumed that the HVA and HA-XXII did not actively support or provide arms to the PIRA and the INLA as has been claimed. Nor is it likely that the Stasi was in touch with the PIRA. HA-XXII would simply have mentioned it in its reports and also the names of its contacts had there been any. Moreover, there would certainly not have been such a sudden and urgent need for more information if previous contacts had existed with Irish republicans. As is shown in Chapter 3 regarding the SIRA documents, at the end of the 1980s the HVA had almost no reports on Ireland and Northern Ireland (see Table 3.27). Evidently, Irish republicans were not a priority in East Berlin.

On 10 October, only a month before the sudden and dramatic end of the Wall, HA-XXII/8 made an assessment about terrorism and the planning of the year 1990. Gorbachev's reforms and their possible consequences seemed to be miles away from the Stasi's mind. HA-XX/8 had nothing new to say on the PIRA and reiterated that no indications were found regarding connections with the GDR. Also, the terrorists would continue to be monitored in 1990. It was mentioned in the report that 'information that the [PIRA] is working together with the "RAF" cannot be confirmed'.[202] Only the month before *Stern* had asked PIRA leader 'Sean' if the Irish republicans were in touch with the RAF. His answer had been: 'No. The RAF does not represent the people, nor is it a movement. The IRA on the contrary comes from a long tradition. It is very strongly supported by the oppressed nationalists in the north of Ireland where also most of the fighting takes place.'[203]

What 'Sean' had said about the RAF/PIRA connections was in all likelihood true. Of course, it would have been in his interest to lie as admitting it would have been counterproductive as it would have revealed that the PIRA was relying on the RAF's logistical support in West Germany and have given the security services a more detailed picture of how the PIRA was operating. But the PIRA's struggle was of a nationalist nature, the unification of Ireland, whereas the RAF's was ideological, the overthrow of what it deemed was a capitalist and fascistic order. Both were not the same. The PIRA had far more in common with ETA in the Basque country, which was fighting for independence from Spain. In fact, in March 1974, a spokesman for ETA declared to the West German *Spiegel* that it had 'good, very good relations with the IRA [PIRA]'.[204] Incredibly as this might appear, in October 1989, the ZAIG (central evaluation and information group) still found time to compile a 64-page media file on the PIRA, consisting almost exclusively of West German press cuttings,[205] while thousands of East Germans were desperately trying to leave the country. A few weeks later, the GDR collapsed. 'That is how quickly history is made', commented Markus Wolf.[206]

A last question must be answered now: were the Irish and British secret services aware that the Stasi had some interest in Ireland and Northern Ireland? It remains difficult to give a precise answer. The archives of the G2, the Irish military intelligence, do not reveal much, if everything is available for consultation. Indeed, the relevant files have promising titles like for example 'East German Intelligence, 10/01/76–23/12/76'.[207] However, the material is scant and consists essentially of press cuttings, mainly from Irish newspapers. The file 'West German Intelligence, 25/04/75–16/12/75' is about the Günter Guillaume affair. There are also press cuttings on the RAF's activities in the FRG. Clearly, the G2 kept itself informed of the latest developments but the material was very far from being original and top secret.

Nevertheless, there is no doubt that the Irish knew that the Stasi was a very active agency. In November 1962, a report entitled 'East German Subversion and Espionage' was prepared for the Irish government.[208]

It was explained that East Berlin was a centre of East bloc intelligence agencies. The KGB had its headquarters in Berlin Karlshorst and had a staff of 800 people. The GRU had a staff of 250 people and was based at Wünsdorf near Berlin, and 'the Polish, Czech and Rumanian intelligence services have large operational agencies in East Berlin, mainly to infiltrate agents into West Germany'. It was stressed in the report that there were 'three main East German organisations concerned with espionage and subversion'. First of all, there was the Stasi, which was headed by Lieutenant-General Erich Mielke. Within the Stasi 'the Main Department of Intelligence [HVA]' was led by 'Major-General Markus Wolf'. Then, details were given about the organisational structure of different sections of the HVA and of the Stasi at large. It was stated: 'The Ministry recruits agents, informers, and collaborators, using bribery, threats (often involving relations in East Germany), and blackmail. It has its own training colleges for teaching the techniques of sabotage and subversion.'[209]

The second main East German organisation was the Ministry of Defence. Here, it was indicated in the report that military intelligence was directed by Colonel Willi Sägebrecht. Colonel Thomas Mrochen was in charge of undermining 'the morale of the West German army'. The third organisation was the *Arbeitsbüro* (the work office), led by a journalist named Erich Glückauf. It had a staff of about one hundred people and coordinated 'all subversive operations against West Germany and West Berlin'. It was also stated that mass organisations such as the Trade Union Federation (FDGB), the Free German Youth (FDJ) and so-called friendship societies were involved in infiltration, subversion and espionage.[210]

The report was rather accurate and begs the question where the Irish had obtained this information. It would seem most unlikely that the G2 was active in Berlin. Did it come from the British, the Americans? That would seem very likely but there is no way of proving it. It is relevant to point out that when the Troubles in Northern Ireland began in 1969, the Gardaí (Irish police) feared that certain pro-Soviet groups in the country might use the opportunity to destabilise the government and seize power. It was especially believed that some members of the OIRA might infiltrate the radio, television and even banks.[211] According to Dr Noël Browne, a left-wing politician and a one-time minister for health (1948–51), the left-wing was closely monitored by the Gardaí which even managed to infiltrate it. Also, the Special Branch installed a hidden camera in front of a Communist bookshop in Dublin.[212] These were certainly techniques worthy of Stasi surveillance operations.

The relevant surviving Stasi material does not reveal that Western intelligence services had taken any counter-measures in Ireland. Regarding the United Kingdom of Great Britain and Northern Ireland, Christopher Andrew in his 1,000-page study of MI5 mentions the Stasi only once in relation with an African country.[213] However, there was definitely an awareness of a possible East German threat. Close encounters between the Irish security services and the East Germans seem to have been of a more amusing kind. Edgar Uher remembers the first visit made by an East German ambassador to Ireland in 1981, a visit he had to prepare:

> By phone we had alerted them all of our coming. By doing so, we equally alerted Irish Security, who consequently then took a keen interest in us. Of course it would also have been in the Irish' interest to make sure that nothing happened to the new ambassador. But it obviously was more than that. We barely had arrived at the Shelbourne [hotel in Dublin], where we stayed, when a blue Renault 18 drew up, installing itself in front of the hotel and from that time on diligently following us. If we walked, two burly guys got out to [follow us]. Why should we make life harder for those guys? We decided to assist them. I walked up to the Renault and informed them about our plans for the following day, so they would know. They had been [completely] surprised, but did not object. We established a very good relationship that culminated the last evening in us presenting them a bottle of whiskey each. Clearly, the picture of the enemy they must have had got shaken that moment ... In return, they offered us their services as pilots for the car-drive back to the car-ferry the last day, for a change not trailing behind, but driving in front with blue flashlights on the roof. My ambassador felt like a king.[214]

The Irish were tenacious in their suspicions and moved one big step forward in their surveillance operations. A few years later, in November 1987, Uher visited Ireland for the last time, accompanying the deputy head of the East German Ministry of External Affairs, Kurt Nier. According to Uher:

> On the way to Dublin I told Nier a bit about my experiences in Ireland. I mentioned [the repatriation of Frank Ryan's body from Dresden], the Irish mentality the problems with appointments kept in time or not quite and the attentiveness of the Irish Special Branch. He first believed none of it. When we left the island two days later he knew better, having been visited in his hotel room in the middle of the night by someone who wanted 'to repair the shower'.[215]

On a more serious note, Uher told this author:

> Let me clearly state that I never had any intelligence function in Ireland; other than to fetch an Irish phonebook which we did not have yet. And

> I am sure that the MfS [Stasi] did not do anything on Irish shores, at least not between 1980 and 88 – here I am pretty sure. I remember that I had been expressly warned by my MfS desk not to establish any contacts with IRA people, which I never purposefully or knowingly did. I surely have met a few people suspected to be IRA.[216]

Uher's statement is certainly corroborated by the lack of evidence in the surviving material, be it from the HVA, HA-XXII or indeed any other department.

It is also relevant to notice the similitude of the Stasi's approach to the PIRA in the 1980s, which Uher describes, to the KGB's: no contact. According to Christopher Andrew and Soviet defector Oleg Gordievsky: 'The [KGB] residency in Dublin was usually reluctant to make contact with any illegal group because of what it regarded as the near-impossibility of keeping secrets in the Irish Republic. KGB officers claimed that merely by listening to conversations in a number of public houses frequented by Sinn Féin supporters they were able to learn a surprising amount.'[217] Of course, 'operation SPLASH' should not be forgotten. But considering all the available evidence for this study, it cannot be stated that the Stasi actively sought to destabilise the United Kingdom by exploiting the terrorist conflict in Northern Ireland one way or another.

Notes

1 BStU, MfS-HA XXII, no. 6083/13, HVA report dated April 1989.
2 NAI, DFA, 2002/19/51, Keating to Hugh McCann, DFA secretary, 15 March 1971.
3 T. Hennessey, *The Evolution of the Troubles, 1970–72* (Dublin: Irish Academic Press, 2007), pp. 35–48.
4 NAI, DFA, 2002/19/51, Keating to Hugh McCann, DFA secretary, 15 March 1971.
5 *Ibid.*, embassy series Bonn, D/101, Keating to McCann, 23 August 1971.
6 NATO Archive, Brussels, record-MC-033-71, summary record of NATO's Military Committee, 26 July 1971 [the author is grateful to Mr Victor Martinez-Garzón (NATO archivist) for this document].
7 *Ibid.*, record-MC-042-71, summary record of NATO's Military Committee meeting, 24 September 1971.
8 *Stuttgarter Zeitung*, 3 February 1972, in Konrad-Adenauer-Stiftung, Sankt Augustin (near Bonn), Pressedokumentation, file: 'Staaten, Irland, 1951–31/07/1983'.
9 NATO Archive, C-R (72) 28, summary record of NATO Council meeting, 4 July 1972.
10 *Ibid.*

11 *Ibid.*, record-MC-032-72, special record of NATO's Military Committee, 28 July 1972.
12 *Ibid.*, PO(72)392, 'Temporary changes in United Kingdom force contribution to NATO', 21 September 1972.
13 BBC4, Timeshift, 'The British Army of the Rhine', broadcast on television on 25 October 2012.
14 V. Mastny, 'Imagining War in Europe: Soviet Strategic Planning', in V. Mastny, S. G. Holtsmark & A. Wenger (eds.), *War Plans and Alliances in the Cold War: Threat Perceptions in the East and West* (London and New York: Routledge, 2006), pp. 24–5.
15 *Ibid.*, pp. 35–6.
16 CIA website, electronic reading room, 'The Balance of Forces in Central Europe', report written by the CIA on 1 August 1977, at www.foia.cia.gov/docs/DOC_0000498556/DOC_0000498556.pdf (accessed 30 November 2012).
17 Bundesarchiv-Militärarchiv (hereafter BA-MA), Freiburg am Breisgau, 'Information über die Aufgaben, die Personalstruktur und die Personalreserven der britische Streitkräfte', March 1972, DVW1–25733/m.
18 Wolfgang Döhnert, Berlin, correspondence with the author, 19 October 2009.
19 B. Yeltsin, *View from the Kremlin* (London: HarperCollins, 1994), pp. 311–12.
20 Andrew, *Defence of the Realm*, p. 605.
21 Treacy, *Communist Party of Ireland*, pp. 375–9.
22 Milotte, *Communism in Modern Ireland*, pp. 250–1, 291.
23 Yeltsin, *View from the Kremlin*, pp. 312–15.
24 *Ibid.*, pp. 315–16.
25 *Ibid.*, p. 316.
26 Boyne, *Gunrunners*, pp. 131–2.
27 Swan, *Official Irish Republicanism, 1962–1972*, pp. 338–9.
28 C. Andrew & V. Mitrokhin, *The Mitrokhin Archive: The KGB in Europe and the West* (London: Penguin, 2000), pp. xxiii, 858 (n. 52), 502–3, 858 (n. 55).
29 See J. O'Brien, *The Arms Trial* (Dublin: Gill & Macmillan, 2000).
30 Andrew, *Defence of the Realm*, pp. 605–6, n. 26 (p. 959).
31 Boyne, *Gunrunners*, p. 132.
32 K. Wharton, *'Sir, They're Taking the Kids Indoors': The British Army in Northern Ireland, 1973–74* (Solihull: Helion, 2012), p. 123.
33 Sloan, *Geopolitics of Anglo-Irish Relations in the 20th Century*, pp. 258, 260.
34 BA-MA, 'MfNV, Verwaltung Aufklärung: Informationsmitteilung, 13 November 1972', 'Kurze Inhaltsangabe des "Informationssammelberichtes über die Streitkräfte kapitalistischer Staaten" (UdSSR) für den Zeitraum vom 16.08 bis 15.09.1972', DVW1-25737.
35 *Limburgsch Dagblad*, 15 October 1969.

36 BA-MA, 'MfNV, Verwaltung Aufklärung: Informationsmitteilung, 17 February 1975', 'Kurze Inhaltsangabe des "Informationssammelberichtes über die Streitkräfte kapitalistischer Staaten" (UdSSR) für den Zeitraum vom 01.12 bis 31.12.1974', DVW1-25724/a.
37 Boyne, *Gunrunners*, see ch. 4, 'The Spooks and the Arms Deal in Prague', pp. 119–38, 432.
38 G. FitzGerald, *Just Garret: Tales from the Political Front Line* (Dublin: Liberties Press, 2011), p. 185.
39 CIA website, electronic reading room, 'Soviet Support for International Terrorism and Revolutionary Violence', report written by the CIA and other American intelligence agencies on 27 May 1981, at www.foia.cia.gov/docs/DOC_0000272980/DOC_0000272980.pdf (accessed 30 November 2012).
40 Andrew & Gordievsky, *KGB*, p. 633.
41 NATO Archive, C-R (76) 1, summary record of NATO Council meeting, 5 February 1976.
42 *Ibid.*, C-M(76)71, 'Half-Yearly Review of Subversive and Intelligence Activities', 24 November 1976.
43 NATO Archive, record-MC-006-77, summary record of NATO Military Committee meeting, 21 February 1977.
44 Rupp *et al.*, *Militärspionage*, pp. 12, 85, 236–7, 238.
45 Gieseke, *Der Mielke-Konzern*, pp. 240–1.
46 *Telegraf*, 3 February 1972; *Tagesspiegel*, 3 February 1972 (BStU, ZAIG, no. 11056).
47 *Neue Rheinzeitung*, 4 February 1972 (BStU, ZAIG, no. 11056).
48 BStU, MfS-HA XXII, no. 19022, op. Mat. 'Feldwebel', file of 'Räther, Willi'.
49 Glees, *Stasi Files*, p. 138.
50 BStU, MfS-HA IX, no. 2451, file containing photographs of the British army in action, no date but probably 1971.
51 *Horizont*, no. 18, 1976 (SAPMO-BA).
52 *Ibid.*, no. 17, 1977 (SAPMO-BA).
53 Geraghty, *Brixmis*, p. 188.
54 BStU, MfS-Sekr. Neiber, no. 13, Lemme to Neiber, 26 November 1979; 'Hinweise zur Präzisierung des Materials der Rechtsstelle des MfS zum internationalen Terorismus', 30 November 1979.
55 Wunschik, '"Abwehr" und Unterstützung des internationalen Terrorismus-Die -Hauptabteilung XXII', pp. 263–4.
56 Wolf & McElvoy, *Man without a Face*, pp. 304–5.
57 *Ibid.*, p. 305.
58 Gieseke, *Der Mielke-Konzern*, pp. 239–40.
59 O'Halpin, *Defending Ireland*, pp. 321–2.
60 Boyne, *Gunrunners*, see ch. 5, 'The Infiltration of the *Claudia* Operation', pp. 139–67.
61 Kopp, *Die Terrorjahre*, pp. 135–8.

62 Boyne, *Gunrunners*, pp. 135, 429 (table for OIRA gun-running operations) and pp. 431–8 (tables for PIRA gun-running operations). The PIRA is by very far the most important gun-runner.
63 I. M. Pacepa, *Red Horizons: The Extraordinary Memoirs of an Eastern European Spy Chief* (London: Coronet Books, 1989), pp. 12–22, 23–36, 239–40, 354.
64 *Ibid.*, pp. 20, 110–11, 112–14, 119–21.
65 Boyne, *Gunrunners*, p. 168.
66 Moloney, *Secret History of the IRA*, pp. 8–9.
67 Pacepa, *Red Horizons*, see ch. 6, pp. 98–114.
68 Moloney, *Secret History of the IRA*, p. 3.
69 Pacepa, *Red Horizons* p. 263.
70 Wolf & McElvoy, *Man without a Face*, pp. 306–7.
71 M. Kopp, *Die Terrorjahre: Mein Leben an der Seite von Carlos* (Munich: Deutsche Verlags-Anstalt, 2007), pp. 183–5, 207–10.
72 J. Follain, *Jackal: The Complete Story of the Legendary Terrorist, Carlos the Jackal* (New York: Arcade, 2011), pp. 182–3.
73 BStU, MfS-HA XXII, nos. 18667, 6065/1 and 6065/2.
74 www.bstu.bund.de, Tobias Wunschik, 'Die Hauptabteilung XXII: "Terrorabwehr"', in K.-D. Henke *et al.* (eds.), *Anatomie der Staatssicherheit: Geschichte, Struktur und Methoden – MfS Handbuch-* (PDF file), p. 47. The BStU website has a most useful detailed book entitled *Anatomie der Staatssicherheit* on the history, organisation and activities of the Stasi published in several PDF files, each file dealing with a particular topic (accessed 7 May 2010).
75 Correspondence with Edgar Uher, Berlin, 31 March 2011.
76 Wolf & McElvoy, *Man without a Face*, pp. 277–8.
77 'Former Stasi master feels free to question the past', by Denis Staunton, *Irish Times*, 2 June 1995.
78 Wolf & McElvoy, *Man without a Face*, see ch. 13, 'Terrorism and the GDR', pp. 277–313, 303 for his mention of the IRA.
79 *Ibid.*, p. 302.
80 J. Holland & H. McDonald, *INLA Deadly Divisions: The Story of One of Ireland's most Ruthless Terrorist Organisations* (Dublin: Torc, 1994), pp. 249–51.
81 *Ibid.*
82 Boyne, *Gunrunners*, p. 346.
83 Holland & McDonald, *INLA Deadly Divisions*, p. 130.
84 Follain, *Jackal*, pp. 129–30.
85 Andrew, *Defence of the Realm*, pp. 649–52, 696.
86 *Der Spiegel*, 34/1979, 20 August 1979.
87 *Ibid.*
88 Kopp, *Die Terrorjahre*, p. 69.
89 BStU, MfS-ZAIG, no. 11056, see West German press cuttings, including 'Rote Armee Fraktion hilft angeblich der IRA' in the *Frankfurter Rundschau*,

13 March 1980.

90 *Ibid.*, MfS-HA XXII, no. 19173, the file has no date and no title.

91 *Ibid.*, MfS-HA XXII, no. 24, 'Wichtigste ausländische Extremisten- und Terrororganisationen und – gruppen', no date, but the most recent date mentioned in the document is 1980.

92 Holland & McDonald, *INLA Deadly Divisions*, p. 129.

93 *Welt*, 18 May 1977 (BStU, ZAIG, no. 11056).

94 Holland & McDonald, *INLA Deadly Divisions*, p. 141 (n. 6).

95 *Ibid.*, p. 130.

96 *Ierland Bulletin*, 23rd year, no. 4, May 2002, at www.antenna.nl/ierland komitee (consulted 14 April 2008).

97 H-Blok/Armagh Komitee (1968–85), at www.iisg.nl, Internationaal Instituut voor Sociale Geschiedenis, Amsterdam (accessed 14 April 2008).

98 BStU, MfS-HA XXII, no. 5749/2, 'Information G/1580/18/02/81'.

99 *Ibid.*

100 C. Daase, *Die RAF und der internationale Terrorismus*, in W. Kraushaar (ed.), *Die RAF: Entmythologisierung einer terroristischen Organisation* (Bonn: Bundeszentrale für politische Bildung, 2008), p. 239, n. 21 (p. 265). Daase has written that O'Hara was an IRA member, but he belonged in fact to the INLA.

101 Holland & McDonald, *INLA Deadly Divisions*, p. 169.

102 BStU, MfS-HA XXII, no. 20488, *Irisch-republikanische Gefangene im Hungerstreik*, published by the WISK, no date but early 1980s.

103 *Ibid.*, MfS-HA XXII, no. 20758, *Revolutionärer Zorn*, no. 6, January 1981.

104 *Ibid.*, MfS-HA XXII, no. 81/1, 'Bericht über das linksextremistische "Westdeutsche-Irland-Solidaritätskomitee (WISK)"', 27 July 1981.

105 *Ibid.*

106 *Ibid.*

107 *Ibid.*, MfS-HA XXII, no. 250, 'Information A/6773/17/09/81'.

108 McDonald & Holland, *INLA Deadly Divisions* (2010 edition), p. 287.

109 BStU, MfS-HA II, no. 18607, Linow to Schenk, 19 October 1982, containing 'Information A/14446/18/10/82'.

110 *Ibid.*, Linow to Schenk, 26 October 1982, containing information 'B/14715/25/10/82'.

111 *Ibid.*, MfS-HA XXII, no. 249 (Band 1 von 2), 'Information A/16381/20/11/82'.

112 Boyne, *Gunrunners*, p. 321.

113 'France 2, 22h45, 'L'affaire des Irlandais de Vincennes', *Libération*, 8 January 1996, at www.liberation.fr/medias/0101169881-france-2-22h45-l-affaire-des-irlandais-de-vincennes-documentaire-de-pierre-pean-et-christophe-nick-irlandais-de-vincennes-le-poids-d-une-balance-treize-ans-apres-une-enquete-sur-cette-affaire-d-etat-t (accessed 26 April 2013).

114 Boyne, *Gunrunners*, pp. 327–32.

115 Gieseke, 'East German Espionage in the Era of Détente', p. 416.
116 R. J. Aldrich, 'British Intelligence, Security and Western Cooperation in Cold War Germany: *The Ostpolitik Years*', in de Graaf *et al.* (eds.), *Battleground Western Europe*, p. 136.
117 BStU, MfS-HA XXII, no. 17219, '4) Iren/Nordiren', no date (last date mentioned in text: 24 March 1987).
118 W. Großmann, *Bonn im Blick: Die DDR-Aufklärung aus der Sicht ihres letzten Chefs* (Berlin: Das Neue Berlin, 2001), p. 149.
119 Krieger, 'German Intelligence History', p. 186.
120 Holland & McDonald, *INLA Deadly Divisions*, see 'Appendix 2: Chronology of INLA actions', pp. 358–68.
121 BStU, MfS-HA XXII, no. 17220, file with no title, including Plunkett, Reid and King's statements, and also other material related to Ireland and Northern Ireland.
122 *Ibid.*, MfS-HA II, no. 18624, 'Information A/03957/09/03/83', MfS-HA II, no. 28369, 'Information A/03957/09/03/83', MfS-HA XXII, no. 248 (Teil 1 von 2), 'Information A/05872/08/04/83' and MfS-HA XXII, no. 248 (Teil 2 von 2), 'Information B/10943/14/06/83'.
123 *Ibid.*, MfS-HA XXII, no. 110 (Teil 1 von 2), 'Information A/33424/01/08/85'.
124 *Ibid.*, 'Information A/35544/03/09/85'.
125 Boyne, *Gunrunners*, p. 113.
126 *Frankfurter Allgemeine Zeitung*, 10 August 2004. See also Koehler, *Stasi*, ch. 9, 'The Stasi and Terrorism: The La Belle Bombing', pp. 325–57.
127 BStU, MfS-HA XXII, no. 17001/7, 'INFORMATION zur möglicherweise zu erwartenden Eskalierung militanter Anschläge in Westeuropa', by XXII/8, 2 June 1986.
128 Moloney, *Secret History of the IRA*, pp. 3–6.
129 *Ibid.*
130 BStU, MfS-HA XXII, no. 17219, 'Übersicht zu terroristischen Aktivitäten der IRA-1986', by XXII/8, 22 September 1986.
131 *Ibid.*, MfS-HA XXII, no. 17220, file with no title, including Plunkett, Reid and King's statements, and also the translation of O'Connell's book and other material related to Ireland and Northern Ireland.
132 *Ibid.*, MfS-HA XXII, no. 16909/1, 'Information Nr. 202/86', 11 November 1986.
133 The author is grateful to Mr Christian Schwack of the BStU in Berlin for this information.
134 BStU, MfS-Abt. X, no. 484, Damm to Krasa, 10 November 1986.
135 O'Halpin, *Defending Ireland*, pp. 337–8.
136 *Irish Times*, 2 June 2010.
137 *Ibid.*, 2 February 2011.
138 Wolf with McElvoy, *Man without a Face*, p. 307.
139 T. Wunschik, '"Abwehr" und Unterstützung des internationalen Terrorusmus-Die -Hauptabteilung XXII', in Knabe, *West-Arbeit des MfS*, pp. 268–9.

140 BStU, MfS-HA XXII, no. 16917, 'AUFGABENSTELLUNG laut Jahresarbeitsplan 1987', 5 February 1987.
141 Daase, 'Die RAF und der internationale Terrorismus', p. 254.
142 'Bomb attack on NATO pipeline', Associated Press News Archive, 7 January 1985, at www.apnewsarchive.com/1985/Bomb-Attack-on-NATO-Pipeline/id-6ea54f9c316116722725528da35ee6ad (accessed 14 January 2013).
143 Alexander Straßner, 'Die dritte Generation der RAF; Terrorismus und Öffenlichkeit', in Kraushaar (ed.), *Die RAF*, pp. 219–20.
144 Daase, 'Die RAF und der internationale Terrorismus', pp. 240, 258–60.
145 T. Wunschik, 'Aufstieg und Zerfall; Die zweite Generation der RAF', in Kraushaar (ed.), *Die RAF*, p. 191.
146 Straßner, 'Die dritte Generation der RAF', p. 208.
147 *Ibid.*, pp. 219–21.
148 BStU, MfS-HA XXII, no. 16917, 'Auszug Jahreslageeinschätzung 1986'.
149 '1987: 30 hurt as car bomb hits army base', BBC, On this day 1950–2005, at http://news.bbc.co.uk/onthisday (accessed 4 March 2011).
150 BStU, MfS-HA XXII, no. 6065/1, 'INFORMATION Nr. 140/87', 24 March 1987.
151 *Berliner Morgenpost*, 25 March 1987; *Tagesspiegel*, 25 March 1987.
152 CIA website, electronic reading room, 'Terrorism review for 9 April 1987', at www.foia.cia.gov/docs/DOC_0000258625/DOC_0000258625.pdf (accessed 23 March 2012).
153 BStU, MfS-Abt. X, no. 484, Kempe to Krasa, 20 April 1987 (MfS, no. 6065/1).
154 *Ibid.*, MfS-HA XXII, no. 19175, [X]; the author has purposefully removed any detail that might lead to the identification of this individual.
155 The author is grateful for this information to Mr Christian Schwack (BStU, Berlin); e-mail exchange, 3 June 2013.
156 O. Schröm, *Im Schatten des Schakals: Carlos und die Wegbereiter des internationalen Terrorismus* (Berlin: Ch. Links, 2002), p. 25.
157 Follain, *Jackal*; for IRA, see p. 225; for ETA, see pp. 122–3, 129–30, 131, 138, 146.
158 Kopp, *Die Terrorjahre*, pp. 132–3, 204.
159 BStU, MfS-HA XXII, no. 6065/1, *Frankfurter Allgemeine Zeitung*, 2 May 1988, *Berliner Morgenpost*, 3 May 1988; *Welt*, 3 May 1988.
160 *Ibid.*, MfS-HA XXII, no. 6065/1, *Welt*, 14 July 1988; *Zeit*, 19 July 1988.
161 *Ibid.*, MfS-HA XXII, no. 6065/1, *Berliner Morgenpost*, 6 August 1988; *Welt*, 8 August 1988.
162 *Ibid.*, MfS-HA XXII, no. 6065/1, *Volksblatt Berlin*, 14 August 1988; *Tagesspiegel*, 14 August 1988.
163 *Ibid.*, MfS-HA XXII, no. 6065/1, AP telex, Aug. 88, DPA telex, Aug. 88, *Welt*, 2 September 1988 and 8 September 1988; ARD, 7 September 1988. HA-XXII's comment that it has no files on Hanratty and McGeough is mentioned at the bottom of the ARD report.
164 *Ibid.*, MfS-HA XXII, no. 6065/1, *Welt*, 22 August 1988.

165 *Ibid.*, MfS-HA XXII, no. 6065/1, untitled document, no author, undated but post 30 August 1988.
166 *Ibid.*, untitled document, no author, undated but post 30 August 1988.
167 Gieseke, *Der Mielke-Konzern*, pp. 240–1.
168 BStU, MfS-HA XXII, no. 17219, 'Die "IRA" ändert ihre Taktik', 21 September 1988.
169 *Ibid.*, MfS-HA XXII/8, nos. 6065/1 and 17219 (same document), 'INFORMATION zu Aktivitäten der "Irisch Republikanischen Armee" (IRA)', 4 November 1988 (marginalia on copy with reference no. 6065/1).
170 The author is grateful to Mr Christian Schwack (BStU) for this explanation; e-mail exchange, 7 February 2013.
171 Glees, *Stasi Files*, p. 126.
172 BStU, MfS-HA XXII, no. 17219, 'Maßnahmen zur weiteren Bearbeitung der "Irisch Republikanischen Armee" (IRA)', 29 November 1988.
173 H. McDonald, *Colours: Ireland – From Bombs to Boom* (Edinburgh and London: Mainstream, 2005), pp. 113–14.
174 BStU, MfS-HA XXII, no. 19156, undated but written in either 1988 or 1989, 'Organisation "IRA"' is mentioned on top (the most recent date mentioned in the text is March 1988).
175 *Ibid.*, MfS-HA XXII, nos. 19156 and 17219 (identical documents), 20 October 1986, '*Einschätzung zur extremistischen Organisation "Irish Republican Army-IRA"*'.
176 *Ibid.*, MfS-HA-XXII, no. 19156, undated document entitled 'Irisch Republikanische Armee ("IRA")' (the most recent date mentioned in the text is 30 August 1988).
177 BStU, no exact reference, index card on the INLA, created on 10 August 1979 and located in the ZMA.
178 Wolf & McElvoy, *Man without a Face*, p. 354.
179 'IRA-Sympathisanten festgenommen', *Tageszeitung*, 16 February 1989 (BStU, HA-XXII, no. 18667).
180 BStU, MfS-HA XXII, no. 17219, 'Einleitung einer Sonderrecherche', HA-XXII/8 to HA-VI, 20 February, 1989.
181 *Ibid.*, MfS-HA XXII, no. 6083/13, report entitled 'Anschlagsaktivitäten der IRA in der Bundesrepublik Deutschland und in den benachbarten westeuropäischen Staaten' by HVA, department IX, April 1989 (no exact date).
182 *Ibid.*
183 *Ibid.*, MfS-HA XXII, no. 5919 (Teil 2 von 2), 'Information A/016157/25/04/89/07'.
184 *Ibid.*, MfS-HA XXII, no. 18667, 'Anschlag auf eine britische Militäreinrichtung', 20 (?) June 1989.
185 'Tödlicher Bombenanschlag der IRA in Hannover', *Tagesspiegel*, 4 July 1989 (BStU, HA-XXII, no. 6065/2).
186 BStU, MfS-HAXXII, no. 5928, 'Information G/026336/13/07/89/07'.
187 *Tagesspiegel*, 18 July 1989 (BStU, HA-XXII, no. 6065/2).
188 See P. Morré's very informative account: 'Joint Operations against the

IRA in the Netherlands and the Federal Republic of Germany', in de Graaf *et al.* (eds.), *Battleground Western Europe*, pp. 253–60.

189 *Süddeutsche Zeitung*, 16 October 1989 (BStU, HA-XXII, no. 6065/2); *Kölner Stadt-Anzeiger*, date not mentioned but very likely October 1989 (BStU, HA-XXII, no. 6065/2).

190 Morré, 'Joint Operations against the IRA in the Netherlands and the Federal Republic of Germany', pp. 253–60.

191 Andrew, *Defence of the Realm*, p. 748.

192 *Quick*, 14 September 1989, found in a compilation of press cuttings by the ZAIG (BStU, MfS-ZAIG, no. 28205).

193 'Belfast liegt im Münsterland', by Marianne Quoirin, 22 September 1989, at www.zeit.de/1989/39/belfast-liegt-im-muensterland (accessed 24 March 2011).

194 *Stern*, 14 September1989, found in a compilation of press cuttings by the ZAIG (BStU, MfS-ZAIG, no. 28205).

195 *Frankfurter Allgemeine Zeitung*, 28 October 1989 (BStU, HA-XXII no. 6065/2).

196 BStU, MfS-HA XXII, no. 17219, 'INFORMATIONSBEDARF zu Aktivitäten der "Irisch Republikanischen Armee" ("IRA") im Operationsgebiet', 25 September 1989.

197 Andrew & Gordievsky, *KGB*, pp. 599–600.

198 BStU, MfS-HA I, no. 18430, 'Handbuch über die Panzer- und Infanterieverbände der britischen Streitkräfte', 2 April 1985.

199 BA-MA, 'Bericht über das Flugplatznetz in Westdeutschland', 1960, Bd. II, DVW1-25811/b.

200 BStU, MfS-HA XXII, no. 6065/2, 'Warnung vor Anschlaegen der PIRA', date unreadable but in all likelihood in July 1989.

201 Follain, *Jackal*, p. 178.

202 BStU, MfS-HA XXII, no. 19826, 'EINSCHÄTZUNG der politisch-operativen Lage für die Jahresplanung 1990', 10 October 1989.

203 *Ibid.*, MfS-ZAIG, no. 28205, 'In jedem Krieg gibt es ziviele Opfer', by Warner Poelchau, *Stern*, 14 September 1989, found in a compilation of press cuttings by the ZAIG.

204 Coogan, *IRA*, p. 543.

205 BStU, MfS-ZAIG, no. 28205, media file on the PIRA compiled by the ZAIG; the most recent press cutting is an article published by *Tagesspiegel* on 4 October 1989.

206 Wolf & McElvoy, *Man without a Face*, p. 363.

207 Irish Military Archives, Cathal Brugha Barracks, Dublin, 'West German Intelligence, 25/04/75–16/12/75', 2006/161/41-G2/C/1684/1; 'East German Intelligence, 10/01/76–23/12/76', 2007/144/72-G2/C/1684; 'Czechoslovak Intelligence Service, 04/01/78–21/08/78', 2008/151/39-G2/C/1258 Pt. 2; and 'Russian Intelligence Service, 08/04/78–31/12/78', 2008/151/64-G2/C/1769 Pt. 9.

208 NAI, DFA, secretary's files, 2001 release, 2001/43/88, report entitled

'East German Subversion and Espionage', November 1962 (no author mentioned).

209 *Ibid.*

210 *Ibid.*

211 M. Mulqueen, *Re-evaluating Irish National Security Policy: Affordable Threats?* (Manchester: Manchester University Press, 2009), pp. 32–3.

212 N. Browne, *Against the Tide* (Dublin: Gill & Macmillan, 1986), p. 249.

213 Andrew, *Defence of the Realm*, p. 470.

214 Uher, 'Last rites', p. 22.

215 *Ibid.*, p. 29.

216 Correspondence with Edgar Uher, Berlin, 14 December 2010.

217 Andrew & Gordievsky, *KGB*, p. 633.

Conclusion

Finally, the history of diplomatic recognition between Ireland and the GDR, involving the repatriation of Frank Ryan's remains, was a most extraordinary one. But the opening of diplomatic relations between the two countries in 1980 did certainly not lead to closer relations generally speaking. Until the early 1970s, successive Irish governments had decided to diligently implement Bonn's Hallstein doctrine, out of ideological conviction and also because they did not want to upset West Germany which was becoming an increasingly important economic partner and which also had a decisive say concerning Ireland's application to join the European Community (EC). Although militarily neutral, Ireland was not ideologically neutral in the East–West conflict.

But unlike other Western European countries, many of them about to become its partners within the EC, Ireland was too systematic and rigorous in its application of the Hallstein doctrine, which need not have been the case. Others like France and Britain, also members of NATO, while not recognising the East German State had not always qualms in doing business with East Germany. It would seem that the Department of External Affairs was too cautious. But also, Irish public opinion was vehemently anti-Communist. This anti-Communism was spearheaded by the powerful Catholic Church, as noted by the East Germans. To defy the church and people in this matter might have compromised the government's chances in re-election. There was little room for a more pragmatic attitude here.

Yet, when Ireland's attitude towards trade with East Germany and Eastern Europe began to change from the mid-1960s onwards, no doubt mainly caused by a desire to find more export outlets as EC membership was out of reach owing to French objections to British membership which was crucial for Irish entry, commercial relations did not change dramatically, not even after the West began to massively recognise the GDR in the early 1970s. The problem of trade incompatibility remained. It was easier for the GDR to export to Ireland than for

Ireland to export to the GDR. In any case, Ireland's eventual entry into the EC in 1973 meant that the country's main trading partners would be located in Western Europe, not in the East. In this respect, Ireland was no different to Britain, France, the Netherlands and others who had little trade with the East bloc. In the end, Ireland's balance of trade with all Communist countries remained largely negative until the collapse of the Iron Curtain. But it mattered little as the volume of trade (export/import) with the East simply paled by comparison with West Germany, even Nigeria, not to mention Britain and the United States. In other words, there was no incentive for Dublin to get closer to East Berlin.

The same was true for East Berlin. Ireland was perceived as being not economically and politically important enough among the Western countries. It was not much different in cultural matters. There were some interesting experiences nonetheless, like the Ireland–GDR Friendship Society and the Ireland Conference in the University of Halle. The lives of the few Irish idealists who settled in the GDR to experience the building of Socialism certainly are worthy of being mentioned. But travel restrictions imposed by the East German authorities, rather weak national economies and distance between the two countries meant that mass tourism was never going to develop. Having said this, the media did pay regular attention to what was happening in each other's country. As to the SED, it accomplished a delicate political tightrope exercise between the CPI and the WP. Under pressure from Moscow to switch support to the WP, it never wavered in its loyalty to Michael O'Riordan.

But now to the all-important question. Was the island of Ireland a relevant target for East German intelligence? As has been established, the Stasi's main objective was West Germany. Not even other European powers such the United Kingdom and France were key targets and major operational areas in Western Europe. As Markus Wolf wrote, East German intelligence 'graded Britain as only a Category 2 country'. According to him, the HVA did infiltrate several people into Britain, 'but very few of these illegals remained in Britain because our government preferred to maintain good relations with London'. Of course, some spies operated from the East German embassy in London. Moreover, Wolf stressed that Dr Hagen Blau, an HVA mole deep inside the West German Foreign Office, gave much valuable information on Britain.[1] If the United Kingdom, arguably NATO's most important member state in Western Europe, was 'only a Category 2 country', then what category was Ireland in? To get something of an answer, the following questions need to be put.

- Was Ireland interesting from a military point of view? The answer is no. Ireland was simply not a significant military power.
- Was Ireland interesting from a political point of view? The answer is no. Ireland was neutral and not a member of NATO. Of course, some initiatives taken by Irish governments could definitely catch the Stasi's attention like for example the various initiatives in the field of nuclear disarmament and troop reduction. But the Irish CND movement was simply too small and could not be compared to the one in the Netherlands which became the object of Stasi surveillance and interference. In any case, US cruise missiles were not going to be installed in neutral Ireland.
- Was Ireland interesting from an economic point of view? The answer is no. For decades, Ireland suffered from a self-imposed economic protectionism that had disastrous consequences on its economic development. It was lagging well behind other Western European countries. In a piece of counterfactual history, there can be very little doubt, however, that had the so-called 'Celtic Tiger' (years of spectacular economic growth) began in the 1980s rather than the 1990s, with the notable development of the computing industries, Ireland would have become a prime target for the HVA continuously in search of the latest progress in the field of electronics. Experts in the GDR knew full well that all the Socialist experts in Eastern Europe could not develop computing systems as quickly as the West.[2] Having said this, there was some industrial espionage as the episodes regarding Pigeon House's pumps and turbines (1969), the Irish steel market and industry (1970, 1972 and 1976) and the Irish telephone network (1975 and 1983) show. But the Stasi obtained this information from *outside* Ireland.
- Was Ireland interesting from a geo-strategic point of view? This question remains difficult to answer.[3] Research in the archives of the former East German military intelligence seems to show that it was probably not the case at least not as far as war planning is concerned. Indeed, the NATO strategic plans for war in Europe that East German spies were able to lay their hands on indicate that direct Warsaw Pact attacks on Ireland with a specific strategic purpose were not anticipated by the West. However, only the opening to research of the Russian military archives regarding the period under consideration could reveal more. But here a crucial difference must be made between the East Germans and the Soviets regarding Northern Ireland, not Ireland. While no evidence can be found that the Stasi intervened in the Northern Irish conflict, in fact that in all likelihood it did not, the same cannot be said of the KGB. 'Operation SPLASH' in 1972 shows

that Moscow was willing to destabilise the United Kingdom. Another point is that Ireland was a handy backdoor to the United Kingdom as there were no border controls between the two countries. This would have been of interest mainly to the KGB as the Soviets had an embassy in Dublin but not the East Germans. The *Irish Times* gave a pertinent analysis of the spying threat when Ireland signed a trade agreement with Bulgaria in 1970: 'Such increased contacts [with Communist countries] could bring its difficulties; Soviet espionage is on a massive level and the fact that we have no military secrets worth while on the world-Power scale will not take away from the advantage that Ireland, relatively a quiet posting, could for that very reason be a valuable centre for agents.'[4] In that sense, Northern Ireland and Ireland were definitely of value.

In the end, by adding up all the negative points it is safe to say that Ireland, not even Northern Ireland, was not a priority for East German intelligence. Of course, it must be stressed here that this did not mean that if some interesting piece of information came from the island, it would not bother analysing it or taking an interest in it. Such an attitude would not be worthy of any serious intelligence service, and the Stasi was a *very* serious intelligence service. Interestingly, most information it obtained on the island came from Brussels. HA-XXII began to have a real interest in the PIRA when the Irish republicans began to massively target BAOR in the 1980s. All of a sudden, the Anglo-Irish conflict was very close to the East German border and Stasi headquarters wondered if the PIRA's operations against British bases in West Germany would not endanger its own. But at that stage, the GDR's years were numbered.

And yet, despite the fact that the island was not a main espionage target, it briefly became a main operational area, not for the Stasi but for the KGB. The fact that Yuri Andropov and the Central Committee of the CPSU – after much hesitation, it is true – eventually decided to send arms to the OIRA during 'Operation SPLASH' in 1972 is most significant for the historiography of the Cold War. Nikita Khrushchev spoke about peaceful coexistence. Leonid Brezhnev was engaged in the Strategic Arms Limitation Talks (SALT). It was all about détente. In 1967, the East had put forward the idea of holding a conference on security and cooperation which eventually became the Conference on Security and Cooperation in Europe (CSCE). It began in November 1972 in Finland. Ironically, the Soviets were essentially interested in so-called confidence-building measures and international cooperation to settle issues peacefully.[5] But how could the Soviets speak about security in Europe while sending weapons to Northern Ireland? 'Operation SPLASH' corroborates the view of those politicians who believed that peaceful coexistence and détente were only a cynical façade. As Ronald Reagan once famously said about détente: '[I]sn't that what a farmer has with his turkey – until thanksgiving day?'. Margaret Thatcher concurred: 'I had long understood that *détente* had been ruthlessly used by the Soviets to exploit western weakness and disarray. I knew the beast.'[6]

Of course, the West was not above cynical interventions throughout the world either. Iran (1953), Guatemala (1954), the illegal U2-spying missions in Soviet airspace (one U2 shot down in 1960) and Chile (1973) seemed to be conveniently forgotten by Reagan and Thatcher, and Nicaragua and the Contras were still to come (1986) to name but some examples. But Andropov and the Central Committee were obviously willing to take huge risks. The Soviets and their allies backed groups in Third World countries which they defined as anti-colonial and anti-imperialist freedom fighters. For example, Moscow invested huge amounts of money in the Movimento Popular de Libertação de Angola (MPLA, people's movement for the liberation of Angola). Besides Soviet pilots and officers who were sent to support the MPLA, there were also about 15,000 Cuban soldiers.[7]

Very obviously, the OIRA never got such massive support from Moscow. But the crucial difference was that unlike Angola, Northern Ireland was deep inside NATO territory. If the British had found out that the Soviets were sending arms to the OIRA, could détente then not be suddenly called into question? What about the SALT negotiations? What about talks to hold a CSCE? Some Irish republicans claimed that the British wanted to maintain their presence in Northern Ireland lest Ireland should be turned into some kind of 'European Cuba'. The republicans believed that these fears were exaggerated.[8] However, 'Operation SPLASH' gives some credence to those like the British Conservative Monday Club who believed in 1974 that Ireland could become 'a potential Achilles heel of British defence'.[9] In September 1971, former Prime Minister Harold Wilson told the then holder of the office Edward Heath that when in Moscow he had persuaded Soviet statesman Alexei Kosygin that Northern Ireland was not worth the Soviet Union's attention.[10] Obviously, Wilson got it badly wrong.

In a brilliantly thought-provoking and analytical article entitled 'The Long Peace: Elements of Stability in the Postwar International System',[11] written in 1986 at a time when the Cold War was not yet over and archives were less available than they are now, John Lewis Gaddis argues that there were a set of unwritten rules between the United States and the Soviet Union that contributed to stability in the world. One of these rules was 'to respect spheres of influence'. He writes that 'despite publicly condemning it the United States never attempted seriously to undo Soviet control in Eastern Europe; Moscow reciprocated by tolerating, though never openly approving of, Washington's influence in Western Europe'.[12] Gaddis concludes that in the end the Cold War might be defined by future generations of historians as the 'Long Peace'.[13] 'Operation SPLASH' and US destabilisation programmes in Eastern Europe, like for instance broadcasts towards Budapest in 1956 inciting the Hungarians to continue fighting, contradict this. Therefore, would it be correct to qualify Gaddis's expression slightly and suggest 'the Long Semi-Peace' instead?

As we have seen, the PIRA was not the Stasi's 'ideological partner' as has been asserted,[14] and nor was the INLA. It should not be forgotten that it was from certain quarters in the United States that the PIRA got much finance and armament, not from the East bloc. What if those Irish-American quarters learned that the PIRA was dancing to East Berlin's tune? One incident perfectly illustrates this. In 1979, Gerry Adams, then vice-president of Sinn Féin, the political wing of the PIRA, wrote a party policy which became known as the 'gray document'. It contained sentences reminiscent of vintage Socialism: 'we believe that the present system of society is based upon the robbery of the working class and that capitalist property cannot exist without the plundering of labour, we desire to see capitalism abolished and a democratic system of common or public ownership created in its stead'.[15] This shocked many traditional republicans and the *Sunday World*, a tabloid in Dublin, claimed that the PIRA was about to become Marxist.

Very soon afterwards, both the PIRA and Sinn Féin leaderships were obliged to issue flat denials and accused the Irish and British governments of using red-scare tactics. In an interview to *Hibernia*, Adams declared: 'First of all there's one thing which should be said categorically… There is no Marxist influence within Sinn Féin; it simply isn't a Marxist organisation. I know of no-one in Sinn Féin who is a Marxist or who would be influenced by Marxism.' The subsequent article in *Hibernia* was then republished in *An Phoblacht-Republican News*, Sinn Féin's mouthpiece. *An Phoblacht-Republican News* also went on to publish one article describing Adams's pilgrimage to Patrick Pearse's home (Pearse had been the republican non-Marxist leader of the Easter Rising of 1916 against the British), and another one praising the actions of Michael Flannery, the very conservative-minded leader of NORAID (Irish Northern Aid Committee, a US-fundraising organisation supportive of Ireland's reunification).[16]

Indeed, the PIRA and Sinn Féin had realised that they had made a serious blunder which could have negative repercussions in the United

States, the free world's leader in its struggle against Communism. NORAID had branches everywhere in the United States and raised millions of dollars, allegedly for families of republican prisoners detained in Northern Ireland. NORAID rejected accusations from the US, British and Irish governments that some of the money was used to procure arms for the PIRA. Whatever the answer, the OIRA, openly Marxist, never got such support from across the Atlantic, which was hardly surprising. The PIRA could rely on networks in the United States to get arms. It is estimated that one such network provided 200 to 300 arms annually between 1973 and 1979.[17] Now, were these amounts of money and arms worth endangering by secretly cooperating with the East Germans? Hardly so. Yet, it must be recalled here that the PIRA did receive arms from the Securitate (or the DIE) in Bucharest through Carlos, according to Magadalena Kopp. This opens a new research avenue although the archives of the former Securitate – and also those of the DIE as there is no reason to believe that it is any different – are very far from being as accessible as those of the former Stasi.[18] Also, it should not be forgotten that from 1972 onwards, the PIRA began to import weapons from Libya as it had obtained the support of Colonel Gaddafi,[19] not exactly a friend of the Americans. So, there can be no doubt that the PIRA did try to get arms where they were available seemingly no matter what regime was in place.

The Stasi was not duped by some of the PIRA's Marxist rhetoric. It got wind of Adams's statement in *Hibernia*. In an undated report, but probably written in 1980, HA-XXII stated the following:

> With regard to the characterisation of the political platform of the Provisional 'IRA' it must be noted that unlike the assertions made by the London government that it has a 'Marxist' orientation, the leaders of this organisation do not consider themselves to be Marxists. As the vice-president of 'Sinn Féin', G. Adams, declared in an interview for the Dublin weekly 'Kaibernia [*sic*: *Hibernia*]: 'There is no Marxist influence within Sinn Féin. I know of no one in Sinn Féin who is a Marxist or who would be influenced by Marxism'. This was also declared by the representative of the Sinn Féin branch in Belfast, T. Hartly [*sic*: Tom Hartley]. 'The accusations levelled against us that we are Marxists are fundamentally false', he said.[20]

In *KGB: The Secret Work of Soviet Agents* published in 1974, the US author John Barron, himself having been involved in intelligence activities, claimed that the Soviets did not make any difference between the Marxist OIRA and the more traditional PIRA 'so long [as the arms they provided] were used in Ireland to the detriment of Great Britain'.[21]

This statement needs to be qualified. The KGB did make the difference. In 1981, the CIA reported that back in 1973, the KGB had labelled the PIRA a '"criminal terrorist" organization' and that it had presently no contacts with it. Yet, it is certainly true that 'Operation SPLASH' shows that the Kremlin was willing to destabilise the United Kingdom. Barron also claimed that the 1972 operational plan of the Dirección General de Inteligencia (DGI, Cuban intelligence service), 'drafted under KGB supervision, stipulated that the Cubans would train Irish Republican Army personnel in the tactics of terrorism and guerrilla warfare. Liaison with the IRA is effected by DGI officers in London through British Communists.' He added that 'the KGB passively watched Ireland after World War II through Czech and East German business firms clandestinely founded to gather intelligence and import strategic embargoed goods to the Soviet bloc'.[22] Regarding KGB and DGI involvement, only the opening of archives of these intelligence services could confirm or otherwise this information. Regarding clandestine East German business firms, there is simply no truth in this.

The Stasi did obtain some very good information on Ireland and Northern Ireland thanks to its vast network of agents and sources. This was especially the case with HA-XXII which watched the PIRA campaign against BAOR. Pro-Irish republican organisations in West Germany like the WISK and the Anti-H-Block Committee were thoroughly targeted. However, the Stasi indulged on occasion in plagiarism, but this was also the case with the KGB which would sometimes not hesitate to turn information obtained in the press into information obtained by conspiratorial means.[23] Perhaps even more surprisingly coming from such a highly efficient intelligence service was a certain amount of sloppiness and factual errors, notably on Irish history. These errors, though not crucial, could have been easily avoided. An important part of the documents the Stasi possessed came from open sources, essentially from the West German media. This definitely indicates that the island on the fringe of Western Europe was certainly not on top of the Stasi's priorities despite its terrorist conflict. Concerning non-open sources, the information the HVA and HA-XXII gathered ranged from the development of the telephone network in Ireland in 1975 to the activities of the PIRA in West Germany in the 1980s thanks to sources and moles within the European institutions in Brussels and the West German security services.

The mass of intelligence obtained was rather diverse ranging from industrial espionage to terrorism. But as Markus Wolf justly wrote, intelligence was a patient game, looking for the relevant detail in a jumble of information. Certainly, as this book shows, espionage is not only a matter of collecting highly restricted information and enemy plans. Some of the Irish and Northern Irish information contained in the SIRA system was very sensitive, but much got only an average grade assessment, below average occasionally. What the mass of information collected about Ireland and Northern Ireland, including many open sources, above all proves is that the Stasi tried to develop an overall picture of the evolving situation. Sherman Kent, a former member of the US Office of Strategic Services (OSS) and later head of the Office of National Estimates, wrote in 1949 in *Strategic Intelligence for American World Policy*: 'Some of this knowledge may be acquired through clandestine means, but the bulk of it must be had through unromantic open-and-above-board observation and research'.[24] The American William Colby, Director of Central Intelligence (DCI) between 1973 and 1976, defined the 'traditional concept of intelligence' as spies trying to steal secret plans and so on. But Colby dismissed this concept and went on to say that during the Second World War, a new concept began to emerge in the United States, one in which the analysis of 'all the relevant information, that was overtly available as well as that secretly obtained' played a key role.[25] Kent also argued that the central idea was that the more knowledge an intelligence service possessed on a specific country, the easier it became to predict the 'probable courses of action' that country might take.[26] Analysing the mass of documents that the Stasi, essentially the HVA and HA-XXII, possessed on Ireland and Northern Ireland, it would seem that it agreed with its US adversaries.

But the question as to what exactly the East German leadership did with all this information remains most difficult to answer. As former KGB officer Victor Cherkashin writes about the information the Americans and British got from the Soviet traitor Oleg Penkovsky: 'Without proof it's impossible to say how much foreign governments base their decisions on intelligence'.[27] It is known that the plans for Pigeon House Generating Station near Dublin were sent to a power station under construction, presumably somewhere in the GDR. So here there is an example of how the fruits of espionage were actually used. For the mass of documents, however, the information it contained was probably simply stored, ready for use if the need arose. The Stasi had found out pretty much everything it needed to know about the WISK and the Anti-H-Block Committee thanks to moles within the West German security services. Yet, what it did with the information remains largely unknown.

Is there a possibility that we might learn more some day about the Stasi's interest in Ireland and Northern Ireland? A definitive answer cannot be given. As Wolfgang Krieger justly notes: '[a] lack of Cold War intelligence sources is nothing unusual. Except for the CIA and a few others, intelligence organisations the world over refuse to declassify their files.'[28] This is perfectly true. On 31 August 1990, the East German State Committee for the Dissolution of the former MfS (Stasi) handed over the hostile target file (*Feindobjektakte*) on the PIRA to the Zollkriminalamt (ZKA, West German customs investigation bureau). What this file contained is anyone's guess. Indeed, apart from a covering letter indicating the handing over of the file and a few blank sheets, one of them containing the Stasi's registration number for the PIRA, XV 5414/85, there was nothing else.[29] The file should be in the possession of the ZKA. It is unlikely that it will be made available for researchers soon as German security services have not released files to date.

In the town of Zirndorf near Nuremberg in Bavaria, a team called Referat AR4 Projektgruppe Manuelle Rekonstruktion has been entrusted with a particular job that requires much patience. When the Stasi shredders gave up the ghost after days of non-stop functioning in 1989, men and women used their hands to tear the documents. However, the bits of paper were collected when the Stasi headquarters were occupied by the people and eventually over 15,000 sacks were filled up. It is the team's job to glue these documents back together. Understandably, work has been slow. It could take months to recreate a single page torn in ninety bits. But a special machine was created, a kind of 'unshredder'. It was initially believed that this 'unshredder' would repair all documents within five years. Unfortunately, that proved to be too optimistic and there were some technical difficulties. So far, it has processed over 400 sacks. As to the team, since 1995 it has managed to process 500 sacks representing about a million scraps of paper.[30] It might well be that there are shredded documents concerning Ireland and Northern Ireland. As we have seen, several documents had been torn but were reconstructed. Therefore, it is a possibility that new information might see the light some day. Whether that information would drastically change the conclusions reached in this book seems unlikely. But in the shadowy world of intelligence, ultimately one never knows.

Notes

1 Wolf & McElvoy, *Man without a Face*, pp. 322–3.
2 H. Müller & K. Rösener, 'Die Unterstützung der elektronischen Industrie', in Müller *et al.* (eds.), *Die Industriespionage der DDR*, pp. 77, 80.
3 The author is currently doing research for a manuscript on this issue.
4 *Irish Times*, 27 April 1970.
5 Stöver, *Der Kalte Krieg 1947–1991*, p. 402.
6 Gaddis, *Cold War*, pp. 216–17.

7 Stöver, *Der Kalte Krieg 1947–1991*, pp. 359–61.
8 M. Cox, 'Northern Ireland: The War that Came in from the Cold', *Irish Studies in International Affairs*, vol. 9 (1998), p. 77.
9 'Not for first time, Ireland represents an Achilles heel', *Irish Times*, 21 August 1974.
10 O'Halpin, 'Intelligence and Anglo-Irish Relations, 1922–73', p. 148 (n. 29).
11 J. L. Gaddis, 'The Long Peace: Elements of Stability in the Postwar International System', *International Security*, vol. 10, no. 4 (spring, 1986), pp. 99–142.
12 *Ibid.*, pp. 133–4.
13 *Ibid.*, p. 142.
14 Glees, *Stasi Files*, p. 126.
15 Moloney, *Secret History of the IRA*, pp. 186–7.
16 *Ibid.*, p. 188.
17 Boyne, *Gunrunners*, pp. 64, 98.
18 'Inside the Securitate Archives; A review of the current state of the archives of the Romanian Securitate', by Lavinia Stan, Wilson Centre, Cold War International History Project, 4 March 2005, at www.wilsoncenter.org/article/inside-the-securitate-archives (accessed 22 March 2013).
19 Moloney, *Secret History of the IRA*, p. 138; see also p. 326, as another example of Libyan support. There are many references to Libya in this book.
20 BStU, MfS-HA XXII, no. 24, 'Wichtigste ausländische Extremisten- und Terrororganisationen und – gruppen', no exact date but most recent date mentioned is 1980.
21 J. Barron, *KGB: The Secret Work of Soviet Agents* (London: Hodder & Stoughton, 1974), p. 26.
22 *Ibid.*, pp. 151, 254–5.
23 Andrew & Gordievsky, *KGB*, p. 618.
24 S. Kent, *Strategic Intelligence for American World Policy* (Princeton, NJ: Princeton University Press, 1949, reprinted in 1966), p. 155, cited in A. N. Shulsky & G. J. Schmitt, *Silent Warfare: Understanding the World of Intelligence* (Washington, DC: Brassey's, 2002), pp. 161–2.
25 Shulsky & Schmitt, *Silent Warfare*, pp. 160–1.
26 *Ibid.*, pp. 162–4.
27 Cherkashin with Feifer, *Spy Handler*, p. 62.
28 Krieger, 'German Intelligence History', p. 186.
29 BStU, MfS-HA XXII, no. 17219, no creation date indicated, the handing over of the file having taken place on 31 August 1990.
30 'Germans piece together millions of lives spied on by Stasi', by Helen Pidd, 13 March 2011, at guardian.co.uk, neweurope; www.guardian.co.uk/world/2011/mar/13/east-germany-stasi-files-zirndorf (accessed 15 April 2011); 'The Stasi files: the world's biggest jigsaw puzzle', by Chris Bowlby, 13 September 2012, in BBC News Magazine, at www.bbc.co.uk/news/magazine-19344978 (accessed 11 February 2013).

Bibliography

Books

aan de Wiel, J., *The Irish Factor, 1899–1919: Ireland's Strategic and Diplomatic Importance for Foreign Powers* (Dublin: Irish Academic Press, 2008).

Adams, J., *Historical Dictionary of German Intelligence* (Lanham: Scarecrow Press, 2009).

Andrew, C., *The Defence of the Realm: The Authorized History of MI5* (London: Allen Lane, 2009).

Andrew, C. and Gordievsky, O., *KGB: The Inside Story* (New York: HarperCollins, 1990).

Andrew, C. and Gordievsky, O., *Comrade Kryuchkov's Instructions: Top Secret Files on KGB Foreign Operations, 1975–1985* (Stanford, CA: Stanford University Press, 1993).

Andrew, C. and Mitrokhin, V., *The Sword and the Shield: The Mitrokhin Archive and the Secret History of the KGB* (New York: Basic Books, 1999).

Applebaum, A., *Iron Curtain: The Crushing of Eastern Europe* (London: Penguin, 2013).

Baring, A. and Schöllgen, G., *Kanzler, Krisen, Koalitionen: Von Konrad Adenauer bis Angela Merkel* (Munich: Pantheon Verlag, 2006).

Barron, J., *KGB: The Secret Work of Soviet Agents* (London: Hodder & Stoughton, 1974).

Becker, B., *Die DDR und Großbritannien 1945/49 bis 1973: Politische, wirtschaftliche und kulturelle Kontakte im Zeichen der Nichtanerkennungspolitik* (Bochum: Universitätsverlag Dr. N. Brockmeyer, 1991).

Berger, S. and LaPorte, N. (eds.), *The Other Germany: Perceptions and Influences in British–East German Relations, 1945–1990* (Augsburg: Wißner-Verlag, 2005).

BI Universallexikon (Leipzig: VEB, Bibliographisches Institut, 1986), vol. 3.

Born, H., Johnson, L. K. and Leigh, I. (eds.), *Who's Watching the Spies? Establishing Intelligence Service Accountability* (Washington, DC: Potomac, 2005).

Boyne, S., *Gunrunners: The Covert Arms Trail to Ireland* (Dublin: O'Brien Press, 2006).

Brown, T., *Ireland: A Social and Cultural History, 1922–2002* (London: Harper Perennial, 2004).
Browne, N., *Against the Tide* (Dublin: Gill & Macmillan, 1986).
Bruce, G., *The Firm: The Inside Story of the Stasi* (Oxford: Oxford University Press, 2010).
Bruce, S., *God Save Ulster: The Religion and Politics of Paisleyism* (Oxford: Oxford University Press, 1986).
Central Statistics Office, Dublin, *Statistical Abstract of Ireland, 1963.*
Central Statistics Office, Dublin, *Statistical Abstract of Ireland, 1978.*
Central Statistics Office, Dublin, *Ireland, Statistical Abstract, 1982–1985.*
Central Statistics Office, Dublin, *Ireland, Statistical Abstract, 1990.*
Cherkashin, V. with Feifer, G., *Spy Handler: Memoir of a KGB Officer* (New York: Basic Books, 2005).
Cohen M. J. and Major, J., *History in Quotations: Reflecting 5000 Years of World History* (London: Weidenfeld & Nicolson, 2008).
Coogan, T. P. *The IRA* (London: HarperCollins, 1993).
Cooney, J., *John Charles McQuaid: Ruler of Catholic Ireland* (Dublin: O'Brien Press, 1999).
Cruise O'Brien, C., *Memoir: My Life and Themes* (London: Profile Books, 1999).
Dáil Éireann, *Election Results and Transfer of Votes in General Election (February 1973)* (Dublin: Stationery Office).
Dáil Éireann, *Election Results and Transfer of Votes in General Election (June 1977)* (Dublin: Stationery Office).
Dáil Éireann, *Election Results and Transfer of Votes in General Election (February 1987)* (Dublin: Stationery Office).
Dáil Éireann, *Election Results and Transfer of Votes in General Election (June 1989)* (Dublin: Stationery Office).
Dalos, G., *Der Vorhang geht auf: Das Ende der Diktaturen in Osteuropa* (Munich: Verlag C.H. Beck, 2010).
de Graaf, B., de Jong, B. and Platje, W. (eds.), *Battleground Western Europe: Intelligence Operations in Germany and the Netherlands in the Twentieth Century* (Amsterdam: Het Spinhuis, 2007).
Delaney, E., *An Accidental Diplomat: My Years in the Irish Foreign Service, 1985–1995* (Dublin: New Island, 2001).
Diedrich, T., Heinemann, W. and Ostermann, C. F. (eds.), *Der Warschauer Pakt: Von der Gründung bis zum Zusammenbruch, 1955 bis 1991* (Bonn: Bundeszentrale für politische Bildung, 2009).
Doerries, R. R. (ed.), *Prelude to the Easter Rising* (London: Frank Cass, 2000).
Fischer, J., *Das Deutschlandbild der Iren 1890–1939* (Heidelberg: Winter, 2000).
Fischer, J., Ó Dochartaigh, P. and Kelly-Holmes, H. (eds.), *Irish–German Studies* (yearbook of the Centre for Irish–German Studies), 1. 2001/2002 (Trier, Wissenschaftlicher Verlag).

FitzGerald, G. *Ireland in the World: Further Reflections* (Dublin: Liberties Press, 2006).

FitzGerald, G., *Just Garret: Tales from the Political Front Line* (Dublin: Liberties Press, 2011).

Follain, J., *Jackal: The Complete Story of the Legendary Terrorist, Carlos the Jackal* (New York: Arcade, 2011).

Fulbrook, M., *Anatomy of a Dictatorship: Inside the GDR 1949–1989* (Oxford: Oxford University Press, 1995).

Fulbrook, M., *History of Germany 1918–2000: The Divided Nation* (Malden and Oxford and Victoria: Blackwell, 2004).

Gaddis, J. L., *The Cold War: The Deals. The Spies. The Truth* (London: Penguin, 2007).

Gallagher, M. and Laver, M. (eds.), *How Ireland Voted, 1992* (Dublin: Folens, 1993).

Garton Ash, T., *The File: A Personal History* (London: Atlantic Books, 2009).

Garvin, T., *Preventing the Future: Why was Ireland so poor for so long?* (Dublin: Gill & Macmillan, 2005).

Geraghty, T., *Brixmis: The Untold Exploits of Britain's Most Daring Cold War Spy Mission* (London: HarperCollins, 1997).

Gieseke, J., *Der Mielke-Konzern: Die Geschichte der Stasi, 1945–1990* (Munich: DVA, 2006).

Glees, A., *The Stasi Files: East Germany's Secret Operations against Britain* (London: Free Press, 2004).

Gray, W. G., *Germany's Cold War: The Global Campaign to Isolate East Germany, 1949–1969* (Chapel Hill, NC and London: University of North Carolina Press, 2003).

Großmann, W., *Bonn im Blick: Die DDR-Aufklärung aus der Sicht ihres letzten Chefs* (Berlin: Das Neue Berlin, 2001).

Hanley, B. and Millar, S., *The Lost Revolution: The Story of the Official IRA and the Workers' Party* (London: Penguin, 2010).

Hartley, S., *The Irish Question as a Problem in British Foreign Policy, 1914–1918* (Basingstoke: Macmillan, 1987).

Hennessey, T., *The Evolution of the Troubles, 1970–72* (Dublin: Irish Academic Press, 2007).

Holland, J. and McDonald, H., *INLA Deadly Divisions: The Story of One of Ireland's Most Ruthless Terrorist Organisations* (Dublin: Torc, 1994).

Hull, M. M., *Irish Secrets: German Espionage in Wartime Ireland 1939–1945* (Dublin: Irish Academic Press, 2003).

Kaufmann, W., *Flammendes Irland: Wir lachen, weil wir weinen* (Rostock: MV/ Taschenbuch, 2003).

Kaufmann, W., *Patrick* (Berlin: Verlag Junge Welt, 1977).

Kennedy, K. A., Giblin, T. and McHugh, D., *The Economic Development of Ireland in the Twentieth Century* (London and New York: Routledge, 1988).

Kennedy, M. and Skelly, J. M. (eds.), *Irish Foreign Policy 1919–1966: From Independence to Internationalism* (Dublin: Four Courts Press, 2000).

Keogh, D., *Ireland and Europe, 1919–1948* (Dublin: Gill & Macmillan, 1988).
Keogh, D., *Twentieth Century Ireland: Revolution and State Building* (Dublin: Gill & Macmillan, 2005).
Knabe, H., *West-Arbeit des MfS: Das Zusammenspiel von 'Aufklärung' und 'Abwehr'* (Berlin: Ch. Links Verlag, 1999).
Koehler, J. O., *Stasi: The Untold Story of the East German Secret Police* (Boulder, CO: Westview Press, 1999).
Kopp, M., *Die Terrorjahre: Mein Leben an der Seite von Carlos* (Munich: Deutsche Verlags-Anstalt, 2007).
Kraushaar, W. (ed.), *Die RAF: Entmythologisierung einer terroristischen Organisation* (Bonn: Bundeszentrale für politische Bildung, 2008).
Leonhard, W., *Meine Geschichte der DDR* (Berlin: Rowohlt Taschenbuch Verlag, 2008).
McCabe, I., *A Diplomatic History of Ireland 1948–49: The Republic, the Commonwealth and NATO* (Blackrock: Irish Academic Press, 1991).
McCauley, M., *The German Democratic Republic since 1945* (New York: St. Martin's Press, 1983).
McDonald, H., *Colours: Ireland – From Bombs to Boom* (Edinburgh and London: Mainstream, 2005).
McDonald, H. and Cusack, J., *UDA: Inside the Heart of Loyalist Terror* (Dublin: Penguin Ireland, 2004).
Macrakis, K., *Seduced by Secrets: Inside the Stasi's Spy-Tech World* (New York: Cambridge University Press, 2008).
Mahon, T. and Gillogly, J. J., *Decoding the IRA* (Cork: Mercier Press, 2008).
Mastny, V., Holtsmark, S. G. and Wenger, A. (eds.), *War Plans and Alliances in the Cold War: Threat Perceptions in the East and West* (London: London and New York: Routledge, 2006).
Mastny, V. and Byrne, M. (eds.), *A Cardboard Castle? An Inside History of the Warsaw Pact, 1955–1991* (Budapest and New York: Central European Press, 2005).
Meyers Neues Lexikon (Leipzig: VEB Bibliographisches Institut, 1964), vol. 4.
Meyers Neues Lexikon (Leipzig: VEB, Bibliographisches Institut, 1969), vol. 9.
Milotte, M., *Communism in Modern Ireland: The Pursuit of the Workers' Republic since 1916* (Dublin: Gill & Macmillan, 1984).
Mitdank, J., *Die Berlin-Politik zwischen 17. Juni 1953, dem Viermächteabkommen und der Grenzöffnung 1989* (Berlin: trafo, 2003).
Mitdank, J., *Die DDR zwischen Gründung, Aufstieg und Verkauf* (Berlin: NoRa, 2008).
Moloney, E., *A Secret History of the IRA* (London: Penguin, 2007).
Müller, H., Süß, M. and Vogel, H. (eds.), *Die Industriespionage der DDR: Die wissenschaftlich-technische Aufklärung der HVA* (Berlin: edition ost, 2008).
Müller-Enbergs, H., Wielgohs, J. and Hoffmann, D., *Wer war wer in der DDR?* (Berlin: Christoph Links Verlag, 2001), DVD edition (2004).
Mulqueen, M., *Re-evaluating Irish National Security Policy: Affordable Threats?* (Manchester: Manchester University Press, 2009).

Murray, R., *The SAS in Ireland* (Cork: Mercier Press, 1990).

O'Brien, J., *The Arms Trial* (Dublin: Gill & Macmillan, 2000).

O'Connor, E., *Reds and the Green: Ireland, Russia and the Communist Internationals 1919–43* (Dublin: UCD Press, 2004).

O'Driscoll, M., *Ireland, Germany and the Nazis: Politics and Diplomacy, 1919–1939* (Dublin: Four Courts Press, 2004).

O'Driscoll, M., Keogh, D. and aan de Wiel, J. *Ireland through European Eyes: Western Europe, the EEC and Ireland, 1945–1973* (Cork: Cork University Press, 2013).

O'Halpin, E., *Defending Ireland: The Irish State and its Enemies since 1922* (Oxford: Oxford University Press, 1999).

O'Halpin, E., Armstrong, R. and Ohlmeyer, J. (eds.), *Intelligence, Statecraft and International Power: Irish Conference of Historians* (Dublin: Irish Academic Press, 2006).

O'Riordan, M., *Pages from History on Irish–Soviet Relations* (New Books Publication, 1977).

Pacepa, I. M., *Red Horizons: The Extraordinary Memoirs of an Eastern European Spy Chief* (London: Coronet Books, 1989).

Pfeil, U. (ed.), *Die DDR und der Westen: Transnationale Beziehungen 1949–1989* (Berlin: Ch. Links Verlag, 2001).

Porch, D., *The French Secret Services: From the Dreyfus Affair to the Gulf War* (London: Macmillan, 1996).

Rimington, S., *Open Secret: The Autobiography of the Former Director-General of MI5* (London: Hutchinson, 2001).

Rupp, R., Rehbaum, K. and Eichner, K., *Militärspionage: Die DDR-Aufklärung in NATO und Bundeswehr* (Berlin: edition ost, 2011).

Salmon, T., *Unneutral Ireland: An Ambivalent and Unique Security Policy* (Clarendon Press, 1989).

Schaffmann, C., *Nordirland: Probleme, Fakten, Hintergründe* (Berlin: Dietz Verlag, 1982).

Schröm, O., *Im Schatten des Schakals: Carlos und die Wegbereiter des internationalen Terrorismus* (Berlin: Ch. Links, 2002).

Schwan, H. and Heindrichs, H., *Das Spinnennetz: Stasi-Agenten im Westen: Die geheimen Akten der Rosenholz-Datei* (Munich: Knaur, 2005).

Sharrock, D., and Devenport, M., *Man of War, Man of Peace: The Unauthorised Biography of Gerry Adams* (London: Pan Books, 1998).

Shaw, E., *Wie ich nach Berlin kam: 'Irish Berlin'* (Berlin: Aufbau Taschenbuch Verlag, 2000).

Shulsky, A. N. and Schmitt, G. J., *Silent Warfare: Understanding the World of Intelligence* (Washington, DC: Brassey's, 2002).

Siegmund-Schultze, D. (ed.), *Irland: Gesellschaft un Kultur*, VI (Halle: Martin-Luther-Universität Halle-Wittenberg, 1989/44, F92).

Skelly, J. M., *Irish Diplomacy at the United Nations, 1945–1965: National Interests and the International Order* (Dublin: Irish Academic Press, 1997).

Skolimowski, J., and Lusiński, C., *Ireland and Poland* (Dublin: Embassy of the Republic of Poland, 2001).

Sloan, G. R., *The Geopolitics of Anglo-Irish Relations in the 20th Century* (London and New York: Continuum, 1997).

Stephan, E., *Spies in Ireland* (Harrisburg, PA: Stackpole, 1965).

Stöver, B, *Der Kalte Krieg 1947–1991: Geschischte eines radikalen Zeitalters* (Munich: Verlag C.H. Beck and Bundeszentrale für politische Bildung, 2007).

Swan, S., *Official Irish Republicanism, 1962–1972* (Lulu, 2008).

Tozzer, K. and Tozzer, M., *Das Netz der Schattenmänner: Geheimdienste in Österreich* (Wien: Holzhausen Verlag, 2003).

Treacy M., *The Communist Party of Ireland, 1921–2011: Vol. I: 1921–1969* (Dublin: Brocaire, 2012).

Weigel, G., *The Final Revolution: The Resistance Church and the Collapse of Communism* (Oxford: Oxford University Press, 2003).

Weiner, T., *Legacy of Ashes: the history of the CIA* (London: Penguin, 2008).

Wharton, K. *'Sir, They're Taking the Kids Indoors': The British Army in Northern Ireland, 1973–74* (Solihull: Helion, 2012).

Whelan, B., *Ireland and the Marshall Plan, 1947–57* (Dublin: Four Courts Press, 2000).

Wolf, M. with McElvoy, A., *Man without a Face: The Autobiography of Communism's Greatest Spymaster* (New York: Public Affairs, 1997).

Wright, P. with Greengrass, P., *Spy Catcher: The Candid Autobiography of a Senior Intelligence Officer* (New York: Viking Penguin, 1987).

Wylie, P., *Ireland and the Cold War: Diplomacy and Recognition, 1949–63* (Dublin: Irish Academic Press, 2006).

Yeltsin, B., *The View from the Kremlin* (London: HarperCollins, 1994).

Chapters in books

Aldrich, R. J., 'British Intelligence, Security and Western Cooperation in Cold War Germany: *The Ostpolitik Years*', in de Graaf, B., de Jong, B. and Platje, W. (eds.), *Battleground Western Europe: Intelligence Operations in Germany and the Netherlands in the Twentieth Century* (Amsterdam: Het Spinhuis, 2007).

Daase, C., 'Die RAF und der internationale Terrorismus: Zur transnationalen Kooperation klandestiner Organisationen', in Kraushaar, W. (ed.), *Die RAF: Entmythologisierung einer terroristischen Organisation* (Bonn: Bundeszentrale für politische Bildung, 2008).

de Graaf, B., 'Stasi in the Polder: The East German Ministry for State Security and the Netherlands, 1977–89', in de Graaf, B., de Jong, B. and Platje, W. (eds.), *Battleground Western Europe: Intelligence Operations in Germany and the Netherlands in the Twentieth Century* (Amsterdam: Het Spinhuis, 2007).

Diedrich, T., 'Die DDR zwischen den Blöcken. Der Einfluss des Warschauer Paktes auf Staat, Militär und Gesellschaft der DDR', in Diedrich, T., Heinemann, W. and Ostermann, C. F. (eds.), *Der Warschauer Pakt:*

Von der Gründung bis zum Zusammenbruch, 1955 bis 1991 (Bonn: Bundeszentrale für politische Bildung, 2009).

Dochartaigh, P. and Kelly-Holmes, H. (eds.), *Irish-German Studies* (yearbook of the Centre for Irish-German Studies), 1.2001/2002 (Trier, Wissenschaftlicher Verlag).

Ebert, G. and Leistner, M., 'Zu den Ergebnissen auf den Gebieten Militärtechnik, Metallurgie und Maschinenbau', in Müller, H., Süß, M. and Vogel, H. (eds.), *Die Industriespionage der DDR: Die wissenschaftlich-technische Aufklärung der HVA* (Berlin: edition ost, 2008).

Gallagher, M., 'The election of the 27th Dáil', in Gallagher, M. and Laver, M. (eds.), *How Ireland Voted, 1992* (Dublin: Folens, 1993).

Gill, P., 'The Politicization of Intelligence: Lessons from the Invasion of Iraq', in Born, H., Johnson L. K. and Leigh, I. (eds.), *Who's Watching the Spies? Establishing Intelligence Service Accountability* (Washington, DC: Potomac, 2005).

Johnson, L. K., 'Governing in the Absence of Angels: On the Practice of Intelligence Accountability in the United States', in Born H., Johnson, L. K. and Leigh, I. (eds.), *Who's Watching the Spies? Establishing Intelligence Service Accountability* (Washington, DC: Potomac, 2005).

Leigh, I., 'More Closely Watching the Spies: Three Decades of Experiences', in Born H., Johnson L. K. and Leigh I. (eds.), *Who's Watching the Spies? Establishing Intelligence Service Accountability* (Washington, DC: Potomac, 2005).

Mac Con Uladh, D., 'The Poor Relations: The GDR and Ireland', in Fischer J., Ó Mac Con Uladh, D., 'The GDR and Northern Ireland', in Berger, S. and LaPorte, N. (eds.), *The Other Germany: Perceptions and Influences in British–East German Relations, 1945–1990* (Augsburg: Wißner-Verlag, 2005).

Mastny, V., 'Imagining War in Europe: Soviet Strategic Planning', in Mastny, V., Holtsmark, S. G. and Wenger, A. (eds.), *War Plans and Alliances in the Cold War: Threat Perceptions in the East and West* (London and New York: Routledge, 2006).

Mastny, V., 'The Warsaw Pact as History', in Mastny, V. and Byrne, M. (eds.), *A Cardboard Castle? An Inside History of the Warsaw Pact* (Budapest: Central European University Press, 2005).

Morré, P., 'Joint Operations against the IRA in the Netherlands and the Federal Republic of Germany', in de Graaf, B., de Jong, B. and Platje, W. (eds.), *Battleground Western Europe: Intelligence Operations in Germany and the Netherlands in the Twentieth Century* (Amsterdam: Het Spinhuis, 2007).

Müller, H. and Rösener, K., 'Die Unterstützung der elektronischen Industrie', in Müller, H., Süß, M. and Vogel, H. (eds.), *Die Industriespionage der DDR: Die wissenschaftlich-technische Aufklärung der HVA* (Berlin: edition ost, 2008).

O'Driscoll, M., 'West Germany', in O'Driscoll, M., Keogh, D. and aan de Wiel, J. (eds.), *Ireland through European Eyes: Western Europe, the EEC and Ireland, 1945–1973* (Cork: Cork University Press, 2013).

O'Halpin, E., 'Intelligence and Anglo-Irish relations, 1922–73', in O'Halpin, E., Armstrong, R. and Ohlmeyer, J. (eds.), *Intelligence, Statecraft and International Power: Irish Conference of Historians* (Dublin: Irish Academic Press, 2006).

Pekelder, J., 'Vom "Sowjetdeutschland" zum "roten Preußen": Niederländische Wahrnehmungen der DDR (1949–1973)', in Pfeil, U. (ed.), *Die DDR und der Westen: Transnationale Beziehungen 1949–1989* (Berlin: Ch. Links Verlag, 2001).

Schmidt, A., '"Aufklärung" des Funkverkehrs und der Telefongespräche in Westdeutschland-Die Hauptabteilung III', in Knabe, H., *West-Arbeit des MfS: Das Zusammenspiel von 'Aufklärung' und 'Abwehr'* (Berlin: Ch. Links Verlag, 1999).

Steffen Gerber, T., 'Zwischen Neutralitätspolitik und Anlehnung an den Westen: Die Beziehungen zwischen der Schweiz und der DDR (1949–1972)', in Pfeil, U. (ed.), *Die DDR und der Westen: Transnationale Beziehungen 1949–1989* (Berlin: Ch. Links Verlag, 2001).

Straßner, A., 'Die dritte Generation der RAF: Terrorismus und Öffenlichkeit', in Kraushaar, W. (ed.), *Die RAF: Entmythologisierung einer terroristischen Organisation* (Bonn: Bundeszentrale für politische Bildung, 2008).

Süß, M., 'Die Arbeitsmethoden der Wissenschaftlich-Technischen Aufklärung', in Müller, H., Süß, M. and Vogel, H. (eds.), *Die Industriespionage der DDR: Die wissenschaftlich-technische Aufklärung der HVA* (Berlin: edition ost, 2008).

Tantzscher, M., 'Datentransfers nach Moskau', in Knabe, H., *West-Arbeit des MfS: Das Zusammenspiel von 'Aufklärung' und 'Abwehr'* (Berlin: Ch. Links Verlag, 1999).

Vogel, H., 'Rolle und Bedeutung der Wissenschaftlich-Technischen Aufklärung der DDR', in Müller, H., Süß, M. and Vogel, H. (eds.), *Die Industriespionage der DDR: Die wissenschaftlich-technische Aufklärung der HVA* (Berlin: edition ost, 2008).

Whelan, B., 'Integration or Isolation? Ireland and the Invitation to Join the Marshall Plan', in Kennedy, M. and Skelly, J. M. (eds.), *Irish Foreign Policy 1919–1966: From Independence to Internationalism* (Dublin: Four Courts Press, 2000).

Wunschik, T., '"Abwehr" und Unterstützung des internationalen Terrorusmus-Die – Hauptabteilung XXII', in Knabe, H., *West-Arbeit des MfS: Das Zusammenspiel von 'Aufklärung' und 'Abwehr'* (Berlin: Ch. Links Verlag, 1999).

Wunschik, T., 'Aufstieg und Zerfall: Die zweite Generation der RAF', in Kraushaar, W. (ed.), *Die RAF: Entmythologisierung einer terroristischen Organisation* (Bonn: Bundeszentrale für politische Bildung, 2008).

Wüstenhagen, J., 'RGW und EWG: Die DDR zwischen Ost- und Westintegration', in Pfeil, U. (ed.), *Die DDR und der Westen: Transnationale Beziehungen 1949–1989* (Berlin: Ch. Links Verlag, 2001).

Ziehm, H., 'Elektronische Datenträger', in Knabe, H., *West-Arbeit des MfS: Das Zusammenspiel von 'Aufklärung' und 'Abwehr'* (Berlin: Ch. Links Verlag, 1999).

Articles

aan de Wiel, J., 'Austria-Hungary, France, Germany and the Irish Crisis from 1899 to the Outbreak of the First World War', *Intelligence and National Security*, vol. 21, no. 2 (April 2006).

aan de Wiel, J., 'The Principality of Thomond and His Royal Highness Raymond Moulton Seághan O'Brien, 1936–1963: Ireland's Greatest Diplomatic Farce', in *North Munster Antiquarian Journal*, vol. 47 (2007).

aan de Wiel, J., 'French Military Intelligence and Ireland, 1900–1923', *Intelligence and National Security*, vol. 26, no. 1 (February 2011).

Chossudovsky, E. M., 'The Origins of the Treaty on the Non-Proliferation of Nuclear Weapons: Ireland's Initiative in the United Nations (1958–61), *Irish Studies in International Affairs*, vol. 3, no. 2, 1990.

Cox, M., 'Northern Ireland: The War that came in from the Cold', *Irish Studies in International Affairs*, vol. 9 (1998).

Doherty, G., 'Ireland, Europe and the Provision of Food Aid to Poland 1980–81', *Irish Studies in International Affairs*, vol. 24 (2013).

Gaddis, J. L., 'The Long Peace: Elements of Stability in the Postwar International System', *International Security*, vol. 10, no. 4 (spring, 1986).

Geiger, T., 'Trading with the Enemy: Ireland, the Cold War and East-West trade, 1945–55', *Irish Studies in International Affairs*, vol. 19, 2008.

Gieseke, J., 'East German Espionage in the Era of Détente', *Journal of Strategic Studies*, vol. 31, no. 3, 2008.

Keatinge, P., 'Ireland's Foreign Relations in 1985', *Irish Studies in International Affairs*, vol. 2, no. 2, 1986.

Keatinge, P. 'Ireland's Foreign Relations in 1989', *Irish Studies in International Affairs*, vol. 3, no. 2, 1990.

Krammer, A., 'The Cult of the Spanish Civil War in East Germany', *Journal of Contemporary History*, vol. 39, no. 4, October 2004.

Krieger, W., 'German Intelligence History: A Field in Search of Scholars', *Intelligence and National Security*, 2004, vol. 19, no. 2.

McNamara, R., 'Irish Perspectives on the Vietnam War', *Irish Studies in International Affairs*, vol. 14 (2003).

Manathunga, C., 'The Evolution of Irish Disarmament Initiatives at the United Nations, 1957–1961', *Irish Studies in International Affairs*, vol. 7 (1996).

Ó Corcora, M. and Hill, R. J. 'The Soviet Union in Irish Foreign Policy', *International Affairs*, vol. 58, no. 2, spring 1982

O'Driscoll, M., 'Hesitant Europeans, Self-Defeating Irredentists and Security Free-Riders? West German Assessments of Irish Foreign Policy during the Early Cold War, 1949–59', *Irish Studies in International Affairs*, vol. 21 (2010).

Salmon, T., 'The Changing Nature of Irish Defence Policy', *The World Today*, vol. 35, no. 11 (Nov. 1979).
Ward, E., '"A Big Show-Off to Show What We Could Do": Ireland and the Hungarian Refugee Crisis of 1956', *Irish Studies in International Affairs*, vol. 7 (1996).
White, S., 'Soviet Writings on Irish History, 1917–1980: A Bibliography', *Irish Historical Studies*, vol. 23, no. 90, 1980.
White, S., 'Ireland, Russia, Communism, Post-Communism', *Irish Studies in International Affairs*, vol. 8, 1997.

Newspapers

Britain

Guardian
Independent

Germany

Der Kölner Stadt-Anzeiger
Frankfurter Allgemeine Zeitung

Ireland

Anglo-Celt
Connacht Tribune
Cork Examiner
Irish Farmers Journal
Irish Independent
Irish Press
Irish Times
Kerryman
Leitrim Observer
Limerick Leader
Nenagh Guardian
Sunday Independent
Westmeath Examiner

DVDs and CD-Roms

BStU, Berlin, 'Die Arbeit der Stasi-Unterlagen Behörde' (DVD), 2011.
Engelmann, Roger, Florath, Bernd, Heidemeyer, Helge, Münkel, Daniela, Plozin, Arno and Süß, Walter, *Das MfS-Lexikon: Begriffe, Personen und Strukturen der Staatssicherheit der DDR* (Berlin: Ch. Links Verlag, 2011).

Kontraste, 13/03/1990, 'Vernichten oder aufbewahren? – Stasi-Akten als politische Zeitbombe', in *Auf den Spuren einer Diktatur*, a series of three DVDs produced by the Bundeszentrale für politische Bildung (bpb) and the Rundfunk Berlin-Brandenburg (rbb), 2nd edition, Berlin, 2005.

Interviews

Reiner Oschmann, former correspondent of *Neues Deutschland*, Berlin, 9 August 2009.

Edgar Uher, former East German diplomat accredited to Ireland and HVA officer, Berlin, 10 January 2010.

Dr Joachim Mitdank, former East German Ambassador to Ireland, Berlin, 12 January 2010.

Wolfgang Döhnert, former correspondent of the ADN in London, Berlin, 13 January 2010.

Institutional archives and public records

Germany

Auswärtiges Amt-Politisches Archiv (AA-PA), Berlin
(archive of the German Foreign Office)
B20-200, Bd. 1825
B31, Bd. 60
B31, Bd. 128
B31, Bd. 197
B31, Bd. 376
B38-IIA1, Bd. 119, 119-4
B38-IIA1, Bd. 318, 318-1

(East German Ministry of External Affairs)
MfAA, A13100
MfAA, C164/77
MfAA, C4459
MfAA, C4460
MfAA, C4461
MfAA, C4463
MfAA, ZR629/97

Bundesarchiv-Militärarchiv, Freiburg im Breisgau
(German military archive)
DVW1-25724/a
DVW1-25733/m
DVW1-25737
DVW1-25811/b

Bundesbeauftragte für die Unterlagen des Staatssicherheitsdienstes der ehemaligen Deutschen Demokratischen Republik (BStU), Stasi, Berlin
(the Federal Commissioner for the Records of the State Security Service of the Former German Democratic Republic)
(all files are related to Ireland and Northern Ireland)
BVfS Leipzig AKG 01967

MfS Abt. Fin./MD/1, MfS Abt. Fin./MD/2, MfS Abt. Fin. 1580, MfS Abt. Fin. 1581, MfS Abt. Fin. 1586, MfS Abt. Fin. 1644, MfS Abt. Fin. 1648, MfS Abt. Fin. 1656, MfS Abt. Fin. 1660, MfS Abt. Fin. 1661, MfS Abt. Fin. 1662, MfS Abt. Fin. 1666

MfS AP 1323/78
MfS BV Cottbus Abt. Fin. 500
MfS DOS 7683/92
MfS F16/HVA
MfS F22/HVA
MfS HA I 18430
MfS HA II/AKG-VSH
MfS HA II 18587, MfS HA II 18588, MfS HA II 18589, MfS HA II 18591, MfS HA II 18592, MfS HA II 18596, MfS HA II 18599, MfS HA II 18601, MfS HA II 18604, MfS HA II 18606, MfS HA II 18607, MfS HA II 18608, MfS HA II 18613, MfS HA II 18615, MfS HA II 18624, MfS HA II 25725, MfS HA II 27015, MfS HA II 28369, MfS HA II 29524, MfS HA II 35670
MfS HA III 16717
MfS HA VI 5665
MfS HA IX 2451, MfS HA IX 13693
MfS Abt. X 484
MfS HA XVIII 4249, MfS HA XVIII 16817
MfS HA XX 5921, MfS HA XX 6819, MfS HA XX 7160
MfS HA XX/AKG 434
MfS HA XXII 24, MfS HA XXII 81/1, MfS HA XXII 110 Teil 1, MfS HA XXII 242/9, MfS HA XXII 248 Teil 1, MfS HA XXII 248 Teil 2, MfS HA XXII 249 Bd. 1, MfS HA XXII 250, MfS HA XXII 342/5, MfS HA XXII 361, Bd. 1, MfS HA XXII 361, Bd. 2, MfS HA XXII 623/2, MfS HA XXII 665/2, MfS HA XXII 736/1, MfS HA XXII 794/37, MfS HA XXII 945, MfS HA XXII 1081, MfS HA XXII 1145/7, MfS HA XXII 1618/1, MfS HA XXII 5310/3, MfS HA XXII 5539/11, MfS HA XXII 5749/2, MfS HA XXII 5915, MfS HA XXII 5919, MfS HA XXII 5928, MfS HA XXII 6046, MfS HA XXII 6065/19, MfS HA XXII 6083/13, MfS HA XXII 6117 Teil 1, MfS HA XXII 16555, MfS HA XXII 16829, MfS HA XXII 16891, MfS HA XXII 16908/1, MfS HA XXII 16909/1, MfS HA XXII 16910/4, MfS HA XXII 16917, MfS HA XXII 17001/7, MfS HA XXII 17219, MfS HA XXII 17220, MfS HA XXII 17920/1, MfS HA XXII 18178/3, MfS HA XXII 18545, MfS HA XXII 19022, MfS HA XXII 19156, MfS HA XXII 19173, MfS HA XXII 19175,

MfS HA XXII 19826, MfS HA XXII 19964, MfS HA XXII 20488, MfS HA XXII 20758
MfS HA PS 212, MfS HA PS 1960, MfS HA PS 1961
MfS HVA 154, MfS HVA 169, MfS HVA 386, MfS HVA 396
MfS Sekr. Neiber 3, MfS Sekr. Neiber 13, MfS Sekr. Neiber 135, MfS Sekr. Neiber 608
MfS ZAIG 6544, MfS ZAIG 10407, MfS ZAIG 10426, MfS ZAIG 10434, MfS ZAIG 10436, MfS ZAIG 10442, MfS ZAIG 10469, MfS ZAIG 10471, MfS ZAIG 10472, MfS ZAIG 11055, MfS ZAIG 11056, MfS ZAIG 14755, MfS ZAIG 19553/1, MfS ZAIG 26968, MfS ZAIG 28097, MfS ZAIG 28205, MfS ZAIG 29548, MfS ZAIG 29661
MfS ZOS 2680

Agents and sources
XV/92/67 'Bettina': F22/HVA, Sira TdB 21
XV/167/71 'Max': F22/HVA, Sira TdB 21
XV/192/73 'Schneider': F16/F22 HVA, Sira TdB 21
XV/268/68 'Löwe': F22/HVA, Sira TdB 21
XV/281/70 'Dorn': F16/F22 HVA, Sira TdB 21
XV/308/71 'Norbert': F22/HVA, Sira TdB 21
XV/367/73 'Korb': F22/HVA, Sira TdB 21
XV/483/68 'Roedel': F16/HVA, Sira TdB 21
XV/502/87 'Mark': F16/HVA, Sira TdB 21, HA KuSch/AKG-KA
XV/750/66 'Walter': F16/F22 HVA, Sira TdB 21
XV/990/60 'Claus': F16/F22 HVA, Sira TdB 21
XV/1093/67 'Rank': F22/HVA, Sira TdB 21
XV/1273/62 'Dräger [Draeger]': F16/F22, Sira TdB 21
XV/1508/75 and XV/1093/62 'Weber': F16/F22 HVA, Sira TdB 21, F16/HVA
XV/1579/68 'Berger': F16/HVA, Sira TdB 21
XV/1586/87 'Aribert': F16/F22 HVA, Sira TdB 21
XV/1619/75 'Herbert': F22/HVA, Sira TdB 21
XV/1762/71 'Fichte': F22/HVA, Sira TdB 21
XV/1815/60 'Jutta': F16/HVA, Sira TdB 21
XV/2091/66 'Komtess': F16/F22 HVA, Sira TdB 21
XV/2171/73 'Weser': F22/HVA, Sira TdB 21
XV/2227/73 'Inge': F16/F22 HVA, Sira TdB 21
XV/2848/76 'Karl': F22/HVA, Sira TdB 21
XV/2873/62 'Anna': F16/F22 HVA, Sira TdB 21
XV/2962/78 'Ahmed': F22/HVA, Sira TdB 21
XV/4070/70 'Lorenz': F22/HVA, Sira TdB 21
XV/4705/63 'Insel': F22/HVA, Sira TdB 21
XV/5485/60 'Angestellter': F22/HVA, Sira TdB 21
XV/6427/60 'Merten': F16/HVA, F22/HVA, Sira TdB 21
XV/6430/82, 'Hans Rosenberg': F22/HVA, Sira TdB 21
XV/13864/60, 'Brede': F16/HVA, Sira TdB 21
XV/15905/60, 'Adler': F16/HVA, Sira TdB 21

Deutsches Rundfunkarchiv, Potsdam-Babelsberg
(archive of German broadcasting)
(documentaries on Ireland and Northern Ireland on GDR television)
'Bringt die Folterer vor Gericht' (Bring the torturers to justice), 7 December 1977.
'Ghettokinder in Belfast' (Ghetto children in Belfast), 9 February 1979.
'Insel des Abschieds' (Island of the farewells), 6 November 1979.
'Nordirland-Ausnahmezustand ohne Ende' (Northern Ireland: state of emergency without end), 11 February 1982.
'Kuppelgrab Newgrange' (Passage tomb Newgrange), 20 June 1982.
'Parlementarier aus Irland bei Horst Sindermann in Berlin' (Parliamentarians from Ireland visit Horst Sindermann in Berlin), 6 September 1988.
'20 Jahre britische Militärpräsenz in Nordirland' (20 years of British military presence in Northern Ireland), 12 August 1989.
'Unruhen in Nordirland' (Disturbances in Northern Ireland), 15 August 1989.
'IRA-Terroristen in Belfast' (IRA terrorists in Belfast), 9 October 1990.

Evangelisches Zentralarchiv (EZA), Berlin
(archive of the Evangelical Church in the former GDR)
5096/11

Konrad-Adenauer-Stiftung, Pressedokumentation, Sankt Augustin
(archive of the German Christian-Democratic Party)
Staaten, Irland, 1951-31/07/1983

Regionalarchiv Ordinarien Ost (ROO), Erfurt
(archive of the Catholic Church in the former GDR)
Vorsitzender/Sekretariat der BOK/BBK (Berliner Konferenz Europäischer Katholiken), K25, K32, K38, K44, K.49, K75, K. 76, and K79 II.

Staatsbibliothek zu Berlin, Preußischer Kulturbesitz Zeitungsinformationssystem (ZEFYS/DDR-Presse)
At: http://zefys.staatsbibliothek-berlin.de/ddr-presse
Three former East German newspapers have been digitalised and can now be consulted online:
Berliner Zeitung
Neues Deutschland
Neue Zeit (East German)

Stiftung Archiv der Parteien und Massenorganisationen der DDR im Bundesarchiv (SAPMO-BA), Berlin
(Foundation Archives of Parties and Mass Organisations of the GDR in the Federal Archive)
DA/1/15657
DA/1/15846
DA/1/15869
DL/2/6679
DO/4/3512
DO/4/4305

DO/4/4347
DO/4/4604
DY/24/11 5724 T2
DY/30/IV/ A2/20/487
DY/30/12881
DY/30/12882
DY/30/12883
DZ/7/64
DZ/22/21

And also the following East German and Soviet newspapers:
Der Neue Weg
Die Neue Zeit (Soviet)
Die Weltbühne
Horizont
Neues Deutschland

Ireland

Cathal Brugha Barracks, Dublin
(Irish military archive)
G2/C/1769 Pt. 3
2003/15/30-G2/C/206
2003/15/31-G2/C/206 Pt. 1
2003/15/34-G2/C/487
2003/15/57-G2/C/1444
2004/16/6-G2/C/206
2004/16/10-G2/C/223/a Pt. 1
2004/16/27-G2/C/743
2004/16/55-G2/C/1444
2004/16/119-G2/C/1927
2005/20/25-G2/C/482
2005/20/61-G2/C/1258
2005/20/81-G2/C/1684/1
2005/20/90-G2/C/1769 Pt. 2
2005/20/113-G2/C/1875
2005/20/137-G2/C/1927
2006/161/41-G2/C/1684/1
2006/161/42-G2/C/1709
2006/161/67-G2/C/1864
2007/144/47-G2/C/1258 Pt. 2
2007/144/60-G2/C/1463
2007/144/72-G2/C/1684
2007/144/73-G2/C/1684/1
2008/151/39-G2/C/1258 Pt. 2
2008/151/58-G2/C/1684

2008/151/59-G2/C/1684/1
2008/151/64-G2/C/1769 Pt. 9
2008/151/116-G2/C/2010 Pt. 1

Dublin Diocesan Archive (DDA)
'The papers of Archbishop John Charles McQuaid C.S.S.p., relating to Communists, 1940–1967' (161-page index file of archival references relating to Communist and subversive activities; descriptive list)

Gilbert Library, Dublin
Communist Party of Ireland papers; Seán Nolan-Geoffrey Palmer Collection
Betty Sinclair diary, box 55, diary numbers 1, 2, 9, 13A, 17, 31 and diary 1980

National Archives of Ireland (NAI), Dublin
DFA, 96/3/97
DFA, 99/2/48
DFA, 305/249
DFA, 305/321
DFA, 313/10A
DFA, 419/33/20
DFA, 2001/43/88
DFA, 2001/43/202
DFA, 2002/19/51
DFA, 2003/17/98
DFA, 2005/145/1403
DFA, embassy series, Bonn: D/2, D/2/1, D/3, D/101, 12/7I, 14/13
DFA, embassy series, Rome: 1918
Secretary's office: A55I, P168

Belgium

North Atlantic Treaty Organization (NATO) Archive, Brussels
C-M (76) 71
C-R (72) 28
C-R (76) 1
IMSWM-061-78
PO (72) 392
Record-MC-006-77
Record-MC-032-72
Record-MC-033-71
Record-MC-042-71

United States

Central Intelligence Agency (CIA)
Freedom of Information Act – Electronic Reading Room, www.foia.cia.gov
'The balance of forces in Central Europe', 1 August 1977

'Soviet support for international terrorism and revolutionary violence', 27 May 1981

'Terrorism review for 9 April 1987'

Private papers

Edgar Uher's unpublished manuscript entitled 'Last rites: East Germany's deal for an Irish patriot's body', in possession of the author.

Index